LORD SOMERS
A political portrait

For Nancy Davis Sachse

William L. Sachse

LORD SOMERS
A political portrait

Manchester University Press

The University of Wisconsin Press

Published by
Manchester University Press
Oxford Road, Manchester M13 9PL

ISBN 0 7190 0604 X

Published in the United States of America and Canada by
The University of Wisconsin Press
Box 1379, Madison, Wisconsin 53701

ISBN 0 299 06890 0
LC 75–885

Printed in Great Britain by
Western Printing Services Ltd, Bristol

Contents

Preface

For a man whose accomplishments have been recognised, and usually extolled, for more than two and a half centuries, John Somers remains remarkably free from biographical treatment. At his death in 1716 a eulogistic memoir, of a type not uncommon at the time, was published by an anonymous writer, and this is still the only biography, spanning his life as a whole, which stands by itself. In 1791 a remote collateral descendant, Richard Cooksey, undertook the task; another attempt was made a quarter of a century later by Henry Maddock, a barrister and legal author. But these do not go beyond the Revolution. Supposedly 'something was expected' of Dr Thomas Birch, and we know that Sir Walter Scott planned to write a biography for publication with the *Somers Tracts*, but in neither case was anything produced. The most extensive treatment is that of Lord Campbell, who devoted six chapters to Somers in his *Lives of the Lord Chancellors* (1845–47). But this work is marred by inaccuracies, unsubstantiated information and a patent Whig bias. In 1863 Thomas MacKnight observed that 'the great statesman and jurist remains to us a mythical personage'; since then little has been done to bring him into sharper focus, the article in the *Dictionary of National Biography* adding little not to be found in Campbell, though taking a more critical approach.

The principal reason for this state of affairs is to be found in the paucity of Somers's personal papers. These were largely destroyed by fire in 1752. Only one substantial collection exists, now in the custody of the Sussex Record Office at Kingston-on-Thames. The biographer must therefore turn to a wide variety of scattered sources, relying heavily upon official materials of a more or less formal sort and upon the papers of those with whom Somers was associated.

The chief aim of this study is to provide an account of Somers's activities as politician and jurist. Since his undertakings in the world of letters, particularly as a patron, were in large measure bound up with his politics, these too are recounted in some detail. And it should be apparent that the many-sided nature of his career, his constant and significant association with the fortunes of the Whigs, and his manifold relations with a wide assortment of men, make his biography a history of his times.

To the many librarians and archivists who have assisted me in the preparation of this work I wish to express my appreciation. I am particularly indebted to the governing authorities and other personnel of the British Museum, the Public Record Office, the House of Lords Record Office, Lambeth Palace Library, the Bank of England, the Honourable Society of the Middle Temple, the Worcestershire, Surrey and Hertfordshire Record Offices, the Bodleian Library and those of All Souls and Trinity, Oxford, the University of Nottingham Library, the Borough of Reigate, the libraries of the University of Wisconsin and Yale University, and the New York Public Library. I am obliged to His Grace the Duke of Marlborough for allowing me to use manuscript materials at Blenheim Palace, and to His Grace the Duke of Portland for the use of the Portland Papers on deposit at the University of Nottingham and the British Museum. I desire also to voice my gratitude for research support from the University of Wisconsin, the Social Science Research Council, and the Institute for Advanced Study. For assistance in research I would mention, in particular, three of my former graduate students: Dr Michael Landon, Dr David Wollman and Dr Robert Frankle.

William L. Sachse

Note on dates and quotations. For days of the month, the Old Style has been employed throughout, except in a few instances indicated by NS. The New Style for the year is employed for dates between January 1 and March 24.

The original spelling and capitalisation have been retained in quotations, but in some cases modern punctuation has been introduced.

I

The early years, 1651–76

John Somers[1] was born on the outskirts of Worcester in 1651. The times
were turbulent. Charles I had been sent to his death. The nation, with
Cromwell at its helm, stood at mid-point in the Commonwealth era. Six
months earlier that invincible Puritan had defeated the Scots at Dunbar,
but a new test of strength was in the offing. Led by the newly crowned
Charles II, the Scots swept south into England, challenging the regicide
regime. It was at Worcester that the crucial encounter occurred. The ancient
city was a prominent royalist centre; it had held out against the parliamentary forces until July 1646. Now, in September 1651, it witnessed the
final rout of the Cavaliers: Cromwell enjoyed his 'crowning mercy'. From
Worcester the defeated prince set forth upon his travels in exile, from which
he would not return for close on a decade. Peace had come, but the city,
numbering over 7,000 inhabitants, bore the scars of conflict.[2]

The infant Somers was six months old at the time of the battle of
Worcester. The exact place of his birth is uncertain. According to one
version, it was his grandfather's house, White Ladies, a one-time nunnery
located just north of the city. Here, we are told, the expectant mother was
taken so that her accouchement might occur in surroundings more tranquil
than might be afforded at her own residence in College Churchyard.[3] But
the latter dwelling, which adjoined the church of St Michael Bedwardine,
has also been described as Somers's birthplace, and with good reason, for the
registers of this parish, where his parents had been married in 1648, include
the entry: 'John the sonne of John Somers Gent. and Katherine his wife was
borne the fourth of March'.[4] The births of two of his four sisters—Mary
and Katherine, both younger than he—are also recorded here.[5] The parish
lay just outside the city limits, to the south. It included the cathedral and
the bishop's palace, in front of which was a 'fair green' with a bowling
alley, extending to the River Severn.[6]

The Somers family, though of Gloucestershire origin, had been established
in Worcestershire since at least the fifteenth century. Nicholas Somers is
known to have held half a knight's fee in Droitwich in the early years of
Henry VI's reign.[7] The family's principal holding was at Clifton, Severn
Stoke, where the parish church of St Denis contains a gravestone with a
punning epitaph to Richard Somers, who died in 1598:

Alas, the flower whom winter hath decayd
Revives in sommer gloriously araid
So sommer shall deths winter at an end
Spring out of dust and unto Christ assend.[8]

In his *History of Worcestershire* Nash has traced the family pedigree from John Somers (1589) to Sir Charles Cocks (1779), a collateral descendant.[9] Among noteworthy members of the family were Sir George Somers, who in 1609 took possession of the Bermudas for England. The Chancellor's grandfather Richard, who became a citizen of Worcester, was described as a man 'of good substance'.[10] His mother was Katherine, daughter of John Severn, of Powick in Worcestershire. Her family had some standing among the Shropshire gentry.[11] Thus, though Lord Somers was sometimes pictured, in the lampoons and satires directed against him in the days of his prominence, as being lowly born, his background was actually that of a minor county family. There is no justification for Swift's remark that he was descended 'from the dregs of the people', or for Mrs Manley's that he was 'by birth a plebeian'.[12]

Somers's father was born in Kidderminster in 1620.[13] Bred to the law, he served as an attorney in Worcester. We can picture him as principally engaged in the usual tasks of a country lawyer, drawing wills, drafting mortgage transactions, arranging conveyances, and the like, though he is said to have frequented the terms in London.[14] But we know little of his professional accomplishments, save that he assisted the famous Dr Fell in recovering rents of St Oswald's Hospital, a Worcester poorhouse.[15] Early in the eighteenth century he was described as 'an Eminent and Wealthy Attorney . . . , possess'd of a competent Estate'.[16] His will, drawn up a few years before his death, makes mention of 'freehold Mesuages, lands, Tenements, hereditaments and premises', located in Worcestershire, without further description or identification. Included among them, certainly, were the Clifton properties, which he had inherited, said to be worth £300 a year. At one time he possessed an interest in Oldington Manor, Kidderminster, but this had passed to Thomas Foley in 1656.[17]

The elder Somers supported the parliamentary cause and appears to have served as captain of a troop of horse in Cromwell's army.[18] According to a family legend, he was so much provoked by a royalist sermon in the parish church at Severn Stoke that he fired a pistol in protest, the ball lodging in the sounding board over the pulpit. Beyond this we know little. However active he was in parliamentary or Cromwellian causes, he saw fit at the Restoration, like so many others, to sue for a pardon under the Great Seal for all 'murders, rapes, felonies and misdemeanours of every kind, by him committed before that time'. His kinsman-biographer, Cooksey, hastens to add that 'malice itself never laid any such crimes to his charge'.[19] In any case, he appears to have settled down under the restored regime, though in 1679 the House of Commons was to take him into custody, along with the under-sheriff of Worcester, for arresting a servant of a Member. The two were released upon apologising and paying fees.[20]

As for the future Chancellor, his early years were spent at White Ladies. This establishment, originally a Benedictine house, was located at Claines, two miles north of Worcester, on the left bank of the Severn. It must have been a sizable place, for during the siege of 1646 it could still be described as 'a strong stone building capable of holding 500 men with safety'.[21] At that time it was in the possession of Richard Somers, the Chancellor's grandfather. But upon his daughter Mary's marriage to Richard Blurton, a Worcester clothier, he conveyed it to her, and here the Blurtons established their residence. Tradition has it that Queen Elizabeth was entertained there in 1585, while on a royal progress, and during his brief sojourn in Worcester before his defeat in 1651 Charles II used it as his headquarters. He would shortly flee to another White Ladies at Boscobel, leaving behind garters, gloves and other personal effects.[22]

According to Cooksey, young Somers's aunt was so fond of him that she 'took upon herself the care of him', and would not suffer her brother to keep his son under his own roof, near the cathedral yard. Here again we are served only by family legend, and left in the dark as to the origin and particulars of this extraordinary arrangement. As for White Ladies, it was a hive of activity. It housed, at least on occasion, not only the Blurtons, but also various relatives of the Foley and Cooksey clans, and was the scene of a variety of enterprises. Besides the management of a large farm, there were the manifold activities of the clothing trade, embracing the manufacture or preparation of teasels, woad, madder and dyestuffs. It was also a centre for the production of brick and tile, for which the necessary reconstruction of the war-torn city provided a ready market; this was recalled in later years by lampoonists, who spoke of the Chancellor's father as a brickmaker's son:

A brickmaker's son in Oliver's days,
One Sommers by name, to his mighty praise.
By turning a rebell his fortune did raise,
    Which nobody can deny.[23]

It is said that some twenty families depended for their livelihood on these operations, and were accommodated in cottages provided for them. A semi-communal life seems to have prevailed: the hall of the old nunnery now provided ample room for a score or more of kinsmen and their friends, who shared a common table in an atmosphere of rural abundance and good cheer. We are told that two boars were annually provided at Christmastide and that, even half a century later, such antique customs as keeping a collar of brawn, as well as a gilt salt cellar, on the table throughout the winter were observed.[24]

It is possible that Richard Baxter, the Presbyterian divine, on occasion visited this menage. Cooksey describes White Ladies as 'a sort of out-settlement of Baxter's, in constant communication and connexion with him'. Baxter was vicar of nearby Kidderminster during the years of the Interregnum; here in 1650 he was to write The Saint's Everlasting Rest. Among Baxter's closest friends was Thomas Foley, to whom he dedicated The Crucifying of the World by the Cross of Christ, and he once spoke of the Foleys as 'that family which I was first indebted to' in Worcestershire.[25] Thomas Foley was a brother of Robert Foley, of Stourbridge, who in 1646 had married Ann Blurton. Richard Blurton, the clothier, was a well-known

Presbyterian. The Somers family, as already noted, were closely connected with Kidderminster. Richard Somers had married a Kidderminster girl.[26] Cooksey, erroneously believing that A *Tale of a Tub* was written at least in part by John Somers, tells us that his grandfather Richard furnished the model for Jack, the Calvinist, and that he was so devoted to Baxter that he spent most of his later days with him in Kidderminster.[27] That White Ladies in these years was a society formed upon Baxter's principles is perhaps an over-statement, but it is not without foundation. But, regardless of the intensity of this Presbyterian atmosphere, its effect upon the youthful Somers eludes us. If we are to judge by his later years, it made no indelible impression, though it may have contributed towards a sympathetic concern for Dissent and a more or less latitudinarian position in religion.

Whatever the religious complexion of White Ladies, there can be no doubt that the Foleys, Blurtons, Somerses, Cookseys, Windsors and others, who met under its roof, gave full attention to local politics. The future Chancellor must have heard, during his early years, many a discussion of political tactics, of who was to stand for the county or the city, or for the boroughs of Droitwich, Evesham and Bewdley.[28] The generous accommodations at White Ladies, where the ancient dormitories of the nuns could still serve an overflow of guests and visitors, made it a rallying point for occasional political gatherings. According to Campbell, 'old Somers' managed the parliamentary elections for the county and the city, as well as the boroughs mentioned above.[29] However this may be, the Foleys were certainly involved in national, as well as local, politics. Thomas Foley, Baxter's friend, who established the family fortune by introducing a new process in the manufacture of nails and by making a rich marriage, was High Sheriff of the county in 1656 and four years later represented Bewdley in the Restoration Convention. His son Paul, born in 1645, sat as M.P. for Hereford in seven Parliaments, and under William III served for three years as Speaker of the House. It is noteworthy that, though a Tory, he was to support Somers's position that the throne was vacant after King James's flight to France. A third generation continued the parliamentary connection. Thomas Foley, who became the first Baron, served both Worcester and Stafford after the Revolution, and was elected for Droitwich in 1698, while Philip Foley sat for Bewdley.

Somers's formal education was begun at the cathedral school, in Worcester. The political alterations of the time were reflected in the management of the school, and it is likely that he was taught both by Thomas Barefoot, master during most of the Interregnum period, and John Toy, whose position Barefoot had taken over in 1653 but who was reinstated following the Restoration. Both were Oxford graduates; Toy published poetical works and held the vicarage of Stoke Prior. He died in 1663, and was succeeded by Thomas Stephens.[30] How long Somers remained at this school is not known; nor can we be sure that this was the only one he attended. According to notes prepared for a biography by Thomas Birch, he also attended a school in Sheriff Hales, Shropshire, kept by a Mr Woodhouse, and possibly another in Walsall, Staffordshire.[31] Unless the family tradition is completely awry, he gained at an early age a reputation for sobriety and studiousness. We are told that, though he was the brightest of the boys at the College School, 'instead of joining his young companions in their boyish amusements, he was seen walking and musing alone, not so much as looking on while they were at play'.[32] We may discount this somewhat as the sort of tale likely to be told about the childhood of a Lord Chancellor, but it is not the only indication that Somers was grave and thoughtful beyond his years.

At the age of sixteen he matriculated at Oxford, and was admitted a Gentleman Commoner of Trinity College.[33] We know virtually nothing of his life there; the Oxford records yield little, and the problem is complicated by the existence of another John Somers, of Exeter, who matriculated in 1674. There was no family connection with Trinity—or, indeed, with any other college. He is said to have been recommended by William Hopkins, himself a Trinity man.[34] Hopkins would have a fairly distinguished career in the Church; though his father lost his Evesham rectory by virtue of the Bartholomew Act, William rose to be canon of Worcester. He was a scholarly man who, in addition to producing the usual sermons and theological treatises, assisted Edmund Gibson with editions of the Anglo-Saxon Chronicle and Camden's *Britannia*.[35] He was, however, only a few years older than Somers, taking his M.A. in 1668; he could hardly have had much influence with the college authorities when Somers went up. It seems likely that Francis Winnington had a greater share in steering the youth to Trinity; he too was a product of that college, and after 1660 a barrister of the Middle Temple. He was, moreover, a close friend of the Somers family, and would play a considerable part in the future Chancellor's legal education.

The Oxford to which Somers came in 1667 was borne on the full tide of reaction against the Puritan restrictions of the previous decade. Anthony à Wood, writing at the end of that very year, exclaimed against 'an age given over to all vice—whores and harlotts, pimps and panders, bauds and buffoones, lechery and treachery, atheists and papists, rogues and rascalls', and so on.[36] We may discount Wood somewhat—he had a gloomy and jaundiced point of view, as well as a persecution complex—but there is foundation enough for his strictures. A superabundance of alehouses helped Oxonians, young and old, escape the restraints of collegiate life, and were the scenes of countless exuberant and disorderly incidents, which sometimes developed into drunken riots and even fatal brawls. In general the standards of behaviour were low: 'dicing and gambling went with carousing: so did easy manners, immorality, loose language, disrespect'. Discipline was ill kept, and the conduct of the 'reverend seniors', as Wood suggests, was not always the model of propriety. The bibulous Rector of Exeter frequently had to be escorted home. When the Dutch admiral Tromp visited Oxford in 1675 he was no match for a hard-drinking crew captained by Dr Speed of St John's; the doughty sea-dog had to be carried unconscious to his rooms. The Vice-Chancellor's court lacked authority; even ceremonial occasions suffered from the rudeness and boisterousness of the undergraduates, and at coursing, or disputations, college challenges often led to blows.[37]

Trinity was in better hands than most of the Oxford colleges, for its President was Ralph Bathurst, celebrated by Dryden as

> . . . a name the learn'd with reverence know,
> And scarcely more to his own Virgil owe.[38]

Bathurst embarked upon his presidency in 1664, holding office for forty years. He was able and energetic, and quite liberal in some respects. A promoter of the Royal Society, he sought to encourage the study of chemistry, and as Vice-Chancellor allowed the King's players to perform in Oxford during the summer. As President he was intimately associated with such notables as Robert South, William Jane, Evelyn, Wren, Boyle, Wilkins and Wallis. A persuasive money-raiser, and himself a generous son of Trinity, he materially enlarged the college facilities and is responsible for the present form of the chapel. Some years after Somers went down, John Harris described Trinity as 'very famous & full of students; gentlemen being very fond of placing their sons under the care of so excellent a governor as yᵉ President of that College'. He goes on to compliment Trinity on its high standards: 'certainly no College ever had more exercise done in it, nor better performed'. He describes the daily regimen:

In the Morning at seven o'clock in Term time, as soon as Prayers were over, there were Logic & Physic Lectures read in the Hall to all yᵉ Students in yᵉ House in distinct classes. Between this time and ten o'clock every undergraduate had a Lecture from his Tutor. At ten there were Disputations in the Hall in Logic and Physics. Every day in Term time there was a Declamation spoke in the Hall in Latin, and at every meal a speech out of some good Latin Author, wᶜʰ was called the Narrare. At two o'clock every afternoon there was an Exposition in the Hall on the best Greek and Latin Authors, where the young Scholars were made to construe, & to give the sense in a manly way: and the Lecturer explained the text grammatically & historically: at 5 o'clock there were Disputations again by the Bach: of Arts at wᶜʰ the Undergraduates were present.

Harris adds that lectures were read in experimental philosophy and chemistry, and 'a very tolerable course of Mathematicks taught', and concludes that the 'Education & manner of Life in this Coll. was Manly and Gentile & free from abundance of the Pedantry and Impertinence in other Houses'.[39] This was in 1683, when Bathurst had headed the college for nearly twenty years; perhaps he had not been able to implement this programme completely in Somers's day. But it seems unlikely that an administrator of his talents and drive would have been slow to enforce the methods and standards which he deemed essential for the proper education of his charges.

There is no evidence that Somers distinguished himself at Trinity. In later years Bathurst would of course boast of having had a part in the education of 'so learned and eloquent a lawyer, so sincere a patriot, and so elegant a scholar as Lord Somers'.[40] But Cooksey, who saw some of his college 'exercises', confessed that he found them in 'no wise remarkable'.[41] His tutor was Abraham Campion, a man some ten years older than his charge. Campion had become a Fellow of Trinity but three years before; he would rise to be professor of moral philosophy and a canon of Lincoln. Somers must have held him in some esteem, for in later years he would recommend him as chaplain to the Archbishop of Canterbury.[42] As for the college, he thought well enough of it to make several benefactions. Twice, in 1675 and again in 1682, he contributed to the repair of the chapel—first five pounds and then a hundred, a generous gift from a young lawyer but recently launched on his career. Ten years later he gave a hundred books to the college library.[43] We can glean but little information regarding his associates among the undergraduates. His lifelong friendship with Henry Newton, who became envoy to Tuscany and an admiralty judge, dated from Oxford days. William Dobson, later Fellow and President of Trinity, came up, like Somers, in 1667; Settle, the dramatist, had preceded him by a year. The legal writer William Nelson probably came to Oxford too late in 1669 to associate with Somers at Trinity, but they must have known each other in the Middle Temple.

Oxford, of course, was more than Trinity, and for all the slackness and incompetence that Wood complained about, it was not without its luminaries and was by no means stagnant. In the year that Somers went up, the Arundel marbles were presented to the university; in that of his departure Elias Ashmole came from London to open his museum and the Sheldonian Theatre was inaugurated. Dr Fell at Christ Church, Ironside at Wadham, and Mews at St John's were redoubtable figures. Fell, the Vice-Chancellor in Somers's undergraduate days, worked to restore discipline and learning, reviving attendance at disputations and lectures, and 'continually hauling taverns and alehouses';[44] Jeames of All Souls likewise fought for the cause of reform. Among the notables that Somers must have recognised was Boyle, who did not leave Oxford until 1668; Wallis, the Savilian Professor of Geometry; and Sir Christopher Wren, who might be observed supervising the rise of his elegant auditorium. And there were occasional visits of celebrities, like that of Cosmo de' Medici, accompanied by twenty servants and pages, about the time Somers went down.

Like many students of the time, Somers did not take a degree. According to Cooksey, his days at Oxford were for the most part spent 'in classical and poetical amusements, rather than studies'.[45] His father probably intended that he should join him in his country practice, which was his to inherit, and it is likely that he spent some time in Worcester acquiring first-hand experience. But in 1669, when eighteen years of age, he had ventured to London in pursuit of the barrister's lore. This turn of events may be credited largely to Sir Francis Winnington. Winnington was by this time a seasoned barrister. In a few years he would become Attorney-General to the Duke of York, and then serve as Solicitor-General. He was increasingly prominent in the affairs of the Middle Temple, of which in 1675 he became

Treasurer. In that year his earnings from the law are said to have exceeded £4000. A hearty man, as much famed for riding and field sports as for legal abilities, Winnington was in a position to observe young Somers and to advise him, for from time to time he joined in the political gatherings at White Ladies, which a decade later would help elect him to Parliament.[46] According to Campbell, Winnington prevailed upon the country attorney to permit his son to study for the Bar, noting how Littleton and other Worcestershire men had won their way to the bench.[47]

In May 1669 he was formally admitted to the Middle Temple upon payment of £3 10s od. Late in the following winter he acquired a small set of chambers in Elm Court, at the Temple, and began to keep his terms.[48] He continued to enjoy Winnington's patronage, having access to his quarters in the Temple, and availing himself so readily of this opportunity that he was regarded by some as Winnington's clerk.[49] Actually, he was never more than pupil and protégé.

The regimen of the Inns in these years was slack.[50] The governing authorities had become negligent in providing systematic instruction for students, and even in requiring them to remain in residence during the terms. 'Readings' and 'Moots' were falling into decay, the 'Exercises' testing legal proficiency were becoming empty forms; a new system of pupilage was under way. The records of the Middle Temple provide evidence that, in the early 1670s, the governors of that Society were not wholly blind to the need for reform, though they showed little zeal. In 1671 they forbade that a Templar be called to the Bar 'without fifteen Exercises', but a year later they reduced this requirement to eight. They also set up a committee 'to consider abuses in Reading times', and gave orders on the conduct of moots. Some attention was paid to the conduct of their charges. Gowns were to be worn on appropriate occasions. An attempt was made to keep the Christmas revels, for which the Middle Temple was famous, within bounds; in 1671 twelve members were subjected to fine or expulsion 'for breaking open the doors of the Hall . . . and setting up a gaming Christmas'. An old order forbidding the porter to let anyone into or out of the Temple after eleven at night was revived; the 'Great Gate' was to be shut at nine. Several were expelled for 'scandalous behaviour in the Courts', and the Lord Mayor was to be questioned regarding the involvement of members in outrages committed upon the watch in Temple Bar.[51]

As with Somers's Oxford terms, the sparseness of the record virtually confines us to speculation as to his Middle Temple associates and the influences brought to bear upon him there. During these years at least three noteworthy figures served as Treasurer, the Inn's principal official. Somers's patron, Winnington, was one. The others were Sir Francis North and Richard Wallop. North became Treasurer in 1671, the same year in which he was appointed Solicitor-General; a decade later he would be Lord Chancellor. His interests transcended the law, and were reflected in the patronage of art, music and science. Wallop rose to be Cursitor-Baron of the Exchequer, but was most prominent as principal counsel for the Whigs in the trials of the later years of Charles II. Among outstanding men called to the Bench (and thus to the governing body of the Inn) at this time, we may mention Vere Bertie, Master of the Benchers in 1674 and a Justice of Common Pleas four years later, and Sir John Hoskins, Master in Chancery, who became President of the Royal Society in 1682. Except for Hoskins, all these men were appointed Readers, or official lecturers, in this period. Other notable Readers were Francis Bramston, eventually Baron of the Exchequer, and Nicholas Lechmere, who served on the Exchequer Bench under William III.

In such a slack age Somers may have seen little of these worthies. In 1676 there was 'a great failure' of attendance by Benchers, and a fine of £50 was imposed for such absenteeism. Some men, though they had chambers in the Inn, never came into Commons. Readers were from time to time mulcted for ignoring their assignments.[52] Much—we may say, nearly everything— depended on the individual student, and while Somers was surely fortunate in his relationship with such a master as Winnington, the knowledge of the law which he was to command must have been essentially the result of his own application and capacity.[53] If Winnington actually reaped such an impressive income, could he have had much time to spare for his protégé?

In the late seventeenth century Readers were still called upon to provide a feast during their term of office. That these were elaborate occasions is attested by John Evelyn, who, as a Member, was invited to Bramston's feast in 1668; it was, he noted, 'so very extravagant & greate as the like had not ben seene at any time'. A year later he described Sir Henry Peckham's feast as 'a pompous Entertainement', and noted the presence of the Archbishop of Canterbury and 'all the great Earles & Lords &c'.[54] Roger North regarded his brother Francis's feast in 1671 as a 'terrible' example of the extravagance of these affairs.[55] It is questionable if an apprentice barrister, without much distinction of birth, would have the entrée to such functions; but we may assume that Somers caught at least a glimpse of some of the nation's great, and even of majesty itself, for Charles II frequently attended feasts and revels at the Inns. In December 1670, for example, the King and Queen, accompanied by the Prince of Orange, 'were present *incognito* at the merriments usual at this season at the Temple, where they were entertained with dances of all kinds to their very great satisfaction'.[56]

In 1669 one hundred and three persons were admitted to membership in the Middle Temple.[57] Nearly all were sons of landed families. Roger North was the only peer's son, but the roster of fathers includes a scattering of knights and a handful of baronets.[58] The rest were sons of clergymen, merchants and lawyers. Most were from the southern half of England, particularly from the south-west. There was but one new member from the far north (Durham), though Ireland was represented by eight. Somers was one of four Worcestershire men admitted. The others were Charles Blount and George Porter, both from Worcester, and Thomas Parker of Longdon. Porter was from Claines, where White Ladies was situated. Except for Somers himself, the most distinguished member of this class was undoubtedly Roger North, the lawyer and historian. But several of them were of sufficient weight to serve as Treasurer in later years; besides Somers and North, the list includes Thomas Brough, Peter Broughton, William Ettricke and Humphrey Hetherington.

Somers was 'called to the degree of the Utter Bar' on 5 May 1676, at the age of twenty-five. For thirteen years we hear nothing of further association with the Inn, except that in 1677 he acquired more commodious chambers in Pump Court.[59] In 1689, however, upon his elevation to the Solicitor-Generalship, he was called to the Bench. The following autumn he was elected Lenten Reader for 1690, and in May of that year, 'having paid 200 l.', was again confirmed as Reader. But it is unlikely that he actually delivered the lectures which had once been a mainstay of the training of barristers. It appears that the last Reader of the Middle Temple to do so was appointed in 1684; readings in the other Inns are known to have ceased about this time. The £200 payment probably gained for Somers the status of the office without the obligations long attached to it. In 1691 he was chosen to succeed Sir George Treby as Treasurer. He occupied this premier office for a year, as was customary; on the basis of the evidence there is nothing to suggest that the character of the Inn was altered through his influence.[60]

According to Cooksey, a lifelong connection with Charles Talbot, twelfth Earl of Shrewsbury, originated about 1672, presumably while Somers was vacationing in Worcester. Four years earlier Shrewsbury had lost his father as a result of a duel with the Duke of Buckingham. We are told that the youthful Earl conceived a distaste for court life, and withdrew to his estates in Worcestershire, in the management of which Somers's father was involved. His principal residence, Grafton, being out of order, he is said to have availed himself of the hospitality of the Somers family.[61] This account does not appear to be supported by any evidence beyond the sphere of family tradition. On the face of it, it seems unlikely.[62] Somers in 1672 was twenty-one years of age, the Earl about twelve; between them was a considerable social gulf. Even if they were thrown together, it could hardly have been for prolonged periods of time. In 1674 Shrewsbury obtained a pass 'to travel beyond the seas for seven years'; shortly thereafter he set out for France.[63] Future years would find the two men closely associated in politics, but for a time they followed separate paths.

NOTES

[1] The family name was variously spelled. The Lord Chancellor preferred 'Somers' (with the circumflex) or 'Sommers'. See Treadway R. Nash, *Collections for the History of Worcestershire* (London, 1781), II, supplement, p. 50; George E. Cokayne, *Complete Peerage* (London, 1910–59), XII, pt. i, 29n.

[2] In 1654 John Evelyn spoke of the cathedral as 'extremely ruin'd', but added that the city was 'neately pav'd and very cleane': *Diary of John Evelyn*, ed. E. S. de Beer (Oxford, 1955, III, 119). See also *Victoria History of the Counties of England: History of Worcestershire* (Westminster and London, 1901–26), IV, 396; Valentine Green, *History and Antiquities of the City and Suburbs of Worcester* (London, 1796), I, 269–77.

[3] For White Ladies as the birthplace, see Richard Cooksey, *Essay on the Life and Character of John Lord Somers* (Worcester, 1791), 5; this is also given in the *Dictionary of National Biography* and in Cokayne's *Peerage*.

⁴ Register Book of St Michael's Parish, 1546–1791, pp. 25, 72. See also Nash, *Collections*, II, 320, 345; John Noake, *Monastery and Cathedral of Worcester* (London, 1866), 394–95.

⁵ On 15 October 1653 and 7 April 1655: Register Book, pp. 73, 79.

⁶ Green, II, 47 and n.

⁷ Nash, *Collections*, I, 346.

⁸ *Victoria C.H., Worcestershire*, IV, 196n. He married Ann Walker of Worcester and had issue, Richard and Elizabeth.

⁹ Nash, *Collections*, II, 54. See also Owen Manning and William Bray, *History and Antiquities of the County of Surrey* (London, 1804–14), I, 286.

¹⁰ *Memoirs of the Life of John Lord Somers* (London, 1716), 9–10. He served as Low Bailiff of Kidderminster: John R. Burton, *History of Kidderminster* (London, 1890), 152, 222.

¹¹ Ibid., 9–10; *The Peerage of England, or an Historical and Genealogical Account of the Present Nobility* (London, 1715), II, 172.

¹² *Prose Works of Jonathan Swift*, ed. Temple Scott (London, 1897–1908), from the *Examiner*, No. 27; Mary de la Riviere Manley, *Secret Memoirs and Manners of Several Persons of Quality, of Both Sexes. From the New Atalantis* (London, 1720), IV, 62.

¹³ Burton, 152, 213.

¹⁴ *Memoirs*, 10.

¹⁵ Nash, *Collections*, II, 345; Green, I, 71.

¹⁶ *Peerage* (1715), II, 172.

¹⁷ P.C.C. Proved, 24 November 1681, Reg. North, f. 174. See also Henry Maddock, *Account of the Life and Writings of Lord Chancellor Somers* (London, 1812), 7; Nash, *Collections*, II, 345; V.C.H. *Worcestershire*, III, 169; IV, 192 and n.

¹⁸ Maddock, 7. See Charles H. Firth and Godfrey Davies, *Regimental History of Cromwell's Army* (Oxford, 1940), II, 562, for a reference to Capt. Somner (or Somners), who had a company, raised in June 1650, in the regiment of Edward Sexby.

¹⁹ Cooksey, 7–8.

²⁰ The M.P. was Sir Scroope Howe. See *Commons Journal*, IX, 596, 603.

²¹ According to the diary of Mr Townshend, 26 March 1646; see also Nash, *Collections*, II, appendix, p. xcvii.

²² Cooksey, 4–5, 9, 121. Cf. Burton, 152, who states that Richard Blurton, Esq., purchased White Ladies.

²³ Noake, 625.

²⁴ Cooksey, 13–15.

²⁵ Frederick J. Powicke, *Life of the Reverend Richard Baxter, 1615–1691* (London, 1924), 158.

²⁶ Cooksey, 118. Richard Somers married Joice Child of Kidderminster: Nash, *Collections*, II, 54. The Childs were 'an old Kidderminster family': Burton, 152.

²⁷ Cooksey, 19, who notes that he desired to be buried in Kidderminster churchyard.

²⁸ Ibid., 15.

²⁹ John Campbell, *Lives of the Lord Chancellors and Keepers of the Great Seal of England* (London, 1857), V, 59. To be used with caution.

³⁰ Cooksey, 10; V.C.H. *Worcestershire*, IV, 487. For John Toy, see also D.N.B.

³¹ Sloane MSS. 4223, ff. 208–13, and see Green, II, 89n.

³² William Seward, *Anecdotes of Distinguished Persons* (London, 1804), II, 114.

³³ Joseph Foster, *Alumni Oxonienses: the Members of the University of Oxford, 1500–1714* (Oxford, 1891–92), IV, 1388.

³⁴ Cooksey, 17.

³⁵ See below, p. 203.

³⁶ *Life and Times of Anthony Wood*, ed. Andrew Clark (Oxford Historical Society, Oxford, 1891–95), II, 125.

³⁷ Charles E. Mallet, *History of the University of Oxford* (London, 1924–27), II, 397n, 423, 428.

³⁸ 'Prologue and epilogue to the University of Oxford, 1674', Epilogue, lines 17–18: *Works of John Dryden*, ed. Edward N. Hooker and H. T. Swedenberg (Berkeley, Cal., 1956), I, 153. And see Thomas Warton, *Life and Literary Remains of Ralph Bathurst, M.D.* (London, 1761).

³⁹ Ibid., 172–73. Harris, a Scholar of Trinity, 1684–88, became Prebendary of Rochester and Fellow of the Royal Society. The excerpts are from a fragment of an autobiography.

⁴⁰ Joseph Ayliffe, *Ancient and Present State of the University of Oxford* (London, 1714), I, pt. ii, 415.

41 Cooksey, 24.

42 Historical Manuscripts Commission, *Buccleuch (Montagu House) MSS.* (London, 1903), II, pt. ii, 636; *Alumni Oxonienses, 1500–1714,* I, 233.

43 Warton, 67; Nash, *Collections,* II, supplement, 49, 55.

44 Mallet, II, 428.

45 Cooksey, 25.

46 See D.N.B., Francis Winnington; Cooksey, 25.

47 Campbell, V, 59, on what evidence is not revealed. There is no reference to this in the *Memoirs,* Cooksey or Maddock.

48 *Register of Admissions to the Honourable Society of the Middle Temple,* comp. H. A. C. Sturgess (London, 1949), I, 178; Campbell, V, 60n.

49 See e.g., *Memoirs,* 10, where Somers is said to have served as his clerk.

50 See William S. Holdsworth, *History of English Law,* VI (London, 2nd edn., 1937), 490–493.

51 *Middle Temple Records,* ed. Charles H. Hopwood (London, 1904–5), III, 1253, 1257, 1262, 1264, 1266, 1273, 1280–81.

52 *Ibid.,* III, 1251, 1276, 1295.

53 According to the author of the *Memoirs* (p. 11), Somers 'vary'd his Studies, and did not spoil the Fineness of his Taste, by confining them to such dry Reading, as is that of the Law'. He was conversant with 'all Parts of Polite Literature', taking particular delight in poetry and history.

54 *Diary,* III, 512, 536–37.

55 Roger North, *Lives of the Right Hon. Francis North* [etc.] (London, 1826), I, 150.

56 Historical Manuscripts Commission, *Twelfth Report,* appendix, part VII. *Manuscripts of S. H. Le Fleming* (London, 1890), 73. In January, 1671, the royal guests were again on hand: *ibid.,* 75.

57 *Middle Temple Admissions Register,* I, 178–80.

58 I omit Charles Lord Clifford, eldest son of the Earl of Burlington, and several others of the nobility, who were given honorary membership in August 1669.

59 *Middle Temple Records,* III, 1296; Campbell, V, 63n, 73 and n.

60 *Middle Temple Records,* III, 1388, 1392, 1394, 1396–98, 1400, 1403. His assistants as Lenten Reader were Mr Morgan and Sir Richard May. Somers was assistant to Anthony Weldon in 1690, and to Edward Crayford the following year.

61 Cooksey, 16.

62 Dorothy H. Somerville, *The King of Hearts: Charles Talbot, Duke of Shrewsbury* (London, 1962), 19n. In a letter to me, dated 25 May 1962, Miss Somerville writes: 'My own impression is that the friendship between Somers and Shrewsbury has been exaggerated. Their relations seem to have been cordial but not intimate.'

63 *Calendar of State Papers Domestic, 1673–75,* 246.

II

The Whig apprenticeship, 1676–88

Though called to the Bar in 1676, several years passed before Somers took up the duties of his profession. By an order issued by Lord Chancellor Clarendon in 1664 no one was to engage in practice before the courts for three years after being called to the Bar. Two years later Sir William Dugdale endorsed such a policy, noting that 'the over early and hasty practice of utter barristers doth make them the less grounded and sufficient, whereby the law may be disgraced and the client prejudiced'.[1] Lord Keeper Guilford likewise condemned too early an appearance before the courts, on the ground that 'no person increaseth his store of law after he is called to the bar and enters upon practice'.[2] One may wonder if Clarendon's order, designed to promote what might be called postgraduate study, had much effect. An eighteenth-century commentator shows another side of the life of young barristers, who

troop down to Westminster at Nine; Cheapen Cravats and Handkerchiefs, Ogle the Seamstresses, take a Whet at the Dog, or a Slice of Roast Beef at Heaven, fetch half a dozen turns in the Hall, peep in at the Common Pleas, talk over the News, and so with their Green Bags, that have as little in them as their Noddles, go home again. Summon'd by pensive Sound of Horn to rotten roasted Mutton at Twelve; Leave a Paper in their Doors to study Presidents and Cases for them all the Afternoon; may be heard of at the Devil, or some neighbouring Tavern till One in the Morning.[3]

Although there is little in the way of evidence, it is likely that much of Somers's time in the late 1670s was spent in the study and the library. Although he acquired in 1677 more spacious chambers in Pump Court, he is said to have made Oxford, rather than London, his usual place of residence, from which he paid occasional visits to Worcester. There is, however, no corroborating evidence from Oxford; if the young barrister lived there it must have been in an extra-mural status.[4] At this time the Inns of Court and the universities were mutually exclusive with regard to their instruction in the law; the former devoted themselves (albeit unsystematically) to the common law of England, while the latter, still wedded to medieval and ecclesiastical traditions, were concerned only with the civil and the canon law.[5] That Somers acquired a familiarity with the civil law that was noteworthy among English practitioners of the day cannot be denied, but how this familiarity was obtained is not clear. Most likely it was from private study. Throughout his life Somers was an avid reader, and the splendid library that he assembled contained many works of jurisprudence apart from those usually consulted by men bred up in the common law. Its catalogue lists nearly 300 printed works under the heading 'Jus civilis'.[6]

During these years he must have perfected and extended his knowledge of modern languages. Greek and Latin he had mastered in the course of his school and college years. He also acquired a command of French, a tongue which gained a new ascendancy among men of affairs in the age of the Sun King; more extraordinary was his knowledge of Italian, a language much less in vogue than it had been a century earlier, when England stood closer to the initial impacts of the Renaissance. We are told that he acquainted himself with the major poets and prose writers of Italy from Petrarch to the contemporary lyric poet (and jurist) Vincenzio da Filicaja.[7] The latter he regarded as one of Italy's greatest literary geniuses. Years later Somers, acknowledging a copy of Filicaja's poems, wrote that he would read them 'with new pleasure every day of my life'.[8] It is pleasant to find that this esteem was reciprocated; Filicaja wrote a Latin ode in praise of Somers in which he lauded him for his ability to speak seven languages without ever having left England.[9]

Meanwhile he was revealing his political colours, and this at a time when the nation was witnessing the beginnings of the Tory and Whig parties, and of the organisation and manoeuvres that we associate with partisan politics. These developments, rooted in the Royalist and Parliamentary causes of the previous generation, were now accelerated and sharpened by a variety of issues and crises: a lack of confidence that Charles II's foreign policy was in the national, or Protestant, interest; hostility towards Roman Catholicism, unleashed in unprecedented fashion by the Popish Plot; and the controversy that raged over the propriety of permitting the Catholic Duke of York to succeed his brother upon the throne. These issues served to align English-men with the Whig Shaftesbury or the Tory Danby; rarely, if ever, have they been so intensely, even hysterically, committed to one side or the other. Somers was no exception, and clearly emerges in these years as an adherent of the Whig interest, with which he was to be prominently identified for the rest of his life.

The groundwork for Somers's Whiggism was laid before these contro-versies rocked the nation. As we have seen, his father held no brief for theories of divine right and passive obedience, and may have even served under Oliver's command. The young Somers's patron and mentor, Sir Francis Winnington, came to be prominently identified with the more aggressive and unscrupulous Whigs. He was among the most notable of those who voted against Danby in 1679, and suffered dismissal from the post of Solicitor-General as a consequence. Embittered by his ouster, he joined the ranks of the Exclusionists, though he had previously opposed them, and denied that James had any right, *jure divino*, to the succession. The crucial years of partisan strife brought new contacts with Opposition figures, some of considerable prominence. Coupled with Winnington as an unqualified supporter of Exclusion was Sir William Jones, the 'Bull-faced Jonas' of *Absalom and Achitophel*, another lawyer, who had risen to be Attorney-General. Jones was a Gray's Inn man; his reputation for legal knowledge was extraordinary, and there can be no doubt that Somers came within his orbit. He is said to have been acquainted with even more notable Whig figures of the time. Here the Earl of Shrewsbury crops up again: family tradition gives him credit for introducing the young barrister to Lord Russell and Algernon Sidney, both shortly to become Whig martyrs.[10] Burnet adds that he was 'much esteemed and often visited by lord Essex', who 'trusted himself to him', while James Ralph (writing two generations later) stresses his political associations with Shaftesbury and others in his camp.[11] In the light of Somers's political orientation these relationships are likely, but there is little substantiation apart from circumstantial evidence.[12]

It is, rather, from what Somers wrote or perhaps helped to write that an alliance with the opposition is discernible. Around 1681 four tracts appeared which have been attributed to him. None bears his name; according to Maddock he never openly avowed any of his productions.[13] One of these, *The Memorable Case of Denzil Onslow, Tried at the Assizes in Surrey, 20 July 1681, Touching His Election at Haslemere in Surrey*—an attack on the practice of fagot-voting, or voting by virtue of spurious qualifications—must be regarded as doubtful.[14] But the other three, which are of more general importance to the student of Restoration politics, have been and continue to be set down under his name.

The first of these is *A Brief History of the Succession, Collected out of the Records and the Most Authentical Historians* (1680). James Ralph tells us that he saw it in the Somers collection, with various notes and 'improvements' in his handwriting, whether as a manuscript or printed piece is not clear.[15] We know that his library contained the 1655 edition of Robert Parsons's *Treatise of the Broken Succession of the Crown of England* and William Lawrence's *The Right of Primogeniture in Succession to the Kingdoms of England, Scotland and Ireland* (1681).[16] In any case, his authorship of the *Brief History* has not been challenged.[17] It is an attempt to answer in the affirmative the constitutional question, recently raised by William Sacheverell, as to whether King and Parliament might not dispose of the succession of the crown.[18] In other words, it was a defence of the Exclusion Bill, supposedly for the information of Lord Halifax, an opponent of exclusion. As such, it attacked the conservative position, to some extent bound up with divine right concepts of government, that Parliament was powerless to change the pattern of succession, which must be left in the hands of providence. This he categorically denied.[19] To show that the Whig proposal to exclude the Duke from the royal inheritance ought not to be regarded as a revolutionary break with English political traditions, he reviewed in detail the history of the crown's descent, from earliest times to the accession of James I. He found that no regular pattern had prevailed, at least for many centuries, and that various principles, depending upon circumstances, governed the succession even in modern times. Written while the crucial bill was still pending, the tract evoked immediate rejoinders, in particular two from Dr Robert Brady, the Cambridge physician and historian who was a strong upholder of the royal prerogative and who represented his university in the parliaments of 1681 and 1685.[20] It is worthy of note that on the eve of the Glorious Revolution the *Brief History* was translated into Dutch, and appeared about that time in a new English edition, as it did again in 1714.[21] Whatever its impact in 1681, it would be read anew whenever the succession to the throne became a critical issue.[22]

In April 1681 *A Just and Modest Vindication of the Proceedings of the Two Last Parliaments* came off the press. The authorship has been assigned to William Jones, Robert Ferguson and Algernon Sidney, as well as to Somers.[23] According to Burnet it was 'first penned by Sidney; but a new draught was made by Somers, and corrected by Jones'.[24] Roger North notes only that it was said to have been composed by Jones.[25] In the following century Lord Hardwicke saw a copy of the tract is Somers's handwriting among his manuscripts which were destroyed by fire in 1752.[26] Hardwicke's Victorian successor, Lord Campbell, appears to have been convinced by this, as well as by strong 'internal evidence' that the work was chiefly from Somers's pen.[27] In our own day Professor Caroline Robbins gives him at least a hand in writing it; it was, she thinks, 'most likely Jones overlaid by Somers', Sidney being at the time too busy with the *Discourses* to have had much of a share in it.[28] We may conclude that Somers bore a considerable responsibility for its published form, and that it represents his considered judgement.

Published shortly after the dissolution of the Oxford Parliament had derailed the Whig exclusionist programme, it was designed to answer a royal declaration, probably framed by Lord Chief Justice North, justifying the last two dissolutions of Parliament and condemning those who had opposed the government by supporting the Exclusion Bill.[29] Burnet describes it as written 'with great spirit and true judgment', a verdict elaborated by Campbell, who proclaims it 'a very masterly vindication of the rights of Parliament, and of the policy of the liberal party under Shaftesbury in their attempt to alter the succession for the safety of the people and the preservation of the monarchy'.[30] In High Tory eyes, however, it was 'one entire begging of the Question, from the Beginning to the End, even of the whole Matter in Dispute', and filled with the 'factious Cant' of the age.[31] This was a much more partisan and polemical work than the *Brief History*: it dealt not with events long past but with a parliamentary crisis of recent months, and one which had left scars and bitter memories.

The tract begins with a reference to the importance long attached to annual parliaments, not to be dissolved until all petitions before them had been 'answered and redressed', a position strongly upheld by Algernon Sidney. That two parliaments had been dissolved within a period of three months could only be regarded as amazing. Attention is then focused on the recent conduct of the legislators, and particularly on the all-important issue of exclusion. On occasion the language is sharp. To the complaint that the Commons had presented addresses 'in the nature of remonstrances rather than answers', a blunt question is put: 'Under what unhappy circumstances do we find ourselves, when our representatives can never behave themselves with that caution, but they will be misinterpreted at court?'[32]

Such strong advocacy of Parliament evoked the charge that the author and his associates were favourers of democracy, or, in the language of the time, 'commonwealth principles'. Indictments of this sort were commonly levelled at the Whigs of these and later times. But they bear about the same relationship to Somers's philosophy of government that the charge of communism bears to most men of liberal political and social sentiments in the present-day United States. Here and elsewhere Somers was to demonstrate an attachment to mixed, or as we should say, limited monarchy:

The preservation of every government depends upon an exact adherence unto its principles, and the essential principle of the English monarchy being that well proportioned distribution of powers, whereby the law doth at once provide for the greatness of the King, and the safety of the people, the government can subsist no longer, than whilst the monarch, enjoying the power which the law doth give unto him, is enabled to perform the part which it allows him, and the people are duly protected in their rights and liberties.[33]

He was no democrat. But he believed that government existed for the benefit of the governed; if these were 'commonwealth principles' he would espouse them:

If they mean by these lovers of Commonwealth principles, men passionately devoted to the public good, and to the common service of their country, who believe that kings were instituted for the good of the people, and government ordained for the sake of those that are to be governed, and therefore complain or grieve when it is used to contrary ends, every wise and honest man will be proud to be ranked in that number.[34]

According to Burnet, the *Vindication* 'had no great effect', party spirit being spent.[35] However true this may be of partisan zeal in general, there is evidence that Somers, at least, was not inclined to forget the recent issues. About the middle of June 1681, an address of thanks for the King's declaration was prepared at the Middle Temple, a day after a similar project had been undertaken at Gray's Inn. In the debate that ensued a struggle developed between the supporters and the opponents of the address as to who should take the chair. The latter 'called for Mr. Somners; on which a poll was demanded, but the addressers refused it, and carried Mr. Mountague and sett him in the chaire', whereupon a free-for-all occurred. In the end, the 'addressers' adjourned to a tavern, while their opponents 'kept in the hall, and fell to protesting against such illegall and arbitrary proceedings'.[36] There can be no doubt of the identity of 'Mr. Somners', and one may assume that he played a consequential part in drafting the protestation, which bore more signatures than the address.

A fortnight later Shaftesbury was sent to the Tower. Denied bail or recourse to trial, the Whig champion seemed to be inextricably enmeshed in the toils of the government. In November he was charged at the Old Bailey with intention of levying war against the king. This, under the Act of 1661, constituted high treason. But, though Justice Pemberton exerted himself to induce the grand jury of Middlesex to bring in a true bill, the jurymen, who had been selected by the Whig Sheriffs, threw out the indictment. Great was the discomfiture of the court, and of those allied with it. From the press came various pamphlets, issued under governmental patronage, denouncing the jury. In reply, Somers brought out *The Security of Englishmen's Lives, or, The Trust, Power, and Duty of the Grand Juries of England*. It was first published in 1681; like the *Vindication*, it has been attributed to another, this time Lord Essex. But according to Burnet it was composed by Somers, who 'wrote the best papers that came out in that time', and there seems to be no doubt in this case.[37] Of all his productions, this is the most ambitious, running to around a hundred and fifty pages, and, if reprintings are an indication, it has best withstood the test of time. The *Catalogue* of the British Museum includes six editions between 1681 and 1771, and this is not a complete list. It was published in Boston, Massachusetts, in 1720 and in London and New York in 1773.

The Security of Englishmen's Lives is in reality a commentary on English justice, though on an early page Somers informs the reader that he will confine himself to a consideration of grand juries, and to showing 'how much the Reputation, the Fortunes, and the Lives of English Men depend upon the Conscientious performance of their Duty'.[38] He emphasises the importance of a full investigation of the facts; judges may advise, but the jurymen 'are bound by their Oaths to present the Truth, the whole Truth, and nothing but the Truth, to the best of their own, not the Judges, Knowledge'.[39] He holds forth at length on the functions and treatment of witnesses, and on the importance of revealing to the jurymen all facts that have been discovered by agents of the government. At this point he underscores the responsibility of the sovereign in seeing that justice is done:

Whosoever hath learnt that the Kings of Engand were ordained for the good Government of the Kingdom in the Execution of the Laws, must needs know, that the King cannot lawfully seek any other benefit in judicial proceedings, than that common Right and Justice be done to the People according to their Laws and Customs.[40]

The protection of the innocent should be of greater concern to a prince than the punishment of the guilty. Clemency in rulers is ever desirable:

If a Criminal should be acquitted wrongfully he may be reserved for future Justice from Man or God, if he doth not repent; but 'tis impossible that satisfaction or reparation should be made for innocent Bloodshed in the forms of Justice.[41]

He returns several times to the theme that the interest of king and subjects in the maintenance of the law should be as one, and that in this enterprise it is of the utmost importance that the grand jury should play an independent role, and should not be restricted in its inquiries: 'The Truth is, that Grand Juries have both a larger field for their Inquiry, and are in many respects better capacitated to make a strict one, than the Petit Juries.'[42] He goes so far as to say that it is a mistake to imagine that the latter were instituted for the hearing of fuller proofs. To those who may object that such careful scrutiny on the part of the grand jury, combined with the normal trial procedures of the petty jury, cannot but result in a double trial, with delay of justice, he replies that this is of slight consequence where the life of a man is in question.[43] 'Therefore,' he concludes, 'let the Grand Juries faithfully perform their high Trust, and neither be cheated nor frighted from their Duty.'[44]

Somers's literary efforts during these years were not confined to the production of political treatises.[45] To the educated man, the man of culture, the classics were then not merely part of the educational discipline of boyhood and early manhood, to be put aside when maturity was reached. They were the very backbone of the arts which enlivened the spirit, and of the philosophies by which they set their compasses. Somers not only continued to read the classics—his extensive library provides ample evidence of his abiding interest in this realm—but essayed translations of the Greek and Latin masters. He was one of a 'mob of gentlemen' who contributed to a new edition of Plutarch's *Lives*, the first volume of which appeared in 1683.[46] Others involved in this venture included Creech, Duke, Knightly Chetwood, Caryll, Rymer and Oldys. Many were friends of John Dryden, who provided the dedication and a life of Plutarch. Somers was responsible for the life of Alcibiades, the Athenian general and statesman. On the face of it, it seems odd that Somers should have co-operated in a project with which Dryden was so prominently associated, even though it was distant from the arena of contemporary politics, for only two years had elapsed since that poet had exposed the Whigs to deadly ridicule in *Absalom and Achitophel*, after which he proceeded to add insult to injury in *The Medal*. But here, it seems, the republic of letters transcended political boundaries.[47] Some, indeed, have regarded Somers as the author of *The Satyr to His Muse, by the Author of Absalom and Achitophel*, an anonymous poem castigating Dryden and vindicating the Whig position, which appeared about this time. It was included under his name in a collection of minor poetic works published in 1750. But Thomas Shadwell's authorship of this piece is now regarded as virtually certain.[48]

Somers did try his hand at versification, contributing translations of 'Ariadne to Theseus' and 'Dido to Aeneas', again anonymously, in *Ovid's Epistles, Translated by Several Hands*.[49] Though Dryden has been described as the editor, it seems more likely that Jacob Tonson, the publisher, collected the pieces, engaging the poet to write a preface. Dryden also supplied translations of three epistles, one of them 'Dido to Aeneas'. Somers's version followed immediately after Dryden's, and bears some striking resemblances, but a modern critic has found it closer to Turberville, Saltonstall and Sherburne than to Dryden.[50] It may be that Somers first met Tonson, with whom he was to enjoy a lifelong friendship and to share various literary adventures, in connection with the publication of this work.

In January 1681 his father died, at the age of sixty. His will, probated in

November of that year, left all his landed property 'scituate and lying in any part of the Countie of Worcester' to his widow, who was to outlive him by nearly thirty years. Drawn in 1676, this will makes specific reference to the 'great Charge' the elder Somers had incurred in the education of his son. It also proclaims his confidence that his wife, who was named executrix, would advance the children 'what shee can, and carrie an indifferent hand amongst them'.[51] The 'children', besides young Somers, were the surviving daughters, Elizabeth, Mary and Katherine, none of them yet married. If the terms of the will were carried out, and the lands went to the widow, James Ralph may have been right in stating that the son was left 'a bare competence, and no more'.[52] Yet the author of the 1716 *Memoirs* declares that he 'inherited a good Estate' after his father's death.[53] It may be that, in due course, Katherine Somers settled property on her son, perhaps after the daughters' marriages had been arranged, but that, for a time, his financial position was not materially improved.

The year 1681 also marked the eclipse of the Whigs, their exclusion programme unfulfilled. Deprived of a parliamentary forum, they were for the rest of the reign impotent. Any hopes of preferment nursed by the youthful barrister were effectively dashed; and, with the succession of the Duke of York presumably assured, more distant prospects appeared equally bleak. The practice of the law was bound to loom larger. Favourable attention and more tangible rewards began to come his way. He was complimented, we are told, by Lord Chancellor Nottingham, who assured him of the pleasure he took in his pleading.[54] For assistance rendered to the Dean and Chapter of Worcester he was in 1681 chosen to be one of the 'standing counsel' for that body.[55] In James II's reign his income as a lawyer is said to have come to £700 a year, an impressive figure; a few years later Gregory King estimated the average annual earnings of 'persons in the law' at one fifth of this amount.[56]

Not until 1683, however, were his professional services of sufficient importance to be noticed in the Law Reports. Early in that year Sir Thomas Pilkington and Samuel Shute were tried, along with Henry Cornish, Slingsby Bethel and Lord Grey of Warke, for riot at the election of the London Sheriffs in June of 1682.[57] Pilkington and Shute were prominent Whigs; as outgoing Sheriffs they had continued the poll several days longer than was authorised by the order of the Lord Mayor, in the Whig interest, of course. Only a few months before, Pilkington had been fined the enormous sum of £100,000 in an action of *scandalum magnatum* for having publicly stated that the Duke of York had been responsible for the Great Fire of 1666. Cornish and Bethel were the new Sheriffs. In various ways they followed in the footsteps of their predecessors, who had been thanked by the freemen of London for their 'provision of faithful and able juries'. Under Cornish and Bethel the Middlesex grand jury that rejected the bill against Shaftesbury was impanelled. Bethel had a reputation for republicanism; Cornish was shortly to be condemned and executed for complicity in the Rye House plot. In the eyes of the court, all were looked upon as trouble-makers, to be discredited and broken. Somers, on the other hand, must have regarded them as champions of the true faith, and been pleased that he was able to play some part in their defence.

In this capacity, he found himself in a distinguished company. Among the eight counsellors for the defence were Sir John Holt, later Chief Justice of the King's Bench; Sir William Williams, recently Speaker of the House and before long Solicitor-General; Richard Wallop, who has been described as the leading counsel for the Whigs in the State trials of the time; and Sir Francis Winnington, Somers's erstwhile mentor and, very likely, responsible for his employment in this case.[58] On the other side he had an opportunity to observe the tactics of Serjeant Jeffreys, soon to be notorious for his conduct of the 'Bloody Assizes'. He appears to have had ample time for observation. The transcript of the trial reveals that he spoke only to 'challenge the array', it being known that a packed jury had been assembled.[59] But he probably assisted his seniors in other ways. As was to be expected, the defendants were all found guilty, and were severely punished.

For the next five years we hear very little of Somers. The constitutional issues of James II's reign—Hales's case, the new ecclesiastical commission, the use of the suspending power—evoked no treatises from his pen. Unlike some of his confreres, he avoided the toils of the Monmouthites, though he was recognised as opposed to James's system of government. But in June of 1688 he suddenly found himself in the limelight of national publicity. He was called upon to assist in the celebrated trial of the seven bishops. This occasion was to prove a climacteric in his fortunes, both with regard to his professional reputation and as a point of departure for the political activities and achievements of the remainder of his life.

The trial arose from the refusal of the bishops (actually, Archbishop Sancroft and six other prelates) to publicise James's second Declaration of Indulgence by ordering it to be read from the pulpit; more particularly, it stemmed from a petition drawn up by these ecclesiastics, in which the royal dispensing power was impugned. This the government chose to regard as seditious libel, and an information was served requiring the bishops to answer the charge in the Court of King's Bench. Seven counsellors were engaged for their defence: Sir Robert Sawyer, Heneage Finch, Sir Henry Pollexfen, Sir George Treby, Sir Francis Pemberton, Sir Cresswell Levinz and Somers, who was paid a retaining fee of £5 7s 6d on 25 June.[60] That Somers should have been included among lawyers of such distinction, in a state trial of such consequence, indicates that he had made his mark in his profession. Even so, his retention was objected to by at least one of the bishops on the ground that he was 'too young and obscure a Man'. But this was overruled at the insistence of Pollexfen, who refused to participate without him, describing him 'as the Man who would take most Pains, and go deepest into all that depended on Precedents and Records'.[61] The prelates may well have looked with some suspicion upon the qualifications of a man whose published writings, whatever his religious beliefs, were hardly consonant with the theories of passive obedience supported by their Church. But they were not to be disappointed in his services.

The defence was handled primarily by Sawyer, Pollexfen, Pemberton and Somers—Sawyer, as senior counsel, leading, and the others assisting. The prosecution rested for the most part in the capable hands of Sir William Williams (Somers's associate in the Pilkington case), who had abandoned his former Whig connections and been raised to the Solicitor-Generalship. After a preliminary hearing, the bishops were given two weeks to prepare their defence, and the trial got under way on 29 June. The royal dispensing power, though not directly on trial, was obviously the underlying issue. Both Sawyer and Pollexfen emphasised the disadvantageous implications of such authority, the latter arguing that if the king's will be not in conformity with the law, the subject is nowise bound. But, in general, they based their defence on the argument that the defendants had done no more than avail themselves of the subject's recognised right to petition. To this Williams retorted that it was only through Parliament (which had not sat since 1685) that the subject could petition, and Justice Allibone, a Roman Catholic, correctly remarked that, as the laws stood, anything spoken or written against the practical exercise of governmental powers was to be regarded as libellous.[62]

Somers, as junior, was the last to speak. His remarks were moderate and succinct; we are told that he spoke for less than five minutes. He availed himself of Thomas v. Sorrel (1674), an Exchequer Chamber case which had involved the validity of a dispensation of a statute of Edward VI, in connection with the sale of wine.[63] The case was appropriate in that the judges had then ruled that there could be no abrogation, either permanently or temporarily, of an Act of Parliament save through the exercise of the legislative function. Somers pointed out how careful the defendants had been 'that they might not any way justly offend the King'. They had not come forward to give their advice as peers of the realm: 'they never stirred till a command which they deemed unlawful was laid upon themselves'. In their petition they had gone only so far as to request that they might not be compelled to read the Declaration of Indulgence; they had not even raised the question of its revocation.

The petition had been described as a false, malicious and seditious libel. On this Somers based his peroration:

My Lord, as to all the matters of fact alleged in the Petition,—that they are perfectly true we have shown by the Journals of both Houses. In every instance which the petitioners mention, this power of dispensation was considered in Parliament, and, on debate, declared to be contrary to law. They could have no design to diminish the prerogative, because the King hath no such prerogative. Seditious, my Lord, the Petition could not be, for the matter of it must be seen to be strictly true. There could be nothing of malice, for the occasion, instead of being sought, was forced upon them. A libel it could not be, for the intent of the defendants was innocent, and they kept strictly within the bounds set by the law, which gives the subject leave to apply to his Prince by petition when he is aggrieved.[64]

In summing up, Justice Wright chose to rule out any consideration of the thorny problem of the dispensing power. The jury was called upon to consider two questions: had publication been proved, and was the petition libellous, in that it had disturbed the governing authority and stirred up the people? To the undisguised satisfaction of Londoners, the jury returned a verdict of 'not guilty'. Though the immediate beneficiaries were seven leaders of the Church of England, the verdict was, in effect, 'against a whole system of government'.[65] We may well imagine Somers's satisfaction. Whether or not the acquittal may be 'mainly ascribed' to his arguments, he had contributed significantly to a winning team, and he had received upwards of £30 in fees. But he had not only helped to win a case. He had bolstered up concepts of government for which he had argued, without immediate success, in years gone by, and which he would implement in classic fashion in the coming Revolution.

While the nation waited to learn the fate of the embattled bishops, the conspiratorial activities which culminated in the Glorious Revolution and the deposition of James II were unfolding. The misgivings which had been mounting for several years had evoked no widespread or sharply focused public opposition. But the birth of a prince on 10 June sounded the alarm. The likelihood that James's policies would obtain a new lease on life with the succession of a Catholic heir, rather than receive their quietus upon the advent of the Protestant Mary, placed the issues in a new perspective. To the man in the street, whose grasp of such technicalities as the dispensing or suspending power was at best vague and faulty, the tale of the warming-pan was quite comprehensible. However absurd and unsubstantiated it may appear to us, to a generation still willing to believe the worst of papists it was but another example of the devious and illicit means such men could be expected to employ to gain their ends. It was but a decade since Oates's revelations had whipped the imaginations of Englishmen into a frenzy and convinced many that James could not be trusted with the crown. Might not the cradle of his son now be, as the Irish Capuchins hoped, 'the tombe of heresy and schism'?[66]

On the very day that the bishops were acquitted, Admiral Russell, a brother of the ill-fated Whig martyr of 1683, embarked for Holland. Disguised as an ordinary seaman, he bore an invitation to William of Orange to invade England in the interests of the Protestant religion and popular liberties; the vast majority of James's subjects, he was assured, would look upon such an enterprise with favour. The signatories, besides Russell himself, were the Earls of Devonshire, Danby and Shrewsbury, Lord Lumley, Bishop Compton of London, and Henry Sidney. William was ready. Since at least 1687 he had been carefully watching the English political scene, and in that year, following Dykveld's mission, had received encouragement from such notables as Nottingham, Shrewsbury and Churchill.[67] Nor did he conceal his opinion that the birth of Prince James was a fraud.

It has been said that Somers probably drew up the invitation to William, and that, if he did not compose the Prince's response, in which he set forth his motives for descending upon England, it 'certainly had his previous approbation'.[68] Granted that anyone involved in such a dangerous business would take pains to cover his tracks, there is virtually no basis for such claims, except, perhaps, in the realm of circumstantial evidence. It is probable that his alleged association with the early phases of the revolutionary movement derives mainly from a remark made by Nicholas Tindal, in his translation and continuation of Rapin's *History of England*, that the young barrister 'was admitted into the most secret councils of the Prince of Orange, and was one of those who concocted the measure of bringing him over'.[69] But Tindal was not born until 1688; he wrote a generation after the events, and, while he may have had access to materials which have since disappeared, his statement is not confirmed in any treatment of the life of William, or in any known contemporary document. Nor is there any proof that Somers was consulted, either by Dykveld or by another of William's agents, Zuylestein, who visited England in 1687 and 1688, and was in contact with the prominent malcontents of the kingdom. That he was working closely with any of the seven signatories also remains to be demonstrated, though here his connection with Shrewsbury may provide a clue, the Earl's house being reportedly the scene of various conspiratorial gatherings.[70] As for William's declaration, it was actually drawn up by Fagel, the Grand Pensionary. But Burnet, who was responsible for the English translation, tells us that 'a great many draughts were sent from England by various hands', these forming the basis for Fagel's text.[71] It may be that one of them was from Somers's pen.

There is, on the other hand, at least a hint that he was regarded as not beyond rendering some service to the existing government. In September 1688 arrangements were afoot for a new Parliament. Circular letters were addressed to lords lieutenant and others in positions of influence, recommending that they 'procure the election of more than a hundred persons' mentioned by name as suitable members of the House of Commons. The list includes the name of Somers. Sir James Mackintosh suggests that he was 'probably selected from a hope that his zeal for religious liberty might induce him to support a government which professed so comprehensive a toleration'.[72] Possibly so; yet it is not apparent that at this time Somers had demonstrated any particular regard for religious toleration. Even after the Revolution his liberality did not extend to the Roman Catholics. And, surely, the junior counsel in the recent bishops' trial seems an odd choice, if the government was thinking along these lines. In any case, Somers's name was stricken from the list after a few days.

Whatever doubt may have existed in the summer regarding the strength of Somers's opposition to James's government must have been speedily dispelled. In October the Court of Aldermen of the City of London chose him to succeed Sir George Treby as Recorder.[73] This event followed by about two weeks the restoration of the City's charter, surrendered five years before with the resultant loss of direct governmental control over the officials and policies of the metropolis. James, with his son-in-law's invasion pending, was anxious to secure loyalty and support wherever he could find it. Aldermen installed by royal commission during the suspension of the charter were ousted; back came the survivors among those who had been in office at the time of the *quo warranto* proceedings. Treby, who had been Recorder during that crisis, now refused to serve. Somers was nominated with several others, of whom Sir Bartholomew Shower and Thomas Jones were the most notable. He was elected and called upon to assume his duties. But to no avail: on 25 October he declined the office in a letter addressed to the court.[74] The entry in its minutes gives no inkling as to his reasons; a month later he would accept the recordership of Worcester. He could hardly have foreseen, a fortnight before the landing of the Prince of Orange, the important political business in which he would shortly be engaged in Parliament, nor even have counted upon a seat. In any case, parliamentary ambitions need not have deterred him, for Treby had held the recordership while sitting as M.P. for Plympton. It is possible that he shunned responsibilities which might, after the recognition won in the bishops' trial, leave him too little time for a more lucrative private practice.

Perhaps he regarded the office as Treby's by right: in the end, after William had come, Treby resumed it.[75] But, in any case, it is significant that the restored Court of Aldermen, freed from royal regulation and pressure, sought Somers's services as the city's principal legal representative. That he was a revolutionary activist requires further proof; that he was generally recognised as a steadfast opponent of the regime is undeniable.

NOTES

[1] *Origines Juridiales, or Historical Memorials of the English Laws* (London, 1666), 323.

[2] *Lives of the Norths*, I, 51.

[3] *Comical View of London and Westminster*; see John Ashton, *Social Life in the Reign of Queen Anne* (New York, 1929), 354.

[4] Campbell, V, 58, 63 and n. Maddock, p. 30, states that he kept his terms at Oxford and London. It is likely that our subject has been confused, with regard to years spent at Oxford, with another John Somers, of Exeter.

[5] There was a renewal of interest in the study of civil law at Oxford during the Interregnum. See Mallet, II, 393; *Cal. S. P. Dom.*, 1657–58, 271–72; D.N.B., Richard Zouche.

[6] Add. MSS. 40, 751, ff. 90–97.

[7] Vincenzio da Filicaja (1642–1707), especially noted for his odes and sonnets. See *Le Vite degli Arcadi Illustri Scritte da Diversi Autori, e Pubblicate d'ordine della Generale Adunanza da G. M. Crescimbeni* (n.p., 1708–14), pt. ii, quoted in Campbell, V, 185–86.

[8] Add. MSS. 36, 270, f. 1.

[9] See Campbell, V, 187, citing *Opere di Vincenzio da Filicaja* (Venice, 1755), II, 50. This may be found in *Aggiunto il di lui Carteggio alle Suddette Poesie* (Venice, 1755).

[10] Cooksey, 25.

[11] Gilbert Burnet, *History of His Own Time* (Oxford, 1823), II, 290; James Ralph, *History of England* (London, 1744–46). According to Caroline Robbins, *Eighteenth-century Commonwealthsman* (Cambridge, 1959), 79, he was also associated with the Onslow family.

[12] See O. W. Furley, 'The Whig Exclusionists: pamphlet literature in the Exclusion

campaign, 1679–81', *Cambridge Historical Journal*, XIII (No. 1, 1957), 26. According to Furley the precise relationship between Shaftesbury and the pamphleteers 'remains a matter of speculation'.

13 Maddock, 65.

14 It may be found in *Somers Tracts* (London, 1747–52), I (1748), 374–80, with no ascription of authorship. Neither the *British Museum General Catalogue* nor Wing lists it under Somers, but Maddock says that he wrote it (p. 47).

15 Ralph, *History*, I, 519, and see Maddock, 50.

16 Add. MSS. 40, 751, f. 169v.

17 The British Museum has some doubts as to its publication date. Wing gives 1680. It may be found in *Somers Tracts*, ed. Walter Scott (London, 1809–15), XIII, 649–67 (where it is ascribed to Somers) and in *Harleian Miscellany* (London, 1803–13), IX, 248–70, where no authorship is noted. A copy in the Beinecke Library, Yale University (British Tracts, Folio Pamphlets 21), bears a handwritten notation that it was 'supposed to be writ by Mr. Petyt', presumably William Petyt (1636–1707), the archivist and antiquary.

18 Anchitell Grey, *Debates in the House of Commons from the Year 1667 to the Year 1694* (London, 1763), VI, 148. The debate in which this question was raised occurred on 4 November 1678.

19 See *Somers Tracts*, ed. Scott, XII, 660, 662.

20 *The Great Point of the Succession Discussed* (London, 1681) and *A True and Exact History of the Succession* (London, 1681). In 1684 Brady, in his *Introduction to the Old English History, Comprehended in Three Several Tracts*, included an enlargement of the latter work. Brady was Master of Caius College, as well as Keeper of the Records in the Tower and M.P. for Cambridge University. In his *Great Point* he rejected the historical examples referred to by Somers; he also accused him of faulty Latin, appending a table listing his 'many willful Mistakes'.

21 Besides that of 1681 there were editions in 1689, 1693, 1714, 1744, 1808, and 1809.

22 Furley, in 'The Whig Exclusionists', 26, regards it as 'probably the best' of the treatments of the subject.

23 See *British Museum Catalogue*, CXVIII, col. 852, with 1681 as date and attribution to William Jones. Wing attributes it to Robert Ferguson, with 1682 as date. According to the *General Biography* of John Aikin and William Johnston (London, 1814) it was originally written by Sidney, but 'new modelled' by Somers (p. 192). Robbins, 2, attributes it to Somers. It may be found in Cobbett's *Parliamentary History of England* (London, 1806–12), IV, appendix, cxxxiv–clxxiv, where it is attributed to Jones; and in *Collection of the Parliamentary Debates in England* (John Torbuck, London, 1738–42), II, 375 ff.

24 Burnet, II, 276.

25 Roger North, *Examen* (London, 1740), 508.

26 *Miscellaneous State Papers from 1501 to 1726*, ed. Philip Yorke, Earl of Hardwicke (London, 1778), II, 399; George Harris, *Life of Lord Chancellor Hardwicke* (London, 1847), II, 20–24.

27 Campbell, I, 65n.

28 I am indebted to Dr Peter Karsten for this information, provided in a letter from Professor Caroline Robbins.

29 *Lives of the Norths*, I, 380–81.

30 Campbell, v, 65.

31 North, *Examen*, 508.

32 *Parliament History*, IV, cxlv.

33 *Ibid.*, IV, clvii.

34 *Ibid.*, IV, clxviii.

35 Burnet, II, 276.

36 Narcissus Luttrell, *Brief Historical Relation of State Affairs* (Oxford, 1857), I, 99–100.

37 Burnet, I, 335. According to James Ralph, Somers was 'more obliged to his Pen than his Pleadings' for the distinctions bestowed upon him. See *The Case of Authors by Profession or Trade* (London, 1758), 33.

38 *The Security of Englishmen's Lives, or the Trust, Power and Duty of the Grand Juries of England Explained* (London, 1681), 12.

39 *Ibid.*, 32.

40 *Ibid.*, 56.

41 *Ibid.*, 61.

42 *Ibid.*, 121.

43 Ibid., 147-49.

44 Ibid., 151.

45 John Oldmixon notes, in his *History of England during the Reigns of King William and Queen Mary* (etc.) (London, 1735), 535, how Somers, Halifax and Sunderland 'distinguished themselves by the Belles Lettres, as well as by Politicks'.

46 *Plutarch's Lives, Translated from the Greek by Several Hands* (London, 1683-86). There are a number of later editions, beginning with that of 1702-11.

47 See below, pp. 201-2.

48 *Supplement to the Works of the Most Celebrated Minor Poets* (London, 1750), pt. ii, pp. 3-11. See *Complete Works of Thomas Shadwell*, ed. Montague Summers (London, 1927), I, clxxxii.

49 Published by Jacob Tonson in 1680, with subsequent editions.

50 See *Works of John Dryden*, ed. Edward N. Hooker *et al.* (Berkeley, 1956), I, 323-24, 341.

51 P.C.C. Proved, 24 November 1681, Reg. North, f. 174. The will was drawn in 1676.

52 Ralph, *History*, II, 784.

53 *Memoirs*, 15; Maddock, 7. According to Nash, *Collections*, II, 55, Somers 'made no addition to his paternal estate' in Worcestershire of about £300 a year 'further than the purchase of the manor of Wadberrow, and a mortgage on Stoulton, though his favour joined to the prudence and parsimony of his successors, laid the foundation of large possessions in this and the adjoining counties of Hereford and Gloucester'. On Katherine Somers's will, see below, p. 299. Campbell, V, 72, suggests that 'ample provision' was made for the sisters.

54 Ibid., IV, 270.

55 John Noake, *The Monastery and Cathedral of Worcester* (London, 1866), 395.

56 *Memoirs*, 15; Gregory King, 'Natural and political observations and conclusions upon the state and condition of England, 1696', in George Chalmers, *Estimate of the Comparative Strength of Great Britain* (London, 1802), 424-25.

57 William Cobbett *et al.*, *Complete Collection of State Trials* (London, 1809-28), IX, 299 ff.

58 Campbell, V, 74.

59 *State Trials*, IX, 226.

60 Ibid., XII, 516-17.

61 White Kennett, *Complete History of England* (London, 1706), III, 513n; James Mackintosh, *History of the Revolution in England in 1688* (Philadelphia, 1835), 359; Thomas B. Macaulay, *History of England from the Accession of James II*, ed. C. H. Firth (London, 1913-15), II, 1022, referring to the recommendation of James Johnstone, Scottish agent for William of Orange.

62 *State Trials*, XII, 183-523.

63 See *Vaughan's Reports* (London, 1677), 330; Laurence Echard, *History of England* (London, 1720), 1106.

64 *State Trials*, XII, 396-97.

65 David Ogg, *England in the Reigns of James II and William III* (Oxford, 1957), 198; Campbell, V, 76; and see Holdsworth, VI, 535, who observes that Somers 'was not only a master of legal principles, but also a master of the art of presenting them in a lucid form', referring specifically to his part in the Bishops' Case.

66 Ogg, *James II and William III*, 201, citing S. P. France, 78/151 (22 June-2 July).

67 See Ogg, *James II and William III*, 196-97.

68 Campbell, V, 77-78.

69 Nicholas Tindal, *Continuation of Mr. Rapin de Thoyras's History of England*, II, 770.

70 Cooksey, 25; Maddock, 195-96, and see above p. 10. In 1708 Robert Molesworth, pleading his services in 1688, referred to Somers as one who could 'vouch for the genuineness of his claims': E. L. Ellis, 'The Whig junto in relation to the development of party politics' (unpublished Oxford doctoral dissertation, 1962), 107, citing Blenheim MSS. D. II, 6, Molesworth to Sunderland.

71 Burnet, III, 286.

72 Mackintosh, 303, citing Lord Sunderland's Letters, September 1688 (State Paper Office).

73 Repertories 94, f. 29 (23 October 1688).

74 Ibid., 94, f. 32.

75 Ibid., 94, f. 77 (13 December, 1688). Somers accepted the recordships of Worcester and Gloucester; see below, p. 67.

III
The Bill of Rights

By Christmas King James's regime had collapsed. Englishmen, regardless of political principles, were faced with the responsibility of establishing a government. The country was leaderless: the King had fled and William was willing at first to assume control only of military affairs, leaving civil administration to an *ad hoc* assemblage of the lords spiritual and temporal, recruited from London and its environs. It was clearly desirable that a Parliament be convened to resolve the crisis, for the results of the political vacuum were already to be seen in the excesses of the common people—particularly the London mob—and in growing disorder in Ireland. The cry, 'No king, no law', which was heard at the time, could not but be deeply disturbing to men of property.[1] The difficulty was that, as things stood, a legitimate parliament could not be assembled. The electoral writs could not be validated, as usual, by the touch of the royal sceptre. But a recent precedent pointed the way. The year 1660 had found the nation in somewhat similar difficulties; these had been resolved by the summoning of a national convention. It was decided that this device should be employed in the current emergency. On Christmas Day the Prince of Orange was asked to direct the issue of writs and to supervise the affairs of the realm until the meeting of the Convention on 22 January, and to this he acceded a few days later.

In the ensuing elections, Somers stood for the city of Worcester.[2] Details of the election have not come down to us. It was customary at this time for the corporation's influence to prevail; a few years later there was agreement that the electorate consisted of freemen not receiving alms.[3] In any case, no local nabob exercised control. On 11 January he was returned, along with William Bromley of Holt, a Whig country gentleman who had represented the city in James II's Parliament.

Although political parties had emerged scarcely more than a decade earlier, they were now recognisable features of the political landscape—however much they might lack organisation and cohesion.[4] Contemporaries were conscious of their existence: those involved in politics would increasingly regard themselves as Tories or Whigs, and, as such, tend to support programmes identified with their party. This is not to suggest a monolithic quality. Over the years there were groupings and regroupings based on a variety of circumstances—the personal influence of magnates, relationships with the court, diverse opinion over party goals and legislative undertakings—tending, more or less, to weaken party unity but rarely causing serious defection. Here the Whigs would have an advantage over their adversaries. More single-minded than the Tories in their support of the Revolution settlement, they possessed a tighter organisation and, in the hands of the Junto, would profit from a more efficient leadership.

When the Convention first met, on 22 January, Somers found himself among a majority in the Commons who were recognised opponents of the Stuart system. While admitting the ambiguities of traditional partisan labels at this time, we may describe these men for the most part as Whigs. Yet, of the 513 members of the Convention, nearly 200 had sat in King James's compliant Parliament of 1685, an indication that the exiled monarch's electoral manoeuvrings (and those of his brother) had not gone for nought. Of these some 160 may be counted as Tories. On the other hand, 183 of the members—some forty above the normal quota—had never sat in St Stephen's before. With parties so evenly balanced and attendance remarkably full, these inexperienced members, many without strong partisan affiliations, must have had a significant influence upon the course of events. Himself a new man, Somers was probably fortunate in the strategic position they occupied in the Convention, for they probably fostered a moderating influence essentially in accord with his political philosophy.[5]

Somers made his maiden speech on 28 January, a day reserved for debating the state of the nation in committee of the whole. It is significant that he was one of the few members to take the floor on this occasion.[6] Most of them appeared somewhat diffident and deferred to such veterans as Sergeant John Maynard, Sir Tomas Littleton and Sir Edward Seymour. Gilbert Dolben led off with a long speech to prove that since James II had withdrawn from the administration of the government, without any provision for a substitute, the throne was vacant. In conclusion he moved that 'King James the Second having voluntarily forsaken the Government, and abandoned and forsaken the Kingdom, it is a voluntary Demise in him'.[7] After around a dozen Members had addressed themselves to various aspects of the problem, weighing the applicability of such terms as 'demise', 'abdicate' and 'desert', and rehearsing the alleged misdeeds of the exiled monarch, Somers rose to speak. Although he jotted down extensive notes on the debates of this and the following day, he did not include his own remarks.[8] But according to Anchitell Grey, the veteran M.P. for Derby, he argued that James II had forfeited his claim to the allegiance of the English people by resorting to Louis XIV and 'casting himself into his hands', and by designing 'to subject the Nation to the Pope, as much as to a foreign Prince'. He recalled that James I had protested that 'if his Posterity were not Protestants, he prayed to God to take them from the Throne'. Precedent was important: 'What you do in this case will satisfy the World abroad, if it be like other cases.' He cited that of King Sigismund, who had inherited the throne of Sweden after having served as King of Poland. A convert to Catholicism, Sigismund had introduced Jesuits, who were disposed to 'disturb the Government, and invade the Laws, as they have ever done'. But popular opposition was too much for him. He returned to his Polish realm; whereupon the Swedes had settled Charles VIII upon their throne. To Somers, Sigismund's conduct was less offensive than James's. Sigismund had merely returned to the land whence he had come, but James had withdrawn to a realm always opposed to English interests, and put himself in the hands of its ruler. In conclusion he moved that Richard Hampden, the chairman, 'appoint a Committee to draw a Vote upon the Debate'.[9]

If Grey's account fully embodies the argument, Somers at this stage of the proceedings made no mention of the social contract theory, so prominently associated with the Whig programme, though Sergeant Maynard had already referred to mixed government having 'its beginning from the people', and Sir Robert Howard (better known now for his dramatic than his political achievements, but a Member of considerable parliamentary experience) presently declared the constitution to be 'actually grounded upon pact and covenant with them'.[10] Somers may have avoided this aspect of the argument, since the theory was anathema to many fellow Members.[11] Nor, apart from observing that James, by throwing himself upon Louis's mercy, had absolved his subjects of their allegiance, does Grey report any reference, on Somers's part, to abdication and the vacancy of the throne, concepts that he would shortly be vigorously supporting in debate with the Lords. But all these points would be made in the resolution which, accepted without division, has been attributed to Somers:

Resolved, That King James the Second, having endeavoured to subvert the Constitution of the Kingdom, by breaking the Original Contract between King and People; and by the Advice of Jesuits, and other wicked Persons, having violated the fundamental laws; and having withdrawn himself out of this Kingdom; has abdicated the Government, and that the Throne is thereby vacant.[12]

On the following day the Commons, again meeting in committee of the whole, framed two additional resolutions. The first declared that experience had proved that it was 'inconsistent with the Safety and Welfare of the Protestant Kingdom, to be governed by a Popish Prince'. This measure passed by acclamation. Somers's contributions, if any, have eluded the record.[13] But we may assume that he was not on the sidelines, for this was a vindication of the position he and the other exclusionists had taken a decade earlier—a position publicised again in a few months in a reissue of the *Brief History*. The second resolution called for a consideration of the constitutional guarantees to be secured prior to the bestowal of the crown: a committee was to recommend 'general Heads of such things as are absolutely necessary to be considered, for the better securing our Religion, Laws, and Liberties'. The forging of the Bill of Rights had begun. Somers was named to this committee, along with thirty-eight other Members.[14]

From the debate preceding the resolution we can obtain some idea of the positions taken by the committeemen. Though there was general attachment to the principles of mixed monarchy, they were of different opinions regarding the extent to which underlying safeguards should be spelled out.[15] The dialogue turned essentially on the simple question of whether the filling of the throne or the settlement of constitutional guarantees was to come first. The committee owed its existence, in a sense, to Lord Falkland's proposal that, now that William had rescued the English people from Catholicism, the Commons should act to protect them against further encroachments on their liberties: 'Before you fill the throne', he enjoined them, 'I would have you resolve, what Power you will give the king, and what not.'[16] Sir Richard Temple had then recommended that the House consider grievances under three main headings: encroachments on Parliament, the behaviour of the judges, and the coronation oath.[17] But others had misgivings about spending valuable time on constitutional details. The venerable Maynard, fearing a long session, cautioned against delay in filling the throne, 'lest, instead of an arbitrary government, we should have none'.[18] Other lawyers, including Somers, supported him. 'A law you cannot make until you have a king,' Pollexfen counselled. To frame detailed provisions 'would necessarily take up much time, whereby Ireland might be destroyed and Holland hazarded', with King James the ultimate beneficiary. Such remarks did not pass unchallenged. 'What care I', exclaimed Edward Seymour, 'for what is done abroad, if we must be slaves in England, in this or that man's power?' But the desirability of speedy legislation could not be ignored. Even William Garraway, who had supported Falkland's original proposal, conceded that he did not advocate extended debate. Christopher Musgrave pointed the way: the business of the Commons was to declare 'wherein King James 2 has broken the laws, and whom you have put by the government'. It was Musgrave, a seasoned parliamentarian, who framed the resolution establishing the committee.[19]

Whatever Somers's contributions to this debate, there is no doubt that he became a leader of the committee, where his knowledge of English constitutional development and his skill as a moderator showed to advantage. This was no mean accomplishment for a fledgling M.P. who had sat in the House for less than two weeks. Two thirds of the committeemen had parliamentary experience going back a decade or more.[20] William Sacheverell has been called the ablest parliament man in Charles II's reign; Sir William Williams was Speaker in that king's last Parliaments; Musgrave had a great reputation with the High Tories. It was not as if Somers had a powerful family interest behind him. He had risen to legal prominence, it is true, but there were others on the committee—Treby, Pollexfen and Maynard, to name but three—whose qualifications in this respect were more generally recognised, and who had the advantage of seniority. Indeed, at the outset Treby appears to have overshadowed Somers, for it was he who would carry the committee's first report to the Commons.[21] Some six years older than Somers, Treby had been a Member of Parliament as early as 1677, and as a counsellor he had been associated with Whig interests and the defence of opponents of the government for a decade.

The committee worked with remarkable speed. Its report was before the House by 2 February. It consisted of twenty-three heads, to which the House added five more.[22] Some referred to infringements of existing rights; others proposed additional safeguards for the liberties of the subject. The former are familiar to all students of the English constitution. The dispensing and suspending power is deemed illegal, as are the Court of Ecclesiastical Commission and the levying of taxes without parliamentary consent; subjects may rightfully petition the king, and, unless they be Catholics, keep arms for their defence; parliamentary elections should be free; Parliament should meet frequently, and its members have liberty to express themselves without interference; excessive bail and fines, as well as 'cruel and unusual punishments' are frowned upon. These, with two or three other provisions, would presently constitute the terms under which William of Orange and his consort secured the English throne, and which, some months later, would gain statutory sanction.

Of the other provisions, some found implementation in other sections of the statute, some were separately dealt with at a later time, and a few were not acted upon, at least in Somers's time. These touched upon the Crown as well as other aspects of the national administration, and upon Parliament, local government, the law, religion and taxation. None of the royal family was to marry a Catholic. Every sovereign, when assuming his royal authority, was to swear to maintain the Protestant religion and the laws and liberties of the land, and to take a revised coronation oath. Over-lengthy Parliaments—such as the eighteen-year Cavalier Parliament of Charles II—were to be prevented. In recommending that no pardon be pleadable to an impeachment, the committee, mindful of the Danby case, strove to sharpen this parliamentary weapon.[23] Various corporations—cities, boroughs, towns, universities, plantations—were to be protected against *quo warrantos* and deprivation of their rights, and such as had been lost were to be restored. Safeguards against the buying and selling of offices were to be provided and abuses in the appointment of sheriffs as well as in the conduct of their offices reformed. As Temple had proposed, the judges were to hold office, not at the sovereign's discretion, but as long as they conducted themselves with propriety; they were to be suspended or discharged only under due course of law, and were to be paid salaries from public funds. The Court of Chancery, as well as other judicial tribunals, was to be overhauled, as were certain official fees. Some reform of procedure in the Court of King's Bench, in the defendant's interest, was also called for.[24] The rights of those accused of treason were to be safeguarded in various ways, both with regard to the construction of statutes and trial procedures. In the sphere of religion, liberty of Protestant worship was to be insured, and steps taken to comprehend all Protestants, as far as possible, in the national religious establishment. The militia acts were condemned as grievous to the subject. The last two heads dealt with the collection of hearth-money and certain features of the excise taxes. These recommendations, taken altogether, form a remarkably complete commentary on the various features of Stuart administration which, over a period of three generations, had aroused suspicion and opposition.

Somers's part in the Convention was not confined to assistance in framing the Declaration of Rights. He was to prove a skilful and trenchant representative of the Commons, as it engaged in conferences with the

Lords on the vital question of the current status of the throne. The resolutions of 28 and 29 January had, of course, been laid before the Lords, who
went into committee of the whole on 29 January, under Danby's chair-
manship. The resolution opposing a Catholic sovereign was carried unanimously. But the one proclaiming the vacancy of the throne occasioned prolonged and searching debate, revealing varied concepts as to its character
and the powers of Parliament and people. Among the Tories of both
Houses was a negligible group who favoured the restoration of King James,
and larger representations of those who supported either a regency or the
acceptance of James's daughter Mary as the natural heir. But the recall of
James was scarcely considered, and the cause of regency appeared likewise
to be lost, for the Lords, by a vote of 51 to 49, had vetoed such a project.
On the following day they moved a step closer to the Whig position when
they agreed, 53 to 46, to accept the Commons' theory that a pre-existent
contract between king and people had been broken by James. But they
refused, 55 to 41, to acknowledge that James had abdicated the throne, or to
accept the idea that the throne was vacant. In place of 'abdication', they
substituted the word 'deserted'; the reference to a vacant throne was also
deleted, being repugnant in that it ran counter to the fundamental principle of hereditary monarchy and appeared to be an entering wedge for
republicanism.[25] Thus altered, the resolution was sent back to the Commons. There the amendments were rejected, and a conference with the
Lords called for.[26]

Somers was one of twenty-seven members named to the committee, also
chaired by Hampden, which was 'to prepare and bring in Heads of Reasons
to be offered at a Conference with the Lords'. Of these, twenty-one were
members of the committee set up on 29 January. To Rapin this conference
was 'the most remarkable that was ever held in England, as well on account
of the Importance of the Thing itself, as for the Ability of the Managers'.[27]
On 4 February, Hampden presented his committee's report as to why the
Commons could not consent to the Lords' amendments. They objected to the
word 'desertion', as not implying a renunciation of the throne. They saw
no reason to alter the word 'vacant', since the Lords themselves had called
upon the Prince of Orange to assume the direction of affairs and had concurred that a Catholic prince was incapable of governing the realm. They
further argued that, since there was no one on the throne to afford protection to the subject, no allegiance was due. The conference with the Lords
followed immediately, with the committee of twenty-seven serving as
managers, and another the following day, but to no avail: the peers resolved
that they would stand by their amendments. A deadlock appeared inevitable. The Tories, taking heart at the course of events, rallied their forces in
support of the Lords' position. But they could not prevail over a widespread
opposition, even though 151 members were disposed to accept the second
amendment. Following this a free conference with the Lords was requested,
to pursue the argument further.[28]

Again Somers found himself called upon to defend and elucidate the position of the majority in the Commons, this time in the give and take of debate. Associated with him as managers were twenty-one other members, all men of considerable political or professional weight, carefully selected for this crucial encounter. Besides Somers, four—Maynard, Pollexfen, Treby and Holt—were able lawyers, the last three destined to achieve the distinction of chief-justiceships. Among the others were Hampden, Sir Richard Temple, William Sacheverell, Colonel Birch, Major John Wildman and Sir Robert Howard. All had participated actively in the debates over the issues at stake.[29] Most of these men were older than Somers, some of them considerably so, Birch and Wildman being survivors of an earlier revolutionary era.

The free conference was held on 6 February in the Painted Chamber. Seated along one side of a table were the managers for the peers—Nottingham, Clarendon, Rochester, Pembroke, and Francis Turner, Bishop of Ely. So large was the attendance from the lower house that its managers had difficulty in taking their places, and the Serjeant at Arms had to be called upon to clear a passage.[30] The debate treated the issues in dispute as questions of law, and involved highly technical discourse on the use of words and on relevant precedents. Somers's stock was obviously rising; after introductory remarks by Hampden, it was he who took the floor. Their lordships, he noted, objected to the word 'abdicate' as unknown to the common law of England, and subject to doubtful interpretation. But neither was the word 'desert' clearly defined. By common acceptance, he declared, 'the word "abdicated" doth naturally and properly signify entirely to renounce, throw off, disown, [or] relinquish any thing or person', by words, writing or action, 'so as to have no farther to do with it'.[31] In support of his interpretation he mustered an impressive array of references to civilians and lexicographers, dipping into the *Lexicon Juridicum* of Calvin and *De Verborum Significatione* of Brissonius, as well as the writings of Grotius, Bartolus, Budaeus and other authorities.[32] Turning to the word 'desert', he argued that it 'hath not only a very doubtful signification; but in the common acceptance both of the civil and canon law, doth signify only a bare withdrawing, a temporary quitting of a thing, and neglect only, which leaveth the party at liberty of returning to it again'. Here, too, he was able to produce extensive supporting evidence derived from the legal usage of the past. In conclusion, he described James II's conduct as a prime example of the act of abdication, noting (with echoes of the recent vote),

That King James II, by going about to subvert the constitution, and by breaking the original contract between king and people, and by violating the fundamental laws, and withdrawing himself out of the kingdom, hath thereby renounced to be a king according to the constitution, by avowing to govern by a despotic power, unknown to the constitution, and inconsistent with it; he hath renounced to be a king according to the law, such a king as he swore to be at his coronation, such a king to whom the allegiance of an English subject is due.[33]

The disputants next turned their attention to the allegation that the throne was vacant. At the beginning of debate, Nottingham had asked whether the Commons meant that James's abdication involved only himself or his heirs as well. The point was of the utmost importance to the legitimists, who, whatever their views of James, were opposed to any solution that would imperil the hereditary rights of the crown. The Lords also challenged Somers to produce an instance where England's government had ever been without a royal head. Clearly, the interregnum of 1649–60 could not serve in this connection, for, in law, the reign of Charles II was recognised as having begun upon the execution of his father. But Somers did not lack a precedent. He referred the lords to a parliamentary roll for 1399, which expressly declared that the regal office had been unoccupied between the reigns of Richard II and Henry IV: 'Sedes regalis fuit vacua'—so ran the Latin of the official pronouncement. Henry of Lancaster had thereupon risen from his place and claimed the throne.

In reply the Lords produced a roll from the first year of Edward IV, a likely place to look in view of the Yorkist claims as rightful inheritors. By this it appeared that the dispensation of 1399 had been formally annulled. The ground seemed to have been cut out from under Somers's position, but not for long. Sir George Treby came to the rescue, calling the legislators' attention to the next significant turning point in the dynastic history of England, the advent of the Tudors. He too could quote parliamentary scripture, this time from a roll of the first year of Henry VII, in which the Yorkist Act had been repealed, and the precedent of 1399 given a new lease of life. Somers's position appeared to be vindicated. Yet, after several hours of claims and counter-claims, the managers separated with neither side converted, and without having wrought a compromise.[34]

But the sands of indecision had, in effect, run out. Conversion came not through the persuasive oratory of the members of the Convention, but at the hands of William himself, and to some extent of Mary. It may be, as Macaulay believed, that the conference was 'a mere form' in that the Lords, informed that Mary was displeased in that she had been advanced over her husband, and worried over the absence of a settled government, had even then been on the point of yielding.[35] In any case, the Prince of Orange, by declaring that he would not be satisfied with a regency, or to act merely as the Queen's consort, but would return to the Netherlands if not accorded full regal authority, had injected a somewhat harshly realistic note into a discussion which must have seemed to him, with his natural economy of speech and practical military mind, incredibly rarefied and academic. At any rate, following the conference the Lords, exhorted by Danby not to persist in a controversy which might have catastrophic consequences, accepted the abdication clause, and by a majority of twenty supported the contention that the throne was vacant. This was immediately followed by a resolution 'that the Prince and Princess of Orange shall be declared King and Queen of England, and the dominions thereunto belonging', which passed in the affirmative without division.[36]

But what of the Bill of Rights? On 4 February the committee of thirty-nine had been ordered 'to distinguish such of the General Heads, as are introductory of new Laws, from those that are declaratory of ancient Rights'.[37] Three days later Treby presented the committee's report. The next few days were principally devoted to a consideration of the 'General Heads' and of amendments to the 6 February vote of the Lords. In these undertakings, and particularly in the negotiations with the Lords that brought about the finished settlement, Somers played a leading part. On 8 February he became chairman of a twenty-one man committee appointed to draw up amendments to the Lords' vote. Finding it difficult to integrate such amendments with the provisions acknowledging existing rights and introducing new guarantees, he sought the direction of the House, which opted for a declaration of rights. Thus instructed, Somers returned the same day with such a statement. Several conferences with the Lords now took place, with the committee of thirty-nine (now actually numbering forty by the addition of Sir John Holt) as managers. On three occasions Somers served as chairman, but the reports made by Sir William Williams and Richard Hampden are evidence that he did not monopolise the chair. Important in the debate was the thorny question of the dispensing power. Somers must have argued for its rejection. A few months earlier he had attacked it in the trial of the bishops, and there is reason to believe that, of all the guarantees in the Bill of Rights, he regarded it as most important in safeguarding the rights of Englishmen. At last, on 12 February, the two houses reached an agreement on a joint declaration. On the following day it was read before William and Mary, who thereupon accepted the crown.[38]

While Somers has been unwarrantably singled out by some historians as the architect of the Bill of Rights, no one can be said to have a better claim to this role.[39] Certainly the concordat worked out in February, and presently to be given full statutory authority, accorded fully with his political philosophy. Some have expressed disappointment that his contributions to debate, and particularly his tactics at the free conference of 6 February, were so narrowly legalistic.[40] Yet the argument on abdication, on which Somers concentrated with such a battery of continental authorities, was obviously germane to the general issue of political reform and constitutional government. Somers and his fellow Whigs were convinced that the permanent rectification of abuses could be assured only by a distinct and permanent break in the succession, and by an effective repudiation of the divine right doctrine, and they feared that a compromise in this area, with some sort of resultant regency, would lead only to political confusion—a confusion in which the forces of the late government might find an opportunity to rally. The initial responsibility of the Conventioners was to determine the status of the exiled Stuart king. Only when this was resolved could other political arrangements be worked out; and only by scrutinising the defection of James in the light of commonly accepted tenets of monarchical behaviour could a sound and enduring judgement be achieved.

Early in 1690 a short tract entitled *A Vindication of the Proceedings of the Late Parliament of England* appeared in print. No author's name was attached, but it has usually been attributed to Somers.[41] Written in answer to an anonymous 'seditious pamphlet', the treatise served to justify the government's policies in prosecuting the war against France and in maintaining internal stability. But it went further in emphasising the beneficent nature of the settlement of the previous year. The first paragraph sets the tone:

The proceedings of the late parliament were so fair, so prudent, so necessary, and so advantageous to the nation, to the protestant interest in general, and in particular to the church of England, that all true Englishmen must needs acknowledge they owe to the then representatives of the nation, their privileges, their liberties, their lives, their religion, their present and future security from popery, slavery, and arbitrary power, had they done nothing else but enacted the rights and liberties of the subject, and settling the succession of the crown.

Later passages spell out what are to be regarded as the most important guarantees of the Bill of Rights. The outlawry of the dispensing and suspending power is put first, followed by the assurance of parliamentary control of taxation, the banning of standing armies in time of peace unless Parliament shall decree otherwise, and the determination of the royal succession.

Of overriding importance is the limitation of the sovereign by law. On the social contract the treatise has nothing to say, though it notes that 'kings generally came out of the peoples' Loins, as being at first made by them'. But the moderate liberal tradition, implicit in Magna Carta and furthered over the centuries through the advance of parliamentarism, is voiced anew:

Our happiness then consists in this, that our princes are tied up to the law as well as we, and upon an especial account obliged to keep it up in full force, because if they destroyed the law, they destroyed at the same time themselves, by overthrowing the very foundation of their kingly grandeur and regal power. So that our government not being arbitrary, but legal, not absolute but political, our princes can never become arbitrary, absolute, or tyrants, without forfeiting at the same time their royal character, by the breach of the essential conditions of their regal power, which are to act according to the ancient customs and standing laws of the nation.[42]

NOTES

[1] Leopold von Ranke, *History of England principally in the Seventeenth Century* (Oxford, 1875), IV, 479, citing dispatch of Ronquillo, in Brussels Archives; see also William L. Sachse, 'The mob and the Revolution', *Journal of British Studies*, IV (No. 1, November 1964), 40,

[2] According to Campbell, V, 78, he had thrice rejected suggestions that he stand in previous elections.

[3] T. H. B. Oldfield, *Representative History of Great Britain and Ireland* (London, 1816), V, 255. He puts the mid-eighteenth-century electorate of the city at 2000. William A. Speck, *Tory and Whig: the Struggle in the Constituencies, 1701–1715* (London, 1970), 130, has 1500. For background, see Alan D. Dyer, *The City of Worcester in the Sixteenth Century* (Leicester, 1973), 214–16.

[4] On party developments, 1689–1714, see especially J. H. Plumb, *The Growth of Political Stability in England, 1675–1725* (Baltimore, 1969); Geoffrey Holmes, *British Politics in the Age of Anne* (London, 1967); W. A. Speck, *Tory and Whig: the Struggle in the Constituencies, 1701–1715* (London, 1970); I. F. Burton, P. W. J. Riley and E. Rowlands, *Political*

Parties of William III and Anne: the Evidence of the Division Lists (Bull., Institute of Historical Research, Special Supp. No. 7, 1968). These works oppose the arguments of Robert Walcott, Jr., for a more kaleidoscopic and fragmented political body, set forth in his *English Politics in the Early Eighteenth Century* (Cambridge, Mass., 1956). See also Dennis Rubini, *Court and Country, 1688–1702* (London, 1967).

[5] Yet he is included in a contemporary list of 'Extreme Partisans', to be found in Browning, *Danby*, III, 172. For the Convention Parliament's composition, see J. H. Plumb, 'The elections to the Convention Parliament of 1689', *Cambridge Historical Journal*, V (No. 3, 1937), especially pp. 244–45. Alan Simpson, in his unpublished D.Phil. dissertation on the Convention Parliament (Oxford, 1940), arrives at a different estimate of party strength.

[6] On 22 January he was among those placed on the large committee of elections and privileges: C.J., X, 10.

[7] Grey, IX, 9.

[8] Hardwicke, *State Papers*, II, 401 ff.

[9] Grey, IX, 16–17.

[10] *Ibid.*, IX, 12, 20; Hardwicke, *State Papers*, II, 402.

[11] In Somers's *Brief History of the Succession* he writes that if men say that fundamental laws 'were made by the diffusive body of the people; they run before they are aware, into the guilt of worshiping that idol the multitude, and make a great step towards placing the foundation of the government upon contract and consent. But then let them produce those laws, or some authentick memorial of them, before it be exacted from us to believe. there were ever any such.' But he goes on to say that the Crown is not merely an inheritance but one 'accompanying an office of trust; ... if a man's defects render him uncapable of the trust, he has also forfeited the inheritance': *Harleian Misc.*, IX, 267, 270. See also above, p. 34 and n. 33. Maddock, p. 209n, suggests that the reference to an original contract 'was more for the purpose of securing unanimity in the House of Commons' than an expression of Somers's real sentiment.

[12] C.J., X, 14. On Somers as author, see Campbell, V, 78–79; Robbins, 79.

[13] C.J., X, 15. Campbell, V, 79, describes this as a 'signal triumph' for Somers.

[14] Somers is listed as twenty-seventh among the committeemen: C.J., X, 15.

[15] See Corinne C. Weston, *English Constitutional Theory and the House of Lords, 1556–1832* (London, 1965), 114 ff.

[16] Grey, IX, 30; cf. Hardwicke, *State Papers*, II, 414.

[17] Grey, IX, 31, and see Ranke, IV, 502–3, where the importance of Temple's speech is emphasised.

[18] Hardwicke, *State Papers*, II, 417.

[19] Grey, IX, 33–37; Hardwicke, *State Papers*, II, 418–22; Dr Williams Library, Roger Morrice MS. Entering Book, II, 447–48 (2 February 1689).

[20] See Weston, 117 and n.

[21] C.J., X, 17; Add MSS. 35, 838, f. 309.

[22] The additional heads dealt with the buying and selling of offices, procedure regarding writs of habeas corpus and mandamus, grants of fines and forfeitures, and hearth money and excise abuses.

[23] Weston, 117.

[24] As in connection with informations, which were to be abolished.

[25] *Lords Journal*, XIV, 110–11; Historical Manuscripts Commission, *Lords MSS.*, 1689–90 (London, 1889), 15–18, where the regency vote is 51–48 and the contract vote 54–43; Rapin, XV, 237, 240.

[26] C.J., X, 18.

[27] Rapin, XV, 242.

[28] Grey, IX, 49–50; C.J., X, 18–20.

[29] Other managers were Henry Capel, Paul Foley, Thomas Foley, Sir Thomas Lee, Garraway, Hugh Boscawen, Henry Goodrick, Sir Thomas Littleton, Waller, Palmes and Guise. John Withers, in his *History of Resistance as Practised by the Church of England* (London, 1710), singles out Somers and Holt as managers for the Commons; see *Somers Tracts*, ed. Scott, XII, 262.

[30] C.J., X, 20.

[31] The *New English Dictionary*, defining the word 'abdicate' as 'to formally give up a right or office', cites this passage second among the references. The first is taken from Bishop Hall's *Hard Texts* (1633).

[32] Guillaume Budé (1467–1540), a friend of Erasmus and librarian to Francis I.

[33] *Parliamentary History*, v, 68–70; also in Torbuck, II, 191–95; *History and Proceedings of the House of Commons* (R. Chandler, London, 1742–44), II, 209–10; Rapin, xv, 244–46. Clarendon raised objections to the reference to the 'original contract'; Treby lent support in this connection: *Parliamentary History*, v, 76, 79.

[34] *Parliamentary History*, v, 94–103; Rapin, xv, 267–71.

[35] Macaulay, III, 1296, and see Burnet, III, 372–75.

[36] Historical Manuscripts Commission, Lords MSS., 1689–90, 14–18: L.J., xiv, 118–19.

[37] According to Douglas Campbell, *The Puritan in Holland, England and America* (New York, 1893), I, 234, Somers used the Dutch Act of Abjuration of 1581 as a model for the Declaration of Rights; but the two documents show little, if any, similarity. A translation of the former, attributed to Somers, is to be found in *Somers Tracts*, ed. Scott, I, 323–29.

[38] C.J., x, 20–27; L.J., xiv, 121–27.

[39] For the importance of Treby's role, see Michael Landon, *Triumph of the Lawyers: their Role in English Politics, 1678–1689* (University, Alabama, 1970), 237–38.

[40] See Macaulay, III, 1296; Campbell, v, 80.

[41] It is attributed to Somers in *British Museum Catalogue*, Wing, and *McAlpin Collection Catalogue*, and by Scott (despite some uncertainty) in his edition of the *Somers Tracts*, x, 257. It is included in the *Collection of State Tracts Published on Occasion of the Late Revolution* (London, 1705), I, 209–18, where the title is given as A *Defence of the Proceedings of the Late Parliament in England*; here it is ascribed to 'Mr. Hampden, Major Wildman, &c.'.

[42] *Somers Tracts*, ed. Scott, x, 257–58, 263.

IV
Member for Worcester, 1689-93

The Convention Parliament lasted for a year. Though many regarded it as merely an *ad hoc* body, a constituent assembly lacking the credentials of a bonafide Parliament, and were to press for its dissolution, there was a natural tendency among the Members to favour retaining their seats. Their first legislative act gave full statutory recognition to their parliamentary status.[1] Most of them, opposed as they were to the Stuart system, regarded their work as only begun. They saw much to be done by way of confirming the Revolution, both in strengthening the Williamite position and in limiting and controlling the actions of government. Early in 1690, unhappy that no visible progress had been made in passing an indemnity act or providing for the militia, worried over revenue and disgusted with the increasingly sharp factional conflicts that slowed the progress of parliamentary business, William dissolved the Convention and issued writs for a general election. The new Parliament convened on 20 March. Over eighty new Members took their seats. While usually described as more Tory than the Convention, it actually represented a more middle-of-the-road position. Oldmixon, the Whig historian, remarked that, while nearly half the Members who had voted against bestowing the crown on the Prince of Orange were not returned, yet 'by the falling off of Others who voted for it, the Government found opposition enough in this Assembly'.[2] Somers, writing to John Locke, observed that in Worcestershire 'the sense of the country' was hostile to the Whigs. But things could have been worse, as far as he was concerned. He was re-elected, as might be expected of the city's recorder. So was his 'old partner', Bromley. And he was pleased that the Earl of Bellamont (an Irish peer), one of the first to join the Prince of Orange, had retained his Droitwich seat.[3]

Somers remained in the Commons until 1693. His activities can be traced in considerable detail, and his influence on certain issues is explicit enough. His appointment as Solicitor-General in May of 1689, raising him to the lower fringes of the ministry, marked him as a coming man, and one to be entrusted with certain kinds of parliamentary business. But this assignment, together with an extensive and profitable private law practice, must have curtailed his legislative contributions to some extent. Altogether, there is evidence for only about a dozen speeches by Somers during William's first Parliament, an output which, quantitatively speaking, lags well behind the recorded utterances of Clarges, Hampden or Musgrave. However active he was as a 'Court Whig'—and serviceable he certainly was,—he was new to the House and cannot be regarded as dominating its proceedings. On the other hand, he was a good speaker, perhaps as gifted as anyone in the House.

Abel Boyer noted his 'manly Eloquence'; Blackmore called it 'more than Roman'.[4] And he was highly knowledgeable. Chief Justice Pollexfen is said to have remarked that no man in Westminster Hall was so well qualified to deal with historical and constitutional problems, a competence not lost when he crossed the threshold of St Stephen's.[5] His approach, in the give and take of politics, remained essentially practical and moderate. Shying away from extreme and doctrinaire views, he gained support on a wider front than would otherwise have been the case.

But then as now the principal work of a Member of Parliament did not consist in making speeches. The seventeenth century witnessed the emergence of committee organisation and functions, essentially along lines that still apply. Having established a reputation as a useful committee wheel-horse in the initial deliberations of the Convention, Somers throughout his years in the Commons was called upon again and again to serve on these bodies. It was, of course, one thing to be named and quite another to be active on a committee. Its work could be effected by a quorum; attendance was not compulsory. The records do not help us here, for they usually refer only to the activities of committee chairmen. But there is every reason to believe that he was a responsible, industrious committeeman. Temperamentally he was conscientious and businesslike; he was keenly interested in the political issues of the day; his official duties as a law officer would sometimes mesh with the parliamentary agenda; busy lawyer that he was, he at least lived in London, a bachelor, with few distractions of family or estate.

As the months passed, his activities were largely concentrated on the implementation and further development of the revolutionary settlement. Already prominent as a framer of the initial provisions which had brought an end to the Interregnum, he was looked upon by fellow Whigs as one who could be expected to contribute to this unfinished business. Prominent on the agenda was the drafting of a new coronation oath. The approaching rites by which the full trappings of royalty would be conferred on William and Mary evoked a scrutiny of the existing pledge, with possible revision to bring it into harmony with the Declaration of Rights. For this purpose a large committee was set up by the Commons on 25 February. It represented a variety of opinion in the House, and included men as politically diverse as Clarges, Seymour, Musgrave and Sacheverell. Somers was not appointed by name, but he was automatically a member, since it included all lawyers. A month later he was named to another committee which was given the task of drafting the bill promulgating the new oath. This body included such legal talent as Sir Heneage Finch, Sir William Williams and Sir George Treby, then Solicitor-General.[6]

Among the points at issue was the phrasing of a guarantee for the national church. Regarding Somers's beliefs in matters of doctrine, and his preferences as to modes of worship, there is little or nothing to guide us. Branded in some quarters as an associate of Toland, he would be charged with deism.[7] But he appears, rather, to have been a churchman of the latitudinarian stripe, somewhat sympathetic to the comprehension of Protestant dissenters, and opposed to Roman Catholicism, though essentially on political rather than religious grounds.[8] If we may take Addison's eulogistic comments at face value, he was a dutiful member of the Church, 'constant to its offices of devotion, both in publick and in his family', sincere but 'not ostentatious' in his religion.[9]

At this juncture Somers demonstrated that his sympathies lay with those who envisaged a possible inclusion of Presbyterians within the Church. In the debate he supported an amendment that the king should swear to maintain 'the Protestant Religion as it is, *or shall be*, established by law'. He was averse to a rigidly prescribed religious settlement, and confident that Parliament could be trusted. There was opposition, of course; the cry went up that the amendment opened the way for altering the government of the Church. It was the warning that the Church was in danger, so frequently heard in years to come. Somers was unmoved by such Tory fears. Whatever men might call him—atheist, deist, Hobbist, latitudinarian,—he was not seeking to wreck episcopacy. But he was a statesman rather than a churchman, and took a long-range view: 'though the constitution be as good as possible for the present time, none can be good at all times'. The more liberal rendition was nonetheless defeated, the Commons supporting the unamended measure 188 to 149. It became law on 9 April, the eve of the coronation.[10]

Somers's position regarding the oath, as well as his reputed latitudinarian sympathies, would lead us to expect firm support of the Toleration Act, which was passed late in May, a reward to Protestant dissenters who had resisted the blandishmens of King James. There can be no doubt that he endorsed it. His interest in the subject is revealed in the catalogue of his library, where, under 'De Toleratione', some twenty works published in the latter part of the seventeenth century are listed.[11] On 9 April he was appointed to a committee of varied composition to draw up an address of thanks for a declaration which William had issued in favour of the Established Church. This pronouncement, apparently accepted without division, gained concurrence from the Lords within a few days, and was thereupon presented to the king. The *status quo* was explicitly supported: the new sovereign was told that the best way to secure the hearts of his subjects was through maintaining a careful stewardship of the Church, 'whose Constitution is best suited to the Support of this Monarchy'. But this recommendation was accompanied by assurances that the Commons, who asked that a Convocation be called, were not opposed to a bill for the 'ease' of Dissenters.[12] Such sentiments could be expressed with some confidence that they would be well received, for as early as 1687 William and Mary had made known their views that no Christian should be persecuted on grounds of conscience, or suffer in any way by differing from the established religion, though Test Acts and other penal measures securing the Protestant ascendancy were to be maintained.[13]

Apart from these general recommendations, Somers's contributions (if any) are lost to view. There is certainly no justification for the claim that he 'carried through' the act.[14] The explanation for this apparent inactivity probably stems from the fact that the bill, unlike the simultaneous and abortive project for comprehending dissenting Protestants within the Church, was an 'agreed measure', enjoying widespread approval, and encountered no obstacles requiring the attention of a busy official. The ways had been greased at a meeting at the Devil's Tavern, where it was agreed that if the Whigs would forget about comprehension the Tories would swallow their opposition to toleration.[15]

One reason, perhaps, why Somers did not play a more prominent part in the religious settlement may be found in his involvement in military affairs. The new regime had to resort to military force to bring Ireland under its authority, and within a few months was at war with France. The authors of the Declaration of Rights had manifested dissatisfaction with existing military arrangements, echoing the national antipathy towards a standing army and indicting the militia acts as grievous to the subject. But now they were called upon to field an army that could look King Louis in the face, and to provide stronger defences for the realm itself. In March, Somers was among those called upon to produce a 'Bill to punish Mutineers and Deserters from the Army' (better known as the Mutiny Act), both at the initial stage as a framer of the measure and as one of thirty-one Members to whom it was committed. His contributions elude the record; William Harbord, the Paymaster General, served as chairman. Designed to provide a code of discipline for the regular soldier, a need recognised for some time, it became law on 28 March.[16]

The Commons now sought to enact legislation regulating the militia, and in April a committee including Somers was set up for this purpose. At the outset the House ordered Sacheverell to 'take care of the Bill', but a week later Somers, along with Garraway and Musgrave, were called upon to assist him.[17] Brought before the Commons in June, it bore several interesting features. The control exercised by the crown and the lords lieutenant was reduced with a view to lessening their political leverage, and provision was made, under certain circumstances, for compulsory military service. The measure has been described as 'a real effort to rescue the militia from decay and make it equal to the perils now facing the country'.[18] But, though passed by the Commons, it failed in the Lords, and with the dissolution of the Convention disappeared into the legislative lumber room.

Perhaps because it was felt that William and Mary's acceptance of the Declaration of Rights had removed much of the urgency, and was a good enough beginning, Parliament moved slowly to give it final statutory form. Varying opinions as to what grievances really cried out for parliamentary attention continued to contribute to the leisurely pace. But, as the Members heard the asthmatic cough of the new sovereign and realised that, though approaching fifty, he was still not blessed with son or daughter, they were spurred on to effect arrangements for the succession. At all costs they must prevent the succession of a Catholic prince: it would be ironic indeed if the Revolution, brought to a head by Jacobite fertility, should be frustrated through Williamite sterility. On 5 March a small committee was chosen to prepare a bill designed to prevent such an eventuality. To this Somers, along with other legal luminaries—Pollexfen, Holt, Williams and Treby—was named. They evidently made slow progress, for about a fortnight later the House found it necessary to 'revive' this committee, afforcing it with fifteen new members. And in addition to its earlier assignment, it was set to the task of drafting, in final form, a Declaration of Rights.[19]

Here Somers was very much in evidence. In a debate on this bill, which occurred 8 May, he opposed a Tory attempt, launched by Sidney Godolphin, to add a proviso 'that nothing in this Act is intended to be drawn into example, or Consequence, hereafter, to prejudice the Right of any Protestant Prince, or Princes, in their hereditary Succession to the Imperial Crown of these Realms'.[20] From this the Whigs drew back. They appear to have regarded it as an attempt to leave the door open for King James's son, should he be induced to turn Protestant. On the other hand, William Ettrick, a Tory lawyer who had voted against offering the throne to William and Mary in the first place, was fearful that it might stand vacant, and a republic emerge by default. 'If there be no Heirs of those in the Entail,' he warned, 'you have left the Government to the People.'[21] Thomas Clarges agreed with him. Somers explored English history to find precedents for his rebuttal. He cited the reigns of Henry IV and Henry VII. Under the former the throne, which had been declared vacant, had been 'settled on the King's sons, and no farther by name'. As for Henry VII, had not Bacon praised his wisdom in that he 'limited the Crown no farther, but left it to descend'?[22] To spell out the succession, Somers argued, might undermine the Revolution itself. 'Let us tread in the steps of our Ancestors; you have declared the Vacancy of the Throne; but to do this now would bring a suspicion on what you have done.'[23] The amendment was rejected, and, after the insertion of a provision virtually eliminating the dispensing power, the bill passed and Treby was ordered to carry it to the Lords.[24]

Though the session continued until mid-August—an extraordinary encroachment on the summertime pursuits of country gentlemen—proceedings bogged down, and it was not until after a two-month recess that further progress was made in enacting the measure. On 24 October, a few days after the Members returned to St Stephen's, Somers, as Solicitor-General, was named to a committee to consider bills pending from the last session, and the same committee was ordered to 'bring in a Bill for establishing the Rights of the Subject'. This third attempt was successful. The bill, reported by Paul Foley on 30 October, passed the House unanimously a week later; it was passed in the Lords 23 November and finally received the royal assent in mid-December.[25] At last the Bill of Rights had statutory sanction.

Guarantees for the future were all very well, but many Members cried out for the redress of old grievances. Whigs, with long memories of the Tory proscriptions of the early 1680s and of royal pretensions of more recent years, turned vengefully upon those who had been parties to either of these programmes. Early in March 1689, Somers was named to a large committee, consisting of more than sixty members, charged with inquiring into the abuses of the last two reigns. Of particular concern were the events which had followed the detection of the Rye House plot, highlighted by the treason trials of Algernon Sidney and Lord William Russell. Convicted and executed in 1683, these men had been accorded instantaneous canonisation as martyrs by the Whigs, who, once opportunity was at hand, lost no time in attacking the attainders that overshadowed their reputations and fortunes. What with his involvement in the Exclusion Controversy, Somers must have been sympathetic. Two committees were set up, one for Sidney, the other for Russell. Somers was a member of both. They dealt primarily with the Lords' bills reversing the verdicts which had sent the two men to the block, measures which passed the Commons with little difficulty. Somers also had a seat on the committee to consider a Commons bill to rehabilitate the reputation of Sir Thomas Armstrong, who had also been involved in the plot. In this case the scales of justice were not so easily adjusted. It was not until late in the second session that a large committee, again including Somers, was charged to consider the bill after its second reading, and the actual reversal of the attainder did not occur until 1694.[26]

Among those once more in the public eye was Titus Oates, still very much alive. An unprincipled opportunist, whose fabrications against the Catholics ten years before had produced a national hysteria, he had met retribution as Charles II's reign gave way to his brother's. But with the Revolution this accomplished liar gained new credit as a victim of the old regime. He petitioned the Lords for rehabilitation, but, though advised by the judges that the sentence was cruel and illegal, they refused to revoke it. Meanwhile, while their decision was pending, he appealed to the Commons, an act which provoked the upper house to commit him to the Marshalsea prison for breach of privilege, and brought the case into the sensitive zone of inter-cameral relations. The result was the first serious rupture between the chambers to occur during the reign.[27]

Here again Somers played a prominent part. In June he was named to a committee to inspect the Lords' Journals in so far as they related to the Popish plot, and the following month he served as a leading manager of a free conference with the peers over amendments to a Commons bill on Oates's behalf. Early in August he was called upon to report these deliberations. The report, which was of considerable length, must have reflected, very largely, his own point of view. Noting that 'the honour of parliaments, public justice and the Protestant religion' were at stake, the committee labelled the judgement as 'cruel, illegal and of ill example to future ages', mentioning specifically the perpetual imprisonment, periodic pillorying and unmerciful flogging which had been prescribed. 'Here', he went on, 'were precedents made, which did not concern this man only, or only this offense; ... the Judgments pronounced against Oates were judgments against every Englishman, subject ecclesiastical as well as temporal; the lords as well as commons.'

It was not enough for the Lords to say that such punishments ought to be prevented in the future. The Declaration of Rights had done as much. Nor was the committee content to express its abhorrence of Oates's judicial fate. It sought to present him as a credible witness, hounded by a government willing to strain the procedural proprieties to achieve its aims. The events of the Popish plot had been carefully examined not only by the committee to which Somers had recently been appointed but by other parliaments and by the law courts. Oates had 'stood upright, his testimony unshaken, till a Papist was upon the throne'. Might not disavowal at this juncture amount to a disclaimer of the plot itself? This was something to give Whigs pause. As for the original judgements, 'violation of law, partiality and corruption were the character of the times; and were visible in everything that moved towards the attaining those Verdicts'. So great had been the government's determination to destroy Oates's credit that 'the prosecutions were notoriously carried on by the express directions and commands of the court'. In view of this and other dubious practices, while there was no proof that jurors or witnesses had been bribed, the Commons thought themselves 'well justified in calling the verdicts corrupt'. And now the Lords were making it impossible for the great informer to demonstrate his innocence; for, with his conviction left standing, the case was closed: there was no legal course for further investigation. 'So severe and extraordinary a thing, as the making a man infamous and taking away his testimony by act of parliament, ought not to be done but upon the greatest consideration.'[28]

Somers was able to convince the Commons; they rejected the position of the Lords. But Oates, though freed at the adjournment of Parliament, was not able to secure the parliamentary absolution he sought. Here we may leave the episode, as far as Somers was concerned. Though largely a wrangle over technicalities, it is not without significance. Granted that partisan considerations loomed large—Oates benefited from the natural inclination to look upon one's enemy's enemy with favour—the argument of Somers and his confreres may yet be regarded as vindicating 'the right of even the worst of mankind to even-handed justice'.[29]

As past innocence (or what the Whigs chose to regard as such) was to be vindicated, so past wickedness was to be punished. As those who had disrupted the monarchical constitution in the heyday of the Puritans had stood suspect at the Restoration, so now the shoe was on the other foot, and the tools of a bankrupt royalism must be brought to account. As in 1660, it was not the principal beneficiary of the political changes that cried out for prescription and outlawry. The new King was eager to reconcile the nation to his leadership. He knew little and cared less about the pretensions and grievances of party men. His principal concerns were the continental situation, with its direct bearing on the fortunes of his Dutch homeland, and the need to subjugate Ireland; and he thought an amnesty a small price to pay for subjects ready, if not entirely willing, to contribute to his war chest. But the Parliament men could not, or would not, forget the past. Not to punish the flamboyant upholders of the Stuart system would, to many of them raise doubts as to the necessity of the recent upheaval. And so, while the King with increasing impatience desired an act of grace, providing a genuine indemnity, the extreme Whigs sought to transform such an instrument of mercy into an act of pains and penalties.[30] They were not satisfied to except certain notorious offenders, but attempted to weave a net fine enough to catch any person guilty of one or more of an extensive catalogue of crimes—a proscription so sweeping, in Roger North's words, as to 'comprehend all mankind'.[31]

Late in March 1689, Somers was among eighteen Members of Parliament directed to prepare an address of thanks for the King's message outlining his desires. Seven months later, at the beginning of the second session, the whole question was still unresolved. The employment of the law officers of the crown in the shaping and amending of bills was common practice, dating back to the sixteenth century. Along with Attorney-General Treby, Somers was now ordered to prepare and bring in a bill for punishing those responsible for the violation of 'Laws and Liberties' since 1660. A few days later Treby was ordered to bring in a bill of indemnity. But the Commons had already singled out certain victims. On 25 October they called for the impeachment of the Earl of Salisbury and the Earl of Peterborough for 'departing from their allegiance and being reconciled to the Church of Rome'; attacked Sir Thomas Jenner, a former Baron of the Exchequer, for his part in subverting the law and government; and furthered an investigation of the misdemeanours of Richard Graham and Philip Burton, former Treasury solicitors who were regarded as notorious agents of James's misrule. Somers was named to a committee to prepare the charges against them.[32]

In the debate Somers stood with those who would concentrate on offences rather than persons. 'It is absolutely necessary', he told the House, 'that some should be punished, for vindicating the King's honour, and to justify without doors what we have done.' But he was opposed to a haphazard catalogue of victims. First there should be a declaration of the offences regarded as unforgivable. It was 'of infinite consequence' that posterity should know why certain persons were punished. He would leave it to committees to decide who were guilty of committing such crimes: 'State the Heads, and leave it to them to adapt Persons to it.'[33] Here, in a nutshell, was the position of the Whigs. Somers, of course, did not allude to the use they could make of such a device to embarrass and handicap their political opponents. The Tories did not need to be told this. They preferred to see particular persons branded as public enemies, and on the same day introduced a motion to this effect. It was lost by a close vote. Two days later the 'Heads' justifying exemption from amnesty were read.[34] But it was too late: in February Parliament was dissolved with the issue still hanging fire. In the end, Somers's efforts went for nought, for in May 1690, an act of grace, emanating from the Lords and exempting only thirty-one persons from a general pardon, was passed. He was involved with eleventh-hour opposition, in connection with alleged procedural novelties in the Lords. But since Parliament was forthwith adjourned, not to sit again until October, nothing came of this.[35]

Partisan zeal is even more evident in Somers's views on the reconstitution of municipal corporations. Among the principal Whig grievances of the foregoing decade had been the surrender, under royal pressure linked with local Tory support, of many borough and city charters during the last years of Charles II. The charters had been reissued, but to the disadvantage of the Whigs: on the grounds of alleged misconduct prominent local figures of that party were excluded from participation in government. This meant more than debarment from urban politics. It effectively removed them, as it was designed to do, from any control over parliamentary elections, and in some boroughs even deprived them of the franchise. It also took from their hands any control over the selection of local juries, an important leverage in an age when the courts of law sometimes served as effective political agencies.

Legislation to restore the old charters was launched early in William's first Parliament. On 2 May Somers was among more than forty Members to whom a bill for this purpose was committed. Two months later he was given a similar assignment with regard to the proposed reversal of the celebrated *quo warranto* judgement against the charter of London—that royal victory which had set in train the rout of the municipalities in the days of Charles II's 'personal rule'. But this legislation lagged, and the Members dispersed for the summer recess without settling the matter.

In October, another committee was ordered to frame a bill restoring the corporations, Somers serving as its chairman.[36] When this bill came up for debate in the House, William Sacheverell, ever zealous in the Whig cause, proposed an additional clause excluding from municipal office, for a period of seven years, all who had taken any part in effecting the surrender of the old charters. Sacheverell's amendment would have reversed the arrangements of Charles II's last years by eliminating local Tory leaders from municipal preferment and its perquisites. Debate raged fast and furious. To the Tory protest that the Sacheverell provision would place the control of corporations in the hands of Dissenters, the Whigs (closing their eyes to the practice of occasional conformity) retorted that the Corporation Act would prevent such an eventuality. The cry of 'Popery and Slavery' went up, raised by Sacheverell and the indestructible Maynard. But the Tories saw in the amended measure 'the total ruin of their interest through the whole kingdom', and they came near to throwing down the gauntlet. In the words of Lord Falkland, 'It is dangerous, now the King is going out of the kingdom, to discontent such a body of people.'[37]

Somers spoke out vigorously for the Sacheverell clause. 'Is there any thing more just and natural', he asked, 'than that these offenders should be laid aside?' The dissenting interest was not to be feared. The corporations would assuredly be served by Church of England men: 'They can have no others.' As for the cry that a bill of pains and penalties was afoot:

You are not doing that; you are only laying them aside, that, you have had experience, would have betrayed the Government. There is no possible inconvenience in this Proviso; you will have better men and unspotted men in their stead; thereupon I would not reject the Clause.[38]

But the clause was rejected, by the narrow vote of 182 to 171: 'We routed Jack Presbyter, horse and foot,' wrote an exultant Tory.[39] Somers, of course, had voted with the ayes, along with five of his Worcestershire colleagues.[40] Perhaps his close association with the men who had fought for the London charter in 1683 impelled him towards this all-out support of Sacheverell. It is not enough to say that he was a Whig. He was also an office-holder under the crown, a 'court Whig', and William was disgusted at what he regarded as a naked grab for power. Somers must have been aware of William's sentiments. On the other hand, he may have genuinely feared reactionary elements among the Tories, and regarded the seven-year ban as no insupportable restraint when measured in terms of the security of the Revolution.[41]

In both Parliaments, Somers played a major role in fiscal deliberations. The business of providing revenue for the government, almost invariably time-consuming and productive of controversy, was made more difficult in these years by unprecedented military demands. In his *Vindication of the Proceedings of the Late Parliament*, Somers admitted that the Convention Parliament had not settled the indemnity and militia problems, but pointed out that more important matters had occupied the legislators:

I would fain know from any not designing man, what was fittest to be done in this case; was the time to be trifled away with the settling of the militia, and passing an act of indempnity before any supplies had been granted his majesty for maintaining this kingdom and his subjects against the formidable French king's fleets at sea, and his Irish forces at land, commanded by the late King James in Ireland?[42]

The question of supply was further complicated by a mounting tendency on the part of Tory squires to weigh the supposed advantages of a full-scale prosecution of the war against the certain burden of the land tax, and to look with jaundiced eye on a 'Whig interest' allegedly bent on reaping the benefits of successful campaigns without contributing in due proportion to the cost.

The Convention lost little time in grappling with finance. The new regime was but two weeks old when Somers and Henry Pollexfen were ordered to draft a revenue bill; it was brought in the very next day. During the course of the Convention Somers was called upon to frame no less than thirteen bills or supplementary provisions dealing with supply. It was important to eliminate all possible loopholes, and the Commons followed the usual practice of taking advantage of the expertise of the crown's leading lawyers. As often as not, he was assisted by Attorney-General Treby. Other legal talent was employed as occasion demanded; in drafting a bill to reimburse the Dutch for their expenses in the expedition of 1688, Somers and Treby were assisted by two Tory lawyers, Serjeant Wogan and Sir John Trevor. But his co-workers were not always lawyers: it was

Sacheverell who assisted him in grafting on the revenue bill of December 1689 a clause appropriating part of the grant for naval expenditures.[43]

The details of fiscal measures were worked out in committees of the whole. From the latter part of 1689 until his withdrawal from the Commons in 1693, Somers almost invariably served as chairman of these bodies. In one month—November 1689—he presided over eight such committees; between October 1690 and March 1693, over no less than eighty-five, all concerned with revenue matters. In the latter period he contributed to the drafting of more than twenty such measures, and was appointed to nine select committees called upon to deal with various questions involving supply. So frequently did he preside that he may be described as a pioneer chairman of ways and means. This function did not emerge, as a definite and salaried position, until 1800, but the practice of relying on a particular Member, rather than passing responsibility from hand to hand, now took root as accepted procedure.

A recital of Somers's activities provides a catalogue of the financial needs of the state, and of the varied devices employed to meet them. The raising of the land tax, the rescheduling of poll taxes, the imposition of special assessments (as on the Jews): all called for attention. In the field of indirect taxation the book of rates might be left as it was for a time, but soon there would be new and complicated customs and excise measures to draft or examine. And there was the efficacy of the fiscal system: public accounts had to be examined to prevent abuses in collection; army and navy estimates called for close scrutiny; the condition of the currency was in itself a problem of massive proportions. Every penny counted in supporting the government and defending it against its foes; it comes as rather a surprise to find Somers on a committee to abolish the hearth tax, a particularly unpopular levy, early in 1689.[44]

Although the ramifications of the nation's fiscal arrangements provided almost boundless opportunity for differences of opinion, two issues in particular received early and widespread attention, both at Kensington and Westminster. The first was whether the revenue granted to James II for life had, upon his deposition, automatically expired; the second involved the length of time for which grants should be made. When, only a fortnight after William's elevation to the throne, a committee of the whole took up the matter of royal resources, some Members contended that as long as James lived his revenues devolved upon his successor. 'Learned men', Sir Thomas Clarges argued, 'are of opinion, that all of the Revenue granted for the Life of the late King is to the benefit of this King Jure Coronae.' But Somers, unlike such eminent Whig lawyers as Holt, Treby and Pollexfen, disagreed. The House, he said, should distinguish between the 'natural and political capacity' of the royal life, in conformity with English law. The legislation conferring the grants had clearly been intended to apply to James's *reign*. An obligation involving a private citizen had no bearing here: 'With a common person it ends [only] with Life,' but with a king it was different: 'a Demise and Abdication of the Crown do extinguish his Title to it'.[45] The House agreed, contenting itself with an act granting an aid to their Majesties.[46]

The other issue was, from the King's point of view, no more happily resolved, though here Somers proved more accommodating. The more extreme Whigs were determined that revenue should be granted for short periods. 'This, they thought, would render the crown precarious, and oblige our kings to such a popular method of government, as should merit the constant renewal of that grant.'[47] There was Tory opposition, both on point of principle and with an eye to courting political favour with William, but initially his supplies were granted for a period of months. In December 1689, a measure was framed to continue the collection of public revenue for a year. To this it was proposed to add the words 'and no longer'. Here was the crux of a debate held on 17 December in which moderate and extreme elements among the Whigs can be sorted out. Somers, though he again pointed out that revenues were related to the sovereign's 'politic Capacity' (hence eliminating any carry-over from James's reign), strove to defeat the amendment. 'So restricted a lease of supply', he argued, would have 'terrible' consequences. He insisted that grants of custom duties lasted for the lifetime of the monarch. But his plea went unheeded.[48]

When the new Parliament assembled the following spring, the King, in his opening speech, gave special priority to two subjects: the settling of the revenue and the framing of the long deferred amnesty. He urged that Members not become entangled in debate while the enemy was in the field.[49] Indeed, conditions were such as to impress upon all but the most refractory the importance of resolving these matters. In Ireland, the 'Protestant interest' was confined to Londonderry and Enniskillen, and on the continent Louis seemed about to establish beyond question a legend of invincibility. Certainly it was time to abandon the adaptations and half-measures of the past year, and work out a realistic and stable budget. Once more debate waxed long and hot, chiefly on the matter of the excise and custom duties. Sir John Lowther, a Tory, moved that these revenues, granted to James for life, should be conferred upon William and Mary for their joint lives. But again the sensitive pocket nerves of his fellow Members frustrated such hopes; 'Whigs and Tories were equally fixed in the opinion that the liberality of Parliaments had been the chief cause of the disasters of the last thirty years.'[50]

In the end a compromise emerged. On 28 March the Commons resolved that the hereditary revenues of James II should pass to William and Mary and that the excise should be theirs for life, but that the customs should be granted only for a four-year period.[51] Somers's part in the debate is not recorded, but he was called upon to draft the bills embodying the resolutions. On 8 April he presented two bills, one conferring the portion of the excise enjoyed for life by James II upon the new sovereigns on the same terms, the other granting tunnage and poundage and other customs duties, with the stipulated limitation. These measures were accepted by the House. A few days earlier, along with Richard Hampden, Chancellor of the

Exchequer, he had been ordered to draft a poll tax bill. This the two men produced within a day.[52] William and Mary could now, at last, count on an annual income of better than £700,000 with which to defray the expenses of the royal household and of certain civil offices. Here Somers may be said to have had a hand in developing the concept of the Civil List, which would be established before the reign was over as a regular feature of the national budget.

One of the stickiest fiscal problems involved the determination of an appropriate income not for the King but for Princess Anne. Should revenues allotted to her while her father was on the throne be continued, in addition to others now to be assigned? The size of her allowance provoked considerable debate; some were proposing as much as £70,000 a year.[53] Somers sought to restrain his colleagues; surely, when the King was finding it necessary to retrench, such expenditure was out of line. He seems to have feared (not without reason) that financial independence would encourage Anne to establish a rival court, which would serve as a haven for the disaffected and dissatisfied, and even as headquarters for a Jacobite restoration. He had no quarrel with Anne. 'No man', he said, 'can more honour the Prince and Princess, or is more highly sensible for her quitting her King, and Father, than I.' But it was 'always dangerous' to provide revenue for a subject through legislative action.[54] In the end a grant of £50,000 was approved, Somers being named to a fifteen-man committee to prepare an address requesting royal approval. The members appear to have been somewhat less than enthusiastic over this assignment, for the committee had to be 'revived' two days later.[55] Anne was watching developments very closely. It is at least probable that her dislike of Somers, which persisted until late in her reign, took its rise from this episode, though it was to be intensified by other considerations.

The latent animosities of Whigs and Tories were partially allayed by the general agreement on the financial limitation of the crown. But other considerations kept them alive. For one thing, what was the legal status of the Convention? On 20 March 1690 a bill was brought into the Lords for declaring the acts of the late Parliament 'to be of full Force and Effect by the Laws of this Realm, and for recognizing Their now Majesties King William and Queen Mary to be, by the Laws of the Realm, our rightful and lawful Liege Lord and Lady King and Queen of these Realms'.[56] According to Burnet, the second part was accepted 'with little contradiction', but the first 'bore a long and warm debate'.[57]

From the outset the Tories had looked askance at the Convention. Some, as Jacobites, regarded it as merely a revolutionary assembly. A larger number, while willing to accept it as a temporary instrument, had sought its speedy extinction in the hope of elections more favourable to the Tory cause. Even when the Convention was no more, and new elections (of indisputable legality to all who were willing to accept the new regime) had returned a House of a more Tory complexion, there were men of that party ready to challenge its authority. Such was now the case. Led by the Earl of

Nottingham, the more unbending Tories, while willing to confirm the validity of statutes enacted by the Convention, balked at recognising that assembly as a bonafide Parliament. To them, it made no difference that immediately after the Interregnum the Convention, 'for preventing all doubts and scruples', had voted itself to be legitimate, notwithstanding the dubious circumstances of its birth.[58] What bastard could remove his own bar sinister?

In the end the measure passed in the Lords, but by only seven votes. It seemed destined for rough treatment in the Commons.[59] That this did not occur was mainly due to the practical arguments set forth by Somers and another Whig stalwart, Thomas Wharton. If, they contended, the acts of the previous Parliament were invalid the Parliament in session had no lawful basis. It was, then, a contradiction to assert that the Convention's acts were extra-legal and at the same time to seek a stamp of approval from the new Parliament: 'This Parliament depends entirely on the foundation of the last.' He further pointed out that if the full legality of the Convention were denied those present with him in St Stephen's were guilty of high treason. The laws repealed by it, in that case, were operative, and so 'they must presently return to King James'; in so far as they had levied and spent public moneys under its acts they had engaged in criminal undertakings. 'This', wrote Burnet, 'he spoke with much zeal, and such an ascendant of authority, that none was prepared to answer it.' It was, he added, 'a great service, done in a very critical time, and contributed not a little to raise Somers's character'. The bill passed within forty-eight hours of its first reading, without a division.[60]

Somers might well bring up the matter of allegiance, for he had been involved with this issue in the Convention Parliament. Although he seems to have played no direct part in drafting the new oaths in April 1689, he was asked, along with the Attorney-General, some six weeks later to examine for errors the act in which they were incorporated.[61] The following October he was named to a committee for framing a bill to enforce the oaths, and in January was among those ordered to consider, after the second reading, a bill requiring the oath of allegiance from all persons over the age of sixteen.[62] Fear of Jacobitism, combined with a Whig desire to embarrass the right-wing Tories, nurtured an obsession. Late in April 1690 the Whigs, led by Wharton—so long and intimately associated with Somers's political fortunes—introduced a measure calling upon all officials, civil, military and ecclesiastical, formally to abjure King James. Somers was a member of the committee instructed to draft the oath, it being stipulated that all refusing to take it were to be committed without bail or mainprise.[63] This loyalty test, however, was never written into law. 'Where you put a Buttress,' Clarges warned, 'there the Building is weak. . . . Nothing will tend more to bring in King James than this Bill.'[64] The Tories rallied to defeat it, 192 to 178. Two years later Somers, along with Trevor, again sponsored such legislation, but again unsuccessfully.[65]

As a law officer of the crown Somers was bound to be involved in measures of security. And not only by way of oaths; he had a hand in other devices for restraining and incapacitating the enemies or supposed enemies of the regime. In March 1689 it was proposed that the government be authorised to seize and detain all who were suspected of conspiracy against it; and, the following winter, that all who had been in arms against the new rulers on 14 February 1689 should be attainted of treason. In April the new Parliament stood ready to prohibit Catholics from venturing more than five miles from their habitations, an old and familiar measure. In the first session of the Convention four other committees dealing specifically with 'Papists' included the name of Somers; they were concerned with the disarmament and apprehension of Catholics, as rebels and conspirators, and an investigation of the practice of educating their children abroad.[66]

It is not surprising, with the regime so untried and vulnerable to enemies both at home and abroad, that Englishmen readily raised the charge of treason, and equated a rigid application of the treason laws with the security of the state and the protestant succession. On the other hand, the Whigs, and especially the younger and more militant ones, recalling what they regarded as the judicial murders of Russell and Sidney, looked for some reformation of procedure, in the interest of the liberty of the subject. Somers had already been involved with the problem in connection with the Declaration of Right: the committee on 'General Heads' had recommended, among other things, the regulation of treason trials.[67] Following the Revolution eight attempts were made to enact legislation reforming treason trial procedure. The Lords led off, and in March of 1689 sent a bill to the Commons. But the lower house set it aside.[68] The Lords were at this time primarily concerned with securing for their members, in cases of treason or felony, the right to a trial before the body of their house (rather than before the Lord High Steward and a panel of peers selected by him) when Parliament was not in session.[69] This was to prove a perennial bone of contention between the two chambers. If Somers joined in the debate on this measure there is no record of it. But in October 1690 he and Clarges, along with several others, were given leave to bring in a bill to regulate 'Tryals in cases of Treason'. This was accorded a second reading within three days, but thereafter passed into limbo.[70] Its provisions have not come down to us. A year later separate treason trial bills were before both houses. A Commons measure was introduced by Sir William Whitlock, who had been associated with Somers in the 1690 venture. It provided counsel and sworn witnesses for the accused, who was also to have a copy of the indictment and a list of the jurors ten days before the trial. No person was to be convicted unless the indictment fell within three years after committal of the alleged crime. This passed the Commons. But it did not satisfy the Lords, who framed amendments again assuring them of trial by the peerage as a whole and extending the new procedure to impeachments.[71]

There was strong opposition to this in St Stephen's, led by the two royal law officers, who advocated strict construction of the original treason act of 1352. Somers vigorously attacked both amendments. The full force of impeachment must be upheld. He agreed that it should be 'like Goliath's Sword, kept in the Temple', to be used only on 'great occasions'. But, he warned, 'the Security of your Constitution is lost, when you lose this Power'. As for the amendment extending trial by peers: to accept this would give 'impunity' to their lordships, for the members of the upper house were in many cases kinsmen or linked by close personal relations. Even should a peer be 'the most abandoned creature in the World, it would be strange he had neither friends nor relations to stand by him'. He cautioned the Commons against any reduction of their powers with respect to the upper chamber. He recognised that the Commons had grown more powerful; on the other hand

The Lords have a Controul upon you in Law-making, and this is a great Power ... What you do now in the Lords Privileges, you take so much from the Crown and yourselves. Whatever you do of this kind can never be remedied; for the House of Peers will not part with any thing they have got; the Crown may, for it must use you.[72]

There was some disposal to accede in the matter of impeachment procedure, but a deadlock over the other issue. Somers was called upon to explain the Commons' objections in a free conference, but to no avail, and the measure died.[73]

A year later Whitlock again introduced a treason trial bill, its provisions identical with those of 1691.[74] Rumours of Jacobite plots rendered its passage unlikely. Once more Somers inveighed against any diminution of the Commons' influence through trenching upon its prerogative of impeachment. He took further exception to the provision limiting the period in which an indictment could be presented to three years following the offence: this would make things too difficult for the crown. He concluded with the bald assertion that the measure was unnecessary and, because of wartime conditions, ill-timed. It was bad to weaken the regime by making it harder to punish treasonable offences. There was no danger from over-severe prosecution, for the government was, if anything, 'too gentle'.[75]

Others joined in the attack, with the result that a resolution passed to lay it on the table until some provision for the 'better preservation' of the royal persons could be framed. By order of the house Somers and Trevor now drafted a rider declaring any denial of William and Mary's right to reign to be treason; it also called for an abjuration oath against James from all office-holders and those suspected of Jacobitism. Designed to embarrass the Tories, it brought them out in full force, and, despite court support, it was defeated, 200 to 175.[76] This spelled defeat for the entire bill. It also marked the end of Somers's association with the project as a legislator, for by the time another bill was introduced (in November 1693) he had left the Commons to become Lord Keeper.

His sensitivity over possible infringements of Commons authority by the Lords was not confined to treason trial issues. He opposed the abortive Triennial Bill of 1693, designed to insure elections at least every three years, which the Lords initiated, sharing the resentment of other Members of Parliament who saw their terms limited by an arrangement which could have no effect on the upper house.[77] In debate early in February he protested that the measure would 'tend to the exalting' of the Lords' powers. He also attacked the bill's provision for annual sessions. To the argument that they had been held in Edward III's reign he replied that this practice had been followed because Parliament then performed extensive judicial as well as legislative functions; with the development of the law courts such justification was largely removed. Annual sessions, he thought, would be looked upon as a 'great grievance'; they would make crown and people 'too weary' of parliaments.[78]

The prospect of William's absence in Ireland raised the question of a regency. The Queen was obviously the natural candidate, though she was inexperienced in public business and is said to have been frightened by the prospect.[79] Somers had no objections to her taking over, provided there should be no question of William's overriding regnal authority. In a lengthy speech before a committee of the whole, having sought in vain for suitable precedents as far back as the reign of Edward III, he urged the Commons that, if they chose to vest authority in Mary, they should 'place it so clear, that there may be no doubt'. The current regime was not a year old; great care should be taken not to weaken it. With some men still dreaming of a republic, the Commons should be 'very considerate in divesting'— that is, in reducing William's official powers. There must be no confusion as to the validity of commissions, or the continuance of Parliament, or the status of Ireland and Scotland. Separating power from authority involved a 'nice distinction', especially when so many regarded William as only *de facto* king. A week later he again warned against any diminution of William's rights. The Queen, he allowed, was 'the best Woman in the World, and she has showed herself so ever since she came hither. But I ask if any good Law was ever proposed, that it is a mistrusting the King?'[80] While Somers was undoubtedly motivated by a concern for the stability of the revolutionary settlement, partisan considerations were also a factor. The Tory Carmarthen (formerly Danby) exercised a marked influence over Mary; under a regency this might be damaging to the Whigs, already smarting from recent electoral setbacks. In its final draft the regency act contained provisions safeguarding William's authority *in absentia*, as well as that of the Parliament.[81]

As the military pace quickened, the manifold problems of war increasingly commanded the attention of the legislators. It was Somers who in May 1689 drafted the declaration of war with France; thereafter he was involved not only in filling the war chest but in various projects for raising and improving land and sea forces.[82] He also participated in general investigations of military policies and activities. In June 1689 he was named to a committee to inquire into the delay in sending relief to Ireland; late in 1692, in a conference with the Lords, he supported Admiral Russell, whose failure to follow up and destroy French forces after the victory at La Hogue was being investigated.[83] In the train of the Irish campaigns came problems connected with the treatment of the rebels, Somers (to his later disadvantage) being particularly active in the matter of forfeited estates. One of the last Commons committees to which he was named was charged, early in 1693, with the task of preparing a 'Humble Address to His Majesty setting forth the Abuses and Mismanagement of Affairs in Ireland'. Somers's name heads the list, though it was Wharton who made the report.[84]

Somers's parliamentary activities were related almost entirely to national rather than local issues.[85] Although more than half the legislation of the period consisted of private bills, he had little to do with such business. He was appointed to several committees of this sort in his early months in Parliament, but to none thereafter: as a governmental official he had more important assignments.[86] Nor did he have much to do with commercial legislation, whether national or local in scope. He appears to have shared the anti-monopolistic sentiment of the age, opposing a bill for the regulation of Thames fishermen on such grounds, and attacking a measure for the encouragement of woollen manufactures as a special interest project of Blackwell Hall. He could not ignore the fact that Worcester was a prominent centre of the cloth industry: we find him among those asked to consider a petition of western 'Gentlemen and Clothiers' for the continuation of free exportation of woollen manufactures, and presenting another from Worcester clothiers to require the East India Company to export a fixed quantity of woollen goods annually.[87] During his last month in St Stephen's he brought in a bill allowing the importation of saltpetre, and another 'continuing the Acts prohibiting all Trade and Commerce with France'. But these were war measures which he was ordered to prepare.[88]

On the whole, Somers's career in the House of Commons confirms the impression that he was a conscientious exponent of the Revolution, and clearly identified with Whig programmes, though less fiercely partisan than some of his colleagues. In an age when Whigs were often dubbed republicans his attachment to the institution of monarchy was beyond question, as was his loyalty to the new regime. Tories would put him among the M.P.s who were 'pensioners and dependants of the state', as one of them put it. As a law officer of the crown he was forced to heed its desires, but his actions in Parliament were not invariably governed by the policies of Whitehall. Sometimes he must have found it difficult to ride the two horses at once, but for the most part he performed to the satisfaction of both King and party. Burnet, explaining why Somers was made Lord Keeper, observed that 'he had always agreed in his notions with the Whigs; and had studied to bring them to better thoughts of the King, and to a greater confidence in him'.[89] He had 'got great reputation', both as Attorney-General and as Member for Worcester.

NOTES

[1] Stat. 1 W. and M., c. 1.; *Cal. S. P. Dom.*, 1689–90, 1.

[2] Oldmixon, 40, gives 54 new M.P.s chosen 'instead of the Disaffected', and notes that, while nearly half the Members who had voted against bestowing the crown on the Prince

of Orange were not returned, yet 'by the falling off of Others who voted for it, the Government found Opposition enough in this Assembly'. See Browning, *Danby*, III, 164 ff., for evidence that 103 of 150 who voted against giving the crown to the new sovereigns were returned, as well as 100 of the 145 who voted for it.

[3] Bodleian Library, Locke MSS. C. 18, ff. 153–54, Somers to Locke, 5 March 1690. *Parliamentary History*, V, 547, inaccurately lists Charles Cocks and Samuel Swift as returned, but they were not elected until 1693 and 1695 respectively.

[4] *History of King William III* (London, 1702–3), II, 322–23; Sir Richard Blackmore, *A Satyr against Wit* (London, 1699), line 129.

[5] Macaulay, II, 1022. It is said that Somers had but one oratorical rival, Charles Montague; see *D.N.B.*, Charles Montague.

[6] *C.J.*, X, 35, 65–66.

[7] 'He is (for Satyr dares the truth declare/Deist, Republican, Adulterer': William Shippen *Faction Display'd*, lines 245–46. And see below, p. 203 and n.

[8] Maddock, 178–79.

[9] *The Freeholder*, No. 39. Trevelyan, in *Anne*, I, 192, describes Somers as a religious churchman of tolerant views, like Addison; to Macaulay, V, 2396–97, he was 'a Low Churchman of the school of Tillotson'.

[10] Grey, IX, 191–98; *C.J.*, X, 85; *L.J.*, XIV, 169. For the old and new versions of the oath, see E. Neville Williams, *Eighteenth Century Constitution, 1688–1815: Documents and Commentary* (Cambridge, 1960), 36–39.

[11] Add. MSS. 40, 751, f. 66v. The listed works were published between 1652 and 1697, four of them after passage of the Toleration Act.

[12] *C.J.*, X, 84–86; *L.J.*, XIV, 177; *Parliamentary History*, V, 217–18.

[13] *A Letter Writ by Mijn Heer Fagel to Mr. James Stewart* (dated 4 November 1687), in *Somers Tracts*, ed. 1748–51, II (1748), 540–45; and see also *Parliamentary History*, V, 218, for William's approval of easing the lot of Protestant dissenters.

[14] Campbell, V, 86. Somers, along with Burnet, Maynard and Newton, is given credit for the Act in *Cambridge History of English Literature*, ed. A. W. Ward and A. R. Waller (Cambridge, 1907–28), X, 373. Burnet, in describing its passage, makes no reference to Somers (IV, 16 ff.).

[15] Grey, IX, 224–25, 241–42.

[16] *C.J.*, X, 47, 53, 67.

[17] *Ibid.*, X, 102–3, 112.

[18] J. R. Western, *English Militia in the Eighteenth Century* (London, 1965), 87. For later measures for punishing mutineers and deserters, with which Somers was involved, see *C.J.*, X, 692, 745, 771.

[19] *Ibid.*, X, 42, 62. The other members were Finch, Eyres, Ettrick, Wyndham, Ventris and Dalton.

[20] *Ibid.*, X, 126.

[21] Grey, IX, 238.

[22] I.e., no further than the heirs of his body; see *Bacon's History of the Reign of King Henry VII*, ed. J. Rawson Lumley (Cambridge, 1882), 15.

[23] Grey, IX, 238–41.

[24] *Parliamentary History*, V, 253; *C.J.*, X, 126.

[25] *Ibid.*, X, 273, 276–77, 280; *L.J.*, XIV, 351, 373. The measure was engrossed as 1 W. and M., sess. 2, c. 2.

[26] *C.J.*, X, 42, 46, 51, 122, 300; and see *D.N.B.*, Thomas Armstrong. Armstrong's case was complicated by his outlawry, imposed when he fled the realm to escape arrest.

[27] Lords MSS., 1689–90, 75–84; *Parliamentary History*, V, 277–28; A. S. Turberville, *House of Lords in the Reign of William III* (Oxford, 1913), 158.

[28] *C.J.*, X, 242, 244–51.

[29] *D.N.B.*, John Somers.

[30] On the differences between these instruments, see Macaulay, IV, 1826.

[31] Add. MSS. 32, 524, f. 2 (North papers).

[32] *C.J.*, X, 64, 275, 278, 281; *Parliamentary History*, V, 406.

[33] Grey, IX, 541–42.

[34] *C.J.*, X, 330 ff. The heads were read on 23 January.

[35] *L.J.*, XIV, 502–3; *C.J.*, X, 422–23. The King had declared his intention of submitting such an Act, in his speech to the new Parliament on 21 March (*L.J.*, XIV, 433–34). It was brought into the Lords on 19 May and passed the following day, being enacted as 2 W. and M., c. 10.

36 *C.J.*, X, 119–20, 215, 277, 284, 313, 324.

37 Burnet, IV, 67; Feiling, 270.

38 Grey, IX, 517; *C.J.*, X, 322–23.

39 Bodleian Library, Ballard MSS. 38, William Helyer to Charlett, 11 January 1690.

40 See Oldmixon, *History*, 36, for a list of those who voted 'to incapacitate all surrenderers of Charters to have any Trust in Corporations'. The Worcestershire colleagues were: Thomas Foley, William Bromley, Sir James Rushout, Bart., Richard Lord Coote and Henry Herbert.

41 See Campbell, V, 87–88, for a defence of Somers. Macaulay, IV, 1783, portrays Somers as disapproving the party violence attending this measure, noting that he did not move the penal clauses.

42 *Somers Tracts*, ed. Scott, X, 267–68.

43 See *C.J.*, X, 37, 39, 258, 303 *et passim*.

44 See *C.J.*, X, 42, 117, 239, 281, 297, 324, 434, 562, 789–92, 805; also *The Parliamentary Diary of Narcissus Luttrell*, ed. Henry Horwitz (Oxford, 1972), *passim*.

45 Grey, IX, 114, 121; New York Public Library, Hardwicke MSS., XXXIII, f. 196.

46 *C.J.*, X, 51; 1 W. and M., c. 8. Campbell, V, 86, appears to embroider on this.

47 Burnet, IV, 23.

48 *C.J.*, X, 310–11; Grey, IX, 490–93; Burnet, IV, 60–61.

49 *C.J.*, X, 349.

50 Macaulay, IV, 1814.

51 *C.J.*, X, 358–59; Grey, IX, 4–23.

52 *C.J.*, X, 360, 368, 372.

53 Kennett, III, 547.

54 Grey, IX, 498, and see Neville Connell, *Anne, the last Stuart Monarch* (London, 1938), 59–61.

55 *C.J.*, X, 312, 314.

56 *L.J.*, XIV, 438.

57 Burnet, IV, 72.

58 Stat. 1 W. and M., c. 1.

59 See Macaulay, IV, 1821–22 and n., referring to Van Citters' comment.

60 *C.J.*, X, 371, 373; Grey, X, 50; Burnet, IV, 74; N. Tindal, *Continuation of Rapin*, XVI, 509.

61 *C.J.*, X, 160. He had also been named to a committee to prepare reasons to be presented to the Lords for the Commons' amendments to their bill abolishing the old oaths and substituting new: *ibid.*, X, 93.

62 *Ibid.*, X, 277, 338.

63 *Ibid.*, X, 388.

64 Grey, IX, 83.

65 *C.J.*, X, 391.

66 *Ibid.*, X, 39, 50, 124, 138, 263, 294.

67 See above, p. 32.

68 *L.J.*, XIV, 132; *C.J.*, X, 54.

69 When Parliament was sitting all the peers served as judges, a majority vote determining guilt or innocence. See Holdsworth, I, 389; II, 232.

70 *C.J.*, X, 430, 433, 437. The others responsible for framing the measure were Sir William Whitlock, Sir Thomas Littleton and Sir Robert Clayton.

71 *C.J.*, X, 555; *L.J.*, XIV, 671, 674. Note below, p. 63, on Somers's opposition to allowing Preston to have a copy of the indictment. See Samuel Reznick, 'The statute of 1696: a pioneer measure in the reform of judicial procedure in England', *Journal of Modern History*, II (March 1930), 5–26 and especially pp. 15 ff. According to Campbell, V, 88, the lower house objected 'on the ground that it would interfere with the supposed right of the Commons to proceed by impeachment for other treasons than those specified in 25th Edward III., and which by that statute are reserved for the judgment of parliament, by the words "in doubtful treasons the judges shall tarry and not proceed till the parliament have declared the same"'. Campbell finds Somers's position in this matter the one instance in which he maintained 'unconstitutional and dangerous doctrine'.

72 There are Harringtonian overtones here, though Somers's library catalogue lists no work by Harrington except the *Life and Works*, not published until 1700. It includes, however, *Consideration on Mr. Harrington's Commonwealth of Oceana* (London, 1657) and Matthew Wren's *Monarchy Asserted, or the State of Monarchical and Popular Government*,

in Vindication of the Considerations upon Mr. Harrington's Oceana (Oxford, 1659): Add.
MSS. 40, 752, f. 30. Grey, X, 210, 213–14.

[73] C.J., X, 582; *Parliamentary History*, V, 681, 689.

[74] C.J., X, 698.

[75] Grey, X, 249–50; Luttrell, *Diary*, 236; Tindal, XVII, 356; C.J., X, 730.

[76] *Ibid.*, X, 744. Difficulties arose over the treasonable nature of words, and waters were
further muddied by some who sought the abolition of oaths: Luttrell, *Diary*, 314–20.

[77] And see below, pp. 191–92.

[78] Luttrell, *Diary*, 407.

[79] See Stephen B. Baxter, *William III and the Defense of European Liberty, 1650–1702*
(New York, 1966), 262.

[80] Grey, X, 102–3, 127.

[81] 2 W. and M., sess. 1, c. 6.

[82] C.J., X, 102–3, 505, 642, 692, 745, 762, and see below, pp. 66–67.

[83] C.J., X, 162, 749; and see Luttrell, *Diary*, 332, for Somers's support of a motion thank-
ing Russell and commending his conduct. In 1691 he opposed a bill to encourage privateers,
as conducive to carrying on trade with France, but espoused a similar measure two years
later: *ibid.*, 94, 424, 454, 458–9, 464.

[84] C.J., X, 113, 283, 367, 380, 494–95, 605, 833, 842.

[85] Some local matters came before him: in 1689 he was called upon to consider bills
dealing with the navigability of the Wye and the regulation of the Droitwich salt works,
and the following year with one for preventing fires in Marlborough: *ibid.*, X, 104, 203,
450.

[86] See *ibid.*, X, 308 (14 December 1689) for the last instance.

[87] *Ibid.*, X, 714; Luttrell, *Diary*, 111, 165–66, 374.

[88] C.J., X, 804, 815, 821, 837, 840, 849–50.

[89] Burnet, IV, 187. For references to Somers's support of the rights of the crown, see
Luttrell, *Diary*, 348, 367, 376.

V
Lawyer and judge

The establishment of the new regime brought a new slate of public officials. That the new king at first chose his principal aides from both of the parties has evoked comment. Yet this was, in large measure, to be expected. William of Orange, however much he would be regarded as the saviour of English liberties, was by nature authoritarian. He had not risked life and fortune to become a mere Doge. He would always keep the conduct of foreign affairs tightly in his grasp, and if his military responsibilities had been less arduous, permitting him to spend more time in England, he probably would have dominated domestic affairs to the extent of being, so to speak, his own prime minister. As for the parties, neither Whigs nor Tories could justifiably claim a monopoly of the royal favour. Though the Revolution settlement bore the stamp of Whiggery, in that it was an application of essentially Whig principles, the moderate Tories had played their part. And now that the Revolution was receding into the past, William might well find it difficult to choose between Whigs who, however zealous in granting him the crown, sought further curtailment of royal authority, and Tories, perhaps faint-hearted or untrustworthy in the Williamite cause, but traditionally exponents of a strong prerogative.

In making his appointments, the new king chose men of various political complexions, though on balance the Whigs were favoured. His Council was predominantly Whig. But Danby, the dean of the Tories, was made Lord President; Halifax, the trimmer, returned to his old office of Privy Seal; and new Secretaries were found in Nottingham, a Tory, as well as the Whig Earl of Shrewsbury. The attorney-generalship went to Henry Pollexfen, who had defended the seven bishops. But not for long; upon Pollexfen's appointment as Chief Justice of Common Pleas, Sir George Treby moved up from the solicitor-generalship. To this office, on 4 May, William appointed John Somers.[1]

For Somers it was the beginning of an association with the ministry, destined to last without a break for eleven years. It was, in a sense, the most consequential appointment in his career, for it put him, as Holdsworth has said, on what had been since the sixteenth century 'the highroad of preferment to the woolsack', in the company of such luminaries as Egerton, Bacon, Littleton, and Finch.[2] The appointment appears to have elicited little comment at the time. This is not surprising. The post was not a great plum, though it brought with it a knighthood, bestowed the following October.[3] But it had some advantages over greater offices: a common law judgeship would have removed him from the effective arena of politics and ended a remunerative practice; a commissionership of the Great Seal would also have been restrictive, and a precarious assignment to boot. As for the attorney-generalship, he could hardly challenge the claims of his senior, Treby. The position commanded a salary of £70 a year. But this represents only a fraction of the income which, after the fashion of the age, was derived primarily from the perquisites of office, the appointment carrying with it 'all the fees, etc. enjoyed by Sir George Treby or any other his predecessors therein'.[4] He shared with Treby the profits from drafting royal grants, and could count on a little patronage.[5]

The office of Solicitor-General, like that of Attorney-General, was of late medieval origin, the earliest known patent dating from the reign of Edward IV. By the beginning of the sixteenth century both functionaries had become important state officials. But the inferiority of the former office, growing out of the relative medieval status of attorneys and solicitors, persisted to Somers's day, and beyond. From Henry VIII's time, promotion from the lower to the higher office became the general rule. Actually, the duties of the two officials were very similar. They served as the principal legal officers of the Crown, in the sense that they were responsible for the prosecution of cases in which the Crown had an interest, and for counselling it in legal matters. As such they held office, at least after the Restoration, during the royal pleasure. But they were also, to a degree, the servants of the House of Lords, which summoned them by writs of attendance to assist in its deliberations. Accordingly, Somers, as Solicitor-General, was called upon to give his opinion in such matters as peerage claims, or the prerogatives of the Earl Marshal.[6]

Both Somers and Treby held office while serving as Members of Parliament. With the increased importance of the House of Commons in affairs of state, it had become desirable that the Crown's legal aides should be in a position to advise that assemblage as well as the Lords. For a time doubts were expressed as to their eligibility, connected as they were with the upper chamber, to sit in Commons, but in Queen Elizabeth's time precedents were established in favour of the Solicitor-General. The Attorney-Generals encountered more opposition: Sir Francis Bacon sat following his appointment in 1613, but as an exception to the rule, and as late as 1673 Francis North's right was questioned. After the Revolution the practice became general, and we find Pollexfen, William's first Attorney-General, as well as Treby and Somers, all occupying parliamentary seats 'without remark and without objection'.[7] But Somers, when Attorney-General, found that the old jealousies were not entirely laid to rest. While serving as chairman of a committee of the whole, he was summoned by the Lords to advise them on the Knollys peerage claim. In complying with the order he had to break up the committee, to the annoyance of the Commons. The peers were also put out; the Solicitor-General had filled in temporarily, but they raised objections to this and proposed that for the future the senior officer should always be available as assistant to their House. The flare-up was short-lived, and Somers and his successors continued to frequent both chambers.[8]

It is safe to say that he soon became almost as familiar with the Lords as the Commons. Apart from his official responsibilities, private suits might bring him before their lordships as a counsellor in cases heard on appeal. Not until 1895 were the King's Attorney and Solicitor prohibited from engaging in private practice; and while, two centuries earlier, the Attorney-General could not appear at the bar of the Lords for a private person, the Solicitor-General might do so. The records show that from time to time the Commons gave Somers leave 'to attend the Lords' in cases being heard there.[9] But sometimes they were not so co-operative. In January 1692 the appellant Samuel Swynock, in Swynock v. Sutton, requested that another day be set for the hearing; his counsel were both tied up with Commons business. One of them was Somers, who was occupied that day as chairman of a committee on supply.[10] Although his private practice is said to have been considerable,[11] he figured but occasionally in appeals to the Lords before December 1691. But in that winter he was frequently involved—seven times in January, eight in February. The cases in which he appeared—sometimes for appellant, sometimes for respondent—covered a fairly broad spectrum of civil issues. Particularly prominent is litigation involving estates, matters of inheritance, marriage settlements, and disputes connected with debts, leases and mortgages. Only rarely did he represent purely commercial interests, which figured much less in the Lord's jurisdiction than did the landed element.[12]

As prosecutor for the Crown, his only case of much importance in these years was that of Lord Preston, whose treason trial took place in the Old Bailey before the three chiefs of the common law courts, Holt, Pollexfen and Atkyns, in January 1691.[13] Preston, who had been Lord President of the Council under James II, and also one of the Council of Five left in London by the fugitive monarch, was arrested en route to France. In his possession were letters outlining a Jacobite programme for the ex-king's restoration with French aid, provided he should return to the Protestant faith. Among others implicated were Queen Mary's uncle, Clarendon, Francis Turner, erstwhile Bishop of Ely, and William Penn.

For some reason the Attorney-General, Treby, stood on the sidelines, and Somers conducted the case for the Crown. Preston and two of the smaller fry caught in the government's net, John Ashton and Edmund Elliott, were charged with having planned the assassination of William and Mary, and with having supplied military information to the French.[14] Somers had first to contend with Preston's persistent claim of peerage, despite the fact that it had already been disallowed by the Lords. While pointing out that no one should expect any court to 'help a person to plead to its jurisdiction', he took pains to explain how the matter had been settled. The judges having found against Preston on this point, Somers took a sterner line in arguing against Preston's claim that he should have a copy of the indictment. But he was willing to allow an extra day for the preparation of the defence, which the judges reluctantly permitted.[15]

On the resumption of the trial he dwelt on the dreadful prospect opened up by the conspiracy: the conquest of England at the hands of a French force. The suggestion that the defendants sought to employ it not only to restore King James, but to preserve the Protestant religion and the laws and liberties of Englishmen, he attacked as beyond the pale of reason:

There can hardly be imagined a greater instance of self-denial, than for the French king, after he had destroyed the Dutch and English fleets, and subdued our forces on land, not to make use of his success, so as to add these three kingdoms to his conquest, and possess himself of the uncontested dominion of the sea for ever, but only to entitle him, at so great hazard and expense, to become a mediator between King James and the people of England, and by his mediation establish the Protestant religion, and the liberties of the people.[16]

The jury, after retiring for but half an hour, returned with the verdict of guilty. Even so, Preston did not go to the block. After a confession implicating Penn and others he obtained a pardon which Somers is supposed to have recommended.[17]

The trial appears to have been conducted with well-nigh unprecedented fairness and humanity. Certainly, in comparison with those connected with the Popish and Rye House plots, still very much alive in the memories of Englishmen, it was exemplary. This was partly due to the restraint of the judges, Chief Justice Holt having shown particular forbearance. But much of the credit belongs to Somers. He was, as he remarked during the preliminaries, opposed to anything 'which should have the least appearance of a hardship'. About to present the evidence, he returned to this theme:

I did never think it was the part of any who were of counsel for the King in cases of this nature, to endeavour to aggravate the crimes of the prisoners, by going about to put false colours upon evidence, or to give it more than its due weight; and therefore I shall be sure to forbear anything of that nature.[18]

He appears to have been as good as his word. An eyewitness reported that 'there was no affected exaggeration of matters, nor ostentation of putid eloquence, one after another, as in former trials, like so many geese cackling in a row. Here was nothing besides fair matter of fact, or natural and just reflections from thence arising.'[19] Nor was it in this case alone that Somers demonstrated restraint and fair-mindedness. They are apparent in other encounters and must have contributed significantly to the process of transforming the royal courts from arenas of persecution into more equitable agencies of justice, despite procedural disadvantages under which those who contended with the government still laboured and which even Somers (as in the matter of Preston's indictment) would exploit.

On 2 May 1692 he moved up to the attorney-generalship, Treby having succeeded Pollexfen as Chief Justice of Common Pleas. While the promotion brought little increase in salary, the gains were much greater.[20] The perquisites and patronage were impressive. The King's Attorney, with his authority to deputise a variety of underlings, was described as 'singulus in omnibus et omnis in singulis'.[21] It is said that the profits of office exceeded by £2000 a year those enjoyed by the Chief Justice of Common Pleas.[22] Somers's private practice presumably continued, at least to some extent.

Now, however, there are few references to activities in the Lords. He could no longer appear there in private suits, and he held his new office for less than a year, during which Parliament was in session only a little over four months.

This period produced the most notorious of the cases with which Somers was involved, the Duke of Norfolk *v.* Sir John Germaine. It demonstrates the difficulties which beset even the prime peer of the realm in securing a divorce. The ordinary courts of justice were of no use for this purpose, but precedents existed whereby an injured husband might gain relief by a special act of Parliament.[23] The Duke had proceeded along this line, claiming adultery between his Duchess and Sir John, only to have his divorce bill thrown out because of doubtful evidence. Advised to have his wife's adultery proved in a court of law, he embarked upon an action against Germaine, seeking damages of £100,000.[24] He engaged Somers as counsel, along with Serjeant Thompson and William Banister, and the case was heard in Trinity Term, 1692, before Chief Justice Holt in the King's Bench.

Somers did what he could for his client, whose reputation was that of the pot that called the kettle black. It was 'sad' that a man of such eminence as the Duke should be embarrassed. As for the evidence, he went on, 'our proofs are such that I am ashamed to repeat them', and, indeed, he left the unsavory details to the witnesses. Some difficulty arose from the necessity of producing proof of adultery, and not mere association, within a period of six years prior to the commencement of the action. In the end the jury found for the plaintiff, but awarded only 100 marks in damages, which drew from the court the reprimand that 'the slightness of satisfaction was almost as great a reproach as the crime itself'.[25] And even with this verdict the Duke was unable to procure his divorce bill until 1700. Once again Somers would deal with the case, but this time from his position on the woolsack.

Scarcely less sensational was Lord Mohun's trial for the killing of William Mountford, a popular actor of the day. It took place before the Lords in Westminster Hall early in 1693, with the Marquess of Carmarthen presiding as Lord High Steward. Baron Mohun, an adolescent rake whose life was 'one long Brawl', had been in the company of Richard Hill, who had stabbed Mountford. The crime arose out of rivalry for the affections of the well-known actress, Anne Bracegirdle. Hill made his escape, but Mohun was seized by the watch. Somers, representing the Crown, again gave evidence of his equitable temperament and regard for courtroom proprieties. It was his part, he told the Lords, 'to give an account of the nature of the evidence', in order that they might 'more easily go along with the witnesses' as they were examined. This, he said,

I shall do as shortly and exactly as I can, without pretending to aggravate any thing, which I could never think did become any one in my station, and I am sure would be to very little purpose upon such a judicature as this; for, after all, your Lordships will found your judgements upon the fact, not as it is represented by us, but as it appears upon the oaths of the witnesses.[26]

But he cautioned the Lords against being swayed by consideration for Mohun's youth or rank: what would 'be murder in the meanest subject, is no less than murder, if committed by the greatest peer'. As one might expect, the key question raised by the Lords was whether Mohun's complicity was sufficient to justify a murder charge. There was also the matter of malice aforethought, for the two men had set off originally not to attack Mountford but to abduct the actress. To these points Somers did not address himself, probably realising that the Crown's case was weak. The judges clearly thought so, and the peers as well, for they declared Mohun not guilty, 69 to 14.[27] A few years later the irrepressible nobleman was again charged with murder, and again acquitted. This time Somers served as Lord High Steward. One wonders what his reactions were when Mohun became a member of his own club, the Kit Cat—to which he was not admitted without opposition.

The King's Attorney and Solicitor did not spend all their working hours in courts of law or legislative chambers. Though not of cabinet rank, they were closely associated with those that were, and who sought their advice on the conduct of public business. In these years Somers learned much of the workings of government and of the problems confronting its principal agents. He advised Secretary Nottingham as to the proper method of dealing with Jacobite activities.[28] The Treasury Lords required his opinion in various matters: what could be done about negligent tax assessors in Ipswich? Had Godolphin forfeited his post as Auditor-General for Wales?[29] Oxford University and the ecclesiastical authorities raised the question of the right of the university to present to livings belonging to Roman Catholic patrons.[30] The 'mad' Duchess of Albemarle had married an earl: did she remain a duchess nonetheless?[31] He was ordered to implement the incorporation of the tapestry manufacturers, to investigate the validity of the charters of Dunwich and Colchester, and to draft a new one for the East India Company.[32] His assignments transcended domestic concernments. He scrutinised bills forwarded from Dublin; his opinion was required as to the grant of escheats in Virginia, or of royal mines which might materialise there or in Maryland.[33]

A few days after becoming Solicitor-General, he was called upon to draft the declaration of war against France. This pronouncement, issued at Hampton Court on 7 May, enjoins co-operation with England's allies against King Louis, 'the disturber of the peace, and the common enemy of the Christian world', whose depredations on the continent were 'in manifest violation of the treaties confirmed by the Guaranty of the Crown of England'. Moving closer to home, it cites infringements of English interests in the old world and the new: commercial warfare, privateering, encroachments and attacks upon settlements across the Atlantic. The persecution of English Protestants in France is deplored; but, despite this ill-usage, Frenchmen in England are given the King's word for the security of their persons and estates, provided they 'demean themselves dutifully towards us, and not correspond with our enemies'. Curiously enough, no direct reference is made to Louis's refusal to recognise the new regime; he is accused, rather, of having for some years 'endeavored by insinuations and promises of assistance' to overthrow the English government, and of now giving active support to rebellion in Ireland.[34] The King must have carefully scrutinised this proclamation; that Somers was entrusted with it is evidence of an already substantial reputation.

A further indication of Somers's growing prominence may be seen in his appointment in August 1690 as Recorder of Gloucester. He held this post, as well as the recordership of Worcester, as long as he lived. Both offices were essentially honorific; they did not require regular attention, and deputies were employed. No doubt the citizens of these communities were pleased to have an official of Somers's stamp, whose influence might be sought when there was need of it. As for Somers, he was moved in 1700 to return £60, due him by way of salary from Gloucester, for the purchase of 'a peece of Plate for the Publick Use of the City'. This took the form of a large silver salver, bearing Somers's coat of arms, which is still in the possession of the corporation.[35]

As for his private life, not much can be said. By virtually all accounts he was by nature a formal, reserved man. He was the 'grave' Somers. In later years Jonathan Swift observed that he had 'little taste for conversation', preferring 'the pleasure of reading and writing'. Yet John Macky described him as 'easy, and free in Conversation', despite his 'grave Deportment'. His long and pleasant association with the Kit Cat Club indicates that he was capable of unbending. Physically he was not impressive, being 'of middle stature, [and] brown Complexion'.[36] A portrait by Kneller, now hanging in the National Gallery, shows well-spaced eyes and a high forehead, a shapely nose and rather full, even sensuous, lips.[37]

Though in his early forties he was still a bachelor. According to the anonymous biography published at his death, he took steps while Solicitor-General towards marriage. The lady was Anne Bawdon, daughter of Sir John Bawdon, a wealthy London alderman.[38] Somers went so far as to disclose his income from rents, engaging, so the story goes, in several meetings with a go-between. But the negotiations were broken off because of differences over the marriage portion and settlement. Dimly seen over the centuries, the project seems far removed from an *affaire de cœur*. But perhaps there was more passion than meets the eye: he is said to have renounced 'ever after' any thought of marrying, because of disappointment. Mistress Anne was to wed a wealthy merchant, but Somers remained single throughout his life.[39]

There is reason to believe that he was 'something of a libertine'. So Macky described him at the age of fifty, though Thomas Birch asserts that 'till turned of 40, he is supposed never to have had any Comerce with a Woman'.[40] Even Macaulay is forced to admit, in his encomium, the possibility that 'the wisdom and self-command which Somers never wanted in the Senate, or the judgment seat, at the council board, or in the society of wits, scholars, and philosophers, were not always proof against female attraction'.[41] But his reputation in this regard has suffered from the imputations of his political enemies, and particularly from the attack of Mrs Manley, in her characterisation of Somers in *The New Atalantis*, where he appears as 'Cicero'. She strikes out particularly at his association, in Anne's reign, with Elizabeth Fanshawe Blount. Though married to a Worcester tradesman, she was of good birth: her father was Sir Richard Fanshawe, Restoration diplomat and author.[42] He was accused of keeping her as a mistress, and of cruel usage towards her husband. 'Cicero', Mrs Manley wrote, 'was whirled about by his lusts, at the pleasure of a fantastic worn-out mistress'. She cannot contain herself:

He prostrated his immutable sense, reason, and good nature, either to revenge or reward as her caprice directed; and what made this commerce more detestable, this mistress of his was a wife! Impious excess! Abominable adultery! Were there not enough of the frail race unmarried?[43]

Jonathan Swift would rake up such charges in *The Examiner*.[44] As an antidote we may read Cooksey, who describes Mrs Blount as a mere housekeeper and nurse at Belbar (Somers's Hertfordshire retreat), whom he had rescued from the negligence of a shiftless spouse.[45] Contemporary gossip also linked him in an 'intrigue' with Lady Harriet Vere.[46] These well-born females notwithstanding, even Cooksey concedes that he 'was by no means nice, or in the least degree delicate' in his sexual behaviour, seeing in this a cause of his ultimate physical and mental deterioration.[47] Cooksey probably drew mainly on family lore. But it was common gossip, by the late 1690s, that Somers had contracted syphilis. Unsympathetic lampooners would make the most of this, as in the lines:

> Here in polluted Robes just reeking, draw
> Th' Adulterous Moderator of the Law;
> Whose wrinkled Cheeks and Sallow Looks proclaim,
> The ill Effects of his distemper'd Flame.
> If more you'd know, consult his friend *Tom Hobbs*
> Who vamps him up with his Mercuriall Jobs.[48]

During these years much of his time was spent at the Middle Temple, where, as we have seen, he had duties as bencher and reader, and was provided with chambers. His associates, however, were not drawn only from the legal fraternity and the ranks of politicians. His literary interests continued, despite official responsibilities. They had already led to friendship with Jacob Tonson, the prominent bookseller and publisher, soon to be the presiding genius of the Kit-Cat Club. With augmented means at his disposal, he could indulge himself in the books, manuscripts and prints which increasingly occupied his leisure hours, and which reveal so pointedly his many-sided interests and tastes. His great collection was in the making, and he stood on the verge of being a patron of arts and letters.[49]

He was also on the brink of top-flight ministerial authority. Since the fall of the notorious Jeffreys in 1688 there had been no Lord Keeper or Chancellor of the realm. Following the Revolution the Great Seal was entrusted to three commissioners, headed by Sir John Maynard. To some extent this reflected the unavailability of a properly qualified candidate (Maynard was renowned as a pleader, but was eighty-seven at the time), but there was also an awareness that the traffic in equity had increased to such a degree that a reconstruction of Chancery was desirable. In 1690 a new commission was appointed, headed by Sir John Trevor. Some favoured this arrangement as a permanent feature. But the experiment was not a success. According to Burnet, 'it made the proceedings in chancery to be both more dilatory and more expensive: and there were such exceptions made to the decrees of the commissioners, that appeals were brought against most of them, and generally they were reversed'.[50] The second commission was dismissed early in 1693.

In March of that year Somers was made Lord Keeper. More was involved than the improvement of judicial machinery. It represented a step in the direction of a Whig government. Political expediency played at least as great a part as professional qualifications in Somers's elevation. Within a year, what with the King's disenchantment with the Tories, the decline of Nottingham and the machinations of Sunderland, the administration would be predominantly Whig. The Tories, recognising Somers's competence but fearing his influence, sought to delay his appointment.[51] But on 22 March he was called before the Council and formally notified that the King, 'being satisfied of his integrity and abilities', had selected him for the post.[52] On 2 May, the first day of the Easter Term, he was installed, taking the usual oaths in the Court of Chancery. As was customary, he proceeded in state to Westminster; close to a dozen peers, and about as many Privy Counsellors, accompanied him in their coaches.[53] He was a day short of his forty-second birthday, and would control the Seal for the next seven years. Only two late seventeeth-century Chancellors, Clarendon and Nottingham, remained longer in office.[54] Four years later he was made Lord Chancellor. The promotion reveals the esteem in which he continued to be held by his sovereign, at a time when the Whigs were visibly declining in favour. Since Nicholas Bacon's day, nearly a century and a half earlier, only three Lord Keepers—Egerton, Francis Bacon and Nottingham—had been so honoured.

As Lord Keeper, Somers gained admission into the magic circle of prime officials of state. The office had been for over a century distinguishable from the chancellorship only in the procedure of appointment: since Sir Nicholas Bacon's time the Lord Keeper had been granted 'like place, authority, preeminence, jurisdiction, execution of laws, and all other customs, commodities and advantages'.[55] Custodian of the Great Seal, he supervised all functions connected with its use. He was Speaker of the House of Lords. He presided in the Court of Chancery, and was the chief exponent of English justice.

In requesting Somers to serve, Carmarthen pointed out that the King had commanded him to say that he would 'admit of no excuse'.[56] Prestigious as the office was, it had its disadvantages. For one thing, it brought to an end Somers's career in the Commons. He would leave an assembly where his influence was considerable to become, for a time, a virtually silent functionary of the peers. The Speaker of the Lords, unlike his counterpart in the Commons, could participate in debate and could vote, but only if he were a peer. Somers was but a knight in 1693. Moreover, with his elevation to the bench he had to surrender his private practice. It was natural that he should show some caution, and that he undertook the office with the assurance of a pension of £2000 a year, to take effect when he should relinquish it.[57] Evelyn may have had this manoeuvre in mind when he criticised Somers for avarice.[58] But the arrangement was to be expected of a man conscious of his own merit, of the spoils system of the age, and of the impermanent nature of high office.

It is undeniable, however, that the perquisites of office offered golden opportunities for self-enrichment. As chief judicial functionary of the realm, Somers commanded an annual salary of £4000, half payable from Post Office revenues and half from those of the Duchy of Cornwall. There were also perquisites of considerable value, including allowances of various kinds, as may be seen in his accounts with the Keeper of the Hanaper in Chancery, for the quarter beginning at Christmas 1698. For 'allowance of diet and fees', at 23s a day, he received £103 10s; for his 'Quarter's annuity' £75; for 'extraordinary attendance' in Hilary Term £50; for 'my Quarter's allowance in lieu of 12 tun of Gascoigne wine by the year' £24; for a similar allowance 'in lieu of impost of 12 tun of wine' £6 6s; and by way of allowance for wax £4. The total came to £262 16s. The following quarter it rose to £277 5s 8d; for that ending at Michaelmas, 1699, it was £270 17s.[59] This does not take into account such gains as the New Year's gifts customarily made to high officials, and not foregone by chancellors until 1706, when Cowper turned them back.[60]

Over seventy dependent functionaries provided the advantages of patronage. These ranged from Masters in Chancery to such underlings as secretaries, ushers and messengers.[61] Little can be said of Somers's operations in this sphere. Lacking an extensive family circle, he avoided the common charge of nepotism, though he was to appoint his brother-in-law Clerk of the Patents in 1699, brushing aside Carmarthen's claim to the place.[62] A few years earlier he was commended for having refused to bestow an 'office of profitt' on one whom he deemed unworthy, despite the offer of a quid pro quo.[63] To the highly sympathetic Burnet he was one of the 'most incorrupt' judges ever to preside in Chancery. But the Duchess of Marlborough, beset with grudges, was not so sure. 'I have heard,' she wrote, 'but I do not know the truth myself, that he got as much money as he could in that post, and some grants not becoming a Chancellor to have.'[64] From our point of view, a general laxness prevailed. Even Cowper, despite his scruples, is said to have made £8000 a year while holding the Seal.[65] Evelyn grumbled that Cowper's predecessor's, 'how little while soever the[y] had the Seale, usually got £10,000, and made themselves Barrons'.[66] But, as Macclesfield would argue in his own defence, such practices as accepting gifts from prospective Masters in Chancery were 'reckoned among the ancient and known perquisites of the Great Seal', and were resorted to by 'great and excellent men' before him.[67]

After his installation Somers resided at Powys House, in Lincoln's Inn Fields.[68] By the time of the Restoration this area had become a fashionable purlieu; in Augustan years it was still 'reckon'd one of the finest and largest Squares in the world'. Powys House was the town residence of the first Marquess of that name, one of the coterie of Roman Catholics close to James II who joined him in exile at St Germain. It was an impressive structure, 'well built of Brick and Stone', good enough for the Duke of Newcastle, to whom it was sold in 1705 for £7500.[69] In his official capacity Somers enjoyed it rent-free. It was equipped with a courtroom, an arrangement which must have been conducive to quieter and more orderly proceedings than could be counted upon among the competing litigants of Westminster Hall, though, when Parliament was sitting, it was more convenient to hold court there.[70]

By 1693 the Court of Chancery had been evolving for centuries as the chief tribunal in which equity, as distinct from the common law, might be administered. Actually, Chancery possessed some common law jurisdiction, but according to Blackstone, this was inconsequential, if not extinct, after Elizabeth's time. Equity was supposed to mitigate the harshness and supplement the inadequacies of a national legal system which had hardened and become formalised, sometimes to the extent of denying justice. By it a means was provided whereby the letter that killeth might be circumvented, and considerations of conscience and reason prevail. For centuries, unlike the common law, it had been free from the brake of precedent, the Chancellors drawing on varied legal authorities and traditions, and particularly on the civil (or Roman) law, so basic in continental systems of jurisprudence. With the passing of time equity would become regular and systematised: Lord Nottingham, 'father of modern equity', did much to introduce regularity; a century after Somers's day its practitioners were as much affected by *stare decisis* and a rigid formalism as any common lawyer. But when Somers took over the Seal it was still possible for an able lord keeper or chancellor to shape the rules of his court to meet contemporary needs. Men could still speak of equity as depending on the Chancellor's conscience, if not the length of his foot. Nottingham himself, in diverging from the opinions of colleagues, had said, 'I must be saved by my own faith, and must not decree against my own conscience and reason.'[71]

Equity jurisdiction was divided into three essential categories. It was described as exclusive when the common law provided no forms of action by which legal relief could be obtained. Especially important were trusts and the rights of married women, infants and lunatics. It provided a concurrent jurisdiction where the common law did not afford adequate relief, particularly in cases of fraud, accident, mistake and specific performance of contracts: in Nottingham's words, 'Chancery mends no man's bargain, though it sometimes mends his assurance.'[72] Finally, in cases where the administrative machinery of the courts was unable to procure necessary evidence, it could exercise an auxiliary jurisdiction. Its involvement with the more important forms of property was extensive; it was said in 1725 that most of the estates in England passed under its review once in a generation.[73]

In most respects Somers was well qualified to uphold equity jurisdiction, and even to shape and extend it to some extent. He was an able lawyer, with an established reputation as a pleader. He had a scholar's interest in the law—not only the municipal law, that of Year Book and Report and Statute, but in the civil law and other branches of jurisprudence. The catalogue of his library amply testifies to a continuation of an intellectual curiosity awakened and served by his studies at Oxford.[74] He was, in addition, a practical man, aware of and involved with many of the main currents of his age. Only one disadvantage might be discerned: he had never sat upon the bench. His professional background was that of the private practitioner and Crown lawyer.[75] As such, within a framework which permitted little deviation in procedure, he had been forced to work with the law as it was, not as it ought to be. He now came, without an interlude of judicial experience, to head a court which, of all courts, placed in the hands of its president broad originative and discriminative powers.

As equity chief, he served capably and conscientiously. The assignment was burdensome; he spent himself freely in its interminable business. His claim, made on the occasion of his impeachment, that he pursued official duties to the detriment of his health was undoubtedly justified. His presence at Westminster Hall soon after seven, when convalescing from an illness, drew comment. Tedious hearings left him exhausted.[76] His duties, moreover, were not confined to the judicial arena. They encompassed top level administrative responsibilities and detailed political management. He was a Chancellor in the mode of Clarendon rather than Nottingham.

As far back as 1621 Edward Coke had declared that there was too much Chancery business for the Chancellor and the Master of the Rolls to handle.[77] Yet their unreformed court was still, at the end of the century, as understaffed with judicial talent as it was encumbered by petty bureaucrats. On occasion some relief was provided by recruiting the services of common law judges. The twelve Masters in Chancery, appointees of the Chancellor and at one time co-judges with him, were in Somers's time no more than expert advisers, having retreated before the burgeoning influence of the Master of the Rolls.[78] This official, appointed by the Crown, was in a sense Vice-Chancellor. Sir John Trevor occupied the post from 1693 until his death in 1717. A relative of Jeffreys (and, like him, rough in the courtroom), he had held the same office under James II, being one of the few judges to be reinstated after the Revolution. There can be no doubt that Somers benefited from the experience and toughness of this veteran. Though deprived of the speakership of the Commons for taking bribes, his conduct on the bench, considering the mores of the age, appears to have been unexceptional. He was undeniably a highly capable equity judge: Holdsworth describes him as one of two notable Chancery officials (apart from keepers or chancellors) of the late seventeenth century.[79]

The pressure of other business may explain, at least in part, why Somers, for all his competence, did little to reform his court, and made comparatively few significant contributions to equity. The need for procedural improvements had long been recognised. About this time that indefatigable tourist, Celia Fiennes, observed that although 'this formerly was the best Court to relieve the subject', it had become 'as corrupt as any and as dilatory'.[80] That fees were high, proceedings sluggish, and settlements too often delayed by rehearings was painfully apparent. Since procedure was based almost exclusively on the written word, an endless proliferation of documents was inevitable; this, in turn, necessitated innumerable fees for the officials concerned, not to mention the pettier claims of minor attendants—crier, usher, bookbearer, and so on *ad infinitum*. Despite a high degree of formalism, the court's practice was perennially in a state of flux; and, strange as this may seem, compared with the common law tribunals it did not enjoy the reputation of being a learned forum. 'A little law, a good tongue, and a good memory would fit a man for the Chancery'—so commented Matthew Hale in Restoration years.[81]

At the Revolution it was expected that some reform might be written into law. Somers himself, as a leading member of the committee on the Declaration of Rights, had included the regulation of the Court of Chancery, as well as other tribunals, in its initial provisions, but action was deferred. Thereafter, as Solicitor-General and Attorney-General, he was called upon by the Commons to give expert advice in framing a variety of measures relating to the administration of justice, some of which introduced elements of reform. Late in February 1689, he, along with the other lawyers, was asked to draft a bill for continuing actions which depended in the Westminster courts, and 'for curing their Defects'. Again, in December 1692, he and Trevor had a hand in preparing legislation 'for the better Discovery of Judgments' in these tribunals; in the following month he was involved in the regulation of King's Bench proceedings.[82] Later, when out of office, he would promote and implement the most substantial legislative reform of the legal system between the days of Praise-God Barbon and Sir Samuel Romilly.[83] But, while holding the Seal, like most chancellors he did little to improve the machinery and methods of his court, contenting himself with half a dozen brief orders on procedure.[84] The status quo was essentially maintained.

It was not easy to make changes. As Holdsworth observes, 'Those who, from their experience of the court, were most competent to reform it, were the most interested in maintaining it in its existing condition.'[85] While its more important offices were at the disposal of the Chancellor or Master of the Rolls, the functions of such officials, who were appointed for life, were largely performed by underlings.[86] Valuable rights of patronage, along with the advantages of sinecures, combined to create vested interests in the system. The rising market value of various offices made incumbents all the more determined to safeguard their property rights. Oldmixon, observing that 'there was hardly any commodity in a market bought and sold more frequently and openly than a Master in Chancery's place', believed that its price had trebled in his own lifetime.[87] Manned by a host of functionaries who regarded their posts as a form of freehold, all engaged in a practice indefinitely and even mysteriously set apart from the mainstream of English law, it is not surprising that reform was resisted for so long.

Among the charges levied against Somers, when he was impeached in 1701, was malversation by delaying proceedings and making 'arbitrary illegal orders' in cases before him.[88] He, of course, denied any improper conduct. But while the impeachment was politically inspired (representing what we would call the smear tactics of partisan enemies), these particular indictments were perhaps not without some foundation. On two occasions Somers and the court he headed came under sharp attack from Sir Robert Atkyns, who in the early years of the reign was Chief Baron of the Exchequer. In 1695 Atlyns published *An Enquiry into the Jurisdiction of the Chancery in Causes of Equity*, a protest against the 'exhorbitant encroachments' of the Chancellor's jurisdiction. Included was an appeal which Atkyns had made against a decree issued by Somers the previous year on a mortgage matter. Atkyns inveighed against the expense and delay in foreclosing mortgages, and more generally against the uncertainty of equitable decisions. In 1699 he again took up the cudgels in a petition to the Commons against mounting equity influence which, he warned, was progressively undermining the common law.[89] The Lords had recently launched an investigation of the costliness and length of lawsuits, ordering Somers, as well as the presiding judges on the common law side, to itemise the fees and perquisites of their courts.[90] But these proceedings appear to have had little, if any, effect.

Of all the cases before Somers, only one is sufficiently well reported to reveal his powers as a judge. This was the so-called Bankers' Case of 1696. Holdsworth has described the judgement as 'the most elaborate ... ever delivered in Westminster Hall, being in fact an historical treatise on the obscure topic of the legal remedies of the Crown.'[91] The case had its origin in the Stop of the Exchequer in 1672, whereby Charles II's government suspended interest payments on part of its debt to certain bankers in order to apply the money saved to the prosecution of the Dutch War. Financial confidence was seriously undermined; no less than five bankrupcies produced tremors in the City. In 1677 the aggrieved creditors were allowed annuities at six per cent, with the hereditary excise as security, but by 1683 these payments fell into arrears which persisted until the Revolution. In 1690 the bankers presented a petition to the Barons of the Exchequer. Somers was Solicitor-General at the time. He, along with the Attorney-General, filed a demurrer; but this was overruled, and the court provided the relief claimed.

In due course, Somers having become Lord Keeper, the matter was brought on a writ of error to the Court of Exchequer Chamber. This was a tribunal created by statute to review the judgements of the Barons: it comprised the Chancellor and Treasurer assisted by common law judges.[92]

Among them was Treby, Chief Justice of Common Pleas. Thus the two law officers who in 1690 had opposed the petition became judges of its validity. But by the practice of the age this was no bar. Progress was at a leisurely pace, which must have been maddening to those whose original grievance dated back more than twenty years. Chief Justice Treby's opinion, in favour of the Crown, was not delivered until June 1695; Chief Justice Holt's, against the Crown, followed in November.[93] In the meantime the six puisne judges had agreed with the Court of Exchequer. The Lord Keeper was yet to be heard from. He was leaving no stone unturned to acquaint himself with the case, and particularly with the historical background of the issues on which it turned. He is said to have spent £700 in collecting relevant books and other materials, and in having searches made.[94]

At last, in June 1696, he delivered his judgement. In Howell's *State Trials* it fills nearly seventy columns.[95] He concurred with Treby. There were two major questions in the case. As to the first—whether the sovereign could alienate the hereditary revenues,—there was no doubt: all the judges agreed that he could. The second, which found Somers, Treby and one of the Exchequer Barons opposed to their colleagues, was whether a petition of right should have been resorted to, rather than the course actually followed. Somers's researches had convinced him that there was no legal alternative to the petition. He argued that no record and no authority could be cited to the contrary, referring to innumerable instances and discussing their relevance to the matter at hand, and decreed the reversal of the decision. Of the thirteen judges, ten had upheld it, but seven of them maintained that the Lord Keeper was not bound by the majority opinion. The common law judges were relegated to the position of assistants. This, however, was not the last word on the case. In 1700 it was taken to the Lords where, despite royal interposition, Somers's judgement suffered reversal. In the end the Court of Exchequer was vindicated, though the bankers had to be content with ten shillings in the pound.[96]

Somers has been criticised, in this case, for his absorption with medieval precedents, particularly his tendency to equate the numerous petitions of bygone days with the petition of right of his time. There is no denying that his outlook was somewhat rigid. He had, he said, great regard for the rights of property, but under William these were safe from royal depredations; it was, rather, necessary to see that the complainants gained no remedy beyond what was available by law.[97] Lord Birkenhead observes that, under the conditions of the time, petitions of right were quite 'illusory' as remedies, and finds Somers's judgement, 'as a contribution to the living science of the law', inferior to Holt's. But he admits the importance of Somers's position for the future application of the remedy. Holdsworth gives him full credit for sanctioning the principle that the petition of right was 'an elastic remedy, which should, so far as possible, be allowed whenever the subject had a claim against the Crown which could be enforced by action against the subject'.[98] This broad view of the remedy's scope would be elaborated by nineteenth-century jurists to serve the needs of the modern state. Somers's arguments (along with Holt's) were invoked in Thomas v. the Queen (1874), where it was ruled that a petition of right lay against the Crown as a means to secure damages for breach of contract.[99] Twentieth-century litigants would in large numbers continue to avail themselves of the remedy.

As for his jurisdiction in Chancery, the sparsity of the record makes it difficult to select cases of particular significance. But even when we allow for the inadequacies of reporting—and possibly for a lack of *causes célèbres*—it is nonetheless striking that a modern catalogue of more than sixty leading cases between the Restoration and the era of Lord Eldon includes none of his decisions.[100] Hyde v. Parratt (1695) deserves mention. The case raised the question of where property was vested when chattels were devised to one person for life, and then to another. Somers held that the former had simply the use, and that the latter had from the outset the property, a decision twice upheld in the early years of George I.[101] The matter of paying debts out of real estate came up in Bampfield v. Wyndham (1699). Before the time of William III real estate was not subject to simple contract debts, 'unless devised or charged for their payment'. The question arose whether, when such an arrangement was made, real estate should be primarily liable, in exoneration of personal property, or be charged only after the latter had been exhausted. Somers took what was essentially the traditional view, holding that where the debts exceeded the personalty 'it must be inferred that the testator intended in charging his realty to relieve the personalty altogether'.[102] However adequate this may have proved as a working rule for the time, it certainly did not satisfy the needs of the late eighteenth century, when Lord Thurlow laid down the rule, subsequently adhered to, that a 'mere charge' was not enough to remove the primary liability of personality, and that, to effect this, clear documentary evidence—in will or deed—of the testator's intention was necessary.[103] In Allen v. Sayer (1699) Somers ruled that 'equity will not suffer an infant to be barred by laches of his trustees, nor to be barred of a trust estate during his infancy'.[104] Another case, in which he signally upheld the equitable custody of infants, was Bertie v. Falkland (1698). Here such jurisdiction was described as inherent in the Crown, as *pater patriae*; exercised of old by Chancery, it had passed to the Court of Wards, only to return to Chancery upon the dissolution of that court. This view, in which he seems to have been historically less correct than in the Bankers' case, has been generally accepted, though he would be partially reversed in his judgement.[105]

In his official capacity, Somers was involved in the judicial business of another tribunal, the House of Lords. While the Lords as a body could and sometimes did participate in judicial business apart from the trial of peers, they were already inclined to leave it to the experts. It was not, however, until 1844 that the rule was laid down that only those learned in the law should vote on appeals: when the peers reversed Somers's judgement in Lloyd v. Carew, he was the only lawyer involved.[106] Nonetheless, the Chancellor's professional expertness and official influence would in most cases weigh very heavily, as would the advice of the common law judges. These, like the law officers, could be compelled to attend, negligence in this respect laying them open to official reprimand. In 1693 Somers felt obliged to warn them that their inattendance had been noted by the House, which would proceed 'with great severity' against them unless they mended their ways. This seems to have had little effect, for the admonition had to be repeated several months later, and in 1694 the Lords ordered that at least two of the judges should be present in the House every day in term time.[107] When the Lord Keeper was absent it was customary for one of the Chief Justices or the Chief Baron to serve as deputy.[108]

The upper chamber had by this time virtually abandoned all jurisdiction at first instance, though it retained such authority in criminal trials of its own members and in conducting impeachment proceedings. But as a court of appeals it had reached full maturity. Appeals from common law courts upon writs of error were fairly common, and sometimes involved a tedious expenditure of time. Appellate jurisdiction in equity, though opposed by the Commons, had nevertheless been secured. Apart from ecclesiastical cases, there were few legal problems of any magnitude which might not come before the Lords.

There seems to be no reason to question Campbell's conclusion that Somers gave high satisfaction in disposing of the proper judicial business of the House upon appeals and writs of error'.[109] It would be tedious to catalogue the cases before the Lords in these years, but some are of sufficient importance to merit attention. Bridgeman v. Holt (1693) shows that the upper House had not entirely laid aside its claim to be a court of first instance. A petition was presented against certain judges for not sealing a bill of exceptions, but upon judicial advice it was withdrawn.[110] Since then the Lords have never attempted to revive the claim. Another case of historical and constitutional interest was the appeal of the Society of Ulster in 1697, an episode of some importance in the long and chequered account of Irish self-government. It arose out of a dispute between the organisation responsible for the building of Londonderry and William King, Bishop of Derry, in the course of which the Irish House of Lords reversed the Irish Court of Chancery. The Ulster Society thereupon petitioned the English Lords against this reversal, arguing that appeal from the Irish Chancery lay to them and not the Dublin peers.[111] This was the most protracted of the cases heard by the Lords while Somers held the Seal, not being determined until December 1699. He must have found himself particularly at home in a dispute where precedents were so abundantly cited, and the Lords' records, as well as his correspondence with the Earl of Galway (one of the Lords Justices of Ireland), show him to have been extraordinarily active. He vigorously maintained the jurisdiction of his chamber, an argument sustained in the decision.[112]

He also wielded some influence in the development of divorce law. Before William III's reign the Lords Journals mention only two divorce acts, those of the Marquess of Northampton in 1552 and of Lord Roos in 1670. But under William several such bills became law. The first such case to come before Somers was that of the Countess of Macclesfield. It excited widespread public interest and occupied the attention of the Lords day after day from mid-January until early March. The adultery of the Countess having been clearly established, the bill was passed upon Somers's advice, despite the fact that (for the first time) no previous judgement had been given in an ecclesiastical court. This occasioned protest, from Rochester and Halifax, as a precedent which might have 'dangerous consequences for the future'.[113] Even more publicised was the chronic case of the Duke of Norfolk. As already noted, Somers had sought as counsel for the Duke in 1692, but to no immediate avail, the bill served by the Duke being twice rejected.[114] But in 1700, as Somers neared the end of his chancellorship, fresh evidence was adduced by the persistent peer. As a consequence, Somers advised the Lords to pass the bill, which not only granted the divorce but gave express permission to remarry. The latter feature makes it something of a landmark in the history of English law, for customarily in divorces *a mensa et thoro* (usually for adultery) this had not been sanctioned. This evoked objections, and there were others directed against the 'short and summary' proceedings in which the ecclesiastical authorities, apart from the prelates in the Lords, had taken no part. Despite this opposition, the bill was passed. The Duke finally obtained his divorce, on terms which, in Ogg's words, 'marked the beginning of the long process whereby the state took over control of divorce from the church'.[115]

As he presided on the woolsack, Somers was from time to time forced to take up cases already adjudicated by him in Chancery. The impartiality with which, on such occasions, he advised the Lords and assisting judges can only be conjectured. The reporting of cases heard in the upper chamber was minimal; parliamentary opposition to the publication of its proceedings would serve as an obstacle until at least the latter years of the eighteenth century. When Bartholomew Shower brought out his *Cases in Parliament* in 1698, the Lords voted it a breach of privilege; Somers reprimanded the bookseller and forbade publication of such deliberations.[116] No further reports of this kind appeared until 1784. There is but a rare glimmering in the records of the House—as in Sir Robert Atkyns *v.* Tooke (1696), where Somers was called upon to give his reasons for regarding the case as belonging on the equity side.[117] Lord Campbell could find but one instance in which he was reversed, Lawrence *v.* Lawrence (1699), a case involving an implied bar of dower. But investigation uncovers at least a half a dozen other reversals.[118] Considering the judicial traffic of seven years, this record is impressive.

About a year before relinquishing the Great Seal, Somers, as Lord High Steward, conducted trials of the Earl of Warwick and Lord Mohun—the same Mohun whom he had once prosecuted as Attorney-General.[119] These noblemen, accused of murdering Richard Coote in Leicester Square, pled their peerage and were tried with the traditional pomp and ceremony. The peers paraded from their chamber, accompanied by a host of functionaries and attendants—clerks of the Lords, Masters in Chancery, the judges, peers' eldest sons, mace-bearing serjeants and a herald. Somers with his entourage brought up the rear, preceded by the Gentleman Usher of the Black Rod bearing his staff of office. For Somers it must have been a profitable occasion. When Carmarthen had served as Steward in Mohun's earlier trial, his remuneration (according to Luttrell) was set at £1000, with a per diem allowance of £500.[120] Apart from due assurances of fair play, Somers's part in the proceedings was confined to comments on points of law and occasional questions to witnesses; he was not responsible for summing up. Despite considerable tumult—in Warwick's trial the disorder provoked him to threaten arrest—the trials appear to have been managed with propriety. In both cases the Lords acted unanimously, Warwick being convicted of manslaughter and Mohun acquitted of murder.

Somers's reputation as a judge was variously estimated by contemporaries. To the Jacobite William Shippen, well known for his anti-Whig satires, he was 'An unjust J[udg]e, and blemish of the M[ace].'[121] Another hostile witness, while acknowledging his 'Art' in expounding the law, accused him of 'Weighing the Party's Merit, not the Cause.'[122] Still another satirical piece, *The Titles of Several Public Acts Agreed to in the Cabal* (1699), includes 'An Act of pardon for all errors and ignorances in the Court of Chancery since May last.'[123] But such jibes usually bear the mark of political malice rather than professional criticism, and are offset by the appraisals of more noteworthy (as well as more Whiggish) observers. John Locke publicly endorsed Somers's 'unbiassed Justice, and steady Care to preserve to every one their Right', while Burnet called him the 'greatest man' he had known as Chancellor, 'fair and gentle, perhaps to a fault'.[124] His protégé, Addison, in eulogising him, observed that 'his great application to the severer studies of the law had not infected his temper with any thing positive or litigious; he did not know what it was to wrangle on indifferent points, to triumph in the superiority of his understanding, or to be supercilious on the side of truth'.[125]

With the passing of a generation or two men of both parties—Nicholas Tindal as well as James Ralph—could afford to be laudatory.[126] It remained for the nineteenth century, with its neo-Whiggism, to bestow the accolade. To Macaulay he was equally eminent as jurist and politician.[127] Lord Campbell, while exhibiting some professional caution in evaluating his contributions to equity, shows almost unrestrained admiration for his capacities as lawyer and judge, as well as for his career as a whole.[128] Only rarely was a more critical judgement voiced. Joseph Parkes, calling in 1828 for equity reform, expressed reservations as to his decrees and general aptitude, adding that 'his complicated and seducing employments as a minister, a courtier, speaker of the upper house, and communicant with foreign ministers, were grossly inconsistent with his office of judge of the court of Chancery'. Yet he admitted that 'his industry, and the principles of his decisions, appear on the whole to have been superior to those of any of his predecessors'.[129] In our own century the estimate of Holdsworth has provided something of a corrective to earlier encomiums, without denying the very substantial basis of his reputation. There is no doubt that he was a distinguished lawyer and a highly competent judge. But he was not, like Nottingham before him and Hardwicke in future years, a notably creative jurist who would give new form and direction to the law. 'It is rather as a constitutional lawyer, a statesman, and a man of letters, than as a great chancellor, that he lives in history.'[130]

NOTES

[1] Royal letters patent constituting Somers Solicitor-General, 'with all the fees etc. enjoyed by Sir George Treby or any other his predecessors', are dated 6 May: *Calendar of Treasury Books, 1689–92*, IX, pt. i, 108.

[2] Holdsworth, VI, 464.

[3] William A. Shaw, *Knights of England* (London, 1906), II, 265. On 10 May 1689 he was made a Bencher of the Middle Temple: *Middle Temple Records*, III, 1388, and see above, p. 10.

[4] *Cal. Treas. Books*, 1689–92, IX, pt. i, 108.

[5] *The Art of Thriving* (London, 1635), in *Somers Tracts*, ed. Scott, VII, 200; and see North, *Lives*, I, 148–49.

[6] Lords MSS., 1690–91, 348, 479–80; 1692–93, 267–71.

[7] Holdsworth, VI, 464–65.

[8] Lords MSS., 1692–93, 267–71; L.J., XV, 146, 177, 183; Luttrell, *Diary*, 366–67. On the assistants of the House of Lords, see John Macqueen, *Practical Treatise on the Appellate Jurisdiction of the House of Lords and Privy Council* (London, 1842), 35.

[9] J. W. Norton-Kyshe, *Law and Privileges relating to the Attorney-General and Solicitor-General* (London, 1897), 7; C.J., X, 204, 470, 485, 501–3. See also Luttrell, *Diary*, 63, 107, and 366–67 (for disagreement concerning Somers's attendance upon the Lords in Lord Banbury's case).

[10] L.J., XV, 23; Lords MSS., 1690–91, 437. For another case where both the Attorney-General and Solicitor-General were prevented from attending a case because of parliamentary business, see ibid., 1690–91, 204 (Lord Lovelace v. Alstone). Sometimes the two law officers were engaged on the same side, as in the Duke of Grafton v. the Lord Chief Justice Pollexfen, when they were heard for the defendant. But this was not necessarily the case: in Leach v. Thompson they were antagonists: ibid., 1689–90, 117; 1692–93, 79. See also ibid., 1690–91, 262 (Browne v. Waight).

[11] Campbell, V, 92.

[12] See Lords MSS., 1690–91, 277, 279–80, 339, 341, 437.

[13] Another case, that of William Fuller, is of some interest in that he proposed to reveal a Jacobite plot in which Lord Halifax was allegedly implicated. Late in 1692 Somers informed the Commons that in accordance with their order he was proceeding against Fuller: Luttrell, *Diary*, 235. Fuller was imprisoned for three years as an impostor.

[14] Ashton was Clerk of the Closet to Mary of Modena.

[15] *State Trials*, XII, 654, 659.

[16] Ibid., XII, 679.

[17] D.N.B., John Somers; *Memoirs*, 38. Somers also participated in Ashton's trial; Elliott was not brought to trial.

[18] *State Trials*, XII, 679.

[19] *An Account of the Late Horrid Conspiracy to Depose Their Present Majesties K. William and Q. Mary* (London, 1691), cited in Macaulay, IV, 1986n. This may have been written by Defoe.

[20] The salary was £40 13s 4d the half-year: *Cal. Treas. Books*, 1689–92, IX, pt. iv, 1889–90.

[21] *The Laws of Honour* (London, 1726, first published 1714), quoted in Norton-Kyshe, 4; and see *The Art of Thriving*, *Somers Tracts*, ed. Scott, VII, 200.

[22] North, *Examen*, 515; North, *Lives*, I, 187.

[23] The cases of the Marquess of Northampton (1552) and of Lord Roos (1670). See below, p. 78.

[24] Luttrell. *Relation*, II, 624.

25 *State Trials*, XII, 927–48; Kennett, III, 668; *Portland MSS.*, III, 508.

26 *State Trials*, XII, 961.

27 *Ibid.*, XII, 1015–47. Evelyn, however, observes that the judges 'declar'd him guilty'; *Diary*, V, 129. Macaulay inveighs against the judgement as inequitable, and cites it as a reason for the Commons not giving in to the Lords on reform of treason trials: V, 2268–70. The proceedings were published, by command of the Lords, as *The Tryal of Charles Lord Mohun before the House of Peers in Parliament* (London, 1693).

28 For example, on seizing Preston's estates and bringing spies to justice. See Hist. MSS. Comm., *Report on the Manuscripts of the Late Allan George Finch* (London, 1957), III, 402, 404. Somers cautioned against improper procedure in dealing with suspected enemies of the state: it was 'scarce legal' for such men to be kept in custody without trial, and 'not fitt' that they be detained upon a single testimony: *ibid.*, IV, 343, 386.

29 *Cal. Treas. Books*, 1689–92, IX, pt. i, 298; pt. ii, 543.

30 Bodleian Library, Rawlinson MSS., D. 742, ff. 30–31; Wood, *Life and Times*, III, 395 and n.

31 Lansdowne MSS., 504, f. 16.

32 *Finch MSS.*, III, 408, IV, 15, 322, 412, 432; Add. MSS. 34,653, ff. 136–37; P.C. 2/75, 23 March 1693. On East India Company charter, see below, p. 137.

33 *Finch MSS.*, IV, 216, 303, 479; *Cal. Treas. Books*, 1689–92, IX, pt. iii 1258; pt. v., 1966.

34 Kennett, III, 563, states that Somers was 'said to have' drafted the declaration. For the text, see Tindal, XVI, 350–54; *State Tracts*, III, 104–5. In the Hardwicke MSS., XXXIII, f. 200, are notes on 'Entering into a War with France'—probably heads of a speech in the Commons in 1689.

35 Gloucester Council Minute Book, 29 August 1690; 5 March 1700; Worcester City Council Minutes, 20 November 1688. At Gloucester Somers succeeded Charles Trinder, who had played a part in the trial of the bishops, and was succeeded by Sir Nicholas Lechmere, Chancellor of the Duchy of Lancaster. In Worcester the town clerk served as deputy; see Dyer, 201.

36 *Works of Jonathan Swift*, ed. Temple Scott (London, 1897–1908), X, 23–24; John Macky, *Memoirs of the Secret Service of J. Macky* (London, 1733). Henry St John once referred to him as a 'little fellow': Hist. MSS. Comm., *Downshire MSS.* (London, 1924), I, pt. ii, 803.

37 On portraits see below, p. 197 and n.

38 A Whig, Bawdon was among the magistrates appointed by royal commission in 1687 and suspended the following year when the old charter was restored. He served for Aldersgate Ward. He was dead by January 1689. See Alfred B. Beaven, *Aldermen of the City of London* (London, 1908), I, 7, 113, 115.

39 *Memoirs*, 25.

40 Sloane MSS. 4223, f. 208v.

41 Macaulay, V, 2397. Campbell defends Somers's morals: V, 192–93.

42 Her mother gained some repute as a musician and French scholar: D.N.B., Lady Anne Fanshawe.

43 *Secret Memoirs and Manners of Several Persons of Quality, of Both Sexes, from the New Atalantis* (London, 6th edn., 1720), III, 200. It was first published in 1709. Mrs Manley spoke more favourably of Somers as critic and patron: *ibid.*, II, 309. John Dennis, in his *Sheltering Poet's Invitation to Richard Steele* (first published in 1714) wrote:

[Wine] makes even Somers to disclose his art
By racking every secret from his heart,
As he flings off the statesman's sly disguise,
To name the cuckold's wife with whom he lies.

See *Poems of Jonathan Swift*, ed. Harold Williams (Oxford, 1937), III, 1098. For some other contemporary allusions to 'Madam Blount', see George de F. Lord *et al.* (eds.), *Poems on Affairs of State: Augustan Satirical Verse, 1660–1714* (New Haven, 1963–), VI, 16n. See also *Private Correspondence of Sarah Duchess of Marlborough* (London, 1838), II, 148.

44 Swift's *Works*, ed. Scott, IX, 171.

45 Cooksey, 27–28.

46 *Wentworth Papers, 1705–1739*, ed. James J. Cartwright (London, 1883), 67. Lady Cowper included Lady Harriet Vere among the young women who 'laid out all their Snares' to catch her husband, the Lord Chancellor, and comments on her 'Poverty and ruined Reputation': *Diary of Mary Countess Cowper*, ed. Spencer Cowper (London, 1865), 34. See also *Horace Walpole's Correspondence*, ed. W. S. Lewis, IX, *Correspondence with George Montagu* (New Haven, 1941), 63, on Lady Harriet being 'forced to live upon her beauty'.

[47] Cooksey, 46.

[48] *Advice to a Painter* (1697), in Lord, *Poems on Affairs of State*, VI, 16. See also *The Golden Age Revers'd* (1703), lines 30–31, and *The Seven Wise Men* (1704), lines 82–84. Birch wrote that Somers's 'Indulgences' were said to have been 'ravenous and eager, and without much Care of Choice': Sloane MSS. 4223, f. 208v.

[49] See below, ch. x.

[50] *Burnet*, IV, 187. As late as December 1692, there seems to have been no intention to dissolve the commission, for when Commissioner Trevor was made Master of the Rolls Serjeant Wogan was appointed in his stead: Wood, *Life and Times*, III, 412 and n.

[51] Campbell, V, 94.

[52] Evelyn gives the date as 19 March, Ogg has February 1693: *Diary*, V, 135; *James II and William III*, 392. Luttrell, *Relation*, III, 59, has 22 March. *The London Gazette*, 23 March 1693, announces the appointment as occurring on that date. For Carmarthen's request in the name of the King, see Macaulay, V, 2324.

[53] Luttrell, *Relation*, III, 58, 60 and 90, where he lists the peers as Norfolk, Devonshire, Dorset, Stamford, Rochester, Newport, Lindsey, Clare, Macclesfield, Manchester and Pembroke.

[54] Taking the period from the Restoration to the retirement of Lord Eldon, Kerly, p. 169, finds the average tenure for Lord Keepers and Chancellors to be seven years. Two of Clarendon's nine years were spent as Chancellor in an exiled court.

[55] Stat. 5 Eliz, c. 18; *Statutes of the Realm* (London, 1810–24), IV, pt. i, 447. The Lord Keepership was bestowed by a mere presentation of the Seal, whereas the appointment of a Chancellor involved the issue of letters patent. The Lord Keepership appears to have involved less official expenditure; see *Journeys of Celia Fiennes*, ed. Christopher Morris (London, 1947), 307.

[56] Macaulay, V, 2324.

[57] *Loc. cit.*; Luttrell, *Relation*, III, 61, erroneously gives £4000 as the figure. North secured the same arrangement; see North, *Lives*, I, 414.

[58] *Diary*, V, 408 and n; Swift absolves him of avarice: Swift's *Works*, ed. Scott, X, 23. Evelyn may have had Trevor in mind.

[59] *Cal. Treas. Books*, 1693–96, X, pt. i, 277, 396, 524; pt. ii, 601, 615, 623; 1702, XVII, pt. ii, 697–98; Add. MSS. 5756, ff. 23–25.

[60] *Private Diary of William, First Earl Cowper*, ed. Edward C. Hawtrey (Roxburghe Club, 1833), 29–30. Ambrose Philips wrote of Cowper:

> He the robe of justice wore
> Sully'd not as heretofore,
> When the magistrate was sought
> With yearly gifts ...

Poems of Ambrose Philips, ed. M. G. Segar (Oxford, 1937), 118. The Lord Chancellor also enjoyed the right to print the Lords' addresses to the throne, though this was 'usually given to the Clerks': Cowper *Diary*, 8. According to Lady Cowper, New Year's gifts came to £3000 a year, but Burnet gives £1500: Lady Cowper *Diary*, 63; Burnet, V, 872.

[61] See Add. MSS. 5756, ff. 65, 113–14; *The Art of Thriving* (1635), in *Somers Tracts*, ed. Scott, VII, 200; Chambelayne, *Angliae Notitiae* (London, 1691), pt. ii, 109–10. Holdsworth, I. 474–75, gives a list of sixty different posts, some occupied by more than one person, in 1740.

[62] Luttrell, *Relation*, IV, 500, 507, 510; *Cal. S. P. Dom.*, 1699–1700, 191.

[63] Add. MSS. 27,382, f. 160 ff.: 'Gravamine Litigatorum et Competitorum, or The Complaint of Such as Have Had Anything to Doe in the Prosecution or Defense of Suites.' The writer was Percival Brunskell; he directed his complaint to the Lords Justices and Privy Council, along with a letter to Somers. Brunskell had held several minor offices, including a clerkship in the Rolls Chapel. He had been heard from before; in a petition in 1690 he stated that he had 'expended or contracted debts of 4,000 l. by the discovery of undue practices in the Courts of Justice, which his oath and duty obliged him to': *Lords MSS.*, 1689–90, 33. North called him 'a very impertinent projector, ... who pretended to make great improvements to the crown, by the revenue of the green wax': *Lives*, I, 219.

[64] Burnet, IV, 388; *Corr. Duch. Marl.*, II, 148–49.

[65] Ashton, 356. Nathan Wright, Somers's successor, allegedly amassed his wealth through the corrupt disposal of patronage: *D.N.B.*, Wright.

[66] *Diary*, V, 611.

[67] *State Trials*, XVI, 786–87.

68 He moved there 24 June 1693; see *Cal. Treas. Books, 1696–97*, XI, 390–91. He displaced Trevor, Master of the Rolls, who moved to 'the rolls in Chancery lane'; Luttrell, *Relation*, III, 72.

69 Edward Hatton, *New View of London* (London, 1708), I, 47; II, 632. For a nineteenth-century illustration, see Charles W. Heckethorn, *Lincoln's Inn Fields and the Localities Adjacent* (London, 1896), 78. The house, as reconstructed in modern times, still stands at the north-west corner of Lincoln's Inn Fields (No. 66). It bears the inscription: 'Anno 1686 / E Flammis Rediviva / Anno 1930 / Vetustate Corrucas Refecta.'

70 *Cal. Treas. Books, 1693–96*, X, pt. iii, 1342; *ibid.*, *1696–97*, 92, 390–91.

71 Duke of Norfolk's case (1681): 3 *Ch. Cases*, 47.

72 In Maynard, *v.* Moseley (1676): 3 *Swanston*, 655.

73 *Parliamentary History*, VIII, 417.

74 See below, pp. 192–95.

75 As early as 1686 Somers was counsel in the Chancery suit of Canning v. Hicks: 2 *Ch. Cases*, 187; 2 *Freeman*, 226; 1 *Vernon*, 412.

76 Add. MSS. 17,017, f. 125. Ranelagh, *v.* Champante (1700) was such a case: 2 *Vernon*, 395. *Cal. S. P. Dom.*, 1697, 207.

77 *C.J.*, I, 594. For comment on the onerousness of the office a century later, see Hughes' letter to Lord Cowper upon his resignation in 1718: Parke, 290n.

78 Masters appointed by Somers include Sir Thomas Pitts (1693) and Dr Henry Newton (1699), a friend from his student days.

79 Parke, 251; Holdsworth, VI, 548. Trevor is supposed to have been rough in the court-room: Edward Foss, *Judges of England* (London, 1848–64), VIII, 70; but cf. the favourable view of the Earl of Ailesbury: *Memoirs*, ed. W. E. Buckley (Roxburghe Club, 1890), II, 411. The Master of the Rolls was not competent for all business before Chancery.

80 Fiennes, *Journeys*, 307.

81 Charles Runnington's account of Matthew Hale's life, prefixed to Hale's *History of the Common Law of England* (London, 1779), x. For defects of the court when North was named Lord Keeper, see North, *Lives*, I, 419 ff.; and see also Holdsworth, I, 423 ff.

81 There were various other assignments of this sort: the setting up a commission to handle the work of the Lord Keeper, the regulation of fees for writs passing the Great Seal, the weeding out of defunct or moribund measures from the statute books, the further abridgement of benefit of clergy. See *C.J.*, X, 34, 90, 200, 653, 729, 731, 761–62, 768, 820, 836; Holdsworth, I, 435–36. An 'Inquiry into irregularities of the Courts of Law' was launched in the Lords on 7 November 1689; see *Lords MSS.*, 1689–90, 313 ff.

83 See below, pp. 239–42.

84 George W. Sanders, *Orders of the High Court of Chancery* (London, 1845), 397, 401–6, 408–12, 414. In December 1695, Somers committed one of the Masters in Chancery, Sir Thomas Row, to the Fleet prison for 'undue practices': Luttrell, *Relation*, III, 563.

85 Holdsworth, I, 425.

86 See *ibid.*, I, 674–75; *Lords MSS.*, 1689–90, 327.

87 Oldmixon, 758. Luttrell speaks of a master's place as worth £400 a year in 1699, but £1500, by 1707: IV, 483; VI, 200.

88 See below, p. 181.

89 Kerly, 172.

90 *Lords MSS.*, 1697–99, 69 ff. A remedial measure was passed in the Lords, but died in the Commons. For the Dean of Guernsey's complaint about the costliness of a patent required by Somers, see *Cal. S. P. Dom.*, 1703–4, 221.

91 Holdsworth, VI, 536, and see Campbell, V, 99–101. Holdsworth mentions only eight other cases in which Somers was involved, six in Chancery and two in the Lords. The Earl of Birkenhead, in his *Fourteen English Judges* (London, 1926), 133–41, comments on seventeen such cases. Somers is best reported in Vernon and Peere Williams, but his decrees may also be found in *Precedents in Chancery*, *Precedents temp. Finch*, Freeman and Shower. For law reports in Somers's time, see Parke, 267; Clyde L. Grose, *Select Bibliography of British History, 1660–1760* (Chicago, 1939), 40.

92 There was no Lord Treasurer at this time.

93 Luttrell, *Relation*, III, 481, 549–50.

94 George Price, *Treatise on the Law of the Exchequer* (London, 1830), xi.

95 *State Trials*, XIV, 39–105.

96 *Ibid.*, XIV, 111; *L.J.*, XVI, 499–501; Stat. 12 and 13 W. III, c. 12, s. 15. Tallard wrote to Louis XIV that King William 'fait touts ses efforts pour que le jugement du chancelier

soit confirmé, et pour éviter l'embaras d'estre obligé de demander à la chambre des communes le remplacement du fond': P.R.O. 31/3, No. 185, 1 February 1700.

[97] *State Trials*, XIV, 44–45.

[98] Birkenhead, 141; Holdsworth, VI, 536; IX, 32–39.

[99] 10 Q.B., 31.

[100] Frederick T. White and Owen D. Tudor, *Selection of Leading Cases in Equity* (6th edn., London, 1886). This work, however, includes only eight cases before 1700, none from William's reign. Even the great Nottingham figures as Lord Keeper in but two of them.

[101] Campbell, V, 97–98; Holdsworth, VII, 476–77.

[102] Kerly, 210–11, citing *Prec. Ch.* (1699), 101.

[103] But an exception to this rule might occur when the enlarged estate 'had come to the testator "cum onere" even though he had consented to pay the debt'; to this extent Somers may be said to have shaped the law in his decree in Magnell v. Howard in 1696; see *Prec. Ch.*, 61, and cf. Lord King's rule in Evelyn v. Evelyn (1728), 2 *Peere Williams*, 659.

[104] Birkenhead, 136; 2 *Vernon*, 368. Laches: remissness in asserting or enforcing a right.

[105] See below, p. 162; Holdsworth, VI, 648; 2 *Vernon*, 342; *L.J.*, XVI, 230, 236–38, 240–41. Some cases, while not noteworthy as to judicial consequences, are procedurally of some interest. Stratton v. Grimes (1698), involving a conditional legacy, was heard by the Chancellor and the Master of the Rolls; it appears that the tradition of these functionaries sitting separately (the latter only as a deputy and at a time when his superior was not holding court) had broken down. See 2 *Vernon*, 357; Campbell, V, 98; Birkenhead, 135. For other instances see Heveningham v. Heveningham (1697) and Leukener v. Freeman (1699): 2 *Vernon*, 355; 2 *Freeman*, 236. Cases were sometimes appealed from the Master of the Rolls to the Lord Keeper or Chancellor; see Shouldham v. Shouldham *et al.* (1694) and Stephenson v. Wilson (1695): 2 *Vernon*, 321, 325. It was not unusual for Somers to call upon common law judges to sit with him: Chief Justice Holt and Treby assisted him on occasion, as in Lord Radnor v. Lord Delaware (1693) and in Cary v. Bertie (1696); in the Duchess of Albemarle and Monk v. the Earl of Bath (1693) Baron Powell was also on the bench: Luttrell, *Relation*, III, 125; 2 *Vernon*, 333; 2 *Freeman*, 193. Other examples are Floyd v. Cary, with Treby and Justice Rokeby assisting, and Kirk v. Webb, with the Master of the Rolls and Powell: 2 *Freeman*, 218, 229.

[106] Holdsworth, VII, 227; John C. Gray, *The Rule against Perpetuities* (Boston, 1906), 145; *L.J.*, XVI, 192–93.

[107] Lords MSS., 1692–93, 268; Macqueen, 39–40; *L.J.*, XV, 364.

[108] When in 1695 Chief Justice Holt begged to be excused from this assignment, on the grounds that he would be absent on circuit, Chief Justice Treby was commissioned to take Somers's place: *Cal. S. P. Dom.*, 1695, 495, 497; cf. *ibid.*, 1697, 149, and see Macqueen, 20.

[109] Campbell, V, 102.

[110] Holdsworth, I, 367–68; Shower, *Prec. Ch.*, 111; Lords MSS., 1693–95, 31–45. A bill of exceptions is a statement of objections to the ruling or directions of a judge, drawn up for the dissatisfied party and submitted to a higher jurisdiction.

[111] See Turberville, *Lords under William III*, 97; Lords MSS., 1697–99, 16–24. The Bishop, concerned over the prevalence of Nonconformity in Derry, had embarked upon the suit with the object of preventing the leasing of certain lands to Presbyterians; see *D.N.B.*, *sub* William King; James R. O'Flanaghan, *Lives of the Lord Chancellors and Keepers of the Great Seal of Ireland* (London, 1870), I, 492–93.

[112] Holdsworth, I, 375; Blenheim Palace MSS., Sunderland Letter Book, 3, letters beginning 18 February 1698.

[113] James E. T. Rogers, *Protests of the Lords* (Oxford, 1875), I, 131–32; *L.J.*, XVI, 194 ff.

[114] For the first two bills, see Lords MSS., 1692–93, 17–27, 278–79.

[115] *L.J.*, XVI, 516–78 passim.

[116] Luttrell, *Relation*, IV, 488; Ogg, *James II and William III*, 78.

[117] Lords MSS., 1695–97, 214.

[118] Somers's ruling that the dower was barred was set aside on a rehearing by Lord Keeper Wright and afterwards, upon appeal, by the Lords: Campbell, V, 98; Brown, *Reports*, III, 484–87; *English Reports*, I, 1448–50. Somers was reversed in Duvall v. Price (1694), Hall v. Potter (1695), Lloyd v. Carew (1697), Peyton v. Brown (1698) and Lester v. Foxcroft (1700); he was partially reversed in Bertie v. Falkland (1697). He was sustained in Tilsley and Pottenger v. Wright (1698), Berkeley v. Cope (1698), Oldbury v. Wynne (1699) and Kirk v. Webb (1698). See Richard Colles, *Reports of Cases, upon Appeals and*

Writs of Error, in the High Court of Parliament (London, 1789), 33–42, 91–96; Lords MSS., 1699–1702, 60.

[119] See *State Trials*, XIII, 939–1060.

[120] Luttrell, *Relation*, III, 28. Considerable expenditure was involved; see Lady Cowper's *Diary*, 72, for a description in 1716.

[121] *Faction Display'd* (London, 1704), line 237.

[122] *The Seven Wise Men*, in *Poems on Affairs of State* (London, 1703–7), IV, 29–30.

[123] *Portland MSS.*, VIII, 63.

[124] See dedication, *Further Considerations concerning Raising the Value of Money* (London, 1695); Burnet, IV, 187–88, 434. Dr Samuel Garth, a close friend of Somers, wrote:

Somers does sick'ning Equity restore,
And helpless Orphans are oppress'd no more.

See *The Dispensary* (5th edn., London, 1703), canto II, p. 16.

[125] *The Freeholder*, No. 39.

[126] Tindal, XVIII, 445; Ralph, *History*, II, 784. Cf. Walpole, *Works*, I, 430; Tobias Smollett, *Complete History of England* (London, 1758–60), IX, 153.

[127] Macaulay, V, 2394.

[128] Campbell, V, 94, 96–98, 202.

[129] Parke, 258–59.

[130] Holdsworth, VI, 530, 537.

VI

Minister of state: the first phase, 1693–95

Custody of the Great Seal raised Somers to the first rank among ministers of state. The prestige of the Lord Keeper was reflected in the protocol of the age: in matters of precedence he was second only to the Archbishop of Canterbury. Although the Chancery had for some time been yielding to the Treasury in the exercise of political influence, its chief had behind him long traditions of leadership in royal councils, a primacy not entirely surrendered until the emergence of the Prime Ministership in the Georgian era. Even so, half a century after Somers's death Blackstone could describe the Lord Keeper or Chancellor as 'an officer of the greatest weight and power of any now subsisting in the Kingdom; and superior in point of precedency to any temporal lord'—noteworthy testimony of how slowly and imperceptibly the office of Prime Minister gained recognition.[1]

As Lord Keeper Somers's duties may be divided into three categories. Besides his judicial functions he was concerned with various administrative responsibilities of a routine nature. He was, in effect, a minister of justice. He oversaw, for the Crown, the appointment of judges and justices of the peace. He served as guardian of infants, idiots and lunatics. In his hands was the general superintendance of all charitable uses, or trusts. In addition, he was King's visitor of all hospitals and colleges on royal foundations, and patron of all ecclesiastical livings in the King's gift under the value of £20 a year. Such duties, along with that of the speakership of the upper chamber, were *ex officio*.

But there was a third category, arising from the fact that Somers—like Clarendon, unlike Hale and North—was a political Chancellor. Prominently identified with the Whig party, knowledgeable in parliamentary as well as legal business, esteemed by the King, he was associated with administrative problems as they arose and with the formulation of such policies as the ruling clique sought to implement. His possession of the Great Seal naturally made him the chief authenticating agent of the regime, even as his office gave him a springboard for high-level participation in administration. Yet without commanding personal qualifications, he could never have weighed so heavily in affairs of state. It was not enough to be Chancellor; a comparison of Somers and his successor Wright is clear enough proof of this.

Upon receiving the Seal Somers was sworn a member of the Privy Council, as was customary. He retained his membership until dismissed upon the accession of Queen Anne. The Privy Council included those holding household offices as well as the responsible heads of the great departments of state. With something like sixty members it was too unwieldy for an effective discussion of policy, but it retained some of its old importance, and there were few matters of public interest which did not at one time or another come before it.[2] It was particularly concerned with a detailed regulation of local administration and with the implementation of policies recommended by departments of state; but it has been well called 'the central clearing house of the administration'.[3] Its responsibilities extended beyond the confines of the realm, embracing the affairs of Ireland, the Channel Islands, and the colonial outposts.

The Council ordinarily met once a week, though additional sessions were sometimes called for, as in 1694, when the King ordered special Sunday meetings 'about the affairs of the Admiralty'.[4] Somers was a faithful attendant. From 1693 through 1695 he was rarely absent; thereafter we encounter a few breaks in his attendance, on occasion covering several weeks, caused by illness or the pressures of other business. In the spring of 1696, for example, he was occupied with the Fenwick plot crisis. He was not easily dispensed with, for the minutes reveal many matters in which the Lord Keeper's advice and co-operation were called for, matters often reflecting the extensive judicial powers which the Council had once exercised. Judges were summoned to hear what they were to 'give in charge' at the next assizes; riots in Worcestershire were to be countered by a commission of oyer and terminer at the Lord Keeper's hands; authors of seditious libels were to be brought to justice, or a rescuer of pressed men arrested. Week after week Somers left the Council table with special assignments: he was to take action 'touching the great abuses and evil practices used in the Collecting of Briefes'; to serve on a committee inquiring into the escape of the Jacobite Colonel Dorrington from the Tower; to meet with the Lords of the Treasury and the judges regarding wartime duties on parchment and paper.[5] Such was the grist of the Council's mill; mostly smallish business, in our eyes, punctuated by occasional issues of larger significance. The very size of the Council had long made the use of committees imperative; we find Somers, joined with Secretary Trenchard, Chief Justice Holt and others, investigating the destruction of the Smyrna fleet in 1693 and participating with other commissioners for hearing appeals in prize causes incidental to the conduct of the war.[6]

But his administrative duties were set in a narrower and more directly effective framework than that of the Council. Throughout William's reign —at least from 1690 on—a cabinet was in existence, consisting of the leading Councillors, meeting ever more regularly, serving to advise the sovereign on virtually all governmental business, to co-ordinate the work of the departments, and, in so far as the King permitted, to take the lead in administration.[7] William's absences from England, first in the Irish campaigns, later on the continent, gave special point to the employment of an effective agency of this kind, although the King apparently would have liked to have got along without it, and tended to oppose meetings which he could not himself attend.[8] But, as Shrewsbury pointed out, it was necessary that 'some people do meet to take the lead'.[9] Thus, whether William liked it or not, whether or not the King was on hand, a cabinet functioned, whether called a cabinet council or a committee (of Privy Councillors). Informal and elusive as it was, it was given status and somewhat clearer definition by the fact that, following Mary's death, most of the major cabinet officials were commissioned Lords Justices, or joint regents, during the King's absences abroad.

Somers, as a great officer of state, served both as a cabinet councillor and a Lord Justice. William would have liked to have confined attendance at Cabinet meetings to the 'great officers of the crown'—the Lord Keeper, Lord President, Lord Privy Seal, and the two Secretaries of State,—but, as has so often happened in the history of the cabinet, the need to secure support and to cultivate particular interests resulted in a body of some size, in this case numbering from nine to fourteen members. Thus Somers was associated not only with the four other office-holders singled out by the King, but, more often than not, with the first Lords of the Treasury and Admiralty, not to mention such household officials as the Lord Chamberlain, royal favourites like Portland and Sidney, and a miscellaneous assortment of highly placed or politically aggressive individuals: Prince George, the Primate of England, Sir Edward Seymour and others.[10]

Unlike the Privy Council, the cabinet did not keep records of its proceedings. A formal secretariat was not established until the present century. But succeeding Secretaries of State—Nottingham, Trenchard, Shrewsbury, Trumbull and Vernon—kept notes which have survived and give us a picture of cabinet activity throughout the century's last decade, save for the year 1692. Somers spent many hours with the cabinet. In 1693, there were seventy-eight meetings, either on Tuesday or Friday; later it became the practice to meet on Sunday. The following year some forty meetings were held between March and September. From October 1695 to May 1696 there were upwards of seventy. Sometimes the Lord Keeper would attend both the Privy Council and the cabinet on the same day.[11] Cabinet meetings were usually held at Kensington Palace (when the King was in residence) or at Whitehall, but sometimes elsewhere. In 1697, when Somers was incapacitated, the cabinet met at least once at his own residence.[12] Business of virtually every kind was transacted, much of it necessitated by the exigencies of war. While it is true that the cabinet was never fully taken into the King's confidence, nor permitted any large measure of independence, it was there that Somers stood closest to the King, and could operate most effectively (before the advent of the Junto) with the principal functionaries of government whether or not William was in England.

But William, in a reign of thirteen years, was out of England over a third of the time. Until Mary's death in 1694 the responsibilities of regency were placed in her hands.[13] Thereafter they were lodged in a committee of prominent individualists called Lords Justices, who had quarters at Whitehall and were provided with guards and attendants as if Majesty were present.[14] For the most part they were selected from the holders of high office. Were it not for the exclusion of one or both of the Secretaries of State from their ranks, it might be said that the Lords Justices 'comprised the cabinet meeting in a formal guise'.[15] The Lord Keeper was clearly marked for membership: Somers served on each of the five commissions from 1695 to 1699, and, as the prime secular official present, acted as the body's President. He may, therefore, be regarded, in a sense, as paramount regent, though the authority was collective, a quorum of four being necessary for the conduct of business. In this respect he over-stepped the bounds on at least one important occasion: when impeached in 1701, one of the charges was that, in affixing the Great Seal to the Partition Treaty of 1698, he had not 'first communicated the same to the rest of the Lord Justices of England'.[16]

Luttrell, among others, believed that the Lords Justices' commission was 'so large as to impower them to call, prorogue, and dissolve the parliament', and 'to break with foreign princes'.[17] But this is an exaggeration. William kept a tight grip on the reins, and all matters of policy were referred to him.[18] They had nothing directly to do with foreign policy. On the other hand, they heard petitions of all sorts; they issued reprieves; they dispatched orders affecting land and sea forces, largely in the realm of supply; they called before them commissioners of the Treasury and Admiralty for questioning; they issued proclamations on a host of subjects. In these Somers and his colleagues coped with problems ranging from deer-stealing in Kent to the peace with France, from the registration of seamen to the debasement of the coinage. Much time was devoted to the approval and recasting of Irish legislation.[19]

However much we may attribute Somers's influence to the rising fortunes of the Whigs, or to connections with such magnates as Shrewsbury or Sunderland, his relationship with the King was all-important. Without winning royal confidence he could not have attained high office, or, having attained it, could hardly have wielded the authority that was his for over half a decade. Of William's autocratic tendencies something has already been said. These did not subside upon his removal from The Hague to Westminster. They were, if anything, sharpened by the military exigencies surrounding and following his acquisition of the British thrones, and perhaps by his awareness of his role as an alien conqueror. But, determined to work out the great design of his life, he could not devote full time to the internal affairs of his new realms; even when Ryswick had set the seal on the labours of a decade, and he had become less Dutch in his outlook, the ties of close to forty years and the patrimony of a son of Orange would bring him back to Holland for several months each year. It was, then, of more than usual importance that his principal English aides should be capable and trustworthy. While she lived, Mary could take up the slack, but, for all her good qualities of affection, dutifulness and common sense, she was no Elizabeth to direct single-handedly the complicated business of government.

Unlike the first two Georges—who, also, found themselves among the alien corn and frequently alienated themselves from their English subjects

—William would never discover a single minister to whom he could entrust the administration. General inter-departmental supervision was a generation away; even then, under Walpole's masterful touch, it would arouse suspicion and resentment. Nor could one party count on the dominance enjoyed by the Whigs in the early Georgian era: fluctuation in party fortunes was the order of the day. But so, too, given the factors of party fragmentation and court influence, were ministerial coalitions. William, essentially non-partisan and suspicious of extremists of the right and the left, linked himself closely with perhaps half a dozen men who in varying degrees managed to gain his confidence. Probably none enjoyed this relationship more completely than Portland—the Bentinck of earlier days. But Portland, like other Dutchmen, could hardly serve as a major political adjutant, however intimate he might be with the King. Such talent must be recruited from the English. William sought it, and in varying degrees found it, first in Halifax, Carmarthen (the former Danby) and Nottingham, later in Shrewsbury, Sunderland and Somers.

Halifax, at the outset of the reign, enjoyed a large measure of the King's confidence. But by 1690, harassed by critics both inside and outside Parliament, he had resigned the Privy Seal. During the next two years he found himself increasingly opposed to the policies of the court, and in 1692 was dismissed from the Privy Council. Nottingham held his secretaryship until the following year; he was then in such disrepute that William was forced to part with him. Carmarthen clung longer to office, but his influence never recovered from evidence brought forth in 1695 of corrupt dealings with the East India Company. Shrewsbury had been given the other secretaryship in 1689; he resigned a year later, then returned to play a consequential part in the middle years of the reign. William held in him high regard, but the retiring, often ailing 'King of Hearts' was not a man to bear the heat of battle, effective as his personal charm might be. Sunderland was coarser-grained; his nerves were stronger, his managerial talents superb. Excoriated by King James, whom he had deserted, yet distrusted by many for ever having served him, his duty to William was inextricably bound up with self-interest. It is possible that, apart from Portland, he was the King's most intimate confidant.[20] But he was best behind the scenes. Had William been a weaker man, and the English government more narrowly based, he might have been a power behind the throne, in the usual somewhat sinister sense. As it was he was a maker of ministers rather than a minister.

Somers lacked some of the advantages that came naturally to these men, heirs as they were of political and social traditions that made men of aristocratic lineage the natural confidants of kings—particularly of a monarch like William III, who regarded even his own consort as ill-born because of her Hyde blood. They enjoyed an entrée which, for all his official eminence, he could not count on. His approaches to William, at least in the earlier stages of his career, were often through Shrewsbury or Portland.[21] Yet the arts of the courtier, in the best sense of the expression, seem to have come naturally to him. His polite and punctilious deportment was acknowledged even by Jonathan Swift:

I have hardly known any man with talents more proper to acquire and preserve the favour of a prince; never offending in word or gesture; in the highest degree courteous and complaisant; wherein he set an excellent example to his colleagues, which they did not think fit to follow.[22]

Swift attributed his 'extreme civility' to an awareness of a 'humble original' and to an iron self-control maintained to check a passionate nature.[23] However this may be, the King was impressed. Other Whigs, he observed, behaved rudely (Wharton was surely in his mind); Somers 'treated him as an ambassador'.[24] The remark is a far cry from any suggestion of an intimate relationship. Given William's nature and his preference for Dutchmen, few Englishmen would attain it. Somers was not among them.

The arts of the courtier were merely incidental. Somers's fortunes depended essentially upon his serviceability to his King and to his party. As a royal aide he could outstrip most, if not all, of his colleagues. Unlike Shrewsbury he was not hampered by the *noblesse oblige* attitude which made that peer an amateur as far as government service was concerned; unlike Sunderland he commanded the respect of his party, as an unwavering, though moderate, exponent of the Revolutionary cause; unlike Portland he was 'mere English', with an intimate knowledge of several branches of government and of constitutional law; unlike Marlborough (and almost everyone else) he was free from the taint of St Germain, at least while William reigned; unlike such stalwart Whigs as Wharton, Russell and Montague, he was personally acceptable to William.[25] Contemporaries were impressed. Addison observed that the King 'consulted no Man so much as him, on all the arduous affairs of the State'. According to Burnet, 'his great capacity for all affairs' made William 'consider him beyond all his ministers'. Abel Boyer wrote that William esteemed him as the greatest man in the realm.[26] Such encomiums obviously call for some discount. Swift was content to say that the King had 'a great value for this Lord and took much of his advice'. Count Tallard gives him full honours, but associates his pre-eminence with the years following Sunderland's resignation in 1697; then, he reported to Louis XIV, no other Englishman had any 'real share in public affairs'.[27]

Unfortunately, the taciturn and preoccupied monarch left no appraisal of his minister. But it is clear that he recognised his ability. He turned to Somers for the composition of the declaration of war against France in 1689, a step of paramount importance in his eyes. Speeches from the throne received final form at his hand, particularly in William's later years.[28] Even after he had surrendered the Seal he performed such service: in 1701, with a new war looming, he framed the royal address in which the King warned Parliament of the dangers likely to result from the establishment of French ascendancy in Spain and her possessions.[29] How much influence he had in the content of these pronouncements is impossible to say, but it is difficult to believe that he would be satisfied with the role of translator or editor. As early as 1693 Bellers, the Quaker, thought it worth while to urge him to persuade the King to put in a word for the poor in his speech to Parliament.[30]

Serviceable as he was to William, Somers's usefulness to his party was, in the long run, more impressive. For, while he was able to accommodate himself to a variety of ministries under William, and at times worked to advance coalition government in the Tory-dominated reign that followed, he was committed, with but rare lapses, to Whig principles and the advancement of that party. That he was associated with a particular element within it, the Junto Whigs, and was primarily concerned with their interests and programmes, is to say no more than that he linked himself with an influential political machine. He recognised the importance of overall party strength, and to some degree embodied it. His judicious and conciliatory disposition was an asset not only within the Junto, but in wooing and winning Whig support beyond its ranks. As the years passed no Whig leader could justifiably pose as a more constant exponent of basic party creeds. His identification with Exclusion under Charles, his freedom from any taint of association with James, his vital role in the Revolution settlement, his 'martyrdom' under Tory impeachment: all solidified his position and enhanced his reputation.

At the outset of his tenure, Somers had to take issue with William over a perquisite of office. As minister of justice, one of the most important of his functions was the appointment and supervision of judges. In this respect, as in others of national significance, the throne was the fountain of honour. But while the formal appointment lay with the sovereign, the right of nomination had long been recognised as one of the perquisites of the Chancellor.[31] During the latter years of Charles II and in James II's reign political considerations, never entirely absent in the appointment of judges, asserted themselves to a perhaps unprecedented extent. While the English system of government had not embraced the doctrine of judicial review, the Crown had its interest in suits at law, and in cases like Hampden's (1637) and Godden v. Hales (1686) it was in a sense attained. And while Charles I had in 1641 agreed that judges were to be appointed during good behaviour, and his son had generally respected this condition during the early years of his reign, beginning in 1668 all judges were appointed during the royal pleasure, and this arrangement prevailed under James II.

Of the ten judges appointed by James II who were living at the time of the Revolution, none had been retained in office. William's first declaration described the judges as perverted by evil counsellors. Charges of high treason against Chief Justice Wright were published at Exeter at his command; seven were exempted from the Bill of Indemnity. It was obviously imperative to reconstitute the bench as speedily as possible. This was done without benefit of Lord Keeper or Chancellor, the Privy Councillors being instructed to bring in lists of worthy candidates. By early May the full complement of a dozen had been appointed. According to

Burnet, the new judges were 'well received over the nation'.[32] The three chiefs, Holt, Pollexfen and Atkyns, were all men of substantial reputation. Somers himself remarked upon their 'known ability' in the law.[33]

The role of the King in this business is not apparent. Apart from military and diplomatic assignments, William was not particularly active in making appointments. In the years immediately following he had little occasion to concern himself with the bench. But in 1693, on the day after Somers's promotion, he ordered him to make out patents appointing Sir William Rawlinson as Chief Baron and Sir William Wogan as Chief Justice of Chester. Edward Ward, who had refused a puisne judgeship in 1689, was to succeed Somers as Attorney-General. The result was a ministerial quarrel. Somers and his fellow Whigs believed that they had royal assurance that Sir Thomas Trevor, Solicitor-General and regarded as Somers's protégé, should have the attorney-generalship, while Ward was to succeed Trevor. This would have been the customary course, but William, influenced by Nottingham and other Tories, had switched to Ward.[34]

Somers was outraged, and lost no time in protesting. On 27 March he sent a message to the King, who, bound for Flanders, was awaiting a fair wind at Harwich. After expressing regret over being forced to disagree with his sovereign so soon after taking office, he proceeded to the heart of the matter:

The lawyers are 'spread over every part of the kingdom' and have great influence among the people. The method used to unite them in their service to the Crown, has been by obliging them to a dependence on the Great Seal for their promotion where they merited it, and this has always given weight to that office in public affairs; and, if I understand you aright, making the Great Seal thus considerable was one of the effects you expected from placing it in a single hand; but I submit it to you how far it is likely to succeed, or any other of your Majesty's ends to be answered, when such eminent offices are disposed of in such a manner at my entrance upon this charge.

After touching on Rawlinson's inexperience in the 'course of the exchequer', and the publicity already given to the appointment of Trevor and Ward, he turned to the matter of his own authority:

This being the case, let me offer it to your consideration whether if the passing of these patents must be the first use I am to make of the seal, it can be supposed I have that credit which ought to go with it, and without which it is impossible it should reach what you aimed at in this change.

Aware of the difficulties of his new post, he had counted upon royal support. Without such co-operation he could not carry on, and he therefore tendered his resignation.[35]

The King refused to accept it. He also refused to back down on Ward's appointment, and Somers did not lay his office on the line again. But Rawlinson did not become Chief Baron, Atkyns having agreed to stay on a while. In 1695 he made way for Ward, and Trevor was able to step up to the attorney-generalship. And so the crisis blew over, partly through compromise, more through the healing passage of time. It appears to have been an isolated case, exacerbated by partisanship; there is no evidence that Somers found further cause to remonstrate in this area. When, in 1695, King and Lord Keeper had different ideas regarding a new Solicitor-General, William's will prevailed without incident.[36] If his proffered resignation was a bluff, it was an audacious one. In the spring of 1693 the Whigs had by no means entrenched themselves as men best able to do the King's business. Apart from this, his manoeuvre may be regarded as an attempt to give new substance to an office which had come to be criticised for subservience. North had been a capable lawyer, but no leader; Jeffreys had associated the Seal with Stuart authoritarianism.

In the course of seven years Somers was able to exert considerable influence in shaping the personnel of the great central courts of common law, each with its chief assisted by three other judges. Altogether, thirty-four appointments and promotions were made in William's reign, involving twenty-eight persons, fourteen of which, involving twelve persons, occurring while Somers held the Seals. Eyre, Rokeby, Turton, Gould, Littleton Powys, the younger John Powell, Blencowe, Ward and Hatsell all took their seats under his auspices. So did Wallop and Simpson, Cursitor Barons of the Exchequer. Something of the mechanics of such manoeuvres, revealing the co-operation of King and minister, is shown in Shrewsbury's letter to William on 5 June 1696:

Judge Turton, whom the Lord Keeper recommends as likely to be promoted to the King's Bench, in the place of Gregory, lately dead, has been a Baron of the Exchequer ever since you came to the throne, and a man very zealous in your interest. Sergeant Blenco whom the Lord Keeper proposes to succeed as a baron in Turton's place, is one who in former parliaments has seemed very well. Though not now in the House, he is an honest and an able lawyer, and son-in-law to Doctor Wallis of Oxford, who deciphers the letters, and will think any-thing done for him at least as great an obligation, as if it were done to himself.[37]

Turton's appointment followed on 27 June, Blencowe's on 17 September.

Despite the Tory ascendancy which developed late in William's reign and marked the early years of his successor, only two judges, Hatsell and Turton, were removed from office, both under Anne. Hatrell, the son of a zealous Roundhead, was but a weak judge. But Turton's ouster was attri-buted by his grandson to 'his honest and firm adherence to the Revolution interest'—that is, his Whiggish predilections.[38] Edward Ward continued as Chief Baron until his death a fortnight before Anne's. Powell remained in office until 1713, Littleton Powys throughout her reign. Ward's long tenure is the more remarkable in that his first important assignment had been as counsel for Lord Russell, and that he retained his Whig connections.

With one exception Somers cannot stand accused of favouring relatives for high places. His brother-in-law, Joseph Jekyll, obtained the chief justice-ship of Chester, a semi-sinecure, in 1697; he was, an unfriendly observer commented, 'a Whig virulent enough in all conscience', who owed his fortune to Somers.[39] Nor was he partial to alumni of his Inn, only two, Hatsell and Wallop, being Middle Temple-bred. On the whole his appointees were solid, conscientious men. With the possible exception of Hatsell none seems to have been unsuited for the bench, though one may wonder at the wisdom of raising up the eighty-year-old Wallop, for all his reputation as a doughty Whig. John Powell was perhaps the only distinguished appointee. His reputation as a learned, humane and enlightened judge— like Holt he was sceptical of witchcraft—makes him an attractive figure. Rokeby, the son of a Cromwellian officer and a man of extraordinary piety, was also highly competent.[40]

Somers's appointment, formalised on 23 March, marked the beginning of a process by which the government would be placed in Whig hands. The same day saw another Whig, Sir John Trenchard, once a member of the Green Ribbon Club, installed as Secretary for the North. 'The bringing of these men into those posts', wrote Burnet, 'was ascribed chiefly to the great credit the earl of Sunderland had gained with the King; he had now got into his confidence, and declared openly for the Whigs.' The manoeuvres were looked upon as a means to placate the Whigs following the royal veto of the Triennial Bill.[41] For some months no further reshuffling occurred. Lord Monmouth described Somers as 'marooned in the midst of a hostile Cabinet' and wanting 'the comfort of his friends'.[42] With Carmarthen, Nottingham and Pembroke occupying influential positions there was some basis for the remark. The Tory ministers were furious over the new appointments; as Sunderland put it, 'A Keeper and a Secretary were made and well chosen; but the clutter at their coming in, by the pressing of the ministers, very much spoiled the good that was designed.'[43] But Somers's isolation did not last long. The King, disgusted with Tory tactics (as he had been with those of the Whigs three years earlier) was increasingly in a mood for a change. Nottingham, despite William's attachment, was the first to go. Dismissed in November, his secretaryship was given to Shrewsbury. By the spring of 1694 the administration had become predominantly Whig.

Somers and Trenchard, as Robert Wolseley pointed out, were expected to use their contacts with the Whigs, especially the uncommitted elements, to 'guide their good affections so as to render them acceptable to the King'.[44] After eight months in office Trenchard could report enthusiastically on the results: 'The Country gentlemen of the Whig party have adhered to the King's interest beyond what could be imagined.'[45] The surest road to royal favour lay by way of ample provision for the war chest. In 1692 the hostilities which had gone on for three years provided little comfort for the English, save for the naval victory of La Hogue—a blow from which the French were not to recover during the war. The following year was to be much the same, the defeat of William's forces at Landen being the bloodiest battle of the war; indeed the English had little reason to expect a favourable outcome until the taking of Namur in 1695. One can imagine the grumbling that went on, as the government turned from one device to another to finance so unrewarding a military programme.

Somers was early involved in rallying the Parliament men and beguiling the City. In April 1693, along with such stalwarts as Sir Robert Howard, Auditor of the Exchequer, Trenchard and Henry Guy, a Treasury official, and of course Sunderland, who was managing the enterprise, he was working to secure the support of the Commons for new excises to be requested the following winter. Early in May Sunderland wrote to Portland: 'I have been severall times with my Lord Keeper and Mr. Secretary. Wee have look't over and consider'd the List of P[arliament] men, and agreed upon the best meanes of Perswading them to be reasonable.'[46] The record touches on the means of persuasion in only a few cases: Lord Brandon would be satisfied with military promotion; Lord Stamford and others in the upper house would respond only to money; Jack Grenville, younger son of the Earl of Bath, who sat for the family borough of Plymouth, apparently could not be bought, and attempts to exert pressure upon the Earl, to get him to 'discipline' his son, were also unsuccessful.[47] In this connection Somers was instructed by Sunderland to stop the reissue (from Chancery) of the Earl's commissions as Lord Lieutenant of Devon and Cornwall. Here he found himself caught in a cross-fire, for Sunderland's influence was countered by that of Nottingham, who was reluctant to withhold Bath's commissions merely on Sunderland's word. In the end Sunderland had to give way.[48]

Such parliamentary influence as Somers was able to exercise had to be indirect. Since he was not a peer, he could do little in the upper chamber except put the question. The old practice of having the Keeper address the Lords at the beginning and end of sessions had ceased. It was his duty, however, to command them to attend, and to receive their excuses for not so doing.[49] Sometimes this called for special attention, as on the occasion of Fenwick's attainder, when no proxies were permitted. And there were other times when the Lord Keeper, through close attention paid to attendance, might exercise some partisan influence in the chamber.[50]

Somers's electoral interest was never large. Upon his elevation to the lord keepership it was so slight that he almost failed to get his brother-in-law, Charles Cocks, returned to the seat he vacated. Cocks's opponent was Samuel Swift, a doughty politician who had been Mayor of Worcester and in 1693 was Sheriff of the county. Among Somers's papers are several letters from Cocks proposing that the Lord Keeper apply pressure on the incumbent Mayor, purchase cloth from the local Clothiers Company, and issue an appeal for the Quaker vote, all for the sake of victory at the polls. The influence of the Company was considerable. Cocks believed that its members, 'except some few', would vote for him, as Somers's nominee. But it was a disadvantage that the great man could not be in Worcester: 'wee drinke and fight and are all in confusion'—a confusion to which Somers may have contributed, since it appears that as late as mid-October he had made no formal nomination. The election was expensive as well as turbulent, costing Cocks £700. Despite this outlay, he was defeated, where-upon he contested the election, accusing the opposition of rioting, bribery, abduction and the illegal swearing of free-men: 'There is an end of all free elections here, if this be passed on.' He hoped his defeat would not alienate his patron, who was assured that 'neither pains nor expenses' had been spared.[51] But a happy ending lay ahead. The evidence for electoral misbe-haviour was skilfully presented, and in February 1694 Cocks was awarded the seat.[52]

In the City of London he was more directly effective—not in shaping elections, but in loosening the purse strings of the burghers. Highly enough regarded in the City to have been offered the Recordership, he appears to have reciprocated this esteem; on one occasion he referred to the commercial element of the nation, in true Whig fashion, as the 'founda-tion of our national dignity' and 'the members that compose the public liberty'.[53] Within a month after receiving the Seal, accompanied by a Secretary of State (probably Trenchard) and the Lords of the Treasury, he went before the Lord Mayor and Aldermen to acquaint them that 'the Queen had great occasion to borrow 200,000 l', which according to Lutt-rell 'they promised to use their endeavours to perform'.[54] In August 1693, he returned to the Guildhall, this time securing a loan of £300,000 to tide the government over its current exigencies. He attributed his success to the King's expert generalship at the Battle of Landen, by which the enemy was largely deprived of the fruits of victory: this, he confided to Portland, 'contributed more than all things else to the Turn in the City, and therefore we are not to put a value upon any little endeavors here'. But the following March Somers was again successful, obtaining £200,000 'on the credit of the land tax'.[55] Ranke's comment that no Lord Keeper ever enjoyed greater credit in the City cannot be far from the mark.[56]

Despite his success as a money-raiser, his connection with the establish-ment of the Bank of England appears to have been entirely formal, its charter being sealed before him in July 1694. Though not among the more than 1200 subscribers who contributed the initial capital of £1,200,000, between 1708 and 1710 he would acquire bank stock valued at £3795.[57] In Anne's reign he was described as 'a friend of the Bank', though opposed to the method of raising money by annuities on lives, in that it would 'mortgage the Nation forever'.[58]

In three other important projects that came to a head before the dissolu-tion of the Officers' Parliament the trail left by Somers is likewise indistinct. According to Campbell he 'manfully concurred' with those who supported the royal veto of the Place Bill, in January 1694.[59] It is logical to assume that a leading minister would have opposed a Country measure by which holders of office under the Crown, increasingly members of his own party, were to be excluded from the House of Commons. But no specific reference from the contemporary record has come to light.

Late in 1694 William finally assented to the Triennial Act, which assured a general election at least once in three years. The proposal was supported by many Whigs as an acceptable alternative to the Place Bill, though it has been described as 'the most effectual of the indirect attacks upon placemen'.[60] William, as already noted, had vetoed a similar measure in 1693, and he remained strongly opposed: he is said to have remarked that the Triennial Act of Charles I's reign was 'the signal for civil war'. Campbell alleges that Somers played a part in dispelling royal fears that the enactment would damage the royal prerogative, pointing out that it lacked provisions cited by Clarendon in his arguments for repealing the original act, and that to employ the veto a second time might make many hitherto loyal subjects look for relief to St Germain.[61] But here again there seems to be no contemporary evidence. The closest we come to it is a remark made by the Earl of Egmont, but this was forty years later in the course of debate on the repeal of the Septennial Act.[62] If Somers did lend support to the measure it represents a change of heart over the course of a couple of years, for, as we have seen, he had opposed the bill of 1693.[63] But he may have found the 1694 enactment more palatable, in that it made no references to annual assemblages, nor (unlike earlier measures) did it impose penalties on lord keepers or chancellors who neglected to perform stipulated duties. And, like other Whigs, he appears to have envisaged substantial partisan advantages from an early dissolution of the existing legislature.[64] On the other hand Bonnet, in a roster of court Whigs whom he lists as favouring the Act, does not include Somers.[65] And when, some twenty years later, the Septennial Act was in the legislative mill, he was reported to have said that he 'never approved the triennial bill'—presumably that of 1694.[66] On the whole it seems doubtful that he expended much energy in persuading the King to sign the measure, certainly not in comparison with the Duke of Shrewsbury, who was so zealous in its behalf that he made its acceptance a condition of his employment in the government.

In 1695 the legislators were forced to turn their attention to the licensing of the press. Here it would be not essentially a question of new legislation (though some was proposed), but of determining whether or not former provisions should be kept in being. These, set forth in the Licensing Act of 1662, required registration of all books and pamphlets by the Stationers' Company, and provided for censorship by civil or ecclesiastical authorities, depending on the character of the printed matter. Passed originally for two years, it was given successive leases on life carrying it down to 1695. Various questions were now raised. Was prevention better than punishment? Could the state rely upon the law courts rather than the censor? Opinion was mixed. William, mindful of the free Dutch press, was inclined to be liberal, but some of his aides argued that it was as much the duty of the state to be forehanded in restraining the perpetration of libels as other crimes.

Somers is said to have been convinced that the regulations were not only vexatious but ineffective, and to have pointed out that, since the Revolution, the press had poured forth more libellous works, affecting both the government and private individuals, than in any former age.[67] We know that he was connected with the 'College', a group of politicians associated with John Locke, and there is ample evidence of the part played by this association in bringing in a bill designed as an alternative for the expiring Act. Somers at first encouraged the members of the 'College' to draft a new measure. But later, under pressure from the court and the bishops, he drew back and himself drafted a clause extending the old Act for another session.[68] In the end the Commons, apparently motivated largely by opposition to the monopoly of the Stationers' Company, would neither enact new legislation nor renew the old. Freedom of the press was, to some extent, advanced by default.

Meanwhile Somers was lending a hand to strengthen England's military position abroad and secure the regime at home. In 1694 Admiral Russell's fleet, operating off the Catalan coast, had saved Barcelona from the advance of the French general, Noailles. It was now decided that the English naval force should winter at Cadiz, a proposal that Russell accepted with ill grace. Somers was all for it, along with others—Trenchard, Pembroke, Romney— who, joining with him to discuss the matter, urged that 'it might be represented with all the advantage the thing will bear' how useful it would be for Russell to be so stationed and supplied that his fleet could be ready for action early in the following campaigning season.[69] Shrewsbury and Pembroke, he said, were like-minded. But, in a letter to Portland, he cautioned against giving opponents of the government cause to complain that England's defences were being neglected, pointing out that for several years there had been fears of French attacks in the winter or early spring, when the fleet was not ready to oppose them:

I do think that it will be necessary to do everything w^{ch} [which] may not only make the kingdom safe in the absence of so great a part of ye Fleet but may make them see that they are safe.

He was sure that the King would do everything possible to ready the English ships earlier than usual, and hoped that he would see that the Dutch came up with their full quotas.[70] He was torn between military advantages and parliamentary reactions, and, as one outside the military coterie, proffered his advice with some diffidence: 'If I suggest anything wrong I hope you will forgive mee. I am sure I do no hurt in it, because I mention it only to y^r L^{dp}, where you will let it dy if it signify nothing.' But, he added, 'I am apt to think nothing would more contribute to the facilitating of business next winter than somewhat of this kind.'[71] 'Business' was, of course, parliamentary business, and especially supply.

There was more involved in securing England than a good defence against French naval attacks. Ever present was the Jacobite threat. No one knew how many could be numbered among the disaffected. Fear and suspicion found fertile soil. Particularly disturbing was the charge that some servants of the state were drinking to the King over the water. The concern was not so much with highly placed men, for their activities could be followed with some certainty; it was rather with place-holders and magistrates of lesser rank. From the time when Sunderland had become William's adviser, he had complained that the government continued to employ men who were opposed to the settlement, and who consequently should be removed from office. There was, of course, general concurrence among the Whigs.

Somers would assist in these purges, primarily of customs and excise commissioners and justices of the peace.[72] In May 1694, before leaving for the continental campaigns, William was prevailed upon to agree to a purge of customs men. As for the excise commissioners, Shrewsbury, Godolphin (who headed the Treasury) and Somers had joined in urging the King that inasmuch as they had in their hands the disposal of £100,000 a year in inferior places, without restriction, it was of the greatest importance to have the right men in their ranks. The subordinate officials, scattered throughout the kingdom, could collectively wield considerable influence in elections; if, as Somers believed, they were the 'worst men that can be picked out' the situation should obviously be remedied.[73] In addition, there was a conviction among the leading ministers that some of the commissioners should sit in the House of Commons, where they could account for their particular department. Both Somers and Shrewsbury were of this opinion, and recommended men already members of the House, rather than men of the 'City'. As Somers wrote the King,

There is one thing necessary for carrying on your service, which was extremely wanting in these two commissions; that there should be somebody of them who might upon all occasions give a satisfactory account in the House of Commons in what related to their proper business.

He expressed the hope that Sir Walter Yonge and Edward Clarke, both reliable Whig wheel-horses, would fill this bill, and be acceptable to William.[74]

But the reconstitution of the commissions did not go smoothly. When Somers, Shrewsbury, Trenchard and Godolphin met in June to decide on the matter, the Tory Godolphin violently dissented from the recommendations of his colleagues (which were supported by Sunderland) and protested to the King that the changes being proposed were not out of interest to the royal service, but were 'for the sake of removing some men that are of one party, and gratifying some that are of another'.[75] He clearly regarded his colleagues' recommendations as a Whig machination, a point of view with which William, opposed to having one party or faction control patronage for its own ends, had considerable sympathy, especially since two of the new commissioners, Tipping and Molesworth, were personally unacceptable to him. He also agreed with Godolphin's objection that the appointment of revenue commissioners was a Treasury patronage right. A partial appeasement was effected by proffering the King a slate from which he might select substitutes for Tipping and Molesworth. But good feeling was not restored. To Somers, Godolphin's reactions were 'so very extraordinary and beyond what his temper does incline him to, that it made everybody wonder', while Sunderland complained that the Whig party 'makes me weary of my life'.[76]

In other ways Somers worked to uncover and to frustrate disaffection towards the new regime. In 1693 he noted, in a letter to Portland, that there was 'a very unhappy mutinous spirit got amongst the meaner sort of people'. It was mainly caused by the dearness of corn—England suffered from an unprecedented series of bad harvests in this decade—but had been 'secretly improved by ill men to very bad designs'. By the efforts of several judges the disorders had been put down. He hoped that Queen Mary would show mercy to those convicted, since they were but tools of cleverer men who had escaped.[77] But an investigation of the justices of the peace, as the key magistrates of the realm, was in order.

Somers was the logical man for such an assignment. The justices of the peace owed their appointment to the Crown, which acted, at various periods, on the advice of different sets of persons. But the Lord Keeper, in a practical sense, exercised the greatest authority in this respect, and has never surrendered his right to appoint, on his own initiative, any person he sees fit. There was no guarantee of life tenure, the lists being manipulated in the interest of the court. It was quite in order for Somers to instruct Secretary Trumbull not to name any justices until he had supplied a list.[78] It was, moreover, the Lord Keeper's responsibility to charge the justices with the performance of various duties. This was usually routine business, witness Somers's injunctions to the Middlesex justices regarding the execution of laws on the observance of Sunday, and against profaneness and debauchery.[79] But in 1693 he went further, calling upon the assize judges for appraisals of the J.P.s whom they encountered on their circuits. He found that, in all of these, there were men who 'have taken the Oaths and yet act directly agst the interests of their maties governmᵗ'. Others had been commissioned despite their 'refusal to act or take ye Oaths upon any occasion'. He reported this, and more, to Portland, and asked him to sound out the King on the retaining of such men in office.[80]

While William's answer is not recorded, there can be no doubt that a reconstitution of the commissions was undertaken under Somers's direction. The purge, which involved the deputy lieutenants of counties and the lieutenancy of London, as well as J.P.s, was the most drastic since the Revolution.[81] Nor were these tactics confined to the year 1693: they were restored to in 1694 and other years, particularly in 1696 following the Assassination plot; in that year at least sixteen justices were removed from the Gloucestershire commission alone.[82] Widespread resentment was inevitable. We shall see that, towards the end of Somers's chancellorship, the Tory House of Commons sought to make amends.

It was not enough to hand-pick the magistrates. Daily vigilance was required to keep abreast of the veiled undertakings of would-be rebels, feckless and inconsequential though they usually were. Somers had intelligence of much of this, though often, conveyed by perjured informers and other interested parties, it would be of doubtful validity. Still, it was well to take no chances. In 1693 we find him writing to the judges on the western circuit, directing their attention to conditions in Bristol, particularly to the 'scandalous rejoicing' of some of its citizens 'at whatever they hear to the disadvantage of their Majesties' interest'.[83] The following year occurred the abortive prosecution of the Lancashire Jacobites. In this Somers had no direct part, though in the summer, several months before the trial, he heard the disclosures of three Lancashire and Cheshire men that they had enlisted 'soldiers' and brought arms for disaffected gentlemen of that region; and after the trial, which resulted in the acquittal or release of all concerned, he received from the judges an account of their proceedings.[84] Well might he do so, for the tactics of the government had brought it nothing but discredit, primarily because of the light which had been thrown on the sources and nature of its so-called evidence.

Late in December 1694 Queen Mary died of smallpox. Subordinate as she was in regnal authority, she had nonetheless served in William's stead for many a month, and the event was not without political repercussions. It appears, however, to have had little direct effect on Somers's career. He was neither among those whom she cherished, like Nottingham and Shrewsbury, nor those, like Sunderland, whom she abhorred. Her regard for the ministers was to some extent shaped by filial loyalty, and in this respect Somers's role in the dethronement of her father may have strained their relations, but there is no evidence that she harboured towards him such aversion as her sister would nurse for so many years.

Upon her death Somers appears to have had a hand in reconciling William and Princess Anne. Such a step was clearly in the King's interest. Estranged from her sister since the dispute over her financial settlement, and offended as well by William's scarcely disguised contempt for her beloved husband, Anne had for several years moved in an orbit of her own, apart from the court, with her own ménage at Sion House or Berkeley House. Had she been clever and unscrupulous she might have proved a serious threat to the regime. She was at least a contingent beneficiary of the Jacobite cause, and perhaps something more, since the unbending Catholicism of her ageing father and the Catholic upbringing of her half-brother raised obstacles which even legitimists could not wholly ignore. Mary's untimely death now made her heiress presumptive. Sunderland, along with Somers and Marlborough, moved quickly to heal the old wounds. Anne, at the instance of Marlborough, wrote a warm letter of condolence. To this the King, distracted with grief, at first paid little heed. But Sunderland pled for a generous accommodation, and Somers is said to have arranged for an interview at which the royal pair, in a formal sense, buried the hatchet.[85] Anne received the recognition that was her due. With St James's Palace assigned to her as a residence, she was physically, as well as politically, brought back into the orbit of the regime.

In so far as Mary had possessed independent authority, it was largely in the realm of ecclesiastical preferment. Here Somers, as Lord Keeper, must have had contacts with her, since he enjoyed extensive perquisites in this area. The King rarely concerned himself with the Church, though he might ask his Lord Keeper to be mindful of the needs of naval chaplains when livings were disposed of.[86] But Somers was not a churchman like Clarendon or Nottingham, and Mary relied primarily on Archbishop Tillotson in such matters.[87]

There was, however, one project dear to her heart in which Somers played a consequential role. This was the conversion of the royal palace at Greenwich into a hospital for ailing and disabled seamen and their dependants. As early as 1691 the Queen had given her blessing to this undertaking. Her concern (so extraordinary in that age) for the plight of the common soldier and sailor was genuine and persistent: 1693 she had sought Somers's opinion with regard to their grievances.[88] Somers's support of the Greenwich project was linked to a conviction that it would contribute to naval morale and make the service more attractive. Writing to the Duke of Portland in the summer of 1693, he commented on the shortage of seamen, the undermanned ships, and the prevalence of desertion, noting that parliamentary attempts to remedy these conditions had proven 'abortive'. He goes on to say, with regard to improvement:

I am convinced it is not to be don by any other way then by giving ye seamen great encouragem[ts] as well as by punishing offenders. I am inclined to think that if some steps were made to the founding a Hospital for the widows and orphans of seamen as were killed in the service of ye King, as also for such seamen as were disabled in the King's service it would be a good ground to work upon in Parlt and would be the most generaly acceptable thing the King could do.

He was aware that the financial circumstances of the Crown made it impossible to launch an elaborate project. But he recalled that 'the King did seem Disposed that the House at Greenwich should be for such purposes', and suggested that William should publicly announce his determination to establish such an institution, underwriting it with small annual subvention 'for setting the work on foot', and encouraging private individuals to contribute to the carrying on the design'.[89]

By the following October the Greenwich facilities had been set aside for the Hospital.[90] Though Mary died in December, William was resolved to carry out her cherished design. Somers, among others, served as a trustee and commissioner for providing suitable accommodations.[91] Such service was to be expected of the Lord Keeper, *ex officio*. We also find him inquiring into abuses at St Katherine's Hospital, near the Tower, and dealing with the financial condition of St Thomas's, in Southwark.[92] But his interest along these lines was not entirely official. He was a charitable man; years before becoming Lord Keeper he was one of the original trustees of a hospital in Droitwich, and both at Reigate and North Mimms, where he possessed property in later years, he made contributions to the public welfare.[93] In the Greenwich Hospital subscription book, which he ordered John Evelyn, as treasurer, to prepare, he was set down for £500.[94]

The death of Mary, thought it occasioned genuine grief in all but Jacobite circles, did not disrupt the regime. There was some uncertainty as to whether that event had automatically dissolved Parliament, but legal opinion held that it could have no such effect.[95] A new Great Seal was, of course, necessary, but there was no rush; Somers did not receive it until the following May, two months after he had participated in the pomp and circumstance of Mary's long delayed obsequies.[96] But her death did have the effect of removing a figure inalterably hostile to Sunderland. To this extent it may be said to have advanced the interest of the combination which that astute manager was shaping into a political directorate.

This group, in addition to Somers, included around half a dozen men in key positions. In April 1694 the versatile Charles Montague, for several years a Commissioner of the Treasury, became Chancellor of the Exchequer. He was Somers's closest friend in high political circles. Edward Russell was First Lord of the Admiralty. Trenchard held one secretaryship and the elusive Shrewsbury, raised to a dukedom, the other. Sir William Trumbull, regarded as a creature of Sunderland, had replaced the Tory Seymour on the Treasury Board, and fell heir to Trenchard's post upon his death in 1695. Of those who came to be prominently associated with the combination known as the Junto, only the rakish Wharton remained without preferment. But this was, perhaps, his own fault. He was continually annoying William with hints of his eligibility for high office, while simultaneously striving to convince the Commons of his independence of the court.

Sunderland envisaged a system in which he and a few 'neutral' associates would control patronage and receive the royal commands, 'while the whigs toiled in the arena below'.[97] His political skill was matched only by his lack of scruple; he was, in contemporary eyes,

A Proteus, ever acting in disguise;
A finished statesman, intricately wise;
A second Machiavel who soar'd above
The little tyes of gratitude and love.[98]

Though without office until 1697, he enjoyed a substantial annual stipend. His usefulness as a mediator between William and the Whigs had been recognised by Somers as early as 1693; he in turn appears to have held the Lord Keeper's abilities in high regard. According to Swift, 'it was alleged that Somers was the only man to whom he would listen'.[99] But there was bound to be opposition, even among the beneficiaries of Sunderland's influence, to his role as a kind of first minister without portfolio. While Somers and Trenchard showed a disposition to co-operate, Montague and Wharton were less amenable. Even had Sunderland stood forth as a party leader, rather than a royal councillor, he would have found it difficult to carry forward his system: the patterns of political discipline were as yet much too indistinct. The still extensive royal authority, the broad cleavages of Whig and Tory, Country and Court, the workings of lesser factions, the subordinate but important influence of various politicians—all contributed to a tangle of relationships and interests that not even Sunderland could unravel. The absence of Russell, wintering off Cartagena, and the death of Trenchard did not help him, but tended rather to strengthen the hands of Montague and Wharton. In the Lords, the disgrace of Normanby was also a blow to his influence, forcing him, as Kenyon says, 'into open competition with Somers and Shrewsbury for the leadership of the government'.[100]

The most pressing problem in 1695 was the condition of the currency. It has been estimated that between 1672 and 1696 the silver coinage depreciated by nearly 40 per cent through the practice of clipping the un-milled coins, which were often irregular in weight and shape, and melting down the scrap. The Mint had for years undervalued silver in relation to gold. Hence it was profitable to export the former, and with the proceeds import the more highly valued metal. This, turned into guineas, was then applied to the purchase of scrap silver, and so a vicious circle evolved. Despite the fact that defacing the coin of the realm was regarded as petty treason, and jails were clogged with those charged with the offence, the practice, so simple in execution, was lucrative enough to induce countless individuals to risk the gallows.[101]

The results were apparent in a sharply depreciated foreign exchange, a rise in prices, and a confusion which affected economic activities on every front, even to the extent of lessening the national credit. For a time the Bank of Amsterdam would prohibit the circulation of English silver. Even the most ordinary transactions at home were rendered more difficult and uncertain. As William Lowndes wrote: 'Persons, before they conclude in any bargains, are necessitated first to settle the price of value of the very money they are to receive for their goods; and if it be in guineas at a high rate, or in clipped or bad moneys, they set the price of their goods accordingly.'[102]

As early as 1694 Somers, at the instance of Charles Montague, who strongly advocated recoinage, was appointed to a committee to consider the rehabilitation of the currency and to draft a bill to this effect.[103] Here Somers's close association with John Locke is manifest. He had probably encountered Locke in the early 1680s. There is evidence that at least one of his political treatises of this period, *The Security of Englishmen's Lives*, was of some interest to Locke.[104] Throughout most of the rest of the decade we lose sight of any connections between them, though it is tempting to suggest that the M.P. for Worcester was in touch with the exiled philo-sopher when he helped pilot the Declaration of Rights through Parlia-ment.[105] It is quite possible. In the autumn of 1689, Somers, as newly appointed Solicitor-General, spoke of former favours received; these, he wrote Locke, 'made me bold to presume upon you, and your judgment is such that I can depend on your instructions as the rules for my behaviour'. This was not mere flattery. In 1690, upon being re-elected M.P. for Worcester, he asked Locke if he should return to Westminster for the opening of Parliament, or continue to attend the assizes. He apologised for his importunity, 'which nothing but yor Kindness to mee upon all occasions as well as my Dependances upon yor Judgement could have drawn mee to'.[106]

As early as 1690 Locke and Somers appear to have corresponded on the value of paper money and the evils of depreciation.[107] The interchange reveals that the two men were like-minded in supporting a highly conservative policy, involving the reissuance of the English coinage at its traditional weight and fineness of silver. Two years later these ideas had sufficiently ripened to be presented to the public in Locke's first publication in the field of economics, *Some Considerations of the Consequences of the Lowering of Interest, and Raising the Value of Money*, a treatise which dealt not only with the cheap money question, but with the problem of the clipped currency. In this Locke was encouraged by Somers and to him it was addressed.[108]

It is clear that he was greatly under the influence of Locke's opinions when, in the course of the 1695 deliberations, he proposed to the Council that all unmilled coin should at one stroke (and without warning) be assessed at its value by weight, although those who immediately yielded it to the assayer were to be given notes assuring payment of the difference between its nominal and real value. But it was not easy to convince the Lords Justices. This was largely due to the arguments of William Lowndes, embodied in a published treatise, for lowering the intrinsic standard.[109] Lowndes had been for over fifteen years associated with the Treasury, and had but recently been made its secretary; even Locke paid tribute to his financial acumen. Again Somers appealed to Locke, asking him to peruse an abstract of Lowndes's essay and join him to discuss it.[110] The result was another treatise from Locke's pen, which was dedicated to Somers; in this he undertook to refute Lowndes's arguments point by point, his major premise being the impossibility of valuing coined silver in lower degree than the uncoined metal.[111] So matters stood for the time; it was not until the new Parliament convened in December that the policy would be determined, essentially along lines drawn in the Locke-Somers position. Somers may well have regretted his dependence upon Locke in this connection. The project, forcing the nation to undergo a substantial deflation in time of war, imposed serious hardships and lacked the safeguards (included in the Lowndes proposal) against profiteering. The recoinage resulted in a deficit of £3,000,000, which had to be made up by levying a special window tax for seven years. The reputation of Montague, who steered the scheme through the House of Commons, was seriously damaged.[112]

Meanwhile, with the King absent from the realm between May and October, Somers and the six other Lords Justices had made their debut as collective regents. In addition to Somers (chosen President despite a serious illness) the board was made up of Tenison, the Archbishop of Canterbury; two members of the royal household, Devonshire and Dorset; and three ministers of state: Pembroke, the Lord Privy Seal, Shrewsbury, Secretary of State, and Godolphin, First Lord of the Treasury.[113] It was virtually a Whig committee, with only Godolphin representing the Tory interest. For five months Somers and his colleagues wrestled with an almost infinite variety of problems. These for the most part may be grouped under military and naval administration, economic matters, and the maintenance of public order. They disposed of naval contingents, pressed men into service, worked out the exchange of prisoners, dealt with prizes and provided for victualling. In connection with the coinage crisis they dealt with valuation, clipping and minting, and, on a broader front, the importation of gold, as well as other aspects of foreign trade. Disorders and riots, the depredations of highwaymen, and Jacobite activities were all on the agenda, as was the composition of commissions of the peace. And there was much other business: it is clear that Somers, as a Lord Justice, became intimately and widely acquainted with the business of running the state.[114]

Since William rarely allowed Parliament to meet when he was not in the realm, the Lords Justices' relations with that body were minimal. The Parliament of 1690 met for the last time on 3 May 1695. During the King's absence it was prorogued from time to time. By the terms of the Triennial Act it might continue in being until November 1696. The fall of Namur in the summer of 1695 brought unwonted prestige to William and his aides and reinforced arguments for an earlier dissolution, since well-timed elections might redound to the advantage of the court. Upon Somers's advice, this action was deferred until the King returned, when it was implemented in customary fashion and a general election ordered.[115]

Somers, of course, took full part in the electoral preliminaries. Fearing that Tories might be returned for the important constituency of Middlesex, he, along with Shrewsbury, strove to gain advantage for the Whigs by resorting to the magic name of Russell. They had in mind Edward Russell, the Admiral, but since he was with the fleet he could not be readily contacted, and it was touch and go whether he would return to England in time. Determined to take no chances, they entreated Lady Rachel Russell (widow of the Whig martyr) to allow her eldest son to be nominated. He was but fifteen, but there was no law excluding minors from the House. If he would, but for a day, stand forth as Lord Russell (putting aside his new title of Marquess of Tavistock), no one could prevail against him; without expense he would gain the seat, and bring in another Whig with him. To such lengths would Somers go to advance his party's fortunes! But Lady Russell refused to allow her son to be a pawn of the politicians. Fortunately for the Whigs, the Admiral returned in the nick of time and was enthusiastically returned, without opposition.[116] Somers also worked with Shrewsbury to get Sir John Houblon elected as Lord Mayor of London, in order that he might influence the City vote.[117]

His personal influence at the polls remained slight. But his brother-in-law, Cocks, was returned, this time for Droitwich, in place of Lord Bellamont, who had become a colonial governor. This probably reflects an arrangement worked out with Swift, now victorious at Worcester. In the Droitwich contest Somers co-operated with Sir Edward Harley, who won the borough's other seat.[118] He could take satisfaction in the return of John Hawles, a lawyer and a strong Whig, for Wilton. Hawles had been unsuccessful in 1690. Some time before the 1695 election Somers advised the King to make him a K.C., pointing out that there was 'a want of lawyers to carry on your service, both in the House of Commons, and in Westminster Hall'. Since there was some prospect that Hawles might be elected, such an honour would be 'a good way to engage him 'in the Crown's interest'.[119] Somers also pressed for Hawles' appointment as Solicitor-General, which was brought about in July 1695. By these manoeuvres he gained a staunch ally. It was also heartening that his protégé, Thomas Trevor, continued for Plympton, and Clarke for Taunton, and that his friend, Richard Dowdeswell (the son-in-law of his old mentor, Winnington), was again returned for Tewkesbury. Dowdeswell would soon be known as a loyal adherent of the Junto; his family enjoyed considerable influence in Worcestershire and Herefordshire. Another associate, Sir James Rushout, managed to hold on to his Evesham seat, despite 'foule practice' encountered in the campaign.[120]

As for the general outcome of the election, the hopes of the government were not betrayed. Many new faces appeared in St Stephen's, but the supporters of the court—that is, the Whigs—would, as a rule, maintain control over the new legislature. The administration's 'hard core of support' rose, at the very least, to above seventy. Somers and other key Whigs were bound to benefit. Never had things been 'more promising in order to set the Kingdom upon a right bottom'.[121]

NOTES

[1] William Blackstone, *Commentaries on the Laws of England*, ed. Robert M. Kerr (London, 1876), III, 48.

[2] It tended to grow larger and larger; in 1711 it had seventy-one members: Edward R. Turner, *Privy Council in England in the Seventeenth and Eighteenth Centuries* (Baltimore, 1927–28), II, 24.

[3] Ogg, *James II and William III*, 333.

[4] P.C. 2/75, f. 508, 18 November 1694.

[5] Ibid., 2/75, ff. 63, 136, 443 *et passim*.

[6] Luttrell, III, 166, 200, 220; *Cal. S. P. Dom.*, 1693, 61; ibid., 1694, 204; ibid., 1695, 111–12; ibid., 1697, 510–11.

[7] See Jennifer Carter, 'Cabinet records for the reign of William III', *Eng. Hist. Rev.*, LXXVIII (January 1963), 95–114.

[8] William's first cabinet council, of nine members, was formed to advise Mary in 1690.

[9] William Coxe, *Private and Original Correspondence of Charles Talbot, Duke of Shrewsbury* (London, 1821), 35.

[10] Ibid., 38–39, and see Edward R. Turner, *Cabinet Council of England in the Seventeenth and Eighteenth Centuries* (Baltimore, 1930–32), I, 402–5.

[11] Carter, 95–96, 100–7. For those who attended regularly in 1694, see p. 105. Besides Somers, five officers—the Lord President, Lord Privy Seal, Secretaries of State and Master General of the Ordnance—and Lord Normanby are listed.

[12] For a reference to a Powys House meeting in 1697, see Turner, *Cabinet Council*, II, 297.

[13] The clause of the Bill of Rights lodging the exercise of regnal power solely in William's hands was reversed in 1690 (2 W. and M., sess. 1, c. 6). For the scope of business before Mary and her advisers, see Finch MSS., III, 378.

[14] Luttrell, *Relation*, III, 469, 474, 522.

[15] Carter, 107.

[16] C.J., XIII, 547, 576; and see below, pp. 180–81.

[17] Luttrell, III, 469.

[18] Regular communication was maintained through William Blathwayt, who, as personal secretary to the King in Flanders (1692–1701), has been described as having 'greater power than any minister': G. N. Clark, *The Dutch Alliance and the War against French Trade, 1688–1697* (Manchester, 1923), 144. On William's control see also Stephen B. Baxter, 'Recent writings on William III', *Journal of Modern History*, XXXVIII September 1966), especially p. 264.

[19] P.C. 2/77, *passim*; see also Cal. S. P. Dom., *passim*.

[20] Evelyn, late in 1695, referred to Sunderland as 'now the great favourite': *Diary*, V, 226.

[21] Coxe, *Shrewsbury*, *passim*; Portland Papers, University of Nottingham, Somers to Portland, 20 June 1693; Add. MSS. 34, 515, f. 195.

[22] *Works*, ed. Scott, X, 23.

[23] Swift includes Somers among the 'New-men' introduced 'into the highest Employments of State, or to the Office of what we now call Prime Ministers; Men of Art, Knowledge, Application and Insinuation, merely for Want of a Supply among the Nobility'. Besides Somers he mentions Montague, Churchill, Vernon and Boyle. See *The Intelligencer*, No. 9, p. 96.

[24] Add. MSS. 34, 515, f. 1.

[25] Baxter, *William III*, 316, remarks that he would 'just do'.

[26] *The Freeholder*, No. 39; Burnet, IV, 388; Boyer, *William III*, 243.

[27] *Tale of a Tub* (London, 1720), footnote to dedication; *Letters of William III and Louis XIV*, ed. Paul Grimblot (London, 1848), I, 467–68.

[28] But Sir John Dalrymple states that William wrote most of his speeches himself: *Memoirs of Great Britain and Ireland* (London, 1790), III, bk. iii, 49. For Somers's composition of a royal speech to Parliament in 1698, see D.N.B., John Somers.

[29] Ogg, *James II and William III*, 483. Devonshire and Vernon perhaps also had a hand in it; see Hardwicke, *State Papers*, II, 459; Turner, *Cabinet Council*, I, 456.

[30] Somers MSS., Bellers to Somers, 18 November 1693.

[31] See Norton-Kyshe, 6.

[32] Burnet, IV, 7.

[33] *Cal. S. P. Dom.*, 1693, 84. For the twelve appointees, see *Cal. S. P. Dom.*, 1689–90, 59. They were to hold office *quamdiu se bene gesserint*.

[34] See ibid., 1693, 83; Henry Horwitz, *Revolution Politicks: the Career of Daniel Finch, Second Earl of Nottingham, 1647–1730* (Cambridge, 1968), 141–42.

[35] *Cal. S. P. Dom.*, 1693, 84.

[36] Nottingham Portland papers, Somers to William, 11 June 1695. According to Campbell, V, 105, William 'promised that in future all such appointments should be made by advice of the Lord Keeper'.

[37] *Cal. S. P. Dom.*, 1696, 216. John Wallis, the mathematician, deciphered dispatches for William III.

[38] Foss, *Judges*, VII, 367, 385–86.

[39] *Portland MSS.*, VII, 447; *Cal. S. P. Dom.*, 1697, 194.

[40] Ailesbury regarded Rokeby as 'a plain man but a sufficient lawyer', but Turton and Eyre as persons 'of a most moderate capacity': *Memoirs*, II, 410.

[41] Burnet, IV, 188; Bonnet report, 3 April 1693, in Ranke, VI, 215.

[42] J. P. Kenyon, 'The Earl of Sunderland and the King's Administration, 1693–1695', *Eng Hist. Rev.*, LXXI (October 1956), 576–602.

[43] Kenyon, *Sunderland*, 256, citing Memoir in Portland MSS., c. June 1693.

[44] Somers MSS., Wolseley to Somers, 16 April 1693.

[45] Dorset Record Office, x36, Papers of Sir John Trenchard, Trenchard to Tewkesbury, 2 December 1693.

[46] Nottingham Portland papers, Sunderland to Portland, 3 May 1693. For this and the following, see Kenyon, 'King's Administration', 584–85.

[47] *Cal. S. P. Dom.*, 1691–92, 64–65; Nicholaas Vapikse, *Correspondie van Willem III en van Hans Willem Bentinck* (The Hague, 1927–35), 1st ser., II, 38–40.

[48] For warrants appointing Bath, see *Cal. S. P. Dom.*, 1693, 92, 98. Somers wrote to Portland, 16 August 1693, pointing out that he was unwilling to do anything without his concurrence, 'but it is now put hard upon mee': Nottingham Portland papers.

[49] For examples, see *Lords MSS.*, 1695–97; 212–13, 263–68.

[50] See Coxe, *Shrewsbury*, 433.

[51] Somers MSS., Charles Cocks to Somers, various letters between 16 September 1693 and 7 January 1694 .

[52] C.J., XI, 82–84; Odlfield, V, 240–42.

[53] Alexander Cunningham, *History of Great Britain* (London, 1775), I, 318.

[54] Luttrell, *Relation*, III, 84. City of London, Journals of the Common Council, LI, f. 251v.

[55] *Ibid.*, LI., f. 272v; Nottingham Portland papers, Somers to Portland, 18 August 1693; Luttrell, *Relation*, III, 279, 288; Common Council Journals, LI, ff. 295v–96.

[56] Ranke, V, 201. Somers and his associates obtained another £200,000 in November 1696: *Post Man*, 26–28 November 1696.

[57] This stock was transferred out of his name between 1710 and 1717, the bulk of it going to Charles Cocks and Sir Joseph Jekyll in the latter year. I am indebted to officials of the Bank of England for this information.

[58] Somers MSS., S. A. Blackerby and W. Moore to Somers, 28 February 1706. Montague regarded the annuity provisions as necessary in order to raise the desired funds. Somers is said to have been impressed by Samuel Lambe's *Seasonable Observations Humbly Offered to his Highness the Lord Protector* (London, 1657), which urged the establishment in England of a bank similar to that in Amsterdam. See *Somers Tracts*, ed. Scott, VI, 446–65; Douglas Campbell, *The Puritan in Holland, England and America* (New York, 1893), II, 326–27. He was opposed to the Land Bank project of 1696: *Cal. S. P. Dom.*, 1696, 250.

[59] Campbell, *Chancellors*, V, 107. See below, pp. 237–38, for Somers's opposition to a similar provision in the Regency Bill (1706).

[60] Dennis Rubini, *Court and Country, 1688–1702* (London, 1967), 104.

[61] Campbell, V, 107: 6 W. and M., c. 2.

[62] The Earl of Egmont notes in his diary that 'the great Lord Somers advised the passing of that Bill': Hist. MSS. Comm., *Earl of Egmont MSS.* (London, 1920–23), II, 56. Somers had been ill during debate on the 1963 Bill. Ellis, 'Junto', 219.

[63] See above, pp. 55–56.

[64] Dorothy Somerville, *The King of Hearts: Charles Talbot, Duke of Shrewsbury* (London, 1962), 98. The Triennial Act permitted the existing Parliament to sit until 1 November 1696.

[65] Bonnet, 10 February 1693, in Ranke, VI, 212.

[66] See below, p. 314.

[67] Campbell, V, 106. For Locke's observations on the Licensing Act of 1662, see Peter, Lord King, *Life and Letters of John Locke* (London 1864), 202–9.

[68] Here I am indebted to Mr Raymond Astbury, of the City of Liverpool College of Commerce, for information derived from Locke's correspondence in the Bodleian Library. On the 'College', see below, p. 116 and n.

[69] Coxe, *Shrewsbury*, 65–68; *Cal. S. P. Dom.*, 1694–95, 251.

[70] Nottingham Portland papers, Somers to Portland, 14 August 1694. In May 1695, Somers with other Lords Justices warned William that the Mediterranean fleet might the following year be 'too Weak and disproportioned to the Enemys strength' unless he took care that the Dutch 'have at least their full Quota of Ships in those Seas': Add. MSS. 40, 771, ff. 21–21v, and see *Cal. S. P. Dom.*, 1694–95, 476.

[71] Nottingham Portland papers, Somers to Portland, 14 August 1694.

[72] See Kenyon, 'King's Administration', 591, and Lionel K. J. Glassey, 'The commission of the peace, 1675–1720' (Oxford doctoral dissertation, 1972).

[73] It appears that he overrated the influence of the excisemen, who were so unpopular that until 1736 they were required to carry arms.

[74] *Cal. S. P. Dom.*, 1694–95, 179–81. Both belonged to the 'College'.

[75] *Ibid.*, 1694, 184.

[76] Nottingham Portland papers, Somers to Portland, 14 August 1694; Kenyon, 'King's Administration', 593.

[77] Nottingham Portland papers, Somers to Portland, 20 June 1693.

[78] Sidney and Beatrice Webb, *English Local Government in the Parish and the County* (London, 1906), I, 379–80; Hist. MSS. Comm., *Downshire MSS.* (London, 1924–40), I, pt. ii, 582.

[79] Luttrell, III, 99, 114, 118; see also *Cal. S. P. Dom.*, 1694–95, 63.

[80] Nottingham Portland papers, Somers to Portland, 20 June 1693. According to Edward Hughes, *Studies in Administration and Finance, 1558–1825* (Manchester, 1934), 188, only one fifth of the excise personnel took the oath of allegiance in the five years following the Revolution.

[81] Luttrell, *Relation*, III, 237; Add. MSS. 34, 515, f. 194; Kenyon, *Sunderland*, 278. In February 1694, forty Tories were evicted from the London lieutenancies 'and replaced by almost as many Whigs': Luttrell, III, 266; see also Burnet, V, 223; Edward Chamberlayne, *Angliae Notitiae* (18th edn., 1694), 750–51.

[82] Webb, I, 322–23.

[83] *Cal. S.P. Dom.*, 1693, 272.

[84] *Ibid.*, 1694–95, 219; 1695, Addenda, 286. See also Matthew Smith, *Memoirs*. Somers's correspondence with Portland touches on the need to pay those who had served the government as informers or witnesses, or might do so in the future: Nottingham Portland papers, 2 May and 2 July 1695; Add. MSS. 34, 515, ff. 6–8, 28 May 1695.

[85] William Coxe, *Memoirs of the Duke of Marlborough* (London, 1847–48), I, 42. But the Duchess of Marlborough makes no mention of Somers in this episode, noting that 'the person who wholly managed the affair between the King and Princess was my lord Sunderland', who had determined to heal the breach before the Queen's mortal illness: *Account of the Conduct of the Dowager Duchess of Marlborough* (London, 1742), 110.

[86] *Cal. S. P. Dom.*, 1693, 438.

[87] But there was close co-operation between Tillotson and Somers in ecclesiastical appointments: Hardwicke MSS., XXXIII, ff. 62–63; Somers MSS., Tillotson to Somers, 8 May 1693.

[88] *Cal. S. P. Dom.*, 1693, 123.

[89] Nottingham Portland papers, Somers to Portland, 14 August 1694. It is noteworthy that in this letter there is no mention of Queen Mary. But a month later Somers wrote that some would envy the King and Queen the glory of beginning such a work: *ibid.*, 14 September 1694.

[90] *Cal. Treas. Books*, 1693–96, X, pt. ii, 796–97; see also p. 926.

[91] *Cal. S. P. Dom.*, 1695, 73, 346.

[92] Somers MSS., documents designated J/8 and J/11, n.d.; Luttrell, *Relation*, IV, 287–88; Portland MSS., VII, 127; Lords MSS., Addenda, *1514–1714*, 505. For the rules of St Katherine's made by Somers on his visitation, 30 September 1698, see Panshanger (Cowper) MSS., box 47, shelf 228.

[93] The Droitwich institution was established in 1688. Somers served as a trustee of the Reigate Parish Library: Wilfrid Cooper, *Reigate: its Story through the Ages* (Sussex Archaeological Collections, V, Guildford, 1945), 63. See also below, p. 315.

[94] Evelyn, *Diary*, V, 209–12, 219; Somers MSS., J/9, petition of Thomas Lane, n.d. Somers's subscription was as large as any except that of the King (£2000): Evelyn, *Diary*, ed. William Bray (London, 1906), III, 132–33.

[95] Bonnet's dispatch, 28 December 1694, in Ranke, VI, 263. And see, e.g. *Whether the Parliament Be not in Law Dissolved by the Death of the Princess of Orange* (London, 1695), by Robert Ferguson.

[96] *Cal. Treas. Books*, 1693–96, X, pt. iii, 1167; Lords MSS., *1693–95*, 409–501; Oldmixon, *History*, 109.

[97] Kenyon, 'King's Administration', 591.

[98] *Poems on Affairs of State* (6th edn., 1716), IV, 90.

[99] Feiling, 295; *Swift's Letters*, ed. Williams, I, 57n.

[100] Kenyon, 'King's Administration', 596–97. Normanby was accused of complicity in frauds and misdemeanours involving Parliament and the City; the charges were dismissed by the Lords for lack of evidence. In 1696 Normanby was dismissed from the Council.

[101] See, e.g. Luttrell, *Relation*, III, 143–44, 155, 157 *et passim*. On 10 September 1695, fifty or sixty clippers were tried: *ibid.*, III, 523.

[102] *Report Containing an Essay for the Amendment of the Silver Coins* (London, 1695), 115.

[103] Henry Lyons, *The Royal Society, 1660–1940* (Cambridge, 1944), 110.

[104] Among the works in Locke's library were three by Somers, including *The Security of Englishmen's Lives*: John Harrison and Peter Laslett, *Library of John Locke* (Oxford Bibliographical Society, 1965), 236.

[105] Maurice Cranston suggests that 'conversations with Locke probably influenced his contribution to the framing of the Bill of Rights', but adduces no evidence: *John Locke, a Biography* (London, 1957), 325.

[106] Bodleian Library, Locke MSS. c. 18, ff. 151, 154.

[107] See Peter Laslett, 'John Locke, the great recoinage, and the origin of the Board of Trade', *William and Mary Quarterly*, 3rd ser., XIV (July 1957), 379 and n.

[108] It was in the form of a 'letter to a Member of Parliament', dated 7 November 1691,

Locke notes, p. 2, that he has particularly 'taken into consideration' a 'printed sheet' entitled *Remarks upon a Paper Given in to the Lords*.

[109] A *Report Containing an Essay for the Amendment of the Silver Coins* (London, (1695). Lowndes proposed a recoinage and, to meet current needs, the raising of the nominal value of silver coins by 25 per cent. Some would have no change. In a letter to an unidentified correspondent Somers wrote: 'there is much Industry and Craft used to continue things in the same ill State they are': Add. MSS. 35,838, f. 325. On the Locke–Lowndes controversy, see Ming-Hsun Li, *The Great Recoinage of 1696 to 1699* (London, 1963), ch. VI.

[110] Bodleian Library, Locke MSS. c. 18, f. 158.

[111] *Further Considerations concerning Raising the Value of Money* (London, 1695). In his dedication Locke notes how Somers and 'other great men' induced him to 'meddle with Money and Trade'.

[112] Li, 116–19; Baxter, *Treasury*, 198–200.

[113] Turner, *Cabinet Council*, II, 191. Of these only three, Tenison, Devonshire and Pembroke, would serve on all seven panels of Lords Justices.

[114] For this see *Cal. S. P. Dom.*, 1694–95, 473 ff., and 1695, 3 ff.

[115] *Ibid.*, 1694–95, 490, 495; Coxe, *Shrewsbury*, 398.

[116] See Macaulay, V, 2650; Coxe, *Shrewsbury*, 401. Edward Russell was returned for both Middlesex and Cambridgeshire, choosing to sit for the latter. The young Marquess may have presented a mature appearance; he was married in 1695.

[117] *Ibid.*, 396–97.

[118] Ellis, 'Junto', 223.

[119] *Cal. S. P. Dom.*, 1694–95, 246. Hawles sat for Old Sarum in 1689.

[120] Somers MSS., Rushout to Somers, 28 October and 4 November 1695. Dowdeswell had married Elizabeth, daughter of Somers's early patron, Sir Francis Winnington.

[121] Hist. MSS. Comm., *Buccleuch MSS.* (London, 1899–1903), II, pt. i, 276 (Capel to Shrewsbury, 10 December 1695).

VII
Junto magnate, 1695–98

In 1695 the Whigs stood on the threshold of unprecedented influence. The favourable results of the elections gave public recognition to a position already enhanced by royal favour and the machinations of Sunderland. In the Lords the death of Halifax had removed one of the most trenchant critics of the government. The support of William's military efforts had at last borne fruit, and it was possible to contemplate the completion of his grand design. While the composition of the new Parliament could not be said to reflect a mandate for unlimited Whig control, it had certainly provided added backing for the party's leaders. Parliamentary management, of course, might not always measure up to royal requirements. As it was, the King was resentful of the joint Tory–Whig attacks on his liberality to Dutchmen, especially his old friend Portland, and he regarded the projected reform of treason trial procedure as at least ill timed. But a ministry that twice in two successive sessions proved able to wring £5,000,000 from Parliament for the war effort could not fail to impress a soldier king.

Somers now held a well-established place among the handful of men in whose hands administrative influence was concentrated. This would come to be called the Junto. When this term came into common use, with this connotation, is hard to say. Shaftesbury had used it as early as 1676 to indicate a political clique; a more public reference is encountered in 1690, in the 'Dutch Junto'.[1] Derived from the Spanish 'junta', it was invariably opprobrious. Although the Earl of Ailesbury listed Somers, Devonshire, Halifax (the erstwhile Montague), the younger Sunderland and Wharton as 'a knot of persons . . . [who] gave themselves the name of a Junto' in 1702, the Whig leaders do not appear to have used it.[2] A pamphleteer gives the year 1701 as the point of origin of the Junto, describing it as a device to promote 'opposition to the Court Party' by evicted ministers.[3] But the label has come to be particularly attached to a hard core of Whig politicians who, in the years 1695–98, made up what one contemporary called 'a ministry within a ministry'.[4] Somers, Russell and Montague were effective ministers: they headed important departments of state and deliberated together on matters of high policy. Wharton, though lacking such preferment, was politically influential (his electoral influence in Buckingham was legendary) and a hard-hitting debater to boot. These men were to provide, for the Whigs, a management which would give in these years a remarkable cohesion and direction to what was a minority interest.[5] Associated with them at the highest levels were Shrewsbury and the elder Sunderland, in a sense patrons of the Junto, but moving in orbits of their own.

Ministries within ministries were not new. What was new was the

Junto's role as a driving force within a recognised political party. It may be said to have been unique. Charles II's cabal was a far different body, embracing men of various persuasions, and born of royal tactics before the advent of Tory and Whig. Even in their palmiest days, late in Anne's reign, the Tories would not assemble such a team. The early Georgian era was familiar with a concentration of power in the hands of a few politicians, but the eclipse of the Tories and the less direct authority of the monarchs (coupled with Walpolean precedents for cabinet domination) provided a different political environment.

Somers has been described as presiding over the Junto. But, while he came in time to be recognised as its head, this is an overstatement. The Junto never acknowledged a presiding officer. Its members were too proud, too influential, sometimes too self-seeking. They comprised a group of politically ambitious and aggressive Whigs, generally (though not invariably) like-minded as to major policies, and usually (but again not invariably) identified with accepted Whig principles and interests. The Junto could by no means always count on the support of non-Junto Whigs, but it provided, collectively, 'a coherent, effective and reasonably united Whig leadership.'[6] Whether in or out of office the Junto lords maintained a close association, not only in the more formal haunts of politicians, but at the Kit-Cat Club, race meetings and country house parties. Varied as its fortunes were in the course of two decades, the Junto remained in being; it never dissolved into factions, though its members might quarrel among themselves.

By Tories and even some within their own party—and by Queen Anne—the Junto lords were regarded as greedy, overbearing and unscrupulous. Such charges are not without some justification. But, for the most part, they stemmed from envy of the extraordinary success achieved through the employment of recognised contemporary tactics. Particularly important was the Junto's more thorough exploitation of the electoral system, as well as of royal patronage. The former was a product of territorial sway, which gave them, collectively, an electoral influence far outstripping what might be expected of so small a group, particularly when, in the course of time, certain recruits or associates were added to the original clique. Reverses would be suffered, of course, but the Junto connection was always to be reckoned with. The benefits of royal patronage would be less constant, with marked differences in the two reigns. But the Junto lords showed remarkable determination and even ruthlessness in securing offices for the faithful, and in insuring that place-holders recognise their political obligations. Such methods were bound to arouse resentment. Yet the purging of the commissions of the peace, midway through William's reign, a major grievance harboured by the Tories against Somers, was resorted to by them once they got in power.

Somers's office did not give him the direct political influence enjoyed by Montague who, as Chancellor of the Exchequer and, from 1697, first Commissioner of the Treasury, presided over a great department, and was in addition a highly skilful political manager. While custody of the Great Seal was still a central function of great importance, providing contact with a great variety of public business, it was essentially Somers's recognised ability, his capacity for business, his staying power, his integrity, that solidified his position and would make him, in time, the leader of the Junto. Material resources were never a consequential factor, certainly not in 1695, though like most men of his station he was showing some interest in the acquisition of land.[7]

He was still a commoner. Not since Orlando Bridgeman's day, a generation before, had a Lord Keeper remained so long in office without a title. Late in 1693 it was reported that he would be made 'Baron of Broughton or Bewdley', and that his patent had passed the Privy Seal.[8] But this was mere gossip. In 1695, however, the King, about to leave for Holland, actually made out the warrant for conferring a peerage. William must have been mindful that Somers, though in effect president of the Lords Justices, was the only commoner among them. More important, probably, was his inability to participate in the Lords' debates. Shrewsbury was given the task of persuading him to accept the honour. Not finding him at home, he wrote:

I had directions to have said everything I could imagine, to persuade you to accept of a title, and the King is really convinced it is for his service you should. I beg the answer I may have may be a bill for the King's signing. As for arguments, I have used all I have already; and by your objections, you may give me leave to tell you, that you are as partial and unreasonable, with too much modesty, as some are with too much ambition. I hope you will not only pardon me for telling you your fault, but that you will correct it.[9]

But Somers refused the peerage, probably because he doubted his ability to support it without substantial grants, which were not assured.

Although he side-stepped ennoblement, he maintained the state associated with his office, such as the levée customary among great persons. He was far from niggardly, noting among his maxims that history was without evidence of an 'illustrious miser'.[10] He was usually to be found at Powys House, his official residence. London he rarely left, though by this time he was making occasional use of a country retreat. What with the pressures of office and an increasing vulnerability to various ailments it was well to escape now and then: in a letter to Portland in 1695 he complained that the business of the term would hardly mend his ill health.[11] He appears to have first resorted to Mortlake, and later, in 1697, to Clapham.[12] In that year he also gave some thought to Tunbridge Wells. But his physician advised him against this watering place as too public and accessible: only the scene would be changed; he would probably have to 'keep a table' and receive 'multitudes of visitors & crouds of earnest solicitors'. Rugby was preferable: the air was better, the waters no worse, and he would be out of range of business.[13] But he seems to have ignored this advice, and certainly sojourned at Tunbridge from time to time. He did not travel much, save for occasional summer visits to the seats of political associates; Worcester appears to have seen little of him, though his mother continued to live there.

The winter months were the busiest time for Somers, for then, in addition to his year-round ministerial duties, he had to preside in the Lords as well as the Court of Chancery. In January 1696 a new assignment, though of an essentially honorific nature, was thrust upon him. The House of Commons had been for some time unhappy over wartime defence of commerce, the state of the coinage, the balance of payments and other economic conditions. The new Parliament now proposed the establishment of a parliamentary committee of trade, with full executive powers. William regarded this as an invasion of his prerogative, and the government lost no time in devising an alternative arrangement.

In this, as in the coinage reform—which was simultaneously upon the agenda—we see Somers and Locke in close co-operation.[14] On 17 December Somers wrote asking the philosopher to come to town. He counted on the 'College' to have informed him of the King's decision to appoint him to the Commission for Trade and Plantations, and on Locke's acceptance, but apologised for having proposed him without his consent.[15] The 'College' was a group of Junto Whigs, including Edward Clarke, M.P. for Taunton, John Freke, a lawyer, Sir Walter Yonge, a Devonshire baronet, Gilbert Heathcote, a banker, as well as Locke and Somers. It was a miniature club, meeting as such when the members were in London and maintaining a correspondence with Locke during the rest of the year. Locke had employed it in his attack on continuing the licensing of the press; later it played a part in the recoinage project. Freke was a sort of secretary; Clarke was the spokesman in Commons, provided with ammunition by Locke, who also, through his publications, worked to inform the public on a broader front.[16]

It is clear that Somers had no intention of allowing prolonged and heated parliamentary debate to deter him from setting up a board under the auspices of the Crown. It is also clear that he wished to work out details with Locke. On the same day that he summoned him, another letter went forth, from Freke, to make assurance doubly sure: 'My Lord Keeper commanded me to write earnestly to you to be here as soon as you possibly could, and said the loss of a day by your absence at this time would be of consequence.' The letter goes on to outline the membership of the proposed commission, and to summarise its functions in detail. With some minor changes it describes the board as it was finally constituted. Locke saw Somers about 20 December. One of the matters discussed was who should serve as secretary. They decided on William Popple, a London merchant and friend of Locke, who was to perform the function with extraordinary success.[17]

The new board was at length set up, after the subsidence of parliamentary debate late in the winter. Its commission was dated 30 April 1696, the first meeting occurring late in June.[18] As an ex-officio member the Lord Keeper was present. Thus began an agency of government that was to last for three generations as the paramount instrument of the old colonial system. Somers would take no part in its regular work. But, as Lord Keeper, he was required (as were the Lord President, Lord Privy Seal and other high officials) to attend it on special occasions.[19] Locke was on the board as a working member. His enthusiasm had evidently cooled somewhat in the spring. Late in March he wrote that he would not be sorry to escape such employment, though it was 'very honourable' and carried an annual salary of £1,000.[20] But he was prevailed upon to serve, undoubtedly by Somers.[21] Keeping him in harness required considerable powers of persuasion. The arduous labours of the commission, combined with the smoke and fog of London, prompted him, after about a year, to submit his resignation. But the Lord Keeper would have none of it. 'I must say', he wrote, 'you are much in the wrong, in my opinion, to entertain a thought of it; and I flatter myself so far as to believe I could bring you over to my sentiments if I had the happiness of half an hour's conversation with you.'[22] Somers prevailed. Locke had marked respect for Somers's intellect and integrity, which he did not conceal. Writing to Somers early in 1697 he remarked: 'I know nobody that can with soe much Right promise himself to bring me over to his Sentiments as your Lordship, for I know not any one that has such a master reason to prevail as your Lordship, nor any one to whom . . . I am soe much disposed to submit to with implicit faith. . . . Your Lordship, who always speaks Reason, is always ready to hear it.'[23] Locke stayed on as commissioner until 1700, though towards the end poor health and the rigours of winter frequently kept him in the 'chimney corner'. Then, with Somers out of office, he made his permanent withdrawal from public life.[24]

Meanwhile the nation stood on the eve of a new flurry of Jacobite activity and of the *cause célèbre* of the legitimists. The more militant among them saw in Mary's death an opportunity to restore the direct Stuart line. Their hopes and underground manoeuvres mounted accordingly. From time to time we catch glimpses of Somers involved in what we would call intelligence operations, as in the spring of 1695, when he sought with Portland to obtain information on what the Jacobites were doing in England. Lord Monmouth, he wrote, was 'uneasy that no care had been taken in it', and had recommended several persons 'deeply in' with the Jacobites, and whose services might be obtained upon easy terms. A few months later Somers was advising payments to informers.[25] Although the Lancashire trials of 1694 had served to discredit such agents, the government could hardly dispense with their services in an age when virtually no police force existed apart from the amateurish ranks of parish constables and watchmen.

Late in 1695 plans were afoot for a rising in England, to be co-ordinated with an invasion from France. The Duke of Berwick came to England to lay the groundwork, to be followed early in 1696 by Sir George Barclay, armed with a commission from James to raise troops for a rebellion. This was to be led by Sir John Fenwick, a north-country man of good connections; his wife was a daughter of the Earl of Carlisle. Fenwick, however, was never to take the field, for before the arrangements could be worked out,

Barclay launched an assassination plot against King William. The date set was 15 February; the place, Turnham Green, near which William passed as he returned from weekly hunting parties in Richmond. But the plot was abortive. The plan was revealed; except for Barclay and Fenwick the conspirators were taken, and within a few days the nation was buzzing with news of the King's providential deliverance.

The attempt on William's life created a sympathetic reaction in his favour, of which the Whigs took full advantage and to which, indeed, they contributed.[26] Somers, along with Montague, is said to have supervised the preparation of Richard Blackmore's *True and Impartial History of the Conspiracy*—by no means the only instance of propagandist activity on their part.[27] An emergency meeting of the cabinet was called at once. Somers was on hand, along with the other Lords Justices of the past summer; Leeds, Prince George and Sir William Trumbull were also there. We can but speculate on what was done. Without doubt Somers and his colleagues set machinery in motion for the apprehension of the plotters and arranged special protective measures for the royal person. But whether he on this occasion suggested the loyalty tests which were soon invoked, and with which his name was prominently associated, cannot be said.[28]

It was but a matter of days, however, before Sir Rowland Glyn rose in the House of Commons to propose that the members, following the precedent of Elizabeth's reign, should enter into an 'Association' to defend William, as their 'rightful and lawful' sovereign, against 'the late King James and all his Adherents'.[29] A great majority of the members swore to honour this pact, and throughout the realm loyal subjects followed suit. By April it had received legislative form, in an 'Act for the Better Security of his Majesty's Person', though not without considerable debate, for the Tories fully recognised the dilemma in which it placed them. 'If they opposed the Association they ran the risk of being branded as Jacobites. If they accepted it they would have to reckon with disunion in their own body, for the more rigid among them certainly would not take it.'[30] But they were powerless to prevent the imposition of the penalties of praemunire on all who would not acknowledge William as rightful king, and the requirement that the Association be tendered to all office-holders and to all members of future parliaments. It came to be a test of loyalty to the existing regime.[31]

In the enforcement of the Act, Somers was bound to play a prominent part, for by its terms the justices of the peace, as well as other magistrates, came under review. As we have seen, he had already given considerable attention to the composition of the commissions of the peace; he now acted promptly to remove from the commissions magistrates throughout the kingdom who refused to comply with the act. The inevitable result was the exclusion of many conservative Tories who (like Nottingham and Rochester in the Lords) balked at giving formal recognition to William as 'rightful and lawful' King, and a natural bitterness against tactics regarded as designed for the benefit of a party rather than for national security. But, while Somers may have been over-zealous, and doubtless took full advantage of this political windfall, it is hard to see, with a fresh statute on his desk, how he could have acted otherwise.[32]

The Whigs, however, were soon to learn that there is no rose without its thorn. The trials of the conspirators, Charnock, King and Keyes—and of five others—proceeded without untoward events, presumably under Somers's direction.[33] William once more showed that he appreciated the value of well-timed clemency as an instrument of policy, and the whole affair might now have blown over, leaving the administration to bask in the sunshine of averted rebellion and strengthened political support, had it not been for the Fenwick case. But in the summer of 1696 this leader of the insurgents was flushed out of hiding. In the hope of saving himself, he made a confession touching on the activities of men close to the throne, and casting doubts on Whig professions of unadulterated fidelity. Marlborough, Godolphin, Russell, and Shrewsbury were accused of treasonable correspondence with the court of St Germain.[34] Of these four all but Marlborough were prominent members of the ministry, and the last two were thoroughgoing Whigs. Though William, in paying no heed to Fenwick's charges, again displayed his statesmanship and magnanimity, it was a different matter with Parliament. Tory intrigues with Jacobites were to be expected. But here were trusted Whig leaders, key men in civil and military affairs, aspersed. Thus, as the Commons set out to test the truth of Fenwick's charges, the ministry, as well as Fenwick, stood on trial.

The story of Somers's activities in the Fenwick affair can be followed in some detail through his correspondence with Shrewsbury. It begins in June, when Fenwick was brought before the Lords Justices.[35] His position was desperate, for in their hands was a letter, intended only for the eyes of his wife, which was an implicit confession of treasonable conduct. It appeared to be an open and shut case. But it was now somewhat harder to secure a conviction for treason. Even as the plot unfolded Parliament had passed the Trials for Treason Act, which required, among other things, that the indictment be supported by two witnesses.[36] The government thought it had its men in Porter and Goodman. Fenwick played for time. First there was the confession implicating William's aides. This occasioned a new examination by authority of the Justices, which produced a second confession, touching but little on the first and creating enough confusion to hold up the trial. Next came news that Goodman had vanished. The Whigs were beside themselves, for they were baulked of their prey, if ordinary judicial procedure were to be invoked.

Somers appears to have been mainly concerned, at this time, lest Shrewsbury make some move that might be construed as a confession of guilt, and thus cast further suspicion on the ministry. The Earl took little comfort from the King's assurances of confidence, and was ready to surrender the seals of office. He found refuge in his Gloucestershire seat; there he stayed despite pleas from Somers and other ministers that he return to London. He was ill, and judged by his doctor 'in no condition to stir'.[37] But though

Somers could not flush him, he could take some credit for keeping him in office. On 19 October he wrote that he was 'infinitely in the wrong' in entertaining any idea of giving up the seals:

I will not at present enter into the dispute of what may be proper hereafter, but I will positively affirm, that all the enemies you have in the world cannot stain your honour so much as such an action would. The world could say nothing else but, either that a consciousness of guilt made you do it, or else, that the King believed the accusation, and called for the seals. Forgive me for speaking after this free manner, for I do own I can scarce be temperate in this matter. There can no possible good come of your quitting: it will not stop the coming of the business into parliament, but it will make it infinitely worse there, than it can be upon the foot it is.

He went on to say that it would also prejudice Russell's position, and handicap the successful resolution of the whole affair, 'which I do not despair may be done'.[38]

It is clear that Somers realised that, much as he desired it, Fenwick's charge could not be kept out of Parliament. This, he told Shrewsbury, must be taken for granted; indeed, the 'endeavouring of it would do mischief'. Nor should the ministry delay in taking the legislators into their confidence, otherwise it might lose the initiative. But how to do it? The King might take the lead, yet there were disadvantages in such a course: 'for if he slighted it, as he ought, perhaps it would be hard to answer the question, why he brought it to the House; and if otherwise, it would give a weight to it'. It would be better, Somers suggested, for Russell to bring the matter up, declaring that the King was 'satisfied entirely of the falsehood and malice of Sir John Fenwick', but that (for his further vindication) he desired the House to 'take notice of the thing'; and that like remarks should be made on Shrewsbury's behalf.

Somers also advocated that Fenwick should be confronted by the King: the idea, he said, 'was mine so much, that I proposed and pressed it from the beginning'. This he regarded as the only way to keep the House from launching an examination of their own. Fenwick's charge, he observed, was 'upon the whole body of the Whigs'; at all costs a vote of lack of confidence must be avoided.[39] This procedure was followed, though William was somewhat reluctant; he had long harboured a dislike for Fenwick. On 2 November, the conspirator was brought into the royal presence at Kensington. Somers was on hand, as were the Crown lawyers and several other officers of state. The interview shed no further light on the matter. Fenwick refused to explain his earlier charges, much less elaborate upon them, save privately to the King himself. This the King would not permit. In a sense the ministry had won the round, in that reputations had escaped further defamation.

In the House, too, events proceeded according to Somers's plan. On 6 November Russell arose to vindicate himself and Shrewsbury. In this he was successful. Fenwick was examined, but he did his cause no good. The Commons resolved that the papers read as Sir John Fenwick's information, 'reflecting on the Fidelity of several noble Peers, divers Members of this House, and others, only by Hearsay, are false and scandalous, and a Contrivance to undermine the Government, and create Jealousies between the King and his Subjects, in order to stifle the real Conspiracy'.[40] It was, in effect, a solid vote of confidence, the resolution passing without a division.

The resolution was followed by a motion to bring in a bill of attainder, which carried by a vote of 179 to 61.[41] Prior to Goodman's disappearance Somers had expected, and apparently desired, that the trial should be conducted in the usual fashion, under judicial auspices: this, he told Shrewsbury, he was inclined to regard as 'the least exceptional way'.[42] Whatever his concern for due process, as a forum for attacks upon the administration Parliament was much more to be feared than a court of law. But with a witness missing—'a most unhappy thing', as Somers put it—he gave full support to the draconian legislative procedure.[43]

The bill of attainder passed the Commons late in November, 189 to 156. It passed in the Lords on 23 December after heated debate, being carried by a majority of seven. Some forty peers protested.[44] So great was the opposition to the use of so terrible an instrument against so 'inconsiderable' a figure as Fenwick: traditionally bills of attainder had secured the convictions of over-mighty subjects. It is obvious that in the Lords (and to some extent in the Commons as well) political leverage had to be applied, and there can be no doubt that Somers contributed his full share to such management.[45] At this time he was plagued with the gout, and so Powys House was the scene of a number of meetings where tactics were decided upon.[46] These backstage operations are largely concealed from our eyes. But, as presiding officer in the Lords, he acted in a more public fashion. In a struggle so close, both sides sought the fullest representation in the chamber. Proxies were not allowed, and Burnet noted how 'extraordinary' it was that messengers should be sent to bring in absent peers.[47] Those who wished to defeat the bill worked with particular zeal to swell their ranks. As the official summoner of peers Somers could hardly play favourites. But he could, and did, resort to particular persuasion with those likely to support the bill. He sent a sharp summons to Wharton 'to come up and assist', and appealed to Shrewsbury to make every effort to be on hand despite his physical ailments:

as the whole business in the House of Commons has proceeded as well as could be wished, and will, undoubtedly, end so in that House, so I am fully satisfied, if you were here, it would take what turn we had a mind to in the House of Lords, which is more than I can yet pretend to say, if your grace be absent when that debate is to come on.

But Shrewsbury either could not or would not comply and was excused by the House.[48]

Shrewsbury, of course, had a particular stake in the outcome of the case, and this intensified Somers's efforts to have him on hand. But the Lord Keeper was aware that every vote would count, and he realised that even among his official Whig colleagues there were those who, when it came to a vote, would not support the measure. Attorney-General Trevor, a lukewarm Whig despite his association with Somers, strenuously opposed it in the lower house.[49] Sunderland disliked the bill, though in the end he supported it.[50] Of Somers's colleagues among the Lords Justices who were peers, only the Archbishop of Canterbury would vote for it. For all the management and intrigue associated with the outcome, for all the rising influence of the Junto, the battle was nearly lost. But, as Somers remarked 'What we aimed at, we had.'[51]

The Fenwick affair left its marks on the ministry. Godolphin resigned and Shrewsbury, secluded in Gloucestershire, became more elusive than ever. The departure of Godolphin, First Lord of the Treasury since 1690, removed the last Tory of any prominence save for Leeds, who clung to the Lord Presidency for another two years. Godolphin had for several years been in communication with St Germain; Fenwick's charges, in his case, came close to the mark. Yet even such a stalwart Whig as Wharton baulked at so bald a partisan stroke as to proclaim them to be valid in Godolphin's case, but invalid for the others. From this predicament the Whigs were rescued by the machinations of Sunderland, and by Godolphin's lack of steadfastness. By Sunderland's advice he was prevailed upon in October to offer his resignation, and the King snapped it up. The episode reveals the extent to which Sunderland was still pulling the wires: as Wharton said, 'there never was more management than in bringing that about'.[52] Somers looked upon the manoeuvre as a piece of trickery; Godolphin, he wrote Shrewsbury, 'has suffered himself to be cozened into an offer to lay down, and is surprised in having his offer accepted'.[53] But he expressed no qualms of conscience: between the two there was little love lost. On various issues—the war, Montague's bank, the recoinage project—the Treasurer had disagreed with his colleagues. Now the Whigs might look for a monopoly of office, and further entrench themselves by an accession of Treasury patronage, especially should the post go to Montague. But at the end of the year it was still vacant.

There was also the problem of Shrewsbury. Though disenchanted with high politics, scarred by the Fenwick publicity, and incapacitated by real or fancied ailments, he was still a man to be reckoned with. Although negligent in the performance of official duties, he was, like Sunderland and Godolphin, a great 'undertaker'. Moreover, he never ceased to be highly regarded by the King, who treated him with a patient consideration which was far from characteristic. Who could best soothe this sensitive soul and gain the advantage of his co-operation for the future? He was almost constantly seeking to unburden himself of the Secretaryship—in effect, he had abandoned the post. Could he be induced to remain in office in a less onerous but still eminent position? Sunderland thought he might accept the Lord Presidency in place of Leeds.[54] But even if he could be retained as a Whig mentor, who would replace him as Secretary?

Here there was disagreement between Sunderland and the Junto. Somers and Russell were for Wharton, despite the King's antipathy. Sunderland was for James Vernon, Shrewsbury's chief clerk. Clearly, in the reshaping of the cabinet a showdown was in the making. Control was all important to Sunderland; he resented any signs of independence. He had differed from his colleagues over the Council of Trade and the Land Bank; in the Fenwick affair he had been averse to the bill of attainder. And so Shrewsbury was courted by both sides, as a man whose support would consequentially affect their influence.

The Junto did what it could to turn Shrewsbury against Sunderland. Russell and Wharton had been playing this game since the beginning of the Fenwick affair. Somers appears to have been less active, but he now sought (after so many exhortations to come to London) to keep him in Gloucester, removed from Sunderland's direct powers of persuasion. He warned him that Sunderland had been spreading it abroad that he was but shamming illness, and that his sudden appearance in London so soon after Fenwick's execution would only bear this out.[55] Somers must have felt that he deserved some co-operation, perhaps even gratitude, from Shrewsbury. During the crucial autumn months he had maintained as close a contact with him as possible, advising him and keeping him abreast of events. In December he had sent him Lady Mary Fenwick's papers, though they had been entrusted to him alone by the peers.[56] But no representations of the Junto could overbear Shrewsbury's sense of gratitude to Sunderland, whom he regarded as chiefly responsible for his absolution in the Commons early in November. He stayed on at Eyton, as Somers advised, but not from mistrust of Sunderland. And when he finally returned to London in March, there could be no doubt that he and Sunderland were the closest of associates and dominated the innermost councils of state. As a contemporary observed, 'the secret and weight of the Administration is wholly in them two'.[57] In April the King insisted that Sunderland accept the White Staff.

Yet Sunderland's advantages were more apparent than real. He had no roots in popular esteem. He was still and ever would be 'a person equally fear'd by all Parties, and belov'd by none'.[58] The Junto was still riding high. The war, so important in linking William with the Whigs, was drawing to a close, but the Treaty of Ryswick was months away, and the argument over retaining the armed forces, so damaging to the Junto, could only be dimly foreseen. Honours and promotions revealed its ongoing influence. Charles Montague became First Lord of the Treasury as well as Chancellor of the Exchequer.[59] Admiral Russell was made Earl of Orford. And Wharton, though disappointed of the Seals (which both Shrewsbury and Trumbull were persuaded to retain) gained some consolation from a lucrative wardenship of the royal forests.

As for Somers, on 22 April he surrendered the Great Seal to receive it back at the higher rank of Lord Chancellor.[60] Now, surely, he would accept a peerage. Save for the republican years of the mid-seventeenth century, all chancellors had been peers since Sir Christopher Hatton laid down the office in 1591. But not until December 1697, on the eve of a new session of Parliament, was this dignity formalised.[61] Again, there was the matter of an endowment to sustain it. Since Somers's holdings were deemed inadequate, the King undertook to bestow on him the manors of Reigate and Howleigh, in Surrey, together with £2100 a year out of fee-farm rents of the Crown.

The manors were located some twenty miles from the metropolis, at the foot of the chalk downs running from western Surrey into Kent. Reigate alone, shortly after the Norman Conquest, comprised 3750 acres. Half the property had been owned by Viscount Monson, the regicide judge, but was forfeited to the Crown in 1661. The other half was acquired by James II in 1686 for £4466. Following James's abdication it remained in the hands of the Crown until 24 April 1697. The grant of that date comprised 'the Maner or Maners of Reigate and Howleigh, with their appertinencies within the parish of Reygate or elsewhere in the County of Surrey', including the site of the ruined castle there.[62] The grant was not to Somers, but to Joseph Jekyll, his brother-in-law, tenable 'in free and common socage, under the yearly rent of £65 8d payable to the Crown'. Jekyll was to hold the property in trust for the Chancellor. Somers, however, was unmistakably lord of the manor; the courts were held in his name, and, after his death, in the names of his surviving sisters.[63] According to the grant, the property was worth £396 5s 3d a year. The income appears to have been notably increased under new management; Jekyll, in a letter bearing no full date but written at least a decade after the acquisition of Reigate, gives its annual value as £999.[64]

The conveyance of Reigate and Howleigh, formalised but two days after Somers became Chancellor, went off without a hitch.[65] But it was otherwise with the fee-farm rents. These were rents paid at a perpetually fixed rate, in this case to the Crown, for estates held in fee simple. Again the device of the trust was employed. This time several trustees were named, including John Warner, a London goldsmith.[66] But before the arrangements could be worked out the Duke of Portland's interests had become involved. He, too, had been granted such rents. Would there be enough for him and Somers as well? Although he had been liberally endowed by the King, his appetite was by no means jaded.

Somers found himself in a ticklish position. He found the fee-farm rents particularly attractive as a form of remuneration, since they need not pass under the Great Seal. On the other hand Portland was a boon companion of the King; it would be unwise to alienate him. And William was determined to make up for the loss of a large Denbighshire grant.[67] On 29 April Somers wrote the King, accepting his grant, but pointing out that he had already advised against such a course if it meant any 'interfering' with Portland. He had been assured that this would not be the case; that William had made, or would make, compensation 'another way'. In any case, he did not question what the King proposed to do for Portland:

I do absolutely submit to it. I have given directions to put a full stop to the carrying on of the Grant [to himself], being resolved neither in this nor any other instance to importune yor Maty wth anything wch relates to my particular interest.

Meanwhile, Portland wrote from Holland that he did not wish to hinder Somers's grant in any way. Perhaps there would be enough to satisfy them both; if not, the King had assured him that he would fill out Somers's endowment from another source. To this Somers replied that he had stopped all proceedings regarding his own interest, lest they might run counter to the King's intentions. Both grants, he said, could not be honoured.[68] The result was an impasse causing some concern. Vernon thought that if Somers's resolution held up it might 'lay a heavier load on all our late grants, and go a great way towards sinking them'. Somers made no move; he would, Vernon reported, 'leave matters as they are'.[69] Meanwhile he was laid low by fever and jaundice. Late in June he wrote to Portland that he was making a very slow recovery, and had taken 'no further step' regarding the fee-farm rents.[70]

In the end Somers got his rents, or at least some of them. Just what manoeuvres were involved is not clear. But an account prepared by trustees of the sale of fee-farm rents, in accordance with orders of the House of Commons dated 1 February 1699, credits the Lord Chancellor with holdings worth £2100 a year. Derived from grants in Berkshire and Buckinghamshire, they included rents of the 'Honour and Castle of Windsor', despite an Act of Henry VIII's reign perpetually annexing them to the Crown. Altogether the Berkshire rents totalled about £520 a year. He obtained other rents from Yorkshire, formerly paid into the hands of the sheriff; there were twelve in all, but they came to only £36. Where the rest came from is not specified.

The new-found income was not an unmixed blessing. Objections were raised on various counts. In a petition to the King, royal officials at Windsor complained that since Michaelmas 1697, they had not received the fees and salaries that were their due. But an opinion obtained from the Attorney-General denied their claims. Still other protests were voiced regarding the manorial rents there. It was alleged that the grant was largely invalid, though Somers's title to as much of the rents as came from assarts and purprestures was described as indisputable.[71] Some rents could not be collected. In 1708 Godolphin, as Lord Treasurer, ordered reimbursement for certain defective rents, but the Commissioners of Account, reviewing the grant as a whole, declared such action injustifiable. They also renewed the charge that the remuneration of officials had been unwarrantably neglected or ignored.[72]

In the meantime the King's work had to be done. Fenwick had gone bravely to the block in January, but much unfinished business connected in one way or another with the plot lingered on, requiring Somers attention. For one thing, there was the Earl of Monmouth. This unpredictable peer had early in the reign moved in the highest circles of government, serving for a time on the Treasury Board and in the Cabinet Council. But those days were gone. No longer in office, and beset with grudges, he would prove a perennial trouble-maker—for Nottingham, Shrewsbury and Somers himself.[73] Through Monmouth, the informer Matthew Smith (believing himself to be ill rewarded for certain services), had accused Shrewsbury of not taking preventive measures despite early information on the Assassination plot. Though Somers counselled restraint, the Earl's tactics antagonised the Lords to such a degree that they sent him to the Tower. This seems only to have stimulated further intrigue. For some time Somers had recognised that he was a man whose impulsive ventures could be dangerous to the ministry. 'His main business', he wrote Shrewsbury, 'is to get out of the Tower, and, in order to do that, he is ready to do anything.'[74]

Of those caught up in the plot of 1696, and still in prison, the most notable was the Earl of Ailesbury. Though a veteran intriguer, he denied that he had ever supported a Jacobite restoration through illicit means. In his *Memoirs* he speaks of Somers as his 'greatest enemy', perhaps not without reason.[75] In October 1696, when the government's strategy was being worked out, Somers had suggested that Ailesbury might be impeached, as 'the most likely way of diverting Parliament from troubling themselves with entering any farther into the inquiry into the plot'.[76] But these tactics were not adopted, and in the following spring Somers was still seeking effective means of bringing the Earl to justice. Again the disappearance of Crown witnesses—three in this case—frustrated the prosecutors. Somers toyed with the idea of making a deal with Peter Cook, who also stood accused; in exchange for a pardon he might serve as a witness. But it was a risky manoeuvre—Cook was 'such an odd fellow, that one may have reason to fear both his folly and knavery'—and this project, too, was abandoned.[77] Shortly afterwards Ailesbury was released. He tells us that the usually self-possessed Chancellor could not conceal his rage when he saw him 'walk down in liberty'.[78] But Somers probably found some satisfaction in the long continental exile on which Ailesbury now embarked.

Meanwhile routine political business called for attention. Important Irish appointments were on the agenda, Baron Capel, the Lord Lieutenant, and Sir Charles Porter, Chancellor of Ireland, having both died. The negotiations now entered upon, revealing the usual competition of would-be patrons, point to the continuing influence of Sunderland and, to some extent, of Shrewsbury, rather than Somers. Somers, who had under Capel's administration exercised some control over Irish affairs, favoured Thomas Vernon for the Chancellor's post.[79] Vernon, a 'noted Chancery practiser', is best remembered for his law reports. Sunderland's candidate was John Methuen, who also had Shrewsbury's support. Though made Master in Chancery in 1685 he had served since 1691 as envoy to Portugal, where in a few years he would conclude the commercial treaty that bears his name. Somers professed to be ignorant of his legal qualifications, but deferred to Shrewsbury's representations.[80] He may have been influenced by assurances that Methuen's appointment would provide a diplomatic assignment for one of the Junto's staunchest adherents, Sir James Rushout.[81] In the end Methuen went to Dublin and Rushout to Constantinople, the King being unwilling to employ an untried man at Lisbon. Thus Somers's negotiations were to some extent rewarded. But he manifested his displeasure when Methuen took up his duties in Ireland.[82]

In the appointment of new Irish Justices there he appears to have played no part at all, the King conferring, in mid-April, with Sunderland and Shrewsbury. On this occasion Sunderland proposed Lord Villiers, while Shrewsbury was for the Marquess of Winchester and Lord Wharton. Villiers and Winchester were appointed, serving with the Earl of Galway, who continued in office. Somers could not have been satisfied with the outcome. He had friendly relations with Galway, but it was becoming abundantly clear that in Wharton the Junto had a colleague for whom William would still do little or nothing, and that Sunderland was ready to fortify him in this regard, though he did agree to a post in the Admiralty for Wharton's younger brother, Goodwin.[83]

Wharton's case apart, there were signs that the King was growing increasingly averse to Whig preponderance. In a letter to Somers after the conference on Irish appointments Shrewsbury reported that William had called for new blood in the customs and excise commissions, adding that preferment 'must not be extended partially to one kind of men, but some should be displaced of different denominations'. Shrewsbury feared that this somewhat cryptic remark might be directed against Sir Walter Yonge and Edward Clarke; if so, he cautioned, 'we are obliged (I am sure I think myself so) to stand by them'.[84] Somers would certainly agree, for these men were useful cogs in the Junto machine. On the other hand, the changes that William made (for the first time) in the composition of the Lords Justices could have given him little cause for complaint. He would now preside over a board still including Tenison, Pembroke and Devonshire, but with Shrewsbury, Dorset and Godolphin replaced by Sunderland, Romney and Orford. Godolphin's dismissal was welcome; Dorset had little political weight. Shrewsbury was a more acceptable colleague than Sunderland, but his semi-retirement could not be ignored. The Junto gained a representative with Orford. Romney (the Henry Sidney of revolutionary days), Master-General of Ordnance, was also a staunch Whig.

The summer of 1697, though quieter than the previous one, was not without crises. Of particular concern to Somers was a major financial scandal which came to light in May, involving Guy Palmes, a teller of the Exchequer. Palmes had been given the place over the protests of Godolphin (who wanted the office for his son) through the influence of Somers, Shrewsbury and perhaps Sunderland. Vernon speaks of him as 'a known creature of the Chancellor's'.[85] In May a shortage of £27,000 was revealed in his accounts. The matter came before the Lords Justices, where Sunderland and Somers quarrelled as to whether he should be dismissed. Though Palmes was working feverishly to make good the deficit, and by mid-June was successful, Sunderland, who was hostile towards the Palmes family, opposed his retention. Somers took the other side. While admitting that the lapse was inexcusable, he deplored the proceedings against the teller.[86] In the end Palmes was kept on, remaining in office until 1702, when he was dismissed for reasons unrelated to official conduct. By twentieth-century standards Somers appears to have condoned a low level of official morality. But the year was 1697; financial machinations of this kind were not uncommon; Palmes had been unlucky in being found out. Nor is it probable that ethical considerations had any substantial bearing on Sunderland's attitude. He was a most unlikely champion of political morality: Somers looked upon his 'transports' as 'above expression'.

Apart from this, there was little until the latter part of August to trouble the routine operations of the Justices. But Fenwick's ghost still stalked abroad. On 22 August, under the sponsorship of Sir Henry Colt, new accusations were made involving a pretended plot for the seizure of Dover Castle, and again touching on the loyalty of the Duke of Shrewsbury. Somers and other Lords Justices were once more involved in tedious investigations. As a result the whole story was discredited. But the tender susceptibilities of Shrewsbury had again been injured, and his determination to withdraw from political office given new life. Once more he took steps to resign. He had already broached the subject to William, claiming ill health, late in August; on 8 September, without consulting his colleagues, he renewed his application. On the same day he informed Somers and Orford of the course he had taken.[87]

Somers was vexed, and did not reply to Shrewsbury for a week. He remarked to Vernon that the latter's conduct 'had put the matter beyond deliberation', and that 'he knew not what to say to it, or what was to be done'.[88] But he soon rallied. It was clear that Shrewsbury was becoming increasingly useless as a minister of state. Still, his influence with the King could not be ignored; it might yet be used to advance the political fortunes of Wharton. Somers therefore did what he could to dissuade him. He thought him 'in the wrong, in taking such a resolution, as well as in giving the King an account of it, before his return'. The recent charges, he added, were so clearly false as to be considered 'a lucky thing, rather than an occasion for your retiring'. With the peace made, official duties would be lighter; Kensington or Chelsea would do as well as a place in town. He urged Shrewsbury to keep an open mind: 'Give me leave to add, that I think a sudden resolution, taken up, without the concurring opinion of any of your friends, ought never to be looked upon as so fixed, but that you should allow them to be heard upon it.' Orford wrote in the same vein on the same day.[89]

But Shrewsbury persisted in this course, and so the question of who was to succeed him again came to the fore, as well as the possibility that he might be kept in the ministry in another capacity. In the meantime he had agreed to retain the Seals until he could deliver them up in person to William. With this, Somers, Orford and Sunderland were in accord. Since the King was not expected until November, there would be some leeway. Somers pressed the Duke no further, and even expressed some sympathy: 'I am too sensible myself of what it is to be perplexed with business against one's inclination, and with no good health, to be very unreasonable in another man's case.'[90] In effect, he adopted a neutral position. Not so Orford and Sunderland, who manoeuvred in support of their respective candidates, Wharton and Vernon.[91]

Across the water the peace negotiations, which had begun the previous May, were at last concluded in October and the War of the League of Augsburg came to an end. Somers took virtually no part, England being represented by Pembroke, Villiers and Sir Joseph Williamson.[92] The King returned from Holland in November. Somers's coach and six was surely among the eighty such conveyances—filled with nobles, prelates and high officials—accompanying him as he entered his capital on the fifteenth. Now, briefly, animosities and jealousies gave way to mutual rejoicing and congratulation, as William, hailed (far beyond any manifestations in 1689) as a deliverer, basked in unwonted popularity.[93] The second of December was appointed a day of thanksgiving, and throughout the realm, from St Paul's in London, where the magistrates appeared in fully panoply, to the most isolated parishes of the north, congregations testified to the wonders of providence. That evening, as the bonfires blazed and the fire-works sparkled, Somers had special reason to celebrate. For on that day the patent creating him Baron Somers of Evesham had at last been issued. He was now not merely the moderator of the peers. He was one of them.[94]

His elevation to the peerage came close to marking the zenith of his fortunes. For several years he had been a key man in a ministry which, from William's point of view and from broader considerations of national interest, had been remarkably successful. As Burnet put it: 'great things had been done; the whole money of England was recoined, the King was secured in his government, an honourable peace was made, public credit was restored, and the payment of public debts put on sure and good funds'.[95] Parliament had been unprecedentedly generous; despite repeated disappointments and widespread isolationist sentiment the war chest had been filled again and again. The Jacobites were ineffectual. On the debit side was the heavy burden of taxation, and an economy depressed in part by war, in part by a series of poor harvests. But the country was beginning to recover. About the only thing to cause the King serious annoyance was the opposition to grants of Crown lands, especially to Dutch favourites.

In the autumn of 1697 the ministerial combination, despite signs of strain, appeared to be still viable. Parliamentary elections were not due for another year. Montague was an expert manager of the Commons. Shrewsbury had been prevailed upon, if not to remain in harness, at least to continue his association with the Whig team. Wharton, though increasingly disgruntled with Sunderland, had not come to the point of open opposition. Somers's knowledge, experience and judgement added prestige to the government. His customarily moderate and conciliatory tactics bound the cabinet together and in particular provided a bridge between his Junto colleagues and the independent Sunderland.

But before the year was out the uneasy alliance had been disrupted, and in the next the Junto was on the defensive. Indeed, at times it appeared that it would be swept away altogether, as threats and charges shook the political framework. To a large extent its difficulties can be blamed on the new peace. Now for the first time in the reign military necessity could not be used as a rallying cry, and discontented men, Tories and Whigs alike, showed greater independence. The issue of the standing army, Dutch favourites, placemen, high taxes—all provided handles by which the government could be wrenched and pushed and possibly defeated. But the reformers and little Englanders were not solely responsible. The over-reaching tactics of Sunderland, the jealousy and resentment of Wharton, the continued retirement of Shrewsbury, the dissatisfaction of the King: all would contribute to the Junto's decline.

The new session of Parliament got under way in December. It was clear from the beginning that the going would be rough. In an address prepared by Somers the King expressed concern that peace had not brought relief from financial burdens—five and a half million pounds had to be found, mostly to make up deficiencies in the military budget,—and went on to make a strong plea for an adequate army. With new-found leisure he could look forward to investigating corrupt practises in the administration and to fighting the good fight against profanity and immorality.[96] This, in essence, was the programme which the Junto was expected to advance. But their leadership, which had in the past greased the ways for so many government measures, would now prove less effective.

The immediate and most heated issue was the retention of a standing army. Antipathy towards such a force, stemming largely from the Cromwellian experience, had been so deep-seated at the outset of the reign that the Bill of Rights had prescribed it altogether in time of peace unless authorised by Parliament. Peace had now come; many Englishmen, of various persuasions, looked for the elimination, or at least a drastic reduction, of the well-trained regulars whom William had done so much to organise, and whose services he suspected might soon be required again. Pamphlets poured from the presses, setting forth the pros and cons.[97] The first was written by John Trenchard and Walter Moyle; its title, *An Argument Showing that a Standing Army is Inconsistent with a Free Government, and Absolutely Destructive to the Constitution of the English Monarchy*, amply states its thesis, which was widely held among Tories and Country Whigs. The authors were both Whigs, Moyle being a member of Parliament at the time.[98]

Thoroughly aware of the importance of the issue, and of William's deep concern, Somers took up his pen. His *Letter Balancing the Necessity of Keeping a Land Force in Times of Peace, with the Dangers that May Follow It* was in print before Parliament assembled. Like so many treatises of this sort, it was published anonymously. But there is no doubt of his authorship.[99] He begins with a plea that the peace should be maintained with as much spirit and courage as had been shown in conducting the war. All were in agreement that a strong fleet was necessary; the dispute lay over whether English security would better be served by maintaining, in addition, a 'land force' (he avoided the invidious 'standing army') or an improved militia. It was foolhardy, he pointed out, to rely too much on the fleet. England had had two wonderful 'Eighty-eights'; she could scarcely expect a third. As for the militia, he gave high marks to its patriotism and courage; he was sure it would be effective against other militias. But this was an age of regulars, and such troops could always defeat the 'untrained multitude'. To be sure, the militia might be improved, but this would take time; it would depend on 'many Particulars' and might be subject to 'many Slips in the Execution'. The nation could not afford so risky a course. With her nearest neighbours, and particularly France, imbued with the 'mistaken notion' of keeping up a mighty force, with England as open as she was to invasion, without internal barriers to hinder the enemy, a highly competent land force was indispensable. It should be kept in being, by act of Parliament, from year to year. According to 'the State of affairs both at home and abroad' it might be 'either increased, lessened, or quite laid aside', as the legislators saw fit. Such an arrangement should lay to rest any fears that an instrument of tyranny might be fastened upon the Kingdom. England, he concluded, could only have liberty if she made the effort to preserve it from both foreign and domestic encroachments, and in this 'we must trust England to a House of Commons, that is to itself'.

Throughout the argument he avoided any personal references, taking a tone of disinterested moderation and common sense, but at the end a subjective note is heard:

You know me to be so jealous of Liberty, to have been always so true to it, to have ventured so much for it, and to have such a stake in it, that you cannot suspect me. You know that I neither have, nor can have any views in this matter but at our present Safety, as well as the Continuance of our Constitution and Liberty for the future.

Obviously Somers expected to be recognised as the author.

The *Letter*, of course, did not end the argument. Among the pamphlets referring unfavourably to his proposal was a rejoinder by Trenchard and a *Confutation* by Samuel Johnson, a divine who differed from his more distinguished namesake in harbouring extreme Whig sentiments.[100] Trenchard, who found an apt scriptural tag in Proverbs XI, 1, saw no difference between Somers's land force and a standing army.[101] He still feared the latter as conducive to enslavement; the yearly review, he argued, would be meaningless since France could be expected to maintain her establishment forever. The militia would suffice. Trenchard knew who had written the *Letter* and some personal animosity crept in: he was sure there was 'Virtue enough yet in England to preserve our Constitution, though a wiser Head than yours designed its Ruine.' Johnson too charged Somers with misleading the public in describing a standing army as a land force, and even accused him of seeking to establish an absolute regime.

The Chancellor did not stand alone; among those ranged on his side was Daniel Defoe, whose three pamphlets in support of William's position complemented the 'Balancing Letter'.[102] But the House of Commons was not convinced. On 10 December disgruntled Whigs as well as Tories joined in a resolution in which the royal proposal to maintain a force of some 30,000 men was cast aside; in its place the standard of 1680 was invoked, providing for about 8000.[103] Confronted by such opposition, borne up by a ground swell of public opinion, the Junto found itself on the defensive as never before.[104]

This challenge to Junto management was accompanied by an attack on Sunderland. By Christmas he had resigned. His downfall was sudden. At the beginning of December his influence was still visible. When Sir William Trumbull, after complaining that the Lords Justices had treated him more like a footman than a Secretary, resigned on 1 December, Sunderland's candidate, James Vernon, took his place.[105] The Whig chiefs had no part in this decision.[106] Somers admitted that the manoeuvre had taken him by surprise, though he had expected that Vernon would get the post sooner or later. The Junto leaders were angry over Sunderland's coup and distrustful of Shrewsbury as undoubtedly privy to it.[107]

It was at this juncture that the Commons levelled their guns at Sunderland. They attacked him on the standing army question and raked over his past to portray him as an evil genius. The Earl lost his nerve as visions of impeachment floated before him—despite support from William, who was furious when he relinquished his gold key of office and fled to Earl's Court.[108] He looked upon the Junto as engineers of his plight, and not without reason. Wharton hated him; despite royal pressure he would not life a finger on his behalf. Montague was glad to see him go. Orford had misgivings, at least, but they were tempered by the hope that Sunderland's retirement might make room for Shrewsbury. As for Somers, he fully appreciated the unique position that Sunderland had attained as a royal confidant, and there is reason to believe that he would have welcomed an accommodation. But he appears to have done nothing to bring it about. He did not regard the Junto as culpable: it was impossible, he wrote, for Sunderland 'or any of his creatures, to give a turn to this affair, as if any thing had been underhand countenanced'.[109]

With Sunderland out of office, the hue and cry abated. Impeachment proceedings were time-consuming as well as unreliable, and the Commons had other fish to fry. The Whigs began to rally, aware that the old 'Machiavel's' fall might bring other men down. But their leaders, whatever part they had played in the skirmish, had little cause for rejoicing. Angry as William was over Sunderland's 'desertion', he was even more enraged with the Junto for its part in the business.[110] They were not only out of royal favour, but cut off from communication with Kensington. One liaison man was gone. The other, Shrewsbury, now seemed about to follow suit. On 29 November he had told Trumbull that he 'would never sign a paper more after this night', and the following day left for Eyford.[111] Again he was seeking permission to resign. The Junto agreed that he should be urged to stay on, though with some reluctance, for they still nursed the vain hope that Wharton might obtain the office. When in mid-December the Duke actually tendered his resignation Somers pled with him to accept the chamberlainship which William had offered him.[112] But to no avail.

The new year, found the Junto still in being, but it could scarcely be called a ministry. The resentful King continued to ignore the Whig chiefs, collectively and singly, issuing no instructions, receiving no reports.[113] Sunderland was gone, Shrewsbury unavailable. William continued to detest Wharton; Orford and Montague he did not care for; Vernon he understandably regarded and treated as a senior clerk. Somers had some credit left. Writing in mid-February to Portland, the King observed that the Chancellor 'is, as you know, the only minister who remains to me'.[114] By Vernon, too, we are told that William regarded himself 'in great want of some he may be free with', and felt that only the Chancellor was left to him. But he 'hath business that keeps him from attending as often as it would be necessary'.[115]

The repercussions of Sunderland's flight followed apace. In or out of office he probably could have affected the decision on the standing army very little. This was a serious defeat for the Junto, for the £350,000 parliamentary grant was sufficient for only about ten thousand men.[116] But the ease with which he had been dislodged caused opponents of the government to fix their sights elsewhere, and offered Sunderland himself opportunity for revenge. The King was to be taken at his word: official corruption should be investigated, and its perpetrators punished. A general onslaught on the Junto appeared in the making.

The attack fell first on Montague. As First Lord of the Treasury and Chancellor of the Exchequer he was legitimate prey; moreover, if he were brought down the Junto would lose its manager in the Commons. Sunderland employed Charles Duncombe, a rich goldsmith who was Receiver General of the Excise, to attack him on the ground of irregularities in the handling of Exchequer bills. It was a foolish move. Duncombe was hardly qualified to lead a crusade for bureaucratic purity. The attack backfired and he, rather than Montague, was sent to the Tower. The First Lord received a resounding vote of confidence.[117]

The Junto survived the crisis. Orford was sniped at, but nothing came of it. Though Vernon feared that Somers might 'have a glance', he was not attacked.[118] But the episode extinguished any hope of accommodation with Sunderland. The ex-Chamberlain had gone so far as to tender the olive branch, offering to live 'in entire confidence' with the Whig chiefs, and to 'labour like a horse'. Wharton could have the Seals.[119] But it was not to be. The Whigs in the Commons were definitely cool: they had not defeated the Sunderland interest in the House to effect the rehabilitation of its leader.

As for Somers, he made no move at this time. He probably believed that, in the current mood of the Commons, Sunderland would be more of a liability than an asset. But even in the following summer, when the possibility of an accommodation again arose, Somers and the rest of the Junto were against it: with elections afoot it was hardly the time to restore so controversial a figure.[120] Without Junto support, Sunderland would not return. He would, he declared, never more 'trouble myself, or anybody else, with public business'. For eighteen months (much longer than Somers expected) he immured himself at Althorp. Somers and his colleagues carried on without him—no easy task, for William was now more than ever convinced that the Whigs had 'a natural sourness, that makes them not to be lived with', and that as a group they were motivated only by self-interest. He did not trouble to conceal his lack of confidence in his ministers.[121]

The new session of Parliament found Somers for the first time able to participate in the debates of the Lords. Until his introduction as a peer he absented himself from the woolsack, Chief Justice Treby presiding in his stead. On 14 December he was installed, with the customary ceremonial.[122] The first debate in which he participated was on a bill requiring Members of Parliament—whether returned from county or borough—to possess landed property as a qualification, a precursor of the Tory Act of 1711. Such a restriction had been agreed upon by both Houses in 1696, only to be vetoed by the King, who did not wish to antagonise the merchants. It had then been proposed that knights of the shire should possess lands worth £600 a year; burgesses could qualify with half as much. The 1697 measure was similar, though it permitted a merchant with an estate of £5000, whether real or personal, to represent the borough in which he resided.

Somers joined in successful opposition. The nation, he contended, 'might reasonably be left to their freedom in choosing their representatives in parliament'. Was it not 'unjust and cruel' to prevent a poor man whose reputation might give him victory at the polls, and who could expect financial support from others, from taking his seat because of his small estate? Corruption in elections was to be feared from the rich rather than the poor, and in any case it was absurd that landed property alone should serve as the all-important criterion.[123] Such high-toned arguments cannot disguise the fact that his principal aim was to protect the Whigs from domination by a Tory squirearchy. His concern for electoral 'freedom' does not appear to have induced him to protest against the manipulation that was becoming increasingly common, save in a few instances where his own clients were affected. He could scarcely be expected to question managerial devices so effectually employed in the Junto's interest by his colleague Wharton.

Another Junto victory, which must have had some effect in soothing the King, occurred in connection with an attempted resumption of Crown lands. On 7 February the opposition undertook to bring in a bill revoking all such grants made since the Revolution.[124] This was a ticklish business. Tories and malcontent Whigs joined forces, as on the standing army issue, knowing that resentment towards Dutch favourites and hopes for lighter taxes would give them widespread support from the public. With a general election approaching it might be fatal to oppose the measure directly. Somers and his colleagues determined to kill the bill with kindness. They proposed to find no fault with it, except that it did not go far enough, and therefore sought leave to bring in supplementary measures designed to annul the grants made under Charless II and James II.[125] The shoe was now on the other foot, for most of these grants had been made to Tories, many to individuals whose claims to such generosity were, to say the least, unimpressive. This did the trick. The three bills, which were treated together, never became law. After suffering various mutilations, they were quietly put aside. Somers's Surrey holdings were safe. More important in the King's eyes, the extensive grants made to such favourites as Portland and Albemarle would remain in their hands.

In mid-February the King was reminded of his avowal to 'discourage Prophaneness and Immortality'. The Commons, calling for effective legislative restraints, asked that vice (particularly among those close to the royal person) be discouraged, and sought the suppression of printed matter containing 'impious doctrines' at variance with Christian orthodoxy.[126] Before the month was out the King had obliged with a proclamation; in the meantime the Lords framed a bill against atheism, sending it to the lower house on 26 February.[127] For some time there had been a growing popular reaction against the moral and religious laxness which had gained some vogue in the years following the Restoration. This contributed to the foundation of societies for the reformation of manners.[128] If, as Defoe wrote in 1698, immorality was 'without doubt the present reigning distemper of the nation', a goodly number of Englishmen were disposed to serve as physicians—or, it might rather be said, as surgeons, ready to cut the malignant growths from the body politic by sharpened laws and vigilante methods.[129]

However Somers regarded the new-found purposefulness of the legislators, there is no doubt that he was suspicious of the motives and activities of ordinary folk enrolled in the cause of reformation. Lacking the zeal of a reformer, he did not view the burgeoning crusade as a moralist, but as a minister of state, concerned with the maintenance of orderly government. And not only Somers, but the King and other royal advisers—not to mention Englishmen of lesser degree—were inclined to suspect that the new societies were not 'the heroic army that was to avert a divine judgment', but rather 'centres of sedition and enemies of the established order in Church and State'.[130]

The part played by Dissenters, in particular, bore watching. When Somers learned of a general meeting of their ministers and congregations, scheduled for Newbury late in June, he bade Vernon bring it to the attention of Shrewsbury, and the junior Secretary wrote accordingly:

It has been taken notice of for some time, that the independent congregations have formed themselves into a fraternity, begun at first for the management of their own societies; and they have since enlarged themselves by the addition of some others, who have associated with them under the pretence of a reformation of manners. They have appointed a general meeting, and there are besides several private cabals, and many discontented persons of all persuasions are endeavouring to herd among them.

The Archbishop of York feared they might have designs on the Church. Somers believed that they aimed rather 'at discrediting the administration, which they represent at atheistical, and designing to drive Christianity out of the world'. According to Vernon, William thought it of 'great consequence' to keep them under close observation. Somers agreed: 'the thing we would know is what discontented churchmen or discarded statesmen mean by insinuating themselves into their familiarities'. He suggested that one Griffith, an Independent minister with whom Shrewsbury had some influence, might serve as a spy and communicate with either himself or Vernon, preferably the latter, to avoid publicity.[131] This arrangement appears to have been followed. The matter soon blew over, as far as Somers was concerned. He had not become a persecutor of dissenters. If they offered no threat to the King's peace he had no quarrel with them, and would support them in the future as he had done in the past.

As usual the winter months found Somers pulled in three directions at once, torn between the Lords, the Court of Chancery and Whitehall. In January he took on an additional assignment as a commissioner of prize court appeals.[132] With increasing frequency he was handicapped or incapacitated with various ailments. Late in January he spent a long weekend at Mortlake in an attempt to shake off a cold. This appears to have done little good, for a week later he was house-bound with a sore throat. By mid-February he was out 'to take the air', and Vernon hoped he could 'fall to business'. He attended a cabinet meeting on 20 February, but a couple of days later he was again 'a little out of order'.[133] It is clear that he was physically run down, and could not find enough time to restore his health.

Nor did the Junto's relations with the King improve. This was largely due to the ambitions of Wharton. Shrewsbury had warned them to take a moderate course in order to alienate William no further. Although Wharton entertained both William and Shrewsbury in March, any good done by this was upset the following month when, at a meeting in Newmarket, the Whig chiefs insisted that Wharton and none other should succeed Shrewsbury as secretary. William now baulked at any further discussion of ministerial arrangements. For his part, he was already planning to bring the Tory Lowther (now Lord Lonsdale) back into his service, and, more important, was relying increasingly on Marlborough. In June the latter was appointed Governor of the Duke of Gloucester, Anne's eight year old son, and took his place in the cabinet. The King seemed prepared to break with the Whigs if there was any possibility of an alternative ministry. Sunderland remained in royal favour and, with his natural aptitude for political intrigue, was still a figure to be reckoned with. Despite the mauling he had received in Parliament, there was still the possibility that a party might 'establish themselves by his means'.[134]

During the latter part of the spring a project for a new East India Company was under consideration. Subject to much criticism, especially by interlopers who sought to gain profitable trading rights, the old company was in a precarious position. Early in 1698, as a means of maintaining its hold on the Indian trade, it had dangled before the government a loan of £700,000 at 5 per cent, only to be countered by a similar proposal from the London merchants, involving £2,000,000 at 8 per cent, which was sponsored by Montague, the First Lord of the Treasury. The House of Commons was almost equally divided on the matter, with some Whigs supporting the Tory opposition. It was largely Montague's managerial and forensic skills that won the day for the new company. But he had the full support of Somers, who a few years before had persuaded the King to impose new regulations, reducing the powers of the Governor, upon the Company.[135] Though a speech made by Montague late in May appears to have turned the tide, the outcome was unpredictable, and Somers worked to get the voters out. On 25 June he wrote to Wharton, who could be counted upon to support the measure, pointing out that the agitation against it was 'very great' and urging him to be present in the Lords when the bill would be taken up there. In the end it passed both Houses, receiving the royal assent in July. In according the London subscribers a monopoly of the East Indian trade until 1711, it gave the Whigs added support in the City and thus improved the position of the party on the eve of the general election. The success of the project, Somers believed, would 'make this session less burdensome to the body of the people, than could have been hoped for, by any other method'.[136] He looked for an improvement of Whig fortunes.

The forthcoming election, made mandatory by the terms of the Triennial Act, began to occupy his attention in the spring of 1698. By May he was discussing tactics with Shrewsbury. Charles Cocks was standing again for Droitwich. Shrewsbury, who was Recorder of the borough, agreed to support him, and worked with Somers to line up the electors. For the city of Worcester, they co-ordinated their efforts in supporting William Bromley, who had been elected with Somers in 1689 and 1690, and again in 1695, it being believed that he had 'by and large the greatest interest' there.[137] Somers was ready to follow Shrewsbury's lead with regard to the county; so, he reported, would other interested parties whom he had consulted in London. He ventured to suggest William Walsh, a political aide in Worcestershire, but with reservations: Walsh was 'very desirous to serve', but Somers thought he would be better advised to aim for a diplomatic post.[138]

As so frequently happened, Somers found it necessary to prod the Duke. Writing a few weeks later, he noted that good men were scarce and that time was of the essence, since Parliament might be called sooner than was expected. The King was inclined that way, and Somers agreed that it was probably advisable to have the writs go out quickly; otherwise the nation would be 'in a ferment all the summer' and the elections would be held 'at a time when the taxes are levying, and, perhaps, when there may be want of money to pay quarters'. A fortnight later he could report that the King had responded favourably to his suggestion that the elections follow immediately upon the dissolution of Parliament. As late as 5 July, when Parliament was prorogued, Shrewsbury was still holding back. But Thomas Foley told Somers that the Duke would propose two new knights at quarter sessions, to replace him and Edward Sandys. The Whigs, he complained, 'were setting up against him in Worcestershire'. This had a bearing on Charles Cocks, for if Foley could not be sure of the county he must oppose Cocks at Droitwich. Foley, of course, was anxious to avoid a contest for his Worcestershire seat. Somers, professing ignorance of Shrewsbury's plans and disavowing any intention to 'meddle' in the county election, decided to ignore Foley's threat. Cocks's chances at Droitwich appeared to be good.[139]

In Reigate, unlike Worcestershire, Somers could play a direct part in managing elections. Here, as lord of the manor, he shared political influence only with Sir John Parsons, a London brewer who had purchased the property once occupied by the ancient priory. A substantial man, Parsons rose to be Lord Mayor of London in 1703. Reigate was a burgage borough, one of forty-three then in existence. In such constituencies the parliamentary vote was still attached to 'ancient tenements' or 'burgages'—old and sometimes ruinous houses, shops, barns, and even gardens and cellars. These could be bought outright, and since the franchise was vested in their proprietors he who controlled them could count on political sway.[140]

After acquiring Reigate Somers lost no time in seeing that his friends and clients were well represented among the burgage-holders there. In 1716 his eulogist noted that 'several of his Lordship's Friends in Town, became Free holders in his Manor, as Mr. *Congreve*, Mr. *Tonson*, and others to strengthen that Interest against the Riotous Expenses, and Factious Cabals of his numerous Opponents'.[141] Shortly before the election of 1698 a large number of Reigate burgages were bought up by George Adney, Somers's secretary, who conveyed them to reliable hands. Tonson and Congreve (the bookseller and the dramatist), both friends and fellow members of the Kit-Cat Club, were but two of the new burgesses on whose votes Somers could count. The legal profession was particularly well represented. Sir Richard Holford, Master-in-Chancery, saw fit to invest, as did half a dozen members of the Middle Temple; there was also a scattering from other inns. One of the new burgesses was Henry Newton, of Doctors Commons, one of Somers's oldest friends; another was his brother-in-law, Joseph Jekyll; still another was Spencer Compton, the future Earl of Wilmington, a fellow Kit-Cat. There is perhaps no better roster of the men in whom Somers had confidence, and whose political orientation was closely aligned with his.[142] This careful political recruitment would pay off.

On 5 July Parliament was prorogued. Only one of William's Parliaments, the Convention, had gone so far into the summer season. It had been, as the King remarked, 'an intolerably long session, very embarrassing and difficult'.[143] Two days later it was dissolved by a proclamation which also made known the King's intention to issue writs for a new Parliament to meet late in August. William was impatient to be off for Holland, and departed on 20 July. Before leaving he set up his fourth regency commission, the first to be called upon to exercise peacetime functions, and now increased to nine members.[144] Again Somers was among them, along with such veterans as Archbishop Tenison, Devonshire and Pembroke. Dorset was back after having been omitted in 1697, Romney and Orford for the second time, but not Sunderland. There were two new members. One, Charles Montague, was to Somers a welcome recruit; the other, Marlborough, must have raised doubts in his mind.

Under the circumstances it was all the more important that the Whig chiefs should not lose credit with Shrewsbury. He still wanted to give up the Seals, but was held back by the King's attachment and his own inability to say no in a final and unequivocal way. Before William left for Holland Somers had spoken to him on the matter. The Duke, he pointed out, was aware that his secretaryship had continued 'too long already in the nature of a sinecure', that it should not be allowed so to continue for another winter, and that it might be impolitic to put off his resignation until William returned and a new Parliament met. But, he told Shrewsbury, he could get 'very little answer' from the King, perhaps because he did not wish to afford his Chancellor 'a pretence to have solicited for a disposal of the place'. Somers still hoped that the Duke might accept the White Staff. He also offered to employ his influence to obtain for him the proprietorship of New York, but Shrewsbury 'judged the thing improper' and so it was put aside.[145] He was inclined to urge him to accept the Spanish embassy, a post of considerable importance in view of the precarious health of King Charles and the international concern over the future of his domains. But he held back, reluctant to press him in a course to which he was averse, or that might prejudice his health—though he probably agreed with Vernon that with respect to the gout there was little difference between Madrid and Grafton. In any case Shrewsbury begged off. Wharton also refused the post; as late as mid-August the King was still seeking Somers's advice on filling it.[146]

By the latter part of July, and on into August, the parliamentary elections were in full swing.[147] Despite the Sunderland crisis and disturbing cleavages in the party, the Whigs had emerged from the session with more credit than could have been foreseen the previous winter. But, as Somers gloomily confessed later in the year, 'the elections were made on an ill foot'.[148] A restless spirit was abroad; and a 'most dangerous division of a Court and Country party'; people were 'tired out with taxes', and resentful of placemen and standing armies. There was many a hot campaign and many an upset.

Actually, Somers fared rather well. At Reigate, Parsons and his son

would have to make way for Stephen Harvey and Edward Thurland.
Harvey, a Middle Temple lawyer and something of a man of letters, was a
recognised client of Somers. He was steward of Reigate manor and lived
in nearby Bletchworth. Thurland belonged to an old family in the region;
his father was Sir Edward Thurland, Baron of the Exchequer. This was the
only time that Somers's influence prevailed in the election of both Members
for the borough; thereafter Parsons was invariably to hold one of the seats
until his death in 1717.[149] As for the Worcestershire front, Cocks 'won
handsomely' at Droitwich and Walsh upset Foley for a county seat.[150]
John Rudge of Worcester, a director of the Bank of England, was victorious
at Evesham. Though a Country Whig, Somers could count on his support.
At Tewkesbury careful groundwork had paid off. Somers had manoeuvred
to secure the office of High Steward, previously held by the pro-Junto Baron
Capel, for his nephew, Lord Essex. Essex had promised that 'no consideration of place or relation' would divert him from his uncle's principles, and
as Portland's son-in-law he could be expected to enjoy royal favour. In the
1698 contest Richard Dowdeswell, a steady Junto man, was returned.[151]
From Eye, in Suffolk, came more good tidings: the burgesses had chosen
Jekyll, Somers's brother-in-law, and Spencer Compton, both of them
Reigate electors. Clarke, as usual, represented Taunton. There were dis-
appointments, of course. Sir Thomas Rouse lost out for both Evesham and
Middlesex, Cary brought up the bottom of the poll at Bristol, and both
Gloucestershire Members were 'enemies'.[152]

As for the Whigs as a whole, and the collective Junto interest, the election was a serious reversal. For all Wharton's influence his candidates went
down in Buckinghamshire.[153] In the important Westminster election Montague and Vernon found the going rough against the persistent and indefatigable Sir Henry Colt. As the summer waned it became clear that in too
many constituencies the verdict had gone against the court. The new
Commons would be of a Tory, Country, complexion. 'Upon the whole
choice' Somers was apprehensive that it would be 'somewhat difficult to be
dealt with'.[154] His fears would all too soon be substantiated.

NOTES

[1] Locke MSS. c.7, f. 69; 'The dear bargain', in *Somers Tracts*, ed. Scott, x, 376; Ellis,
'Junto', 247–48.

[2] *Memoirs*, II, 534. In 1712 Defoe wrote: 'These Gentlemen had a double Appellation,
according as the People who spoke of them are to be understood, (viz.) The Tory Party,
and the Court, called them the Juncto, the Dissenters called them the Whig Lords';
The Conduct of Parties in England, 14. The terms 'Junctonians' and 'Summerian Whigs'
were also employed. According to Holmes the term 'Junto' was not applied until 1696;
before then and for some time thereafter they were 'Court Whigs,' 'Modern Whigs', or
sometimes 'Prerogative Whigs': *British Politics*, 14 and n., 494 and n.

[3] Ellis, 'Junto', 247.

[4] *Faults on Both Sides* (London, 1710), in *Somers Tracts*, ed. Scott, XII, 691.

[5] On management see J. H. Plumb, *The Growth of Political Stability in England, 1675–
1725* (Baltimore, 1969), 139; A. K. Powis, 'The Whigs and their relations with William III
in the period 1689–1698', unpublished M.A. thesis, University of London, 1948.

6 Plumb, *Stability*, 139.

7 In 1695 Somers's mother, noting that a neighbour was prepared to sell land to him, offered advice: Somers MSS., January 1695.

8 Luttrell, *Relation*, III, 223–24.

9 Hardwicke, *State Papers*, I, 429; *Cal. S. P. Dom.*, 1695, 329.

10 Add. MSS. 32, 095, f. 413.

11 Luttrell, *Relation*, III, 404, 408, 470; Nottingham Portland papers, Somers to Portland, 2 May, 11 June 1695. He was very ill in 1695, according to Henry Guy: Japikse, XXIV, 58.

12 *Cal. S. P. Dom.*, 1695, 333; 1697, 184; Luttrell, *Relation*, IV, 234; R. J. Kerr and I. C. Duncan, *Portledge Papers* (London, 1928), 260.

13 Somers MSS., Dr Hobbes to Somers, 5 August 1697.

14 The idea for a council of trade may have originated with John Cary, who corresponded with both men. There is a long letter from Cary to Somers in Hardwicke MSS., XXXIII, ff. 102–5, proposing such a scheme.

15 Locke MSS. c. 18, f. 161, and see Laslett, 'John Locke', 388. Locke had been secretary to the 1673 council of trade.

16 *Ibid.*, 381–82. Professor Robbins, in her *Commonwealthsman*, 62, includes Gilbert Heathcote, London banker and merchant, in the group. Another member was Richard Neville, M.P. for Berkshire: Locke MSS. c. 17, ff. 205–6, Popple to Locke, 2 March 1693. See also Cranston, *John Locke*, 386–87, 393, and above, pp. 98–99.

17 Laslett, 'John Locke', 389–90; D.N.B., William Popple (d. 1708); R. M. Lees, 'Parliament and the proposal for a Council of Trade, 1695–6', *Eng. Hist. Rev.*, LIV (January 1939), 49.

18 *Cal. S. P. Dom.*, 1696, 154.

19 See M. P. Clarke, 'The Board of Trade at work', *Am. Hist. Rev.*, XVII (October 1911), 20 and n.

20 *Works of John Locke* (London, 1714), III, 545.

21 Clarke, 'Board of Trade', 38.

22 Locke MSS. c. 24, f. 226.

23 *Ibid.*, f. 227, 1 February 1697.

24 Coxe, *Shrewsbury*, 400.

25 Add. MSS. 34, 515, ff. 6–8, 198–99.

26 See Horwitz, *Revolution Politicks*, 156.

27 Lord, *Poems*, VI, 519n.

28 Browning, *Danby*, I, 531 and n.; see also Kenyon, *Sunderland*, 277–78; Feiling, 321; Macaulay, V, 2602.

29 Goodwin Wharton claimed the credit for originating the Association of the Commons: MS. autobiography in Add. MSS. 20,006–7. C.J., XI, 466–67.

30 Browning, *Danby*, I, 532; 7 and 8 W. III, c. 27.

31 See Jennifer Carter, 'The Revolution and the constitution' in Geoffrey Holmes, ed., *Britain after the Glorious Revolution* (London, 1969), 41. About a hundred Tory M.P.s and some twenty peers refused to sign.

32 Ellis thinks that Somers did little more than provide information needed by the council and obtained from judges: 'Junto', 296, citing Hist. MSS. Comm., *Fitzherbert MSS* (London, 1893), 38–39). Glassey finds that he effected substantial changes, and in some cases a purge: 'Commission of the peace', 162 ff.

33 Hardwicke, however, did not 'recollect any thing amongst lord Somers's papers relative to this plot': Burnet, IV, 302n.

34 Macaulay, VI, 2644–46. Others named were the Earl of Bath, Lord Brudenell, Admirals Killigrew and Delavall, Generals Kirk and Tollemache, Brigadier Mayne and Commander Crawford: Oldmixon, *History*, 151–52, 156–57.

35 According to Bonnet, Somers urged Fenwick 'à faire une confession ingenue, et l'asseurant que quoy qu'il pût alleguer, l'on n'en tireroit point d'avantage contre luy': Add. MSS. 30,000 A, f. 256v.

36 Somers could take no direct part in this legislation, and his activities behind the scenes are not apparent. It was enacted as 7 and 8 W. III, c. 3.

37 Somers also urged Wharton to come to town; he was sure that his presence would be of service to Shrewsbury and Russell '& would assist in the governing of a thing which does very much concern them': Carte MSS. 223, f. 34. See also Somerville, *King of Hearts*, 126.

38 Coxe, *Shrewsbury*, 412.

[39] *Ibid.*, 414–15, 420.

[40] *C.J.*, XI, 579.

[41] *Loc. cit.* For details see Burton, *Political Parties*, 20–26.

[42] Coxe, *Shrewsbury*, 408.

[43] *Ibid.*, 420–22; *Buccleuch MSS.*, II, 421; *Letters Illustrative of the Reign of William III* by James Vernon, ed. G. P. R. James (London, 1841), I, 58–59.

[44] Burnet, IV, 334; *C.J.*, XI, 598; Rogers, *Protests*, I, 128–30; *L.J.*, XVI, 48, which gives forty-one as the number of protesters.

[45] Coxe, *Shrewsbury*, 436, states that the bill of attainder was 'accomplished principally by the spirit and activity of lord keeper Somers, and the Whig chiefs'. Ellis, 'Junto', 304–5, speaks of Somers as supporting his colleagues of the Junto 'in annexing—or rather by-passing—the law for frankly political reasons'.

[46] Thus on one occasion there was a meeting 'to hear what hath past in relation to Fenwick's examination and to resolve what is next to be done': Egerton MSS. 9086, f. 89; see also ff. 76v, 78v; *Vernon Letters*, I, 30, 33, 35, 42.

[47] Burnet, VI, 324.

[48] Coxe, *Shrewsbury*, 435.

[49] Burnet, IV, 334n.

[50] Coxe, *Shrewsbury*, 428.

[51] Shrewsbury was not present. Pembroke, Devonshire, Dorset and Godolphin voted against it: *State Trials*, XIII, 755–56; Coxe, *Shrewsbury*, 452. Somers thought Devonshire would support the bill: *Vernon Letters*, I, 73–74. There are division lists in L'Hermitage's dispatches, Add. MSS 17,677 QQ, f. 172, and (for the Lords) in Cobbett's *Parliamentary History*, V, 1154–55.

[52] Coxe, *Shrewsbury*, 429. Feiling's remark (*Tory Party*, 323), that Godolphin's ouster was 'rather improbably attributed to Sunderland' is unaccountable.

[53] Coxe, *Shrewsbury*, 415, 420, and see Hugh Elliott, *Life of Sidney, Earl Godolphin* (London, 1888), 182.

[54] Kenyon, *Sunderland*, 287.

[55] Coxe, *Shrewsbury*, 472.

[56] *Vernon Letters*, I, 149 and n.

[57] *Hist. MSS. Comm., Fourteenth Rept.*, iii, 132.

[58] Boyer, *William III*, III, 343.

[59] He became First Lord 1 May 1697; he had been Chancellor of the Exchequer since April 1694.

[60] *London Gazette*, 22 April 1697. For Somers's letter of thanks to William, see Ellis, *Original Letters*, 3rd ser., IV, 329.

[61] The *Post Man*, 24–27 April 1697, reported that Somers had been created 'Baron Esham'.

[62] See Manning and Brady, *Surrey*, I, 271–72, for a detailed description of the manor. Howleigh (Hooley) was located east of the town of Reigate; it included a residence called Hooley House, in 1702 the property of Robert Savage, yeoman. There was also an ancient priory, used around 1800 as a country seat, and pictured in *ibid.*, I, facing p. 294.

[63] *Ibid.*, I, 271, 283, 284; Hooper, *Reigate*, 32 and n. On 4 April 1717 the court was held in the names of Mary Cocks and Elizabeth Jekyll, and of their husbands. Mrs Cocks died late in 1717. Sir Joseph Jekyll appeared as lord of the manor at the next court, 28 April 1718, and continued as such until his death: Manning and Brady, I, 284.

[64] Somers MSS., Jekyll to Somers, 4 April, no year (o/1/15). Luttrell, *Relation*, II, 214 gives £900; the *Memoirs*, 42, 'not above £600'. Nash remarked of Somers, in connection with his impeachment, that his 'contempt for money' and indignation at the accusations against him led to his refusal 'to collect the chief rents at Reigate, by which many of them were lost to his posterity'. See H. L. S. Cocks, *Eastnor and the Malvern Hills* (Hereford, 1923), 253.

[65] But evidently there were some complaints: see *Vernon Letters*, I, 224.

[66] According to the *Memoirs*, 43, the others were Humphrey Hetherington, Richard Adney, Samuel Newton and Leonard Hancock. Only three (Hetherington, Adney and Newton) are mentioned in a report of the Commissioners of Accounts: *Lords MSS.*, 1712–14, X, 39.

[67] The Commons had unanimously protested against this alienation of a part of the principality of Wales.

[68] Nottingham Portland papers, Somers to William, 29 April 1697; Portland to Somers, 4 May 1697; Somers to Portland, 11 May 1697; *Vernon Letters*, I, 271–72.

69 *Ibid.*, I, 224, 237, 263.

70 *Portledge Papers*, 260; *Vernon Letters*, I, 259, 262, 278, 284; *Private Correspondence and Miscellaneous Papers of Samuel Pepys*, ed. J. R. Tanner (London, 1925), I, 142; Coxe, *Shrewsbury*, 483; Nottingham Portland papers, Somers to Portland, 25 June 1697.

71 Stowe MSS. 597, ff. 55 ff.: *C.J.*, XIII, 166. Assarts: lands cleared for cultivation; purprestures: encroachments on royal lands. On the Windsor rents, see Reports of Commissioners of Accounts (2955), *Lords MSS.*, 1712–14, X, 39.

72 A list of rents in the Somers MSS. (J/13) shows most of them eleven years in arrears in 1708—as long as Somers had held them.

73 Monmouth had been on sufficiently good terms with Somers to assist him in his translation of Demosthenes: Harold Williams (ed.), *Poems of Jonathan Swift* (Oxford, 1937), II, 397.

74 Coxe, *Shrewsbury*, 473. For these and subsequent machinations of Monmouth, see Somerville, *King of Hearts*, 132–34, 137–39.

75 *Memoirs*, II, 419.

76 Coxe, *Shrewsbury*, 410.

77 Ellis, *Original Letters*, 3rd ser., IV, 327–28. In the end Cook was banished.

78 So Ailesbury was told; in his opinion Somers was linked with the 'slaves of the Court': *Memoirs*, II, 426, 432.

79 The Somers MSS. include many letters from Capel to Somers on Irish affairs in 1695 and 1696. See also *Vernon Letters*, I, 146, 152.

80 Coxe, *Shrewsbury*, 456; A. D. Francis, *The Methuens and Portugal, 1691–1708* (Cambridge, 1966), 68.

81 Somers MSS., Rushout to Somers, 18 July 1696; Coxe, *Shrewsbury*, 463, 473–74. On Rushout's Worcester connections, see Oldfield, V, 249; Jones, *First Whigs*, 198n.

82 Boyer, *William III*, III, 242, and see *Vernon Letters*, I, 238–39. Methuen was appointed 11 March, but was removed 21 December 1697. Rushout died in 1698 before leaving England.

83 Coxe, *Shrewsbury*, 477–78.

84 *Ibid.*, 478–79. Yonge served as M.P. for Honiton (1678–81, 1690–1711) and for Ashburton (1689–90).

85 *Vernon Letters*, I, 256, where the name is given as 'Palmer'. Kenyon, *Sunderland*, 270, says Sunderland had a hand in recommending Palmes. Somers had importuned Portland in 1694 in connection with the appointment: Nottingham Portland papers, Somers to Portland, 14 September 1694.

86 For a detailed treatment, see Baxter, *Treasury*, 157–65; also *Cal. S. P. Dom.*, 1697, *passim*; *Vernon Letters*, I, 265, 275, 283, 288, 302; *Buccleuch MSS.*, II, 472–73. Because of illness Somers lost touch with the case; on 15 June he wrote to Shrewsbury that he did not know what had become of Palmes, adding that the matter 'might have been set right, without giving him any wound, or occasioning any loss to the king': Coxe, *Shrewsbury*, 485.

87 *Ibid.*, 172–73, 175–76.

88 *Vernon Letters*, I, 375.

89 Coxe, *Shrewsbury*, 176, 491–94.

90 *Ibid.*, 497, 500.

91 Kenyon, *Sunderland*, 293–94; *Vernon Letters*, I, 379–81.

92 But his opinion was solicited, along with Sunderland's, with regard to mentioning the King by name, as 'William the Third, King of Great Britain,' in one of the articles. They advised that such a course was 'of consequence for preventing future cavils': *Vernon Letters*, I, 87.

93 Grimblot, I, 137.

94 Cokayne, XII, pt i, 29.

95 Burnet, IV, 397.

96 *L.J.*, XVI, 174–75. Kennett, III, 740, notes that it was criticised for containing some expressions that were 'too magisterial'.

97 On this see E. Arnold Miller, 'Some arguments used by English pamphleteers, 1697–1700, concerning a standing army,' *Journ. Mod. Hist.*, XVIII (December 1946), 306–13; Lois J. Schwoerer, 'The literature of the standing army controversy, 1697–1699,' *Huntington Library Quarterly*, XXVIII (May 1965), 187–212.

98 Trenchard must not be confused with the Secretary of State of the same name, who died in 1695.

[99] The pamphlet may be found in *State Papers of the Reign of William III* (London, 1706), II, 585–89.

[100] Trenchard's pamphlet was entitled *A Letter from the Author of the Argument against a Standing Army, to the Author of the Balancing Letter:* Johnson's, *A Confutation of the Late Pamphlet Intituled, A Letter Balancing the Necessity,* etc.

[101] 'A false balance is an abomination to the Lord, but a just weight is his delight.'

[102] See Miller, 307.

[103] C.J., XII, 5. In committee Harley had proposed £300,000, maintaining that this, exceeding Charles II's 1680 establishment by £15,000, was a fair allowance. See Rubini, 140.

[104] The Whig ministers could not decide whether they should make an all-out stand for a sufficient army, or put their emphasis on the retention of foreign troops.

[105] Coxe, *Shrewsbury*, 504–5.

[106] *Vernon Letters*, I, 434.

[107] Somers regarded Lord Tankerville, a vigorous supporter of the government in the Lords, as Sunderland's candidate. Coxe, *Shrewsbury*, 505–6; Kenyon, *Sunderland*, 295–96.

[108] *Vernon Letters*, I, 448.

[109] Coxe, *Shrewsbury*, 510–12, 519, 521–23. Vernon agreed; to him the attitude of the Junto had been 'hostile and perhaps ill-judged, but not treacherous or even disloyal': Kenyon, *Sunderland*, 299.

[110] *Ibid.*, 301.

[111] *Ibid.*, 295, citing Turnbull's diary, 29 November, Downshire MSS.

[112] Coxe, *Shrewsbury*, 521–22. Somers feared that it would now be 'utterly impossible' for the King 'to transact any longer with our party'.

[113] *Ibid.*, 560; Baxter, *William*, 362.

[114] Grimblot, I, 181.

[115] *Vernon Letters*, I, 450.

[116] Grimblot, I, 147; *Parliamentary History*, V, 1168.

[117] C.J., XII, 132–33; L.J., XVI, 225, 235.

[118] *Vernon Letters*, I, 466.

[119] *Ibid.*, I, 470.

[120] See Grimblot, II, 80, where Tallard reports that the 'cabal' has declared that 'they could no longer take a part in his [William's] affairs' if the Earl of Sunderland either returned to office or resided in London: cf. Coxe, *Shrewsbury*, 541–42. According to Vernon, Somers was for an accommodation and thought it 'inconvenient to put it off to the end of the Session'. He feared that, with 'moles' working underground, new measures might be provoked, and that it would be bad to carry the problem over till the new session convened. But the King wrote to Portland late in February that the Whigs 'by no means desire the return of Lord Sunderland, and they make no mystery of it: he appears to have a mind to return': *Vernon Letters*, II, 16; Grimblot, I, 213.

[121] Coxe, *Shrewsbury*, 530, 549; Kenyon, *Sunderland*, 307. According to Methuen, Sunderland was (in May 1698) 'the only person to whom the king talks of business, or trusts in his affairs', what with Portland out of the country: Coxe, *Shrewsbury*, 538.

[122] L.J., XVI, 174 ff.

[123] Tindal, XIV, 373.

[124] C.J., XII, 90.

[125] *Ibid.*, XII, 99.

[126] *Ibid.*, XII 102–3; *Parliamentary History*, V, 1172–73.

[127] Steele, *Proclamations*, I, 507 (No. 4246); L.J., XVI, 217; C.J., XII, 132.

[128] For detailed treatment, see Dudley W. R. Bahlman, *Moral Revolution of 1688* (New Haven, 1957); Garnet V. Porteus, *Caritas Anglicana* (London, 1912); and see Tindal, XVIII, 433–34.

[129] *The Poor Man's Plea* (London, 1698), 2.

[130] Bahlman, 83.

[131] *Vernon Letters*, II, 128–29, 130, 133–34, 155–57.

[132] *Cal. S. P. Dom.*, 1698, 62.

[133] *Vernon Letters*, I, 485; II, 4, 20.

[134] Feiling, 329; *Vernon Letters*, II, 15.

[135] *Cal. S. P. Dom.*, 1694–95, 246, 297, 317; Coxe, *Shrewsbury*, 74.

[136] Carte MSS. 233, f. 54; Coxe, *Shrewsbury*, 539; C.J., XII, 331; L.J., XVI, 341, 343.

[137] Somers MSS., Shrewsbury to Somers, 11 May 1698; Coxe, *Shrewsbury*, 536–37.

[138] *Ibid.*, 541–42. Walsh was a member of the Kit-Cat Club. According to Ellis, 'he seems

originally to have been Shrewsbury's follower and to have transferred his allegiance to Somers after Shrewsbury's retirement overseas': 'Junto', 364n. On his services to Somers in Worcestershire, see Philip Styles, 'The corporation of Bewdley under the later Stuarts', *University of Birmingham Historical Journal*, I, (1947–48), 116.

[139] Coxe, *Shrewsbury*, 539–41.

[140] Walcott, *English Politics*, 14 and n. See also Oldfield, IV, 616, who writes (1816): 'the inhabitants of Ryegate have no more concern with the election of their nominal representatives than the people of Birmingham', noting that voting rights lay in about two hundred freeholds, nearly all the property of the Earl of Hardwicke and Lord Somers. Some had little value, apart from political leverage; see William Bryant's list of Reigate's burgesses (1786) in Surrey County Archives, 318/1.

[141] *Memoirs*, 42.

[142] For the complete list, see Bryant. Later others were added to the roster, among them the painter Kneller and Joseph Addison: Hooper, *Reigate*, 119–21.

[143] Hardwicke, *State Papers*, II, 358.

[144] *Cal. S. P. Dom.*, 1698, 368.

[145] Coxe, *Shrewsbury*, 180, 522–26, 538, 540, 549–50, 553.

[146] *Ibid.*, 541, 550, 553–54; *Vernon Letters*, II, 127–28, 132; Somers MSS., Alexander Stanhope to Somers, 28 July, 27 August (?), 5 October 1698; C.J., XIII, 492.

[147] On 12 July Somers wrote Wharton that he hoped to put the writs into the hands of the Sheriff of Buckingham within a day, adding that he need not be concerned with election expenses provided none were incurred thereafter: Carte MSS. 233, f. 70.

[148] Hardwicke, *State Papers*, II, 435.

[149] The arrangement is said to have resulted from a political deal regarding the mayoralty of London, wherein Parsons was induced by Somers to cast the decisive vote for Sir Thomas Abney, as opposed to Sir Charles Duncombe: *Memoirs*, 77–79. Speck, *Tory and Whig*, 121, lists Reigate among constituencies having one safe Tory seat in the period 1701–15, and notes (p. 130) that, with an early eighteenth-century electorate of 240, only fifty-five lived in the town. Ellis, 'Junto', 361 ff., has interesting detail on this election. The poll was close: Harvey, 120; Thurland, 119; Sir John Parsons, 111; John Parsons, 100; Bryant. See also Hooper, *Reigate*, 119–21; Manning and Brady, *Surrey*, I, 292.

[150] Coxe, *Shrewsbury*, 554; *Vernon Letters*, II, 152. The poll was 1400 for Sir John Packington, 1200 for Walsh, 693 for Foley: 'Members chosen to serve in the ensuing Parliament', Carte MSS. 233, f. 53.

[151] Hardwicke MSS., XXXIII, f. 61; Add. MSS. 34, 515, ff. 199–200; Nottingham Portland papers, Somers to Portland, 19 June 1696; Coxe, *Shrewsbury*, 539. Somers also appears to have used his influence to obtain the election of Richard Neville for Berkshire: Downshire MSS., I, 559.

[152] Elis, 'Junto', 369–70.

[153] *Vernon Letters*, II, 142; Coxe, *Shrewsbury*, 554. For a list of the old and new Commons, see Henry Horwitz, 'Parties, connections, and parliamentary politics, 1689–1714: review and revision', *Journal of British Studies*, VI (November 1966), 62–69.

[154] Coxe, *Shrewsbury*, 524.

VIII
Decline and fall, 1698–1700

The summer of 1698, with the nation no longer at war, found the Lords Justices' load lighter. Apart from naval preparations to counter supposed military designs of the King of Portugal, and the voting of a pension for Titus Oates, their business was largely of a routine character. Early in August they prorogued the new Parliament, scheduled to meet later that month, until 27 September.[1] For Somers there was no inkling of the difficult days that lay ahead. He took advantage of the lull to allow himself the longest vacation since he had assumed official duties. Chancery business occupied him until mid-August, but by the 19th he had left for Tunbridge Wells.[2] He was worn and spent. Late in July he had intimated to Shrewsbury that he looked forward to retirement; his health, he wrote, was 'so much impaired, that I must endeavour to recover it by some little retreat from my continued toil, at present, in hopes of an entire retirement to follow'. His 'strength of body and mind' were not up to the demands of the Chancery.[3] The change of scene and his 'course in spa waters' seem to have done him good. Early in September Vernon reported that he was looking very well, and planning to stay another fortnight. He did not return to London until 15 September.[4]

But even at Tunbridge Wells he could not escape the responsibilities of office. He had no sooner arrived than he was called upon to take part in the final stages of the long-projected Partition Treaty, designed to implement the liquidation of the Spanish Empire once the feeble Charles II should expire. Negotiations between England and France had been going on since March, when Portland had been sent to the court of the *Grand Monarque*; the following month Louis had dispatched Count Tallard to England. The English ministers had no part in these deliberations, and knew little about them. In foreign affairs, as in war, William saw fit to be his own minister, and he took only his Dutch favourites, Portland and the rising Albemarle, into his confidence. 'His chief characteristic is great distrust', remarked a French observer, 'so that very few persons, even amongst those who are in office, are acquainted with his secrets.'[5] Neither of the Secretaries of State was informed of what was going on. Orford, though head of the Admiralty, could write on 16 August that he knew of no provisions to take effect upon Charles's death—a neglect, he feared, that would 'prove very fatal to England'.[6]

About that time the ministers gained their first intimation as to the form the long-awaited treaty would take. Writing to Vernon on 14 August, Portland described the terms in a few terse lines:

The conditions are pretty near of this nature: that the Electoral prince of Bavaria shall have the kingdoms of Spain, the Indies, the Low Countries and all that depends upon the Spanish dominions, except the kingdoms of Naples and of Sicily, Sardinia, the province of Guipuscoa on this side of the Pyreneans, Fontarabia and St. Sebastian, Final and the places of Tuscany, of which Spain stands now possessed, in consideration of which France is absolutely to renounce the right it pretends to the succession of Spain. Milan is to be given to the Archduke, second son to the Emperor.

Since William was unwilling to 'enter too deeply into this matter without knowing something of their opinions in England', he commanded Portland to convey this information to Vernon, in order that he might discuss it with Somers.[7]

On the following day William wrote to Somers, pointing out that Vernon had been instructed to communicate only with him, and that he was to use his own judgement in discussing the matter with others. Besides secrecy, speed was of the essence—'according to all intelligence' the Spanish King could not outlive the month of October. If it should prove advisable to proceed with the treaty, Somers was to send on 'full powers under the great seal, with the names in blank'. Care was to be taken that not even the clerks should comprehend the nature of the document.[8]

Somers regarded it as 'very unlucky' that he should have left London with such consequential business afoot. He instructed Vernon to see that Orford, Montague and Shrewsbury were informed. These three, with the junior Secretary, could determine if others should be let in on the secret. Like William, he emphasised the need for secrecy; he was sure that nothing could 'be more ruinous than that such a negotiation should be in the least entertained, unless it were very probable to succeed'. The preparation of the necessary documents he left to Vernon. He was willing to come to town on 26 August, and thus save Orford and Montague the troublesome journey to Tunbridge. But Vernon wrote that they had 'too great a consideration for him' to interrupt his cure, and saw no reason for it.[9] So Somers remained at Tunbridge. Montague, along with Vernon, joined him at the spa.[10]

On 28 August he was able to report their reactions to the King. In view of the attacks later made on him for his part in this transaction, the points in his letter deserve close attention. Though the question of Louis's good faith had naturally occurred to them, they had put it aside, assured that the King 'would not act but with the utmost nicety in an affair wherein the glory and safety of Europe were so highly concerned'. They deferred, too, to William's judgement that it was important, in view of France's military might, to make some provision for the Spanish domains before Charles's death. But they sounded a note of caution on the morale of the English people:

So far as relates to England, it would be want of duty not to give your Majesty this clear account, that there is a deadness and want of spirit in the nation, universally so, as not at all to be disposed to the thought of entering into a new war, and that they seem to be tired out with taxes to a degree beyond what was discerned, till it appeared upon the occasion of the late elections; this is the truth of the fact upon which your Majesty will determine what resolutions are proper to be taken.[11]

Turning to specific provisions in the treaty, Somers raised some doubts regarding the disposition of territory. Would not Sicily in French hands make them 'entirely masters of the Levant trade'? And if the French should possess Finale and other western ports, shutting off Milan from access by sea, might not that duchy 'be of little signification in the hands of any prince'? Fears were also expressed that by Pyrenean gains the French king would be able to invade Spain more easily. While no one could expect that France would 'quit its pretences to so great a succession without considerable advantages', he was confident that William would hold out for as moderate terms as possible. He hoped that England might secure some commercial advantages from the treaty:

If it could be brought to pass that England might be in some way a gainer by this transaction, whether it was by the Elector of Bavaria (who is gainer by your Majesty's interposition in this treaty), his coming to an agreement to let us into some trade to the Spanish plantations, or in any other manner, it would wonderfully endear your Majesty to your English subjects.

As for the enforcement of such a treaty, Somers and his colleagues were obviously worried. Was France alone to be entrusted with it? If so, how could one be sure that she would not overstep the bounds of the agreement?[12]

The overall reaction of William's English advisers can only be described as unfavourable. We may discount the dutiful expressions of confidence in the King's diplomatic grasp and good intentions: what remain are doubts, warnings, objections. But Somers and the rest had been consulted too late. They probably realised that things had gone too far for them to exercise much influence on the outcome. They were aware of Charles II's precarious hold on life, of the political vacuum his death was likely to create, and of the forces that could rush in to fill it. They were fearful that France might sweep all before her. To put things off might prove fatal, nor could they be sure that a delay would result in more acceptable terms. For William—none knew this better than he—was handicapped in diplomacy by the military weakness of his island realm. The land force of the 'Balancing Letter' did not exist.

And so the ministers took no stand against the treaty, but salved their consciences by noting its defects, and hoped for the best. Somers concluded his letter by apologising for any delay that his absence from London had caused. Blanks, as William had requested, were left for the names of the commissioners, who, Somers suggested, should be Englishmen or at least naturalised English subjects. Vernon had supposed that he might be averse to affix the Great Seal without a royal warrant, and had called this to Portland's attention. But Somers did not insist on such authorisation. By 28

August the commission was sealed 'in such manner that no creature has the least knowledge of the thing', save for the handful who had discussed it. Somers must have sealed it himself. In so doing he issued a blank cheque to any commissioners William might appoint to conclude the negotiations, either on the terms which had been proposed or on others which circumstances might dictate. The King naturally employed Portland as one of the plenipotentiaries, and chose Sir Joseph Williamson as the other. Under their auspices the treaty was signed in September.[13]

Somers now received a blanket warrant, regularising his action with regard to the commission and directing that the Great Seal should be affixed to two ratifications of the treaty, as well as to several secret articles related to it. These articles were designed to fortify the pact in case of the death of the Electoral Prince without heirs, or of the ailing Prince Vaudemont, who governed Milan for Spain. Of the English ministers only Vernon and Somers were supposed to have knowledge of them. The Chancellor complied with the warrant. With this, his part in implementing the treaty was accomplished. In the interest of secrecy he saw to it that neither it nor the commission was enrolled in Chancery, and advised delay in informing the Emperor of its contents.[14]

He could not foretell that within a few months it would be invalidated by the death of the Electoral Prince, and that he would be called upon to authenticate a second treaty.[15] He may have foreseen how his political enemies would use the negotiations against him. But he could hardly have anticipated or comprehended the strictures of Victorian historians who labelled his conduct as unconstitutional.[16] This it was not, however inexpedient and ill-advised it may have been. Though connected with a ministry which, in its relationship to Parliament, has been called England's 'first real cabinet',[17] collective responsibility of ministers belonged to the future. Somers had broken no law in following royal instructions, though he appears to have strained correct procedure in not insisting on the identity of the commissioners.[18] The conduct of foreign policy, like war, was still a sport of princes, even in England, and it is safe to say that no minister or Member of Parliament possessed the knowledge of continental affairs that William had acquired through years of painful experience. Somers was in no way obligated to secure a broader consensus; secrecy and dispatch, as the King made clear, had been the order of the day. As for the treaty itself, it was unthinkable, once it had been worked out by Portland and Williamson, that the Privy Council or any other English agency should nullify it. These men were, after all, plenipotentiaries. To suggest that, once Somers saw that his opinions would be disregarded, 'it was his duty to resign' ignores the political realities of the age. It probably would have been a good move, but duty was not involved, unless self-preservation be regarded as such.[19]

The King did not return until early December. For the most part domestic affairs were in a state of suspended animation, awaiting that event and the debut of the new Parliament, successively postponed over the months. It would prove troublesome to Somers. But long before it met anxieties began to crowd in upon him. For one thing, Captain William Kidd, a naval officer whom Somers (among others) had dispatched to make war on sea raiders had himself turned pirate. More disturbing at the time were signs that the Junto might disintegrate, or at least lose influence. It was bad enough that Shrewsbury was edging towards retirement. But his usefulness had been diminishing for some time. Far worse was the strategic retreat of Montague: unlike Shrewsbury he was a key figure in the ministry and the House of Commons, and a Junto man through and through.[20]

Early in September Montague secured from the Treasury Board the Auditorship of the Receipt, recently vacated by the death of Sir Robert Howard.[21] The office was highly desirable, being worth at least £4000 a year. As First Lord he could not hold it himself, but bestowed it upon his brother, Christopher. This decision was taken without consulting Somers or the other ministers, or even making application to the King. It was, without doubt, an insurance scheme: Montague was looking out for his own interests in view of the uncertain days that lay ahead. Though he did not resign as Chancellor of the Exchequer until the following spring, and as First Lord for over a year, the handwriting was on the wall; Vernon, at the time, spoke of the financeer's resolution to quit these places.[22] His friends, mollified by the promise that he would not immediately withdraw, rallied to support him, and the King was induced to confirm the appointment. But Somers had deep misgivings:

The business of Mr. Montague gives me great disquiet. It was done much on the sudden, without the advice or knowledge of many of his best friends. I wish it may turn out well for himself, but I do not see how it can turn out well for the public.[23]

For 'the public' we may read 'the Whig party', though the First Lord's financial skill had, for the most part, proved a boon to the nation as a whole. Somers's concern was well-founded. Montague had made new enemies by beating out other contenders and had shaken the confidence of his adherents. Whether the step materially affected his parliamentary influence is hard to say, but we can agree with Macaulay that the 'flinching of the captain, just on the eve of a perilous campaign, naturally disheartened the whole army'.[24]

Nor was James Vernon's conduct regarded as impeccable. As the opening of Parliament approached, the appointment of a Speaker became a lively issue. The results of the elections made the choice of a Tory a distinct possibility. Paul Foley, Speaker in the late Parliament, was in failing health, and was too Whiggish in his sympathies for many Tories. They were therefore on the lookout for a new candidate to oppose the Junto's able friend, Sir Thomas Littleton. A few days before Parliament assembled, Vernon fell under suspicion for caballing with the Tory leaders. He was still regarded as to some extent Sunderland's man, and Littleton was notoriously hostile to Sunderland. Somers did what he could to smooth things over with the Whigs. He conceded that the 'more than ordinary familiarity' between the Secretary and the Tory leaders gave cause for concern, but assured them that 'there was no umbrage to be taken at it'. He told Vernon that he would be his 'compurgator as to Sir Thomas Littleton', and offered to do whatever the Secretary thought best to remove the 'jealousies' that had arisen. In the end his representations and Vernon's endorsement of Littleton's qualifications cleared the atmosphere. Somers, he reported

> took occasion to tell my Lord Orford and Mr. Montague, how instrumental I had been in the accomplishment of their desires, and gave me a larger share of it than I pretended to, whereupon the tide turned immediately, and I was loaded with compliments, and assurances of friendship.[25]

Littleton's appointment, a few days later, ended the incident. Somers had rendered valuable assistance as a conciliator.

The new Parliament finally met on 6 December. It was now clear that the ministry could no longer count on a majority. Harley's country party had gained added influence, linked as it was with the adherents of Rochester and Nottingham. No one knew what Sunderland might do. As yet this master politician had not recruited a following, but Somers was apprehensive. His only comfort lay in the disunity of the Tories: 'Were not the difficulty equal, in finding a number of Tories, capable of uniting, I take it for granted, the Whigs would, long since, have been laid aside.'[26] In any case, careful management was essential.

The Members took their seats in a somewhat irritable mood. The opening of Parliament had been fixed for 29 November, which was unusually late, but the King's continued absence (due to adverse winds) forced the Lords Justices to prorogue it for yet another week. The delay, during which the Members cooled their heels, gave ample time for reflection on their sovereign's partiality for Holland, a subject that always rankled. But, to begin with, things seemed to go well for the government. Littleton was chosen Speaker despite Edward Seymour's impassioned objection to calling a courtier to the chair: the Tories had no candidate. The address from the throne, which Somers as usual composed, was favourably received. It underscored, first, the importance of a decision regarding the requisite military and naval forces for the nation, and second, the need to reduce the debt incurred through the recent war. In addition William called for the provision of employment for the poor, the framing of 'some good Bills for the Advancement of Trade', and the 'further discouraging of Vice and Profaneness'.[27]

William had confessed to Heinsius that he had 'every reason to be afraid as far as the troops are concerned'. Events proved that he was right. He was probably thinking in terms of a force of 20,000, but, Vernon reported, 'I am afraid there is no great disposition in the House to allow of more than 10,000 men, if they can now be brought to it'.[28] This was an understatement. To the Commons the foreign situation wore a peaceful aspect.

The old fears, real or fancied, of a military establishment had not been allayed. Besides, here was a stick with which to beat the government. They proceeded to use it. Seven thousand men would suffice for England, less by a thousand than had been countenanced the previous winter. Ireland was to be allowed 12,000. To this end a bill was introduced by Harley, tacked to a supply measure to insure its passage in the Lords.[29]

The ministry found itself in a difficult position, and not only because of parliamentary recalcitrance. William was of little help. For one thing, he had shut his eyes to the limitations of the previous session, save in so far as he evaded them by sending part of the foreign troops to Ireland. And now, despite his consuming desire to maintain a substantial force, he continued his distant treatment of his ministers. While they wrestled to work out a compromise, he did not even specify the number of troops he hoped to keep in arms. The success of the Whigs in securing the Speakership for Littleton, on the other hand, strengthened his hope that the ministry could pull his chestnuts from the fire. Somers did not conceal his misgivings from Shrewsbury:

I should tell your grace, that, upon a meeting with Mr. Secretary, lord Coningsby, and divers others of the House of Commons, we are all agreed in an opinion, that this business of the army could not be carried higher than 10,000, and that with the utmost difficulty, and not unless the country gentlemen would enter into the debate, which they would never do, unless it might be said to them, that it would be an acceptable service to the king, and that he would make the best of that number.[30]

In other words, the opposition, opposed as it was to any increase of the forces, would certainly not yield to the proposal, modest as it was, unless it could be presented as carrying the royal approval—and perhaps not then. But the King was adamant. 'When this was told him,' Somers reported, 'he was very much dissatisfied'; rather than agree to a proposal he could not embrace 'he would leave all to Providence'.[31] But here providence was not on William's side. On 18 January the Commons—ignoring a rider that, in addition to the 7000 men, the King might retain his beloved Dutch Guards, numbering 2500—passed Harley's bill and sent it to the Lords. Although 132 Whigs voted against it, the ministry had proven impotent; from the day of Harley's fateful motion it had been unable to seize the initiative.[32] The King was resentful and disgusted; even before the end of December he was blaming his ministers 'for their easy giving way' and nursing thoughts of abdication.[33]

The bill still had to pass the Lords. There Somers and Wharton might exercise a direct influence. According to Bonnet the King summoned the Chancellor on 28 January and spent five hours discussing what action should be taken.[34] But there was little hope. 'Some of the House of Lords have a great mind to oppose it,' Vernon wrote, 'but I suppose they will well consider before they come to a rupture with the House of Commons on so ticklish a point.' He read the situation correctly. Apart from the strong determination the Commons had shown for reducing the forces, the measure was regarded as a money bill; the Commons 'would be jealous of the Lords mending it under any pretence whatsoever'.[35] Curiously enough, it was the Tories—Leeds, Normanby, Rochester—who were expected to oppose it as an attack on the privileges of their chamber, while Somers now gave it his support. It was not that he approved of it; the author of the 'Balancing Letter' still believed in the necessity of an adequate standing army and criticised the bill as endangering the national security. But what useful purpose could be served by its rejection when financial support for any force, regardless of size, could come only from the lower house? Anything, he argued, was preferable to a bitter conflict in which King and Lords would find themselves embroiled with the Commons. Supported by Lord Tankerville, who contended that the King would gain more by conciliating his subjects than by securing additional troops, he was at his best.[36] The House was convinced; the bill was passed without a division. It was, on Somers's part, a demonstration of political courage and good sense: no easy course to take, what with the King's sensibilities to be considered. William rose to the occasion. He cloaked his bitter frustration, accepting the measure in good part with remarks cast in the English tongue by Somers, but suggesting that a compromise might be worked out whereby he could retain the Dutch Guards.[37]

Somers's contribution to parliamentary co-operation was accompanied by a service in the interest of the regime itself. The favourable reception of Harley's motion had so disillusioned the King that he talked of abandoning the government and returning to Holland. In a letter to Heinsius late in December he hinted that an 'extreme course' might take him to The Hague sooner than he had expected.[38] When Somers learned of this he at first regarded it as mere bluff, 'meant for an appearance only, and to provoke us to exert ourselves'. But a few days later William convinced him that he was in dead earnest. His plan was to go before Parliament and tell them that since he saw that they were 'entertaining distrusts and jealousies of him', and neglecting to take necessary steps for their own self-preservation, he was determined to leave the country. Before departing, he would consent to any arrangements they might make for appointing parliamentary commissioners to take over the government.

Somers was aghast at the suggestion, and could hardly contain himself as he remonstrated with the King:

When he first mentioned this to me, I treated the notion as the most extravagant and absurd, that was ever entertained, and begged him to speak of it to nobody, for his own honour.

For two hours he strove patiently but in vain to dissuade him. He discovered that William had unburdened himself to Montague, Orford and several others, including Marlborough, a particularly foolhardy confidence in Somers's eyes because of his close association with the next in line, Princess Anne. The Chancellor returned to the charge several times, but the King was not to be swayed. He refused to permit further discussion of the subject, telling Somers plainly that he 'was resolved'. In desperation, Somers played his final card, putting his own office to hazard:

I told him, I hoped he would take the seal from me, before he did it; that I had it from him, when he was king, and desired he would receive it from me, while he was so.[39]

It is difficult to judge the King's seriousness of purpose. To renounce a crown that he had worn for a decade, to dissociate himself from a realm whose resources had proved so valuable in his great contest with King Louis: it is almost impossible to take such threats at face value. On the other hand, who can weigh the effect of disillusionment, poor health and the strain, if not loneliness, of a life among foreigners?[40] Whatever the answer, Somers's efforts did not go for nought. Sham or real, the crisis passed. The farewell address was never delivered; William remained in England as her King.

The King's acceptance of the disbandment measure, for all his good grace, did not produce a more amenable legislature. And the following months witnessed a progressive weakening of the Junto. Somers managed to escape personal attack, though there had been rumours in December that an impeachment might be launched 'on Kidd's account'. But the other members of the triumvirate, Orford and Montague, were not spared. Late in December Vernon noted that 'Lord Orford grows weary of being the mark, of being so often shot at, and talks of quitting as soon as he has justified himself.'[41] But his roughest treatment lay ahead. On 29 March the Commons framed an address on the corruption and inefficiency of the Admiralty, one clause of which declared that his dual role as First Lord and Treasurer was 'inconsistent with the service'. In the end an unvarnished demand for his removal was defeated by but four votes. He had survived by a hair's breadth, but it was obviously impolitic for him to continue in both offices. Here a decision was not easy, for while one was more honorific the other was far more lucrative. The Admiral's disposition, naturally peppery, was not improved by this dilemma, and he became an increasingly disgruntled colleague.[42]

As for Montague, whose successes in the last Parliament had done so much for the Junto, his influence was greatly diminished. Furthermore, his appropriation of the auditorship for his brother had won him the bitter emnity of Leeds, who claimed a reversion of the place to his son, and who sought revenge by launching a parliamentary inquiry into the enforcement of an act of 1695, by which Members of Parliament had been prohibited from farming or collecting any tax. In the end Christopher escaped the net, but it could not have been a comfortable experience for the Montagues. Nor could the Whigs ward off a Commons inquiry into grants of forfeited Irish lands, which, despite royal assurances in 1691 that they would not be made until Parliament had formulated a policy, had been extensively bestowed on William's servants and friends. Here Somers must have been touched upon, if only because of the nature of his office, but there is no evidence that he was singled out for attention. It was disturbing, however, that of the seven commissioners selected, four were connected with the opposition; one, the violent Trenchard, had been Somers's antagonist in the standing army controversy.[43]

However unsettling these attacks, Somers showed little inclination to retire. As colleagues moved partially or completely off the political stage, he went about his business.[44] But he had admitted, when Parliament convened, that there was 'no face of government', and conditions had not improved.[45] By early March Vernon had written Orford off; Somers and Montague were still called ministers, but he could see none 'who take upon them any management'.[46] The French ambassador agreed: in domestic affairs all things were 'at a stand', with nothing decided 'but by Act of Parliament'.[47] The King was restive; he expressed concern that the new Commons was endangering his position as well as the Junto's. To bolster up sagging party fortunes Somers again turned to Shrewsbury, who was persuaded to see the King at Newmarket. There he agreed not to withdraw from politics altogether, and William asked him to try to make peace between the Junto, Sunderland, Godolphin and Marlborough.[48] This was no easy task: it would take time, if it could be done at all.

But William was impatient to be off to Holland, and determined to leave behind him a more effective administration. On 4 May he prorogued Parliament, and within a fortnight had turned to the Tories for three appointments. The Earl of Jersey took Shrewsbury's secretaryship, vacant since December. Leeds finally retired, 'Long Tom' Pembroke taking his place as Lord President. Pembroke's Privy Seal was given to Lord Lonsdale. All three were moderates, unexceptional men, but undistinguished. The Tories could rejoice, but it was a makeshift, patchwork arrangement.

Even as the ministry was being adulterated, its old Whig core, the Junto, was further diminished. Late in March Somers thought that Orford's 'mortifications, this session, in both Houses, are got pretty well over', and could hope that he would rest content with his First Lordship. But the Admiral was no sooner free from castigations of the Commons than he became involved in a bitter dispute over his right to determine the composition of the Board of Admiralty, an issue which gave new life to an ancient feud with his professional rival, Sir George Rooke. On 15 May, while Somers, along with Shrewsbury and Montague, was seeking to effect a compromise, he tendered his resignation, and this without any consultation with his colleagues.[49] Before the month was over he was replaced by the Earl of Bridgewater. In the same month Montague took another step towards retirement, stepping down as Chancellor of the Exchequer. It was not unexpected, but it was a blow nonetheless.[50] Even at court the old associates were disappearing. Portland, resentful of the new-found favour of Albemarle, gave up the Groomship of the Stole. Somers had had his difficulties with Portland, but at least he was a Whig: Albemarle was inclined to favour the Tories.

There were various appointments to be worked out before William departed for Holland—chiefly seats on the Treasury and Admiralty Boards, as well as the Board of Trade, and Irish posts. Troubled by Orford's retirement from the Admiralty, Somers hoped that Lord Tankerville, a staunch supporter of the government, might be pressed into service. Tankerville shied off: 'he would rather', he said, 'be drawn through a horse-pond before he would take that employment'. But he was willing to take the second Treasury seat. Since the Earl of Jersey was now Secretary, a new governing commission for Ireland had to be worked out. Berkeley, who had introduced Somers as a peer, took his place. Galway and the Duke of Bolton, both sound Whigs, stayed on, Somers seeing that the latter, a useful Junto associate, received a lord lieutenancy as well as the wardenship of the New Forest. He also saw that Lord Stamford, 'who began to show himself very dogged for his being neglected', gained a seat on the Board of Trade; his parliamentary influence was not to be ignored.[51]

As usual, the commission of Lords Justices was not announced until the eve of William's departure. Again it was made up of nine members, and again, while Archbishop Tenison headed the list, Somers was the effective president. The veterans Pembroke and Devonshire, who had served on all previous commissions, were reappointed; Marlborough and Montague, first named in 1698, were also back. But the recent ministerial changes brought three new members to the body: Lonsdale, Jersey and Bridgewater. As a result, the board had a more Tory complexion that had ever been the case.[52]

It was to be another quiet summer, so much so that Somers appears to have taken little part in their counsels. It was just as well. The strain and disappointments of recent months had taken their toll. The usually self-possessed Chancellor, Vernon reported, was 'more out of sorts than he would let appear'.[53] For the first time, so it seems, he was keeping to himself. Chancery business had to be attended to, of course. But once the term was over, he withdrew from the capital. Vernon hoped that he might join Shrewsbury at Bath: 'I think those two meeting would be of more significance than if half a dozen more were added to them.'[54] As it turned out, he journeyed in mid-August into Cambridgeshire where, along with Montague and several other 'persons of note', he visited the Earl of Orford. One can imagine the licking of wounds and laying of plans that took place. He then moved on to Tunbridge Wells, rather than Bath, and there he remained for over a month. He was not without company: Treby was there and 'many persons of quality'. The waters seemed to benefit his health. Back in London on 27 September, he took some time to get back into harness. 'I think my Lord Chancellor has seen very few since he came to town,' wrote Vernon. He excused himself from meeting with the Lords Justices on the 26th, but a couple of days later he was again holding his levees, and on the 30th sat with them for the first time.[55]

For the second time that year attention was focused on Anglo-Spanish relations. Late in May, along with other cabinet members, Somers had joined with Scottish officials to examine the circumstances of the Darien project.[56] This ill-fated venture, which had aroused such enthusiasm in Scotland as a means whereby a great trading base could be established on the Isthmus of Panama, had naturally evoked sharp resentment in Madrid as an unwarranted trespass, not to speak of deep misgivings in English commercial circles. Now the grievance, involving the conduct of the Spanish ambassador, the Marquis de Canales, was on the other foot. In September the Marquis had addressed a public protest to the Lords Justices regarding William's involvement in the partition arrangements, and was threatening to appeal to Parliament. Such conduct was regarded as insupportable. The Justices, acting on William's orders, proceeded to expel the high-handed diplomat. It was Somers who worked out the terms of the message of dismissal, following precedents of Charles II's reign.[57] Apart from this, and the examination of some Irish officers, who had returned from France and 'talked big, as if their day were a coming', there was little that required the Chancellor's attention.[58] Even the burden of Chancery business was unaccountably light.

The King returned on 20 October, an unprecedentedly early date. It was believed that this might contribute to better public relations, and even William dared to hope that the new session of Parliament would be more harmonious than the last.[59] Somers was not optimistic. Late in September he told Vernon that he hoped the King 'would keep himself upon the defensive' at the opening of the session, 'and not propose anything for angry people to lay hold of, who watch for such an occasion'.[60] But in his opening speech William turned at once to the unfinished business of the first session, calling for further provision for the national security by land and by sea, and the discharge of the war debts. He regretted 'the necessity of so often asking aids', but assured the legislators that nothing was for his personal use, or would be diverted from its designated purpose. He concluded with an appeal for co-operation: 'Since then our aims are only for the general good, let us act with confidence in one another.'[61]

But it soon became apparent that the new session was likely to prove as troublesome as the last. On 28 November the Commons, sitting as a committee of the whole on the King's speech, showed that they had not forgotten old grievances and were prepared to entertain new ones. They called for marks of royal displeasure against those who misrepresented the proceedings of the House; they wanted a committee to look into charters granted during the reign, and another to inspect the commissions of the peace.[62] Somers was specifically mentioned; it was increasingly clear that he stood in jeopardy. Vernon realised this, although at first he thought he would 'not be hurt'. On 29 November the faithful, some twelve or fourteen strong, caucused at Powys House to discuss the general situation and, in particular, the projected Commons investigations. 'I think', Vernon wrote, 'it was rather to show we should stand by one another, though there was nothing said of it.'[63]

The charters and commissions were but the beginning. If Vernon had any illusions about Somers's position, by 2 December they had evaporated.

'It is now plain', he observed, 'that my Lord Chancellor is aimed at, with a great deal of bitterness.' For on the previous day the Commons, in a debate staged ostensibly for a discussion of trade, turned their attention to piracy, and particularly to Captain Kidd. Kidd, it was alleged, had 'plundered with a commission under the Broad Seal in his pocket, and was encouraged to it by those who were in partnership with him, and had obtained a grant of all he should steal'.[64] A tremendous furore was generated; in Tallard's words, 'Jamais affaire n'a fait plus de bruit'. What, asked Howe, 'would become of this nation, if those in authority were not content to plunder and sweep away by grants all that could be got here, but likewise sent out their thieves to rifle whatever was to be met with elsewhere?' A political lampoonist took up the theme more pointedly:

> The Earth's my own, I give it as I please
> And to my Vice-Roy K--d, I gave the Seas.

Musgrave, a fierce Tory, urged that the perpetrators not be spared should the allegations be proved.[65] In the end the Commons ordered that Kidd's commission should be laid before them, as also the grant to the subscribers, together with complaints about his activities that had been made from time to time by the East India Company. Any defence of the subscribers' conduct would have to wait until these documents had been produced.[66]

Somers was in an awkward position. He had affixed the Seal to Kidd's commission. With piracy so prevalent, the practice of empowering private or semi-private agencies to suppress it was not uncommon. In the *Memoirs* Somers's eulogist points out how under James II a 'creature' of Somers's enemies, Sir Robert Holmes, had procured a similar grant, 'wherein not only all Pyrates Goods, but even Bona Depredata were granted in express terms'.[67] Somers's embroilment in the Kidd affair went back to 1696. At that time piracy had reached such proportions that a counter offensive was called for. The normal procedure would have been to dispatch warships, as was done in 1699 when Somers formalised various commissions authorising captains 'to fight and seize all pirates in the seas of India or elsewhere'.[68] In 1696, however, no funds had been available for this purpose, and the King called upon private enterprise in a way reminiscent of Elizabethan days. Subscribers were asked to contribute to the undertaking, and in return, with some reservations for the Crown, could reap whatever harvest there might be. William himself promised £3000 (which in the end was not forthcoming); Somers contributed £1000; Shrewsbury, Romney and Montague £500 each, not to mention others.[69] Accordingly, the *Adventure Galley* was fitted out and her command given to William Kidd, a naval officer of good reputation.[70] Kidd sailed out of Plymouth with the usual commission to 'sink, burn and destroy pirates', but once in distant seas he succumbed to the temptation of plunder and turned pirate himself. At length, after an encounter with an English frigate, he was captured and eventually brought home in irons. He did not reach England until the spring of 1700, but his exploits had been well publicised before Parliament met.

On 3 December another meeting was held at Powys House, attended by Orford, Montague and Vernon, among others. There they discussed the problem, deciding what papers they should hold in readiness and in general planning their defence. Somers was opposed to any delay 'in owning who they were that fitted out the ship, and what they paid towards it'—a position deemed prudent in view of the publicity the venture had already received. The House of Commons might thereby be convinced that all had been above-board from the beginning. But Vernon feared that, whatever the outcome of the inquiry, Somers might be driven beyond endurance, might be so 'teased and baited' in Parliament that he would seek withdrawal from public life.[71]

The Commons returned to the charge on 5 December. An angry debate ensued. Vernon had made sure (doubtless following instructions at Powys House) that they would have before them documents proving that, as soon as Kidd's conversion to piracy became known, orders had gone forth to seize him and convey him to England. But these were grudgingly accepted: they 'had a mind to pass their censure only on the grant that was previous to all this'. Howe was not to be placated. After a 'warming speech' he moved that the grant be declared illegal, a motion supported and refined by Harley. But Montague, Smith and other Whig stalwarts called for a scrutiny of all the papers before the question should be put, and the House voted without division that this course be followed in a committee of the whole. It was clear to Vernon, however, that the opposition, if it could, 'would lay the sole blame of the grant on my Lord Chancellor'.[72]

The debate on the following day lasted from noon until nine in the evening. Vernon had been right: much of it was a direct attack on Somers. He had authenticated Kidd's commission: surely the Captain's bad character must have been known beforehand. Even more objectionable was the order that virtually all goods that fell into Kidd's hands were to go to those who had subsidised him, Somers among them. The Crown, it was alleged, could not bestow the rights to such booty in advance to individuals. The Old East India Company interest, bitterly anti-Whig, took up the hue and cry with a vengeance, charging that Kidd had seriously damaged the Company's remaining trade and its relations with the Great Mogul. The judges, on the other hand, came to Somers's aid. In the past, they advised, the Lord High Admiral had possessed a right to all goods taken from pirates. But now there was no holder of this office; consequently the right had lapsed to the Crown, which might do with it as it would. The frankness of the interested parties turned out to be a good tactical move. As the Commons heard the names of Shrewsbury, Romney, Orford and Bellamont, they drew back somewhat, fearful of offending at one fell swoop so many magnates of the realm. Some insisted that the House should 'censure miscarriages wherever they were to be found'. But Cowper turned this aside: 'as nobody ought to be influenced by great names, so neither should there be any envy or prosecution against men because they were great'. They, like all others, 'ought to have their actions weighed in equal balances'. And so, in the end,

Somers was justified. The Commission was declared, by a vote of 189 to 133, not to be illegal. The majority of fifty-six was thought by Vernon to be 'no small matter as this House is constituted', and he was probably right.[73]

It was a vindication of the Chancellor's judgement, rather than a vote of confidence. Among the opposition a good many did not stay the course, but 'slipt away', apparently unwilling to vote on a doubtful point of law. Perhaps, had the attack been more restrained, some sort of censure would have resulted; some were 'offended at the heap of enormities that were charged upon the grant'. This had been done deliberately, so Vernon thought, with a view of bringing the Chancellor down. The manoeuvre had backfired, 'the two houses being juster than to be led blindly by other men's passions'. But the episode revealed that hostility to Somers, first manifested in the previous spring, had not cooled over the summer. It had grown more determined and rancorous, and its professors, baulked in this encounter, would neither forget the Kidd affair nor let slip other opportunities to discredit the Chancellor.

Such occasions presented themselves during the winter months. The long deferred problem of the forfeited Irish lands now received full-scale attention. Since the last session public opinion had been further aroused by Charles Davenant's *Discourse upon Grants and Resumptions*. The author, a bitter foe of the Junto,[74] set out to show how ministers who had procured Crown revenues for themselves had been dealt with in the past, and argued that the forfeited estates should be applied towards payment of the public debt. No mention was made of contemporary figures, but the reader could recognise Somers in Ranulf Flambard, Portland in Gaveston and Montague in Jean de Montaigu.[75] A reply, *Jus Regium*, a defence of the King's right to dispose of Irish forfeitures, as well as other revenues, appeared in 1701. The authorship is uncertain; it has been attributed to Somers, but also to Defoe.[76]

On 15 December the House heard the report of the investigators appointed the previous spring, and on the same day resolved that a bill should be introduced applying the Irish lands to the use of the public.[77] In other words, the extensive grants made by the King should be expropriated and disposed of anew for the benefit of the English taxpayer, at the discretion of thirteen trustees owing their appointment to Parliament. The Christmas recess delayed deliberations, but with the return of the legislators early in January the fat was in the fire. Lords and Commons, Whigs and Tories, clashed with almost unprecedented rancour in a contest that was not resolved until April, and that brought in its train threats and attacks on the responsible ministers. On 18 January the Commons resolved:

That the advising, procuring, and passing the said Grants of the forfeited and other Estates in Ireland, hath been the Occasion of contracting great Debts upon the Nation, and Levying heavy Taxes on the People; and, That the advising and passing the said Grants is highly reflecting on the King's Honour; and the Officer's and Instruments concerned in the procuring and passing these Grants have highly failed in the Performance of their Trust and Duty.[78]

This reprimand, which struck squarely at Somers, was conveyed to the King in mid-February. In a terse reply, probably composed by Somers, William touched briefly on the sense of obligation that had led him to reward those who had assisted him in the reduction of Ireland, and went on to suggest that the Commons were neglecting their duty in not providing supply. But this merely provoked the retort that 'whosoever advised it, had used his utmost endeavours to create a Misunderstanding and Jealousy between the King and his people'.[79]

A week earlier the Commons, in endeavours to discredit the ministers, had ventured beyond the issue of Irish lands. A resolution was framed to the effect that the procuring of a grant of any Crown property by a minister concerned with its implementation, for his own benefit, while the nation was at war, 'was highly injurious to his Majesty, prejudicial to the State, and a Violation of the Trust reposed in them'.[80] Here was a more useful handle. Somers and most of his colleagues had not benefited from the Irish grants. But English grants were another matter. Somers had received Reigate and had been promised the fee-farm rents well before the war came to an end at Ryswick. As early as December 1699, Vernon had expressed concern that the Junto's foes would attack Somers for his Windsor grants, as well as Orford and John Smith for the advantages they had obtained or sought.[81] That a man raised to the dignity of the Seal required a peerage, and that, in most cases, some endowment was called for; that the office was precarious and, once lost, rarely reassumed; that an ex-Chancellor was, in effect, debarred from returning to the private practice of law as a livelihood—all these considerations were put aside. Doubtless the substantial pension appeared to be more than adequate to most country gentlemen.

But Somers's account was far from bankrupt. His enemies were simultaneously impelled by hostility and restrained by fear. They hoped to become strong enough to carry an address against him, but were 'apprehensive of miscarrying in it'.[82] It is significant that in the debate on 13 February neither the Chancellor nor any other minister was singled out by name; the opposition sought to arouse mistrust but avoid the risk of rebuttal on specific charges. But the reference to Somers was obvious, even to the densest Tory backbencher. Sir Rowland Gwyn, a stalwart Whig, was not deceived. 'Why this reserve?' he inquired. 'Everybody knows your meaning. Everybody sees that you have not the courage to name the great man whom you are trying to destroy.' A heated debate ensued. Somers's defenders now exerted themselves, taking a line they had not dared to use for some time. Gone was the silence, the inertia, which had too often, of late, characterised the Whig benches. The Tories fell back, amid protests that they had no intention of attacking the Chancellor. Even Howe hedged: 'My Lord Somers is a man of eminent merit, of merit so eminent that, if he had made a slip, we might well overlook it.' He had, according to report, no personal dislike for the Chancellor; it was, rather, that 'the applause he has from his party will lead him in any thing they are fond of'.[83] The House sat until a late hour. At last the question was put. It failed to pass by a majority of fifty in a division of over four hundred members.[84] It was hard to remember when there had been so large an attendance.

It was a victory for the court interest, and a testimonial to Somers's reputation and influence, but scarcely a comfortable margin of security.[85] There had been talk of impeachment in some quarters. Somers found the uncertainty trying. He wished his opponents would produce specific objections against him, and thought it 'much the most uneasy condition to have their accusations kept in suspense'. Vernon was not sure what Somers would do if this situation continued; there were rumours that he would resign, but others said he would not 'gratify his enemies so far'.[86] He had recently suffered the judicial rebuff of having his decree in the Bankers' case, which he defended before the Lords, decisively overturned by that body.[87] It was worrisome, too, that the Kidd affair could not be laid to rest. There were indications of a desire to renew the investigations; in March the King complied with the Commons' request that Kidd should not be 'tried, discharged or pardoned until the next session of Parliament', and that the Earl of Bellamont should transmit to them all papers relating to the case. While this was perhaps indicative that the opposition lacked adequate grounds on which to base a successful attack, it was nonetheless disconcerting.[88]

By the end of the month Somers talked of resigning. As if he was not sufficiently badgered, the unaccountable Peterborough (the Mordaunt of earlier days) was still vengefully working to discredit Shrewsbury, and Orford as well, and was angry that Somers was not disposed to co-operate.[89] Peterborough, he confided to Vernon, was very ill-natured. But, he added cryptically, 'there were others as bad as he': he could tell an extraordinary tale of 'very barbarous contrivances' against him. Vernon thought he referred to Lord Sunderland, for one, though he had never heard the Earl speak of Somers but 'with great esteem for his abilities', and believed that the Chancellor was deceiving himself. But there was no doubt of his low state of mind: 'The Lord Chancellor seemed very weary of continuing under these agitations, and said people could not be more desirous of his quitting, than he was to gratify them in it.' Would he have the resolution to 'bear up against this constant baiting?' His friends felt called upon to remind him that resignation would be looked upon as an admission of guilt.[90]

Deliberations on the Forfeitures Bill were to some extent delayed by preoccupation with another issue directly affecting Somers. His appointments to commissions of the peace were sharply attacked. As has been shown, the Tory grievances on this score went back to the early days of his authority, and had been heightened by the part he had played in implementing the Association of 1696. In 1699 the Tories were again complaining that he had made 'a partial and undue Distribution' of the commissions, and the following spring included among their grievances his use of the Seal to discharge justices of the peace and fill their places with less substantial persons.[91] It was further alleged that in his charge to the J.P.s he had called upon them to disparage the existing Parliament, as being so opposed to the government that it had undermined the credit of the nation by its refusal to grant supply, and had gambled with its very security by reducing the military establishment. But, as Burnet wrote, 'a clamour and murmuring was all that could be raised'.[92] Bigger guns would have to be fired to bring the Chancellor down.

From the beginning of the session Somers sat regularly on the woolsack, not missing a meeting until mid-January, when he was absent for three days. According to tradition he was so mortified by his reversal in the Bankers' case that he never presided in the Lords thereafter. This is untrue; through the rest of January and all of February he was constantly on hand. In March, however, he was absent half the time. He occupied the woolsack for the last time on 28 March, save for a brief appearance on 1 April for the purpose of commissioning the Earl of Bridgewater in place of Treby. Physical rather than political discomfiture probably accounts for his absence. By his own testimony he was too ill for business. According to Vernon he was suffering from a cold and 'advised to take a little country air'; Bridgewater was expected to take his place for the week.[93] In any case he took no direct part in the inter-cameral struggles over the final form of the Irish Forfeitures Bill.

This measure, as it emerged from the Commons, went beyond earlier specifications. All grants made since 1685 were at one stroke invalidated and placed at the disposal of the trustees. Informers were encouraged by the prospect of rewards to disclose grants which for some reason might remain undiscovered. From the findings of the trustees there was to be no appeal. Finally, to apply the utmost pressure on the House of Lords, the provisions were tacked to the land tax. Opposition in that chamber was inevitable. The peers had but recently bowed to the tacking device; to do so again, at least without a struggle, would bring their house into contempt. They did not object to reappropriation in principle. But they moved to curtail the powers of the parliamentary trustees; in particular they altered passages by which they were vested with property never forfeited to the Crown, or never alienated by it.[94]

Somers's absence notwithstanding, he was accused of being responsible for these amendments, which the Commons found entirely unacceptable.[95] They were in a fever of excitement as they inveighed against such obstruction. The Lords had no right to amend money bills; they must either accept the measure or, by rejecting it, leave the nation beggared and underdefended. 'They object to tacking, do they?' exclaimed one member: 'Let them take care that they do not provoke us to tack in earnest. How would they like to have bills of supply with bills of attainder tacked to them?' It was, the Dutch ambassador believed, a direct attempt to intimidate the Chancellor. But Somers, at the time, indicated his disapproval of the peers' resistance. The Lords had to give way. On 10 April they passed the measure 39 to 34, the Earl of Bridgewater continuing as deputy on the woolsack.[96] The alternative seemed to be a dissolution, and cooler heads, at least, realised that this would be but to jump from the frying-pan into the fire. For it would never do to make the bill an election issue: public opinion, which was severely inflamed, was far too favourable towards it. The Commons had on 8 April ordered the printing of all important documents relating to the matter, thus carrying the dispute to the electorate.[97] Who could tell what a new and perhaps even more Tory chamber might propose?

But if, in their retreat, William and the peers thought that the pressure against Somers would be withdrawn, or at least lessened, they were sadly mistaken. The Commons, as they awaited the Lords' action, had continued to pillory the Chancellor. At the head of the pack, Sir Edward Seymour had named him as 'one that was more to blame than all the rest'; he went on to reflect on his judgement in the Bankers' case and to accuse him of Hobbism in religion.[98] Somers could only decry his harsh treatment: it would be 'better to live in Poland than in this country'. Vernon now thought he had no intention of retaining the Great Seal.[99]

With Irish forfeitures out of the way, the Commons could bring their attacks closer to home. On 8 April they had resolved 'that the procuring or passing exorbitant Grants, by any member now of the Privy-Council, or by any other that had been a Privy-Councillor in this or any former reign, to his own use or benefit, was a High Crime and Misdemeanour'. They also referred in a general way to their need to secure themselves 'against an ill ministry, and the influence of foreigners'.[100] But they were aiming chiefly at the Chancellor, and the mention of his name produced a long debate. One after another of the leading Tories spoke against him. His grant was called exorbitant, his ministry 'partial and offensive'. They blamed him again for unsatisfactory answers from Kensington, and for the recent opposition of the Lords. Godolphin declared that the incompetence and negligence of persons recommended by Somers for the customs service had cost the kingdom £20,000. But he had his defenders. Sir Walter Yonge proved loyal. Godolphin, he said, was merely piqued that his own nominees had not won out in the scramble for office. William Cowper made 'a very handsome defence'; Lord Hartington and Henry Boyle also spoke in his behalf.[101]

At length John Leveson Gower, one of the most acrimonious of the Tories, along with Simon Harcourt called for his impeachment. Had the Commons then known of Somers's participation in the Partition Treaties (the second of which he had validated that very winter) they probably would have embarked on once upon this course. But these transactions were not revealed for another year. As it was, the more prudent members shunned a procedure which would call for charges sufficiently precise and demonstrable to hold good in a court of law. They fell back on Musgrave's motion 'that an Address be made to his Majesty, to remove John lord Sommers, lord chancellor of England, from his presence and councils for ever'. Once more the moderates rallied, and when the House divided the motion was lost, 167 to 106. Many who had supported the Forfeitures Bill would have nothing to do with this proposal. Some, expecting the Chancellor's early retirement, thought the address unnecessary. And so the hue and cry died down, for the moment, the House contenting itself with an address to the King that no foreigner except Prince George should be admitted to his councils, either in England or Ireland. It had been a long day; the Members had sat by candle-light until ten.[102]

For Somers a battle had been won. But no one could tell what new campaign might erupt on the morrow. The House would doubtless find other amunition. Captain Kidd was expected momentarily, and, while it was perhaps too late in the session to undertake a full scale parliamentary investigation, his presence in England might give a new handle to the Chancellor's foes. Somers had concurred with Orford and Vernon that, as far as possible, the arch-pirate should be kept under wraps. They wanted to have him examined by the cabinet, then committed to the Marshalsea. But the Commons had other plans. Harley warned against allowing the examination to be conducted by any who 'were suspected as an accomplice of the crime'. He was supported by Musgrave, who proposed that if Parliament were sitting when Kidd arrived he should be brought to the bar of the Commons; otherwise the examination should be undertaken by the Admiralty. Although Kidd was in the Downs by 11 April, Parliament was prorogued (until 23 May) that very day. Three days later he was brought before the Admiralty; there it was decided that he should be kept close prisoner until Parliament sat again.[103]

Somers was disturbed by this turn of events and blamed Vernon for contributing to it. The Secretary, he felt, had been far too obliging in furnishing whatever the Admiralty required in the case; he should have held back in the hope that the cabinet might gain the advantage of conducting the examination. In any case, he should not have allowed a packet of letters from Lord Bellamont to be sent to the Lords of the Admiralty. When Somers learned that his own secretary had been called upon to be present, in the expectation that the packet would be opened, he was highly incensed, regarding this as an 'unheard of indignity to one of his character'. He refused to participate in these proceedings, or to allow his aides to do so.[104] Yet, as he admitted to Montague, on the whole things did not go badly. The story Kidd told squared with the version given to the House of Commons. He produced a 'plain account' of the cost of fitting out the ship and the identity of its owners, noting that he had been once with Romney, oftener with Orford, but had never seen either Somers or Shrewsbury.[105]

But would the King retain him in office, and was he willing to remain?[106] These were the questions which set the coffeehouses buzzing and were thrown back and forth wherever politicians gathered. Clearly, some changes were in the offing. The Tories were optimistic. A new day was predicted for Leeds, Rochester, Godolphin and even Sunderland.[107] The King, though he had never been so disgruntled with his English subjects, was aware of the need to court Tory opinion. It was clear that the cashiering of Somers would go far to placate that party. During the struggle over the Forfeitures Bill it had been suggested that the Tories might be willing to drop the measure if the Whigs were ousted. Rumour had it that Lady Orkney, once William's mistress, who had a sizeable vested interest to consider, had been sounding them out regarding their position on the lands if Somers could be deprived of the Seal. And there had been a hint, at least, that William, if assured of £200,000 from the lands, might dismiss his Chancellor.[108]

This would mean dropping an experienced pilot, but one who had obviously lost much of his effectiveness. Somers was aware of his diminished usefulness. He was, he told the King on several occasions, becoming 'a weight on public business'. The French ambassador believed that he wished to retire, and that it was William, and William alone, 'qui le retenu jusqu'à cette heure'. But he continued to look upon voluntary retirement as a confession of guilt; he would relinquish the Seal only at the King's command. He was following for himself the advice he had given Shrewsbury, Orford and Montague. And it seems he had not lost the will to govern. He feared the uses the Seal might be put to in other hands. With royal support, a shuffling of the ministry, and perhaps a new Parliament, he might still be useful, even influential.[109]

Among those who believed that Somers was not yet to be written off was that master of political manoeuvre, the Earl of Sunderland.[110] Although he had crossed swords with the Junto in the past he insisted throughout 1698 and 1699 that any scheme of government in which he might participate would have to rest on an alliance between the King, Shrewsbury and the Junto. But the remodelled ministry must include some Tories, and particularly Robert Harley, who headed the 'new' or moderate wing of the party. Shrewsbury lent assistance, both in making peace with the Junto and negotiating with Harley. It was not easy to overcome Junto suspicions, especially those of Orford and Wharton. Somers, tracked by Shrewsbury and Montague to Tunbridge Wells, apparently pledged his support. Meanwhile Sunderland's credit with the King was rising. In January William asked him to invite Harley to form a coalition ministry with Somers, along with Marlborough and Godolphin. The project had much to recommend it. The Tories were disunited, with no 'Junto' of their own to give political direction. Harley was the only opposition figure with sufficient ability and influence to form a ministry. It might be viable, if properly shorn up. But it was not to be. Harley baulked at joining a ministry not of his own choosing; William would not give him a free hand.

By the end of April Somers was out of office. On 25 April he went to Hampton Court, where he sat, as Lord Chancellor, with the Council for the last time. On the agenda was a matter of particular concern to him: the personnel of commissions of the peace. Pursuant to the address of the Commons, the King had already removed several justices and deputy lieutenants. Somers discovered that the Council had in its hands a list of all the justices, with a view to making further alterations. No longer could the Whigs expect to control this important agency of government.[111]

On the following day Somers was called upon by Lord Jersey, who requested the surrender of the Seal. The King had finally made up his mind. He would seek to establish a more harmonious relationship with Parliament by dismissing this personification of Whiggery. In the King's eyes an act of resignation would have been preferable. But to this Somers remained opposed. There was a day's delay while Jersey obtained the necessary warrant. Somers was well aware that his hour had come; he had already called upon Powys to sit for him in Chancery.[112]

NOTES

[1] Luttrell, *Relation*, IV, 408, 414–16; L.J., XVI, 346.

[2] *Cal. S. P. Dom.*, 1698, 379, 381.

[3] Coxe, *Shrewsbury*, 551, 553.

[4] *Vernon Letters*, II, 173. Vernon saw him on 16 September and wrote: 'I think he looks very well, but he says he found himself better the first fortnight he drank the waters, than he has done since': *ibid.*, II, 176.

[5] Probably the Abbé Renandot: Grimblot, II, 191.

[6] Coxe, *Shrewsbury*, 552.

[7] Japikse, XXIV, 88.

[8] Grimblot, II, 121, 129–30.

[9] *Ibid.*, II, 131; *Vernon Letters*, II, 155.

[10] Japikse, XXIV, 90.

[11] Grimblot, II, 144.

[12] *Ibid.*, II, 145.

[13] *Ibid.*, II, 134, 146, 156; Add. MSS. 40, 772, f. 15, Somers to Vernon, 22 August 1698.

[14] Japikse, XXIV, 102 ff.

[15] See below, pp. 176–77.

[16] See, for example, Campbell, V, 123; Lodge, 419–20. Macaulay makes no comment on constitutionality.

[17] Ogg, *James II and William III*, 337.

[18] And possibly in not effecting enrolment; see Roberts, *Responsible Government*, 312. But a few years later Somers assured Bishop Nicolson that before he became Lord Chancellor there were no treaties registered in Chancery after that for Dunkirk: Nicolson MS. diary (Tullie House, Carlisle), 1 November 1705.

[19] But cf. Chester Kirby, 'The four lords and the partition treaty', *Am. Hist. Rev.*, LII (April 1947), 477–90, especially p. 487.

[20] For Somers's high opinion of Montague as a political manager, see Christian Cole, *Memoirs of Affairs of State* (London, 1733), 22.

[21] On this office, see Baxter, *Treasury*, 125–28.

[22] *Vernon Letters*, II, 166, 170.

[23] Coxe, *Shrewsbury*, 560.

[24] Macaulay, VI, 2874.

[25] *Vernon Letters*, II, 221–22, 225.

[26] Coxe, *Shrewsbury*, 560.

[27] *Vernon Letters*, II, 230; L.J., XVI, 352.

[28] Grimblot, II, 210; *Vernon Letters*, II, 230.

[29] C.J., XII, 361; cf. *Vernon Letters*, II, 236.

[30] Coxe, *Shrewsbury*, 566, 571, 573.

[31] *Vernon Letters*, II, 240–41.

[32] C.J., XII, 440; Henry Horwitz, 'Parties, connections, and parliamentary politics, 1689–1714; review and revision,' *Journal of British Studies*, VI (November 1966), 57; Browning, *Danby*, III, 213–17.

[33] *Vernon Letters*, II, 241.

[34] Add. MSS. 30,000 E, f. 25, 30 January 1699.

[35] *Vernon Letters*, II, 252, 255.

[36] *Ibid.*, II, 257; Turberville, 197–98. L'Hermitage, in his dispatch of 31 January 1699, reports that Somers's speech received 'un applaudisement general': Add. MSS. 17,677 TT, f. 83.

[37] Bonnet reported that this speech was apparently the result of the five-hour conference of 28 January: Add. MSS. 30,000 E, f. 29, 3 February 1699.

[38] Macaulay, VI, 2866.

[39] Coxe, *Shrewsbury*, 572–73.

[40] Rubini, p. 146, suggests that 'part of William's design was perhaps to make sure that

the ministry would do its best out of fear of what the commons would do to them after the king left'.

[41] *Vernon Letters*, II, 233, 241.

[42] *Ibid.*, II, 273. The vote on Orford was 164 to 160.

[43] *C.J.*, XIII, 66. See *Parliamentary History*, V, 1202–3, for an abstract of the commissioners' report.

[44] But in April he presided over the Lords on but two occasions, Treby serving as deputy. Ill health was probably the reason, though we hear only of a bout with rheumatism late in the month. He laid the blame on the troublesome trials of Warwick and Mohun: these, he told Shrewsbury, had almost killed him. The Lords appear to have recognised the pressure of business under which he laboured; he was named to but one committee, dealing with problems of the woollen industry. See *L.J.* XVI, 404, 441 ff.; Luttrell, *Relation*, IV, 511; Coxe, *Shrewsbury*, 582.

[45] Hardwicke, *State Papers*, II, 435–36.

[46] *Vernon Letters*, II, 268.

[47] Grimblot, II, 316.

[48] Coxe, *Shrewsbury*, 582, Kenyon, *Sunderland*, 311.

[49] Coxe, *Shrewsbury*, 579, 583. Orford had not concealed his intention to resign, should he not get his way.

[50] *Ibid.*, 584; Grimblot, II, 322.

[51] *Vernon Letters*, II, 287, 296, 298, 300; *Cal. S. P. Dom.*, 1699–1700, 212; Speck, *Tory and Whig*, 70. Stamford became President of the Board.

[52] *Cal. S. P. Dom.*, 1699–1700, 208–9. Those replaced were Dorset, Orford and Romney.

[53] *Vernon Letters*, II, 287. In June Lord Abingdon defeated Somers for the High Stewardship of Oxford and Wallingford: *Wiltshire Archaeological and Natural History Magazine*, XLVI, 76–77; *Portland MSS.*, III, 605.

[54] *Vernon Letters*, II, 295, 330; Nottingham Portland papers, Vernon to Portland, 1 August 1699.

[55] Luttrell, *Relation*, IV, 549, 563; *Vernon Letters*, II, 354–58.

[56] Luttrell, *Relation*, IV, 521; *Vernon Letters*, II, 297.

[57] *Vernon Letters*, II, 359–60. See also Luttrell, IV, 566–67; Gromblot, II, 351, 354–56; Ogg, *James II and William III*, 452. The case referred to was that of Don Bernardo de Salinas.

[58] *Vernon Letters*, II, 363; Luttrell, IV, 581.

[59] Grimblot, II, 361.

[60] *Vernon Letters*, II, 359.

[61] *L.J.*, XVI, 476–77; Grimblot, II, 379.

[62] *Ibid.*, II, 382; Luttrell, IV, 587; *C.J.*, XIII, 8.

[63] *Vernon Letters*, II, 368–70.

[64] *Ibid.*, II, 371–72; P.R.O. 31/3, bundle 184, f. 552v.

[65] *Vernon Letters*, II, 372–73; *The Triumph of the Great L–d S——* (London, 1701).

[66] See *C.J.*, XIII, 10, and 11–36 for the documents.

[67] *Memoirs*, 89. The East India Company was to petition for similar powers in 1700: P.R.O., P.C. 1/54, 25 April.

[68] *Cal. S. P. Dom.*, 1699–1700, 278; see also p. 398 (8 December 1699).

[69] This according to Graham Brooks, *Trial of Captain Kidd* (London, 1930), 12; but L'Hermitage says he contributed £500: Add. MSS. 17,677 ww, f. 204v.

[70] On Kidd's character, see 'A Full Account of the Proceedings in Relation to Capt. Kidd', *Collection of State Tracts* (London, 1705–7), III, 233. Burnet points out that Somers 'understood nothing of the matter, so that he never saw Kid, only he thought it became the post he was in, to concur in such a public service': IV, 423.

[71] *Vernon Letters*, II, 373–74.

[72] *Ibid.*, II, 375–76.

[73] *Ibid.*, II, 378–81.

[74] Somers had made at least one attempt to get Davenant a place at court, but was unsuccessful: Nottingham Portland papers, Somers to Portland, 19 June 1696, where he describes him as 'a very honest usefull Gentleman'.

[75] See Davenant's *Political and Commercial Works* (London, 1771), III, 199–203, 250–51. Montaigu was *surintendant des finances* to Charles VI of France. He accumulated a great fortune, but was accused of malversation and executed in 1409.

[76] It is attributed to Somers in D.N.B. (John Somers) and in Lord, *Poems on Affairs of*

State, VI, 328n. It is not included in John Robert Moore, *Checklist of the Writings of Daniel Defoe* (Bloomington, Ind., 1960).

[77] *C.J.*, XIII, 66–67; *Parliamentary History*, V, 1202–3.

[78] *C.J.*, XIII, 130.

[79] *Ibid.*, XIII, 228.

[80] *Ibid.*, XIII, 208.

[81] *Vernon Letters*, II, 398.

[82] At least, so Vernon believed: *ibid.*, II, 425.

[83] Macaulay, VI, 2956–58; *Vernon Letters*, II, 425

[84] *C.J.*, XIII, 208. The vote was 232 to 182.

[85] Bonnet refers to 'l'estime generale' in which Somers was held: Add. MSS., 30,000 D, ff. 51–59.

[86] *Vernon Letters*, II, 411, 425–26.

[87] *L.J.*, XVI, 499–501; Luttrell, *Relation*, IV, 606.

[88] *C.J.*, XIII, 286, 297; *Vernon Letters*, II, 428. Richard Coote, first Earl of Bellamont, as Governor of New York, had arrested Kidd. He and Somers were on friendly terms.

[89] See Coxe, *Shrewsbury*, 596–98, for details, including a letter from Somers to Shrewsbury dated 16 December 1699. In addition Somers was being 'pressed' by the Bishop of St David's for a writ of error, in order that the Lords might review his sentence of deprivation for simony and extortion: *Vernon Letters*, II, 441, 445, 450; Luttrell, IV, 617.

[90] *Vernon Letters*, II, 416–19, 446; Burnet, IV, 445. On Sunderland's professed desire to come to terms with the ministry, and especially the Chancellor, see Coxe, *Shrewsbury*, 595.

[91] Bonnet in Add. MSS. 30,000 D, ff. 159–59v, 30 April 1700, speaks of the substitution of persons 'moins riches'.

[92] P.R.O. 31/3, bundle 184, f. 544v., Tallard to Louis XIV, 13 December 1699; Burnet, IV, 433.

[93] *Vernon Letters*, III, 3, 9–11.

[94] *Turberville*, 204–5.

[95] Evelyn *Diary*, ff, 401, 407n; Burnet, IV, 429; *Vernon Letters*, III, 22. Cf. the lines in *On My Lord Somers* (London, 1700): 'Vain thy Efforts the Houses to divide,/They'll close again and crush thy daring Pride.'

[96] Macaulay, VI, 2973; *L.J.*, XVI, 576.

[97] *C.J.*, XIII, 318.

[98] *Vernon Letters*, III, 13. Tallard reported that Seymour 'fit une harangue contre le chancelier dans laquelle il dit que c'était un ministre dangereux': P.R.O. 31/3, bundle 185, Tallard to Louis XIV, 22 April 1700.

[99] *Vernon Letters*, III, 10–11.

[100] *C.J.*, XIII, 318.

[101] As did Sir Edward Blackett, M.P. for Northumberland, and Richard Norton, M.P. for Southampton County.

[102] *C.J.*, XIII, 321; *Vernon Letters*, III, 322–23; Luttrell, *Relation*, VI, 633. Yonge and Boyle served as tellers on Somers's side.

[103] *Vernon Letters*, III, 9–10, 12, 18; *C.J.*, XIII, 322; Luttrell, *Relation*, IV, 634–35, 638.

[104] *Vernon Letters*, III, 34; Ellis, 'Junto', 422. The packet was sent in the spring of 1698: Bodleian MSS. 16,188, ff. 19–20v, Bellamont to Somers, 12 May 1698.

[105] *Vernon Letters*, III, 32, 35; *Portland MSS.*, VIII, 78.

[106] Vernon was in the dark; the Chancellor was 'very reserved in this particular': *Letters*, III, 30.

[107] Feiling, 340, citing Bodleian Ballard MS. 10.

[108] See Feiling, 338, citing Harley's autobiographical fragment; *Vernon Letters*, III, 3, 8. According to Tindal, XIX, 47–48, the Earl of Jersey sought to convince the King's favourite, Albemarle, that Somers's ouster would placate the Tories. Baxter, *William III*, 377, states that one of William's personal reasons for the dismissal was to make room for John Methuen, a friend of the King.

[109] *Vernon Letters*, III, 53; cf. Coxe, *Shrewsbury*, 615, for a statement that William privately and repeatedly urged the Chancellor to resign in order to avoid the embarrassment of a dismissal. See also P.R.O. 31/3, bundle 185, 7 May 1700 (NS); Ralph, *History*, II, 855; Oldmixon, *History*, 208; Tindal, XIX, 49–52.

[110] On this see Kenyon, *Sunderland*, 311 ff.

[111] Luttrell, *Relation*, IV, 634, 638. According to one report Somers did not see the King

in the month before 25 April: *Portland MSS.*, III, 618. See also Bonnet, Add. MSS. 30,000 D, f. 160v; Burnet, IV, 432–33. Over a week before Somers's ouster Tallard wrote to Louis XIV: 'L'on croit que le chancelier sera obligé de quitter sa charge, s'il se retire le Roy son maistre perdra le meilleur sujet qu'il ait en Angleterre': P.R.O. 31/3, bundle 185, 27 April 1700 (NS).

112 *Cal. S. P. Dom.*, 1700–02, 26, gives 26 April as the date of the warrant. Jersey first tried to gain possession of the Seal without a warrant, but Somers protested that it was of too great importance to be relinquished without a formal order, and would not comply: Bonnet, Add. MSS. 30,000 E, ff. 89v.–90. Tallard, writing 7 May (NS), reports that the Chancellor supposedly delivered up the Seal the previous day at 8 p.m., and confirms this in his letter of 10 May (NS): P.R.O. 31/3, bundle 185; see also Luttrell, *Relation*, IV, 639. Notices of his dismissal appeared in the *Flying-Post* and *Post Man*, 30 April.

IX

Impeachment

The leader of the Junto had fallen. Reactions were what might be expected. The Tories exulted. They looked for a new alignment of government. Montague had given up the Treasury; Wharton was said to be seeking retirement. Seymour addressed the King in the tones of an indispensable man.[1] To the Whigs, William seemed to have lost at the council table the courage that had never failed him in the field. To dismiss a minister with such a record of accomplishment, and who, despite the decline in Whig fortunes, had managed to weather all personal attacks in the House of Commons, was at least highly impolitic: who would be willing to do the King's business if they were to be so treated?[2] Bonnet, despite his familiarity with the vagaries of English politics, still found it remarkable that the Chancellor's difficulties arose out of dutifulness to his sovereign.[3]

As for the victim, he appears to have laid down his charge with good grace and equanimity. 'Though it displeased many people', wrote Kennett, 'yet it seemed not to affect his Lordship, who retired with content and temper.'[4] He could take comfort from the support, not only of his Whig confreres, but of moderate opinion generally. The loyalty of an old friend like Montague might be expected; that the Tory Allen Bathurst, the nephew of Somers's undergraduate mentor, should continue to show his personal regard was especially heartening.[5] He could take some satisfaction, too, in the difficulties encountered by the government as it sought to find a qualified successor.

For a time, as his eulogist remarks, 'the Seals were said to go a begging'.[6] There were few candidates in the field, and these were looked upon as inadequate. If, as Bonnet declared, the English believed that chancellors should be rich (and thereby supposedly incorruptible), versed in affairs and able to expedite them, firm in upholding the law and effective in maintaining a balance between king and people, this is understandable. Harley's candidate was John Methuen, and William was inclined that way. According to Bonnet, he might have got the post had the Duke of Leeds and Chief Justice Holt not warned the King of his inadequacy: it was not enough to have been Lord Chancellor of Ireland.[7] Nottingham and Justice Powell were also reported to be in the running. But they seem to have received little serious attention. This was reserved for Attorney-General Thomas Trevor and Chief Justice Holt. On the day of Somers's fall Luttrell reported that it was 'generally said' that Trevor would succeed him, but by the middle of May he had definitely refused. He was unwilling to risk his practice at the bar for what might prove to be an ephemeral custody of the Seal. In the meantime it had been tendered to Holt. He too turned it down.[8] Meanwhile, business depending on the Seal was at a standstill. To provide a stop-gap remedy the King entrusted it to the two Chief Justices and the Chief Baron, as commissioners, Holt being willing to serve as their head. At the same time, Sir John Trevor, Master of the Rolls, and nine other Chancery officials were authorised to hear all Chancery cases until a new chief should be appointed.[9]

For Somers there was no new post. But, though omitted from the panel of Lords Justices commissioned late in June, he continued as a Privy Councillor until the end of the reign. Strained as his relations with the King must have been, there was no breakdown. On the eve of William's departure for Holland he was on hand with other notables to kiss his hand and wish him *bon voyage*. He remained, after all, a power among the Whigs: the political influence of a decade could not be nullified in one fell swoop. More than a year later his nominees were still to be found manning the commissions of the peace. His knowledge of the workings of government was so extensive that he could not be entirely dispensed with; Vernon, for example, continued to turn to him.[10]

Meanwhile the indefatigable Sunderland saw fit to include him, once again, in his schemes for reshaping the government. These were to some extent encouraged by the King, who was all too conscious of the disarray of the administration, and was believed in some circles already to be regretting his dismissal of the Chancellor.[11] Sunderland's manoeuvres at this time appear highly paradoxical, for many, Somers included, regarded him as primarily responsible for the Chancellor's dismissal. On the eve of that event a placard had been tacked to the doorway of the Court of Chancery: 'This house to let; for information apply to the Earl of Sunderland.'[12] But now he assured Shrewsbury (one of the few that showed signs of believing him) that it had always been 'his notion that the King's business never could be so well carried on as by my Lord Chancellor, and his friends', and that he had been 'against my Lord's going out'.[13] He claimed that he had advised William to have a frank discussion with Somers on 'the present posture of his affairs', and to assure him of his support for such methods as he should propose 'for the carrying on the public business'. He had expected the King to take this course, and was 'very much surprised when he heard in what manner they had parted'. Now he was recommending

that the King and my Lord Somers may be brought to rely one on the other, and that all dissatisfactions may be removed; that my Lord Somers forbear shewing any resentment for what is past, but, on the contrary, that he dispose his friends to carry on the public business next session, they being satisfied that the King will desire nothing unfit or unreasonable from them.

He knew of no engagements entered into by the King in opposition to Somers. Orford, Wharton and Montague, as well as Somers, should be acquainted with the proposal, but no one else for the time being.[14]

Airy as this scheme appears it seems to have been taken seriously by Vernon, for one. But he wondered if Somers would be willing to hold the

Seal again. Might he not prefer 'his own quiet, and not to expose himself to new attempts?' Vernon thought it best, for the present, to put the Seal in commission; it could be restored to Somers at an opportune time, perhaps when a more amenable legislature had been elected. Even if a new Lord Keeper were appointed—and this the King appeared more inclined to do—it could be with the understanding that his tenure would be brief, though made worth his while.[15]

But Sunderland's days of ministry-making were over. He could not rehabilitate himself in the eyes of the Junto. Montague was highly suspicious; Wharton and Orford were downright hostile.[16] And with some reason, for, as Vernon put it, Sunderland was 'almost afraid of his own project', and it unfolded in something like cloak and dagger fashion. Perhaps it was but a trick 'to amuse the Whigs and keep them quiet this session'.[17] Could a man so generally regarded as having brought about Somers's downfall now be expected to deal sincerely in raising him up again?

Somers, who learned of the project through Montague, remained on the sidelines. His usage at William's hands afforded him some claim to martyrdom, in Whig eyes, and had certainly not undermined his leadership of the Junto. This would have to be shared, at least, if he were to be reinstated under Sunderland's auspices. He was in no hurry; the lightning that had been playing about his head, the political atmosphere still so dangerously charged, made him cautious. Early in June he wrote to Shrewsbury that he would like to see him, but without arousing suspicion that the two were 'caballing':

For though I neither do nor ever will meddle with public affairs, nor have the least resentment against any persons who may be imagined to have been most active in getting me displaced, yet I find it very hard to convince men that it is so.[18]

Shrewsbury, like Somers, was now in retirement. He had yielded up the White Staff and refused the lord lieutenancy of Ireland. And he too had rejected Sunderland's proposals. 'Seven years ago', Sunderland reminded him, 'there was as little faith as now, though many things were brought to pass which seemed impossible.'[19] But history would not repeat itself: Shrewsbury's refusal marked the end of the project.

On 21 May Nathan Wright, Serjeant at Law, was named Lord Keeper. He was a moderate Tory, who as junior counsel for the prosecution had been Somers's opposite in the trial of the bishops. Although he had built up a considerable practice since then, he would never rise above official mediocrity. Sunderland, it seems, envisaged a short tenure. Yet, though held in low regard even by his own party, he managed to retain the Great Seal until the Whig revival in 1705. Somers immediately offered him Powys House; by late in September the bulk of his furnishings had been removed, and he delivered the key to the new tenant.[20]

Though considerably reduced, his income was still substantial. His 'allowance 'of £4000 was continued to 1 June; thereafter he could count on his £2100 pension, and income from rents and grants.[21] During the summer he was occupied with house-hunting. In May he had taken a house in Leicester Fields, but this was a stop-gap arrangement. Archbishop Tenison, trying to be of help, suggested a place in Ealing.[22] But Somers wanted a town house, and in the end took a lease on No. 21 St James's Square. This was perhaps the most fashionable quarter of the metropolis. The house had first been occupied by Arabella Churchill, Marlborough's sister and mistress of James II. Somers took it over from his friend and colleague, Montague.[23] Meanwhile he found time to visit Tunbridge Wells for relaxation and the water cure. In August he journeyed to Petworth; in September, along with Montague and Tankerville, he spent some time in Hampshire and the Isle of Wight.[24]

While he was adjusting himself to a new way of life, death twice materially affected the fortunes of the kingdom. Late in July the eleven-year-old Duke of Gloucester, Anne's only surviving child, suddenly sickened and died. Jacobites could now take heart, as another obstacle in the way of a legitimist restoration was removed. Three months later Madrid announced the long expected demise of Charles II. The death of the Duke called for a new definition of the succession. The Spanish King was but a fortnight dead with Louis XIV, ignoring the Partition Treaty of the previous March and taking advantage of Charles's will, formally acknowledged his grandson, the Duke of Anjou, as Philip V of Spain. With the former project, which resulted in the Act of Settlement, Somers had little to do. But the dramatic episode at Versailles produced a sequence of events which within a few months led to his impeachment.

Before this occurred, a new Parliament came into being. William had returned to England in October, earlier than usual. The news of King Charles's death and its dynastic aftermath reached him at Hampton Court. Utterly disillusioned with France, he turned again to the earlier policy of alliance with Austria, an alignment that would persist for half a century. But he was faced with manifest difficulties in effecting it. However little the Whigs might appreciate the partition treaties, their aversion was nothing compared to that of the Tories, who looked upon Charles's will 'not merely as a lesser evil, but almost as a positive good'.[25] And it was with the Tories that William would have to do business. This he realised: by the end of the summer Harley, Godolphin and Rochester had formed something of a team, and in September Godolphin was offered the Treasury. And, as if the existing Parliament was not Tory enough, there were designs afoot to elect a new one. In any case the mandate of 1698 would expire in another year; and 'partitions and successions' were 'too great to be begun in the fag end of a parliament'.[26] So Seymour and Musgrave thought, and the King concurred. Apart from any commitments he may have made with his new aides, he was not averse to dissolving the legislature that had passed the Irish Forfeitures Bill, and this he did on 19 December. By this time Rochester and Godolphin had taken their seats in the cabinet. Charles Hedges, another staunch Tory, was now Secretary in place of Jersey, who in the summer had obtained Shrewsbury's vacated chamberlainship.

The election was hard fought. Close to three thousand candidates appealed to the electorate.[27] Somers lost no time in deploying his forces. On the very date of dissolution, Harley was informed that the ex-Chancellor was mustering his 'last list' against the Reigate election.[28] His brother-in-law Cocks prepared to stand for Worcester and Jekyll for Eye. Both were returned, though Cocks had to be content with his old constituency, Droitwich. Walsh was re-elected for the county. Four others well known as associates of Somers gained seats. Edward Clarke, of 'the College', was again returned for Taunton; as a Commissioner of Excise he had been excluded in 1699. Richard Dowdeswell, the son-in-law of Somers's early patron, carried on for Tewkesbury, and Stephen Harvey was back for Reigate, the Tory Parsons regaining the other seat. New to Parliament was Thomas Wylde, a Middle Temple lawyer and friend of Somers, who defeated William Bromley in the Worcester election.[29] Thus Somers's 'connexion' in the new House was maintained, his official downfall notwithstanding, though his representation was still a far cry from the twenty-five members in Wharton's stable. 'Being discharged from all his Employments,' wrote Macky, 'he still keeps up a great Interest in both Houses. A Thing very uncommon for an *English* disgraced Minister.'[30] His showing was of a piece with the returns as a whole, which resulted in very little change, the Tories securing a majority of sixty-five. Their leaders were all returned, and the Court-New Country coalition, as Walcott terms it, succeeded by a narrow margin in electing Harley Speaker, in place of Littleton, the friend of the Junto.[31]

The new Parliament did not get down to business until 10 February. In his speech from the throne the following day, William stressed the importance of providing for the Protestant succession and of taking steps against any dangers that might arise from the enthronement of a Bourbon in Madrid. The Commons lost little time in taking up the succession problem; within a month the resolution providing the framework for the Act of Settlement had been drafted. The finished measure, conveying the crown to Sophia of Hanover and her descendants, and imposing various limitations on the royal power and the conduct of government, was first read in the House of Lords on 14 May.[32]

Somers, though no longer on the woolsack, attended the Lords with much greater regularity than in the previous session. He first appeared, in his altered capacity, on 11 February, when he took the customary oaths; thereafter he was rarely absent save in March, when he missed five meetings. It must have been pleasant to have Charles Montague, recently created Baron Halifax, sitting beside him. He was evidently ready to roll up his sleeves, and in the months that followed—even after the shadow of impeachment hung over him—was named to a variety of committees. Most of them had to do with private bills, but there were some of more general importance. Late in April he was on a committee to consider an act to restrain 'trifling and vexations suits in law', as well as one for the regulation of prisons. And it is noteworthy that he was placed on an enormous committee charged with considering procedures involved with impeachments.[33]

Though the settlement bill was essentially a back-bench Tory measure, it encountered little resistance in the Whig-dominated Lords. Within a week it was accepted in committee of the whole, and on the 22nd it was passed without amendments. Somers was present on each of the four days that the bill was before the peers. Instrumental as he had been in framing the Bill of Rights, he now appears to have taken no formal part in enacting the measure that filled various gaps in that statute. But he may have worked behind the scenes at an earlier date. General outlines had been prepared by the party leaders, and Somerville goes so far as to say that Somers 'projected the bill for extending the Protestant settlement'.[34] It may be that, once this objective was attained, in the only way that seemed feasible, Somers, like the King and many others, took little interest in provisions which would not come into effect until an unforeseeable date, and which might prove abortive—as two of them did. But there is a more immediate explanation for the former Chancellor's silence. On the very day that the bill was read for the first time in the Lords, the peers heard the articles of impeachment against Orford; five days later, with Somers on the barons' bench, the clerk read similar articles against him.

Just before the opening of Parliament Louis XIV had obtained a decree confirming the new King of Spain's right to the French throne should his older brother, Louis of Burgundy, die without issue. The possibility that Spain and France might merge into one giant empire moved a step nearer. More immediately disturbing was the movement of French forces into the Spanish Netherlands, with the resulting expulsion of the Dutch from frontier garrisons and the occupation of strategic locations, and indications that the French King was determined to monopolise the Latin American trade. These developments prompted the Commons to frame a resolution that they would support William and his government, as well as a request that he enter into such negotiations with the Dutch as would contribute to the national interest. But a complaisant attitude, which augured ill for the military preparations that William judged necessary, was rife. To awaken his insular subjects, he attempted to play on the age-old fear of invasion. He presented to the Houses a letter from the Jacobite Earl of Melfort, which told of a strong legitimist party in Scotland and of a projected French descent upon England.[35] It was a dangerous manoeuvre, and he soon had cause to regret it, for the letter provoked a highly critical investigation of the Partition Treaties.

The second Treaty, that of March 1700, was taken up first, there being no public knowledge, at the time, of the negotiations of 1698. Made necessary by the untimely death of the Electoral Prince, it had assigned to the Archduke Charles the share—Spain, the American provinces, and the Low

Countries—previously allocated to him; the Dauphin was to have the bulk
of the Italian possessions and Lorraine; the Duke of Lorraine was to be
compensated with Milan. These terms had been communicated to Somers in
January 1700; and after the treaty was signed by Portland and Jersey he
had affixed the Great Seal.[36] Although his part in these proceedings had
been essentially formal, the Tories were more than ready to make the most
of his failure to confide in Parliament, which had been sitting at the time.
Late in March, in a full-dress debate in the Lords, Normanby, Rochester,
Godolphin (and even Devonshire) took this line.[37] But Somers, as well as
Portland, Halifax and other chiefs of state, appear to have acquitted
themselves well, and the involvement of Jersey, as well as other Tories,
served to blunt the attack. It was revealed that Somers had raised objections
to certain provisions, such as the presence of the Archduke in Spain, at a
conference called by Jersey (at William's request) in February 1700.[38] In
neither House, at this time, was Somers's action in finalising the instrument
(despite his admitted misgivings) successfully exploited as evidence of
delinquency. But he had a narrow escape in the Commons. On 24 March
they rebuked William for procedural lapses; on the 29th a motion that the
Chancellor, in affixing the Seal, was guilty of high crimes and misdemeanours, failed to carry by only seven votes—182 to 189.[39]

Portland was not so fortunate. Three days later he was impeached.[40] This
redounded to the disadvantage of the former Chancellor. Indeed, the Prussian resident regarded the attack on the Dutch peer as an attempt to prepare
the way for Somers's destruction. If a foreign courtier was to be brought to
justice, so much the more should a veteran English statesman, learned in
the law and versed in constitutional usage, be held responsible.[41] Portland's
star had for some time been waning, but Somers, though forced on to the
defensive, seemed able to withstand every attack; might he not be on the
verge of reasserting his old mastery? The desire to discredit him continued
unabated. A new opportunity came when Portland, in the course of
questioning, revealed that there had been an earlier treaty—that of October
1698—in which Somers had played at least as indefensible a role, and
which was a much more satisfactory weapon in Tory hands in that it had
been negotiated entirely under Whig auspices. By 9 April William had
agreed to provide the Commons with a copy of the mysterious document,
and with Vernon released from the obligation of silence the stage was
prepared for unbridled debate.[42]

14 April was a day full of sound and fury in St Stephen's. The proceedings began with the reading of the Portland–Vernon letters dealing
with the negotiations. Although Portland had declared in the Lords, upon
questioning by Somers himself, that the Chancellor's name did not appear
in these communications, his involvement, along with that of Orford and
Halifax, soon became apparent and was discussed in the House to his disadvantage.[43] During the long-drawn proceedings Somers got wind of what
was going on, and asked permission to appear in his defence. Peers of the
realm were rarely favoured in this way: between 1523 and 1779 only

twenty were accorded the privilege.[44] There was considerable opposition on this occasion. The Tories had just been frustrated again in an attempt to make something of the Kidd affair;[45] they had a healthy respect for Somers's eloquence and were not overly confident of the robustness of their charges. But after some wrangling he was permitted to appear.

Night had fallen when he entered the House. Candles had been lit. He sat for a moment on a chair placed for him just within the bar, then rose and stood behind it to speak for more than half an hour.[46] Like Secretary Vernon he had secured a royal release from bonds of secrecy. He began by observing that, since all his actions had been undertaken with a view towards the well-being of the state, it was unfortunate that his connexion with the treaty had bred suspicion. He confessed that he had opposed it in various particulars, and had advised the King to this effect. But, informed that the negotiations would be completely frustrated unless it were accepted, he 'thought it was the taking too much upon himself, if he should have put a stop to a treaty of such consequence'. As evidence of good faith he presented William's letter asking him to forward the commission, and his own reply, together with the ratification. There were Tory demurrers. Constitutional practice, it was alleged, had been ignored in that William's letter could not be regarded as a formal warrant for the use of the Seal; objections were also raised to the authentication of an instrument not fully drafted.[47] But Somers regarded the letter as his warrant; it was true that he had desired such a formal document for his protection, but he had not insisted upon it, fearing that the delay might not be in the public interest. As for the treaty itself, he had felt himself bound, as Lord Chancellor, to affix the Seal; having given the King his best counsel, he thereafter merely exercised a formal function of his office. He refused to reveal who it was who had informed him of the Commons' proceedings, remarking that:

he was strangely surprised at a question, that he never knew was put to any man, that came to desire the favour of being heard; and that, if that question was asked to bring the least prejudice to any man in England, he would not only be content to lie under the censure of the house, but suffer the worst thing, that might befall him upon earth, rather than do such a dishonest thing.

With this he withdrew, leaving the documents he had presented.[48]

The reactions to his defence varied according to the political vantage point. The Tory Dartmouth, noting that he had never seen the House 'in so great a flame as they were upon his withdrawing', claimed that Somers's attempt 'to throw everything upon the king' backfired, so that 'he left them in a much worse disposition to himself than he found them' and many of his best friends 'heartily wished he had never come thither'. But Bishop Burnet reported that 'he spake so fully and so clearly, that, upon his withdrawing, it was believed, if the question had been quickly put, the whole matter had been soon at an end', and the Dutch envoy, L'Hermitage, agreed, noting that even his enemies could not but admire his presentation.[49]

In any case the Tories still had some shot in their locker. A vigorous defence by William Cowper called for rebuttal, in the course of which the edge of Somers's apologia was blunted. When, late that night, it was moved that his actions regarding the treaty constituted a high crime and misdemeanour the yeas had the edge, 198 to 188. It was forthwith resolved that he should be impeached, and Simon Harcourt, the Tory lawyer who would one day hold the Great Seal, was ordered to notify the Lords to that effect.[50] On the same day Orford and Halifax suffered a like fate, by more decisive margins.

Somers could now anticipate specific charges, to be drawn up by the Commons committee already involved with Portland's impeachment, now enlarged and entrusted with all four cases. But the Commons adopted a leisurely pace, and the articles were not presented to the Lords for five weeks. Instead they attempted to secure beforehand the advantages of an adverse judgement. On the day following the impeachments they resolved, 162 to 107, to petition the King to remove from his 'council and presence for ever' the four lords who had advised and transacted a treaty 'of so dangerous consequence to the Trade and Welfare of this nation'. Ten days later the address was formally presented.[51] The King could do no wrong: such was the principle (in so far as any principle entered into the partisan manoeuvre) that underlay this move. It made no difference that the King himself had sponsored the arrangements, and that the ministers (save possibly for Portland) had done little but carry out his orders. At one blow the Tories could crucify the Whig chiefs and voice their objections to William's foreign policy.

The Commons, however, had bitten off more than they could chew, for this address produced the first of a series of clashes between the chambers which ultimately served to render the impeachments abortive. Many of the lords were angered by this tactic. They—and others, too—regarded it as condemnation without trial, and a breach of their prerogative as judges in impeachments.[52] The Commons were asking for a royal sentence. The Lords informed them to this effect and countered with an address to William that he 'pass no censure or punishment upon the Lords impeached during the dependence of the Impeachments in this House'. This passed by a vote of 40 to 27.[53]

Although William was reportedly touched to the quick by the Commons' address, he sought to avoid embroilment in the dispute. His main interest was in securing an ample grant, so that he could get on with his military preparations. It was obviously important to remain on amicable terms with the Commons. To them he replied that he would 'employ none in [his] service but such as shall be thought likely to improve that mutual Trust and Confidence between us'.[54] With his soft and evasive answer he hoped to turn away wrath, but the names of the impeached lords remained on the Council books.[55] To the Lords he deemed it best to make no reply at all, a procedure regarded as so extraordinary that they appointed a committee (of which Somers was a member) to search the Journals to find if there was any precedent for it.[56]

The Easter recess came and went, the month of April passed. The Lords were still awaiting the impeachment articles. According to Burnet, the Commons now believed that they had sufficiently injured the Whig chiefs, and, trusting that the King would not henceforth employ them, could let the matter drop.[57] On 5 May their lordships saw fit to prod them.[58] This and several subsequent reminders were irritating, for the lower house was as jealous of its rights as prosecutors as were the Lords of their judicial functions. Meanwhile Somers and the other victims received support from an unexpected quarter. The Kentish Petition, a brief address to the Commons from the magistrates and others at the Maidstone quarter sessions, condemned the way the House had been acting since the beginning of the session. It directed the Members' attention to the dangerous continental situation, lamented the delay in granting supply, and attacked the partisan prosecutions. One can trace a personal nexus, for Somers had been instrumental in commissioning some of the justices of the peace who now rallied to his defence.[59] But the petition was more than a repayment of political debts, and was not the only expression of this sort. On 30 April Somers's brother-in-law, Jekyll, wrote him of the indignation of the people of Chester over his impeachment.[60] The petition was followed by Defoe's so-called *Legion's Memorial*, which included, among the sins of the Commons, their request that William oust the impeached magnates and their delay of impeachment proceedings in order 'to blast the reputation of the persons, without proving the fact'.[61]

Somers and his colleagues did not profit from such manifestoes. The House of Commons was particularly enraged by the Kentish Petition, and committed five of its signatories to prison.[62] Some Members were persuaded that the Whig chiefs (and especially Somers) were responsible for it.[63] There is no evidence for this, but he may have come to the petitioners' defence in *Jura Populi Anglicani, or the Subject's Right of Petitioning Set forth* (1701).[64] Its author contended that the action taken by the Commons was an invasion of the rights of Englishmen, as an unwarrantable extension of their authority, and that, in any case, the petitioners had broken no law. The right to petition he declared to be incontrovertible, being 'justify'd by the Law of Nature, the Practice of all States in the World, and ... allow'd by the Laws of this Land'. But such arguments did not deter the extremists, who strove to drive on the impeachments even as the House was forced, by inexorable circumstances, to ready the nation for the eventuality of war against a power-complex that their victims had striven to prevent.[65] The articles against Orford had been sent to the Lords on 5 May. Two weeks later Simon Harcourt carried up those against Somers.[66]

In all there were fourteen. The first six dealt with the treaties. In Article I Somers was charged with encouraging and promoting the Treaty of 1698, without consideration of previous commitments to Holland. The second referred to the commission, alleging that he had affixed the Great Seal 'without any lawful warrant' and 'without communicating the same to the then lords justices of England, or advising in counsel with his majesty's privy council thereupon', and noting that 'no certain persons of known honour, fidelity, and experience' were at the time nominated commissioners, despite the unlimited powers conferred upon them. In the third and fourth articles Somers was attacked for procuring, *ex post facto*, a warrant for the commission, and for affixing the Seal to the ratification of the Treaty, again without consultation and regardless of the blanks to be filled in at a later date. The fifth was a similar indictment in connection with the Treaty of 1700, while the sixth scored Somers's neglect in not arranging for the enrolment of the documents in Chancery, 'as by the duty of his place he should and ought to have done'.

But the Commons did not rest their case upon these indictments. They turned again to the matter of grants and emoluments. In the seventh article they declared that, contrary to his oath of office, Somers had passed 'many great, unreasonable, and exhorbitant Grants', both of properties and interests belonging to the Crown and of the forfeited estates in Ireland. Furthermore, not content with the perquisites of office, a generous pension, and other profits and advantages, he had 'begged and procured for his own benefit' many grants of 'manors, lands, tenements, rents, hereditaments, and revenues, belonging to the crown of England'. These were particularised in Article VIII. In the following articles he was castigated for elaborate dealings and allegedly fraudulent practices aimed at uncovering and securing fee-farm rents to the value of £33,600, procedures smacking of bribery (or something close to it) and collusion with trustees. Article XI made special reference to his appropriation of quit-rents set aside for the maintenance of Windsor Castle and the payment of officers and servants there. The final articles further broadened the indictment by raking up once more the commission to Captain Kidd, and by accusing the former Chancellor of delay of justice, arbitrary orders, and other judicial delinquencies, with particular reference to the Bankers' case.[67]

Within five days, on 24 May, Somers's answer was in the hands of the Commons; it was read three days later.[68] He dwelt at greatest length on the first article, which charged him with promoting the first treaty. After rehearsing the preliminaries in which he was involved, he pointed out that he had no knowledge of the progress of negotiations until the latter part of September 1698, when Secretary Vernon had informed him that the treaty had been 'adjusted, concluded, and signed by the commissioners named by his majesty for that purpose' and by the representatives of the King of France. Nor had he 'at any time whatsoever' promoted the treaty or advised the King to enter into it. As for the next three articles, charging him with authenticating incomplete documents relating to the negotiations of 1698, without proper warrant or adequate consultation, he continued to shield himself behind the King's express commands. He saw no illegality in signing a blank cheque regarding the identity of the commissioners. Less convincingly, he admitted that he had retroactively sought a warrant for issuing the commission, 'not that he doubted his majesty's said letter to be a sufficient warrant', but that such authorisation might more properly be produced should occasion arise.[69] As for the fifth article, dealing with the Treaty of 1700, he had been without knowledge of its contents until he had occasion to peruse a draft, along with other Privy Councillors. He had then raised objections, but had been informed that the treaty 'was so far perfected, that nothing could then be altered therein'. Accordingly, upon receipt of a warrant, he had affixed the Seal, conceiving that he was obliged to do so. Even more than the first, the second treaty had been a *fait accompli* by the time he was apprised of its contents. As for dereliction in not enrolling the documents, he blamed the prothonotary of the Court of Chancery, remaining silent on the matter of secrecy.

In the matter of grants, he denied any malfeasance whatsoever. He had diligently attempted to adhere to his oath of office. In a dig at the Tories, he observed that 'more considerable' grants had been allowed 'in the like number of years, in most of his predecessors' times'. All had been processed in a regular manner, nor did he at any time 'advise, promote, or procure, any grant to be made to any person whatsoever, of any forfeited estate in Ireland'. As for allegations that he had profited unduly and illegally at the public expense: he had received Reigate and the fee-farm rents 'from his majesty's own motion, and of his mere bounty', without solicitation on his part. No contracts had been 'colourably or fraudulently contrived' to deceive the King or evade the law. Though he admitted that several rents granted in trust for him had turned out to have been previously disposed of, and that others were not in the power of the trustees to bestow, he placed the blame on misinformation; similar mistakes had frequently occurred in the past. In any case, to the best of his knowledge, none of his rents had ever been annexed to Windsor Castle; no one had suffered 'oppression or vexation' because of his grants; and they had involved little or no charge to the Crown, and no financial loss save to Somers himself.

Turning to the thirteenth article, involving his relations with Captain Kidd, he admitted, as he had done before, that he had affixed the Seal to his commission, as well as to the grant by which the backers of the venture were to be recompensed. He admitted, too, that he was one of the grantees, with Samuel Newton serving as trustee in his behalf. But he denied that Kidd had at that time been 'esteemed a person of ill fame or reputation', or that the venture could in any way be regarded as prejudicial to the merchants or other subjects of the King—or to William himself, who had been assured of a tenth of the winnings. He reminded the House that since Kidd had proved faithless he, along with the other grantees, had suffered financially. Finally, he denied any judicial misconduct, as alleged in the concluding article. His reversal of the judgement in the Bankers' case had been entirely regular. He had never upheld a position dangerous to the constitution or destructive of the rights of property. He had constantly applied himself to the dispatch of judicial business, even 'to the very manifest impairing of his health'. With this defence he rested.[70]

It was now the Commons' turn. But their replication was not forthcoming; instead, the two Houses became increasingly involved in arguments over procedure, and in defending what each regarded as indisputable prerogatives. To some extent these arose from the fact that the impeachment process had never been fully defined. A number of questions emerged. What about bail or security for impeached persons? Were there time limits affecting the presentation of articles and the answer of the accused? Were there procedural differences between cases of high crimes and misdemeanours and those of treason? Could peers impeached at the same time and on similar charges vote at one another's trials? And could they sit at their own trials as members of their House? Most important, were the Lords alone to determine procedural questions, or were the Commons as well to have a share? Such problems could and did create endless discussion.

But in large measure the delay stemmed from one cause: the realisation, on the part of the Tory-dominated Commons, that they would be unlikely to secure a conviction in the Whig-dominated Lords. Better that the sword should be kept dangling over the heads of the Whig leaders than that their conduct should be vindicated and their reputations refurbished by formal acquittals. As the days passed it seemed less and less likely that the former Chancellor would be tried during that session, and it was he whom the Commons had chosen to try first.[71] Poussin, who had succeeded Tallard as Louis's ambassador, was of this opinion. Congreve, the dramatist, wrote on 7 June: 'tho they are impeached I believe they will never be tryed; for their is neither matter nor proof against them'.[72]

Whether or not there was matter or proof, Congreve was right. The Commons called for a joint committee of both Houses to work out procedural details; the Lords, though willing to answer questions posed by the Commons, set their faces against such co-operation. The peers insisted that none of their House was to be prevented from voting on any occasion except in his own trial. They also held fast to determining the dates for such trials. That for Somers had been set for 13 June. The Commons refused to participate on that date, claiming that it did not afford them sufficient time to prepare their case, and hammered away for the joint committee. The Lords relented to the extent of agreeing to a free conference; judicial matters, however, were not to be discussed. This encounter, on 13 June, drove the final wedge between the chambers. The Commons stalked out, infuriated by remarks of Lord Haversham, particularly by his insinuation that the lower house was deliberately attacking, on partisan grounds, men whom it knew to be innocent.[73] He had touched upon a very sensitive nerve. If the four Whigs were suspect, why had the Tory Earl of Jersey, who as plenipotentiary had signed the second treaty, gone scot-free? Why was his co-signer, Sir Joseph Williamson, not in the dock? Were Seymour's hands clean with regard to Irish grants? In effect, the Commons' participation in the impeachments was over, though they belatedly produced articles against Halifax. They preferred to nurse their grievances. Though the Lords twice sought the continuance of the conference, it was in vain. On 16 June they rescheduled Somers's trial for the morrow. On the same day Harcourt informed them that the Commons would not participate, giving as their reasons the Lords' refusal to accept a joint committee, their insistence that the impeached peers should sit in judgement upon one another, and the absence of satisfaction regarding the Haversham insult.[74]

Undaunted, the Lords proceeded to wind up the business. Westminster Hall had been fitted out for the occasion, under the supervision of Sir Christopher Wren. On the appointed day they resolved, 57 to 36, to take their places there for Somers's trial, notifying the Commons to this effect, the protest of thirty-two peers notwithstanding.[75] To a man the knights and burgesses shunned the proceedings, and the Lords, with all due ceremony, seated themselves in solitary splendour. Somers was present; since this was only a case of misdemeanour he was allowed to sit within the bar. His successor, Wright, was in the chair.

The proceedings began. The articles and Somers's answer were read; all persons concerned were called upon to come forward and make good the charges. But the peers could not but laugh at this formality: there were no accusers, no presentation of evidence, no prosecution. After a few minutes, Somers moved that his own counsel be heard, and the case for the defence was presented.[76] This completed, the Lords adjourned to their chamber, where they heard a motion for acquittal. Some confusion now arose as to what course should be taken with an accused person who pled not guilty without evidence presented against him. The Tories protested that while they could not, without such evidence, declare Somers guilty, neither could they declare him not guilty: after all, though the prosecution had defaulted, he might have committed the offences charged against him.[77] But the motion as finally phrased read: 'That John Lord Somers be acquitted of the Articles of Impeachment against him exhibited by the House of Commons, and all Things therein contained; and that the said Impeachment be dismissed.' This was resolved in the affirmative, 55 to 33, not without a protest from thirty-one peers, who still maintained that it contravened accepted rules of justice to acquit a person without hearing his accusers or admitting the matters charged against him.[78] Several hours were spent in this debate, and it was not until eight in the evening that the peers once more wended their way to Westminster Hall. The question being put, each peer was asked by the Lord Keeper whether he was content or not content with acquittal. The contents numbered 55, the non-contents 32. Orford and Halifax chose not to participate in their colleague's trial, but Portland was there, voting with the majority. The Lord Keeper now declared his predecessor acquitted, upon which the peers returned to their chamber and ordered that the impeachment be dismissed.[79]

Perhaps the most striking feature of the vote was the number of participants: only very important issues could line up nearly ninety peers in Augustan England. Apart from Orford and Halifax, about the only consequential figure not voting was Shrewsbury, who was living abroad.[80] Of other living signatories of the revolutionary invitation to William of Orange, Scarborough, Romney and Devonshire supported Somers, while Bishop Compton opposed him. Compton was joined among the bishops by Sprat and Trelawney. All three had been consecrated before the Revolution. But they were outnumbered, four to one, by the prelates appointed by William. Among the temporal peers Somers gained his margin of victory (nine votes) through the barons rather than the higher ranks. Basically, the vote represented the partisan cleavage one might expect. All the major Tory figures—Godolphin, Marlborough, Nottingham, Rochester, Lindsey, Weymouth—voted against Somers. Nearly all the Whigs supported him, two major exceptions being Oxford and Somerset. The latter was perhaps influenced by his friendship with Anne and his kinship with Seymour.[81]

The Commons inveighed against these proceedings as a miscarriage of justice, and ordered that no Member, upon pain of the utmost displeasure, was to appear at the forthcoming trial of Lord Orford.[82] But they were powerless to undo what had been done, and the only result of their intransigence was that the remaining impeachments were dismissed—not only those against Halifax and Portland (against the latter they had not even proffered charges), but also the long dangling indictment of the Duke of Leeds.[83] But perhaps they saw no other course. Time, in a sense, had passed them by. They had launched their attack upon the Whig chiefs when public opinion on the Spanish crisis seemed favourable and when isolationist sentiment was undoubtedly considerable. But, as the weeks passed and the aggressive character of the French government grew more apparent, a reaction set in. The old Francophobia reasserted itself; a new warmindedness was in the making, and with it a mounting sympathy for the party most identified with the checking of French aggression, and for its leaders who had borne the heat of battle. According to Bonnet, an eyewitness, Somers's acquittal was enthusiastically acclaimed by the spectators in Westminster Hall, and there were bonfires and other demonstrations in the metropolis.[84] Nor was satisfaction limited to those of Whiggish allegiance. In Reigate Sir John Parsons 'order'd the Bells to be rung; tho' he was far from being a Man of his Lordship's Principles in Politicks'.[85]

Somers's impeachment left no mark on the English constitution, save in so far as it was to demonstrate the clumsiness of the device. But, since no minister of state had been convicted on an impeachment for half a century, this was already apparent. Whether or not he was justified in his conduct regarding the treaties—and it is here that even his admirers concede that the opposition had a case[86]—was not thrashed out at the time: nothing, for that matter, was proved right or wrong. Like Danby he shielded himself behind the King's express orders. This had done Danby little good. Had Somers been subjected to a bonafide trial, such a defence would probably have been overborne, in his case too, by the concept that the King can do no wrong, with its tacit corollary of ministerial responsibility. Even so, with the Whigs as entrenched in the Lords as they were, it is almost impossible to conceive of a conviction, with the guidelines that such a judgement might have furnished. Somers had served the nation well: his reputation could withstand prying and probing. But, no less important, he had served his party well, and his party did not let him down.

NOTES

1 P.R.O. 31/3, bundle 185, f. 97v, Tallard to Louis XIV; Feiling, 340.

2 Kennett, III, 783.

3 'Les Anglois, qui ont des maximes particulieres, ne lui disputent pas la fidelité pour le Roy; ils avouent mais c'est pour lui en faire un crime, et pour l'accuser de n'avoir pas en autant d'égard pour les engagements de sa charge': Add. MSS. 30,000 D, f. 160v.

4 Kennett, III, 783.

5 *Annual Register* (1775), 23. The Duke of Bolton, among others criticised the King for ingratitude, declaring his 'unalterable friendship and respect' for Somers: *Buccleuch MSS.*, II, pt. ii, 651. His electoral influence in Hampshire and elsewhere was of great importance to the Junto in later years.

6 *Memoirs*, 51–52.

7 On 26 May (NS) Tallard wrote to Louis that so far no one had been found who wanted to be Chancellor, 'aumoins de ceux que la cour auroit désiré': P.R.O. 31/3, bundle 185, f. 110v. See also Bonnet, Add. MSS. 30,000 D, f. 160v, ff.; Macky, 143; Browning, *Danby*, I, 550.

8 Luttrell, *Relation*, IV, 639–40, 646. According to Tallard, Trevor was to be Lord Keeper, but without the ministerial duties Somers had borne: P.R.O. 31/3, bundle 185, ff. 107–7v.

9 Luttrell, *Relation*, IV, 641; *Cal. S. P. Dom.*, 1700–02, 33; *Flying Post*, 7 May 1700.

10 *Vernon Letters*, III, 44, 107–8; Feiling, 351.

11 It is said that William on his deathbed expressed remorse over his ingratitude to his Chancellor: Cunningham, I, 252. Hardwicke merely states that he 'repented it immediately after': Burnet, iv, 434n. Tallard reported on 8 May (NS) that William had derived no benefit from ousting Somers: P.R.O. 31/3, bundle 185, f. 102v. William Shippen (?), in *A Conference between King William and the Earl of Sunderland in a Letter to a Friend* (London, 1700), lines 57–58, has the King say:

By displacing a Lord Chancellor so much Esteem'd,
More Credit I've lost than can ere be redeem'd.

12 Bonnet, Add. MSS. 30,000 D, ff. 164v–65.

13 There is some evidence that he favoured resignation, not the cashiering of the Chancellor: Hardwicke, *State Papers*, II, 439. But cf. lines 42–44 in Shippen (?), *A Conference*:

The remove of the Seal I [Sunderland] lament and disown;
Twas not from my Lord taken, himself laid it down.
A better Lord Chancellor never was known.

14 *Vernon Letters*, II, 43–45; Hardwicke, *State Papers*, II, 437–40.

15 *Vernon Letters*, III, 46, 59; cf. 65. See also Somerville, *King of Hearts*, 181, for Sunderland's suggestion that the Seal be put in commission, with Somers as head.

16 See Montague to Somers, Hardwicke, *State Papers*, II, 436–37. 'I know not what to make of all this', he wrote; he thought it merely 'a shift to lessen the odium' of Sunderland's suspected role in Somers's dismissal.

17 *Vernon Letters*, III, 40.

18 Coxe, *Shrewsbury*, 619–20; *Buccleuch MSS.*, II, pt. ii, 652.

19 Coxe *Shrewsbury*, 621.

20 *Cal. Treas. Books*, 1699–1700, 442; Luttrell, *Relation*, IV, 693; Arthur Dasent, *History of St. James's Square* (London, 1895), 244.

21 *Cal. Treas. Books*, 1699–1700, 73.

22 Somers MSS., Tenison to Somers, 4 May 1700; Lambeth Palace, Gibson MSS., vol. XIV, f. 155.

23 Dasent, 157. According to Hatton, *New View of London*, I, 41, it was 'a very pleasant, large and beautiful Square, . . . mostly inhabited by the Prime Quality'.

24 Somers MSS., Tenison to Somers, 29 August 1700. See also Luttrell, *Relation*, IV, 685.

25 Lodge, *History*, 437.

26 Feiling, 341, citing Edward Seymour.

27 *Ibid.*, 343.

28 *Portland MSS.*, III, 639.

29 *Somers MSS.*, Charles Cocks to Somers, 7 December 1700; Mary Cocks to Somers, 1701 (o/1/9); Walcott, *English Politics*, 200, 202; Baxter, *Treasury*, 138.

30 Macky, 53.

31 See Feiling, 343, who speaks of 150 new Members who, it was thought, 'would probably go with the tide which was still swinging against the Junto'. See also Speck, *Tory and Whig*, 123; Walcott, 88.

32 *L.J.*, XVI, 681.

33 *Ibid.*, XVI, 636 ff., especially 663–64 and 672.

34 *History*, 257.

35 *C.J.*, XIII, 333, 335–36; *L.J.*, XVI, 598–600.

36 *Lords MSS.*, 1699–1702, 270. Somers seems to have been the only English minister informed of these negotiations. See Morgan, *Political Parties*, 271.

37 P.R.O. 31/3, bundle 187, f. 318 and v, 20 February 1701.

38 *Lords MSS.*, 1699–1702, 221.

39 *C.J.*, XIII, 425; Luttrell, V, 33. According to Bonnet, Harley declared that if Somers's 'crime' in affixing the Seal should go unpunished one 'pouroit datter dès ce moment là la ruine de la liberté Anglicane': Add. MSS. 30,000 E, f. 121, 1 April 1701.

40 *C.J.*, XIII, 465.

41 Add. MSS, 30,000 E, 1 April 1701, ff. 121–21v; see also L'Hermitage in Add. MSS. 17,677 ww, ff. 212v–13, 12 April 1701.

42 *Lords MSS.*, 1699–1702, 223; *L.J.*, XVI, 646; *C.J.*, XIII, 478–79; P.R.O. 31/3, bundle 188, f. 382, Tallard to Louis XIV.

43 *L.J.*, XVI, 643; *C.J.*, XIII, 484–89; Torbuck, III, 155–56; Luttrell, V, 39.

44 John Hatsell, *Precedents of Proceedings in the House of Commons* (London, 1781), I, 110–15; II, 1–7.

45 According to L'Hermitage, the Kidd investigation continued to make 'beaucoup de bruit'. Tallard reported to Louis that the Tories sought to ruin Hartford for having given the commission to Kidd, 'et Sommers chancelier d'alors pour l'avoir scélé', but that after a hot eight-hour debate the legality of the commission was upheld: Add. MSS. 17,677 ww, f. 204; also f. 211; P.R.O. 31/3, bundle 188, f. 378v.

46 *C.J.*, XIII, 489.

47 Torbuck, III, 158–61.

48 *Parliamentary History*, V, 1245–46; Burnet, IV, 478–79.

49 *Ibid.*, IV, 479 and n.; Add. MSS. 17,677.

50 Burnet, IV, 479–80 and n.; *C.J.*, XIII, 489.

51 *C.J.*, XIII, 491–92; *L.J.*, XVI, 653.

52 Bonnet wrote: 'Cette conduite irreguliere et emportée est blamée de tous ceux qui ne sont pas prevenus pour les Tories': Add. MSS. 30,000 E, 22 April 1701.

53 *L.J.*, XVI, 654; according to Turberville, 214, the vote was forty-nine to twenty-nine.

54 *C.J.*, XIII, 506; P.R.O. 31/3, bundle 188, Poussin to Torcy, f. 398v., and f. 408 v., where Poussin reports that the King assured Seymour in a private audience that the Commons would be satisfied with the course he would take regarding the four peers; see also Kennett, III, 803.

55 Turberville, 214.

56 *L.J.*, XVI, 657.

57 Burnet, IV, 482.

58 *L.J.*, XVI, 667.

59 There is no specific reference to Somers in the Petition, or in Daniel Defoe's *History of the Kentish Petition* (London, 1701).

60 *Somers MSS.*, 30 April 1701. See also *Notes and Queries*, 2nd ser., X, 325.

61 *Somers Tracts*, ed. Scott, XI, 455 ff.; *Parliamentary History*, V, 1252–56.

62 *C.J.*, XIII, 518.

63 See Ranke, v, 263 and n.

64 See William T. Morgan, *Bibliography of British History (1700–1715) with Special Reference to the Reign of Queen Anne* (Indiana University Studies, Bloomington, 1934–42), I, 180; John Locke, *Two Treatises of Government*, ed. Peter Laslett (Cambridge, 1960), 379n.

65 On 9 May, the day after the Petition was received, the Commons resolved to provide

such military assistance to the States General as the Treaty of 1677 had stipulated: C.J., XIII, 523.

66 *Ibid.*, XIII, 553.

67 L.J., XVI, 689–94.

68 C.J., XIII, 568 ff.

69 See above, p. 178.

70 L.J., XVI, 700–5.

71 *Ibid.*, XVI, 714; Burnet, IV, 500.

72 William Congreve, *Letters and Documents*, ed. John C. Hodges (New York, 1964), 23. Bonnet agreed: 'La vérité est qu'il n'y a aucune accusation importante a alleguer contre ces deux Lords' (Somers and Orford): Add. MSS. 30,000 E, f. 233.

73 L.J., XVI, 731 ff.; C.J., XIII, 629–30; *Parliamentary History*, V, 1298–99; Torbuck, III, 202; Burnet, IV, 500, 502–3 and n., 512.

74 L.J., XVI, 742, 746, 749, 753–54.

75 *Ibid.*, XVI, 752–56; Rogers, Protests, I, 155–57.

76 Bonnet, in Add. MSS. 30,000 E, ff. 276v.–77v. Bonnet was present. L.J. XVI, 755.

77 Lords MSS., 1699–1702, 299–300; *Parliamentary History*, V, 1313–14.

78 L.J., XVI, 755; Rogers, Protests, I, 158–59. Rivers and Abingdon were tellers.

79 P.R.O. 31/3, bundle 188, f. 470v, Poussin to Torcy.

80 For a letter from Shrewsbury expressing his 'sincere concern', see Coxe, *Shrewsbury*, 632–34; *Buccleuch MSS.*, II, pt. ii, 653–54.

81 The Jacobite Huntington, curiously enough, voted for acquittal.

82 C.J., XIII, 636.

83 Leeds had been impeached in 1695 for taking a bribe to procure the East India Company charter. His impeachment, along with those of Portland and Halifax, was dismissed on 24 June. Orford was acquitted the previous day: L.J., XVI, 767–69.

84 Add. MSS, 30,000 E, f. 280. There was 'a great shout in the Hall, and clapping of hands for a considerable Time': *Memoirs*, 104,

85 *Loc. cit.*; Bonnet, Add. MSS. 30,000 E, ff. 291–91v; Luttrell, *Relation*, V, 62.

86 Campbell, V, 136; Birkenhead, 127.

X

The pursuits of leisure

Somers's dismissal in 1700 released him from pressures of business which, save for the fag-end of the summer, were virtually unremitting. Though he was still a member of the Privy Council, his ministerial duties were a thing of the past. Never again would he be bound by the timetable of a judicial term. The House of Lords would continue to rely upon him, in both legislative and and judicial matters: he was a seasoned authority on legal and constitutional matters, a parliamentarian who knew the ways of both Houses from long experience, a leader of the Whigs, a veteran administrator who was familiar with court and council. But Parliament was not a continuous enterprise; its sessions rarely lasted as much as half the year. There were additional hours now, in which to cultivate his friends and the interests of his leisure time, to pursue his hobbies and to spend his substantial income.

Whether in or out of office Somers was ever the Londoner; once embarked on the regimen of the Middle Temple he was rarely very far away from the metropolis. Had he married and produced a family he might have established it in one of the more or less elegant country seats so characteristic of the age. But he remained a lifelong bachelor, and seemingly took little pleasure in the amenities of country living. The law, politics and literature were all centred in London, and these were his consuming interests.

All three were interwoven with his social life, the last two to a remarkable degree in the great Whig club, the Kit-Cats. According to the historian Oldmixon, this club 'grew up from a private meeting of Mr. Somers, afterwards Lord Chancellor, and another Lawyer, now in very high station in the Law, and Mr. Tonson, sen. the Bookseller, who before the Revolution, met frequently in an Evening at a Tavern, near Temple-Bar, to unbend themselves after Business, and have a little free and cheerful Conversation in those dangerous Times'.[1] This is quite probable; we know that Somers and Tonson were closely associated by 1688. The Kit-Cats, however, seem to have borne some relationship to an earlier society known as the Knights of the Toast, a convivial group whose pursuits are obvious from their name. For a time it is impossible to distinguish the rising Kit-Cats from the Knights, but the former appear to have formed themselves into a club by 1697.[2] The club's name has been variously explained, but the version now generally accepted is that it derives from Christopher Cat, the proprietor of a tavern where the early meetings were held. We may picture Somers seeking good talk, food and drink at one or another of the places frequented by the Kit-Cats, first at Cat's establishment near Temple Bar, later at other London taverns and particularly at Tonson's residence at Barn

Elms, near Putney. This became the club's headquarters, with a special room hung with Kneller's portraits of the members. In summer it occasionally met at the Flask Inn, in Hampstead.[3]

While it kept Cat's name, it might better have been called Tonson's club, for he continued to be its guiding spirit and perennial secretary and was regarded as indispensable.[4] In 1703, when he was in Holland, Vanbrugh, the playwright and architect, assured him that 'the Kit-Cat wants you, much more than you can ever do them', and that the club would never assemble without him.[5] This is the more remarkable in that it included a substantial cross-section of the great families of England—Berkeleys, Cavendishes, Montagues, Howards and Sackvilles—blue bloods unlikely even to associate with a London bookseller, much less regard him as an arbiter. But Tonson was no ordinary bookseller. Well might he be called 'chief merchant to the Muses'. He was financially successful, largely from government printing contracts, later through speculation in the ill-fated South Sea Company. His list of publications included works of such notables as Milton, Dryden, Addison, Steele and Pope. But he had more than business acumen: he was a man of parts. Pope described him as a perfect image of Bayle's Dictionary—'so full of wit, secret history and spirit'.[6] He was good company, and his knowledge of literary London was unsurpassed. He could be useful to patron, writer or collector, and the Kit-Cat roster was studded with their names. Over the years Somers enjoyed friendly relations with him.

For Somers the Kit-Cat Club had obvious attractions. Most important, perhaps, it was the Whig party in its social aspect. Here was the Whig élite—and some of the rougher diamonds as well. Besides Somers, two of the Junto stalwarts—Montague and Wharton—belonged to the club. In a membership never exceeding forty-eight, with not more than thirty or so at any one time, half were, or were to become, peers of the realm. The political weight of these men, directly brought to bear through seats in the Lords and indirectly through their influence over elections, was formidable. Fully half the membership, moreover, sat at one time or another in the Commons. There was a considerable age-spread: the members had not all 'arrived', many were on the way up. Among them were no less than four future chief Ministers.[7] To Somers the club afforded contact, in an atmosphere of relaxation and congeniality, with the leaders of the party and its rising men, like Stanhope and Walpole. One can imagine the political strategies and bargains that Somers, Wharton, Montague, and other politicos worked out over their bottles of claret. The caucus, as we know it, would not come to England for a century and a half, but its functions were to some extent fulfilled in such social gatherings.[8] There is no minute book to aid us. But we know that a meeting was called to investigate the dalliance of the Duke of Somerset with Harley, with the result that the Duke was expelled from the club. The Kit-Cats certainly arranged for a demonstration in 1711 against the Tory peace policy; it is likely that they engaged in preliminary debate on the procedure to be followed in the Sacheverell case, and they may have laid secret plans for a possible military coup should a Jacobite rising occur upon Anne's death.[9]

The club set great store on conviviality. Indeed, it was criticised at the time (by Tories, of course) for its frivolity if not downright immorality.[10] The High Tory Shippen, satirically providing a voice for their accomplishments in *Faction Display'd*, allows their claim of 'Direction to the State', but goes on:

'Twas there we first instructed all our Youth
To talk Prophane and Laugh at Sacred Truth.
We taught them how to Tost, and Rhime, and Bite,
To Sleep away the Day, and drink away the Night.[11]

And this is nothing compared to some allegations of irreligion and even treason. These, while admitting the latitudinarian and deistic views of some of the members, we may dismiss. But Somers and his confreres did enjoy in full measure the pleasures of the bottle and the table. New members provided special feasts, and it was the pleasant custom to toast the ladies introduced at meetings—usually daughters of aristocratic Whigs, like Lady Sunderland, who was known as 'the little Whig',—commemorating their charms in rhymed couplets inscribed on toasting glasses:

When Jove and Ida did the Gods invite
And in immortal Toastings past the Night
With more than Bowls of Nectar they were blest
For Venus was the Wharton of the Feast.[12]

The wine at times flowed pretty freely. There is no evidence that Somers had to be escorted home, but it happened at least once with Sir Richard Steele. One may conclude that its members shared to a considerable extent the shortcomings of polite society, as inveighed against by moralists and parsons, but apart from young Mohun, the homicidal duellist, and perhaps Wharton, described by Lady Mary Wortley Montagu as 'that most profligate, impious and shameless of men', they do not seem to have deviated far from generally accepted standards of conduct.

But the club was more than a convivial group sharing common political interests. It was a place—perhaps *the* place in London, and hence in the nation—where patron, collector and writer (at least those of the Whig persuasion) could meet on something like an equal footing. Somers himself was all three rolled into one. Though he wrote little for publication after his dismissal,[13] his interest in men of letters and their works did not flag, and at the Kit-Cat Club he rubbed shoulders with most of the outstanding literary figures of Anne's reign. Swift's jibe at the club as a 'set of wits' who claimed 'a monopoly of our critical sense' was not far from the mark.[14] Somers's own protégé, Addison, was a member, as was Steele. The stage was represented by Congreve and Vanbrugh, co-managers of the new Queen's Theatre in the Haymarket. This the Kit-Cats helped to build, in return for life subscriptions to the entertainments there, and they attended en masse, occasioning Mary Astell's disparaging remark on how they showed 'their Value for Religion by the Proportion between their Offerings to the Temple and their Bounty to the Theatre'.[15] Such professional craftsmen provided a distinct leavening in the aristocratic group, though they were linked to the rest by the common bond of Whiggery and to some extent esteemed for their services in its cause. And there were others, of higher social station, though of less durable literary reputation: William Walsh ('the best critic of our nation', according to Dryden),[16] whom Somers supported for a parliamentary seat, and who collaborated with Congreve and Vanbrugh; Samuel Garth, who as a physician ministered to Somers's ailments and as a poet is remembered for *The Dispensary*; George Stepney, something of a poet, though a much better diplomat and conversationalist. With Tonson presiding at the board, and the bottle going round, there must have been many a memorable evening. Walsh and Edmund Dunch, who became Master of Anne's Household, were known as great wits, and Swift was to describe Charles Dartiquenave, the leading bon vivant of his age, as 'the greatest punner of this town' next to himself.[17]

As a collector and patron, Somers could share his interests and keep abreast of events through his association with the Kit-Cats. His old friend and co-worker Montague, made Baron Halifax in 1700, was a well-known Maecenas, serving as patron of Addison, Congreve and Prior and assembling a notable collection of pictures and antiquities. But the club had other prominent figures of this sort: as Ned Ward wrote, it was 'strengthen'd by the awful Presence of Right Honourable Wits, and other wealthy Pretenders, who, tho' not quallify'd to be Poets, they were rich enough to be Patrons, and ready with an open Hand to bespeak the Honour of the next flattering Dedication'.[18] One was the elderly Earl of Dorset, to whom Wycherley and Dryden as well as other literary men were indebted. Another was Charles Howard, Earl of Carlisle, who was not only a patron of the arts but an author and poet, and who commissioned Vanbrugh to design his vast country house, Castle Howard.

The late seventeenth century saw the establishment of the first great private libraries to be assembled by laymen in England. Pride of place has been given to the Earl of Anglesey, who died in 1688. However this may be, by Anne's reign it is not difficult to name ten or twelve aristocrats who had acquired substantial reputations as collectors. Somers's opposite, Harley, and his son, brought together one of the truly distinguished collections of all time, while that of Sunderland (not the arch-politician, but his son) has been described as the 'choicest' to be gathered before 1720. Among the Kit-Cats Howard and Montague built up libraries of some size. But it appears that Somers outstripped them.

Fortunately, we have a detailed catalogue of his books, in two folio volumes, and a similar record of his manuscript holdings.[19] Altogether the collection numbered more than 9000 printed works and hundreds of manuscript items; the Bodleian, at the time, had about 30,000 books and 6000 manuscripts. How long it was in the making is impossible to say. No doubt he began to acquire legal materials in his younger days. But the great bulk of his library, and its more valuable items, must have been obtained in the years of prosperity, and particularly in the more leisurely ones following his partial eclipse in 1700. It is noteworthy that Wormald and Wright make no reference to this collection in their account of English libraries before that date.[20]

The sections into which the catalogue is divided give evidence of the breadth of Somers's interests. As we might expect, his holdings in British history and English law were very rich, the former numbering over 350 items in the catalogue, the latter around 300. Some 250 deal with civil law —clearly a reflection of his early concern with this branch of jurisprudence, which contributed so much to his reputation as a learned and scholarly jurist. But, while the law and other relevant disciplines are abundantly represented, the collection was not merely a lawyer's library. It reveals, in countless ways, the broad intellectual interests of a highly cultivated collector, not wedded to any one field or period, a buyer of current medical books as well as the works of the Greek poets. As Burnet remarked, 'he was very learned in his own profession, with a great deal more learning in other professions, in divinity, philosophy, and history'.[21] In addition to historical works dealing with Great Britain, he brought together impressive arrays in the Roman, Byzantine, French and ecclesiastical fields. It comes as something of a surprise that the most numerous classification on the shelves of this latitudinarian Whig was neither historical nor legal, but theological, where we have upwards of 1300 entries.[22] He is said to have possessed virtually every printed edition of the Bible.[23] Perhaps he acquired some large collection, or it may be that these extensive holdings merely reflect the superabundance of such materials in the market. After theology comes philology with over 400 works, and geography with around 350. 'Philology' is but a division of a varied complex under 'Humane Letters', which includes poetry, grammar, rhetoric, antiquities, and other branches of the subject. Philosophical literature is well represented, as are the fields of natural history, politics and economics, medicine, mathematics and the arts.

Somers was not merely a seeker of antiquities and rare books, to be prized as collector's items. Of Robert Harley, his rival in book-collecting as well as politics, Prior wrote:

Fame counting thy books, my dear Harley, shall tell
No man had so many, who knew them so well.[24]

The same could be said of Somers. In 1697 he was described as 'a great Judge of learning and bookes'.[25] He was a reader—and something of a supporter—of the writers of his age, and their works make a long list in his catalogue. In English history, for example, one can point to few significant publications in the twenty-five years following the Revolution which Somers did not acquire. Gibson, Temple, Echard, Madox, Kennett, Bohun —all are there. So are Clarendon's *Rebellion*, Ludlow's *Memoirs* and those of

Sir Thomas Herbert, Whitelocke's *Memorials* and Fairfax's *Short Memorial*. Nor were foreign works ignored. Whatever Somers's mastery of other tongues he read French with ease; on his shelves were such items as de Larrey's *Histoire d'Angleterre*, Samson's *Guillaume III* and Massolier's *Henri VII*, to note but a few. The English poets and playwrights take up five folio pages of the catalogue, and are represented by 142 individual works, published between 1561 and 1715. Here are included all the notables of the past, from Chaucer to Milton, but there is no dearth of the writings of contemporaries. Among his books were publications of Addison, Behn, Shadwell, Rochester, Sedley and Dryden. In a somewhat younger group, he had those of Tate, Blackmore, Settle, Garth, Coward, King, Philips and Prior, among the poets, and of Congreve, Dennis, Lady Chudleigh and Susannah Centlivre among those primarily connected with the stage. Of the latter group, Somers had at least one work by each writer, published after the year 1700.

As in any collection, we may to some extent link items in his library with personal relationships and specific concernments engrossing his attention at one time or another. Had his catalogue been devised on other principles, it might have contained a category headed 'Association Pieces'. Here we would find essays by Addison and Steele, poems by Garth and Walsh, plays by Congreve, historical works by Gibson, Rymer and Madox. Some of these were presentation copies, perhaps testimonials to Somers's interest and generosity. As for the reflection of personal involvements, the legal works, printed or manuscript, in various instances evoke some particular case, of which the Bankers' was but the most famous. Another example is found in the project for Anglo-Scottish union.[26] There are a number of works on this subject, including Sir John Heyward's *Treatise* of 1604, and John Bristoll's *Discourse* of 1641. Similarly, we may attribute to his activities in reforming the coinage a variety of relevant treatises, including the two by John Locke, as well as those of Lowndes and Pratt.[27] It may be, too, that the large number of medical works stems from Somers's bouts with ill health. There are no less than 181 items in this category, nearly a third of them published in the quarter of a century following the Revolution.

Yet, in the great majority of cases, his books suggest a ranging intellectual curiosity rather than any practical motivation for acquiring them. Though he never travelled by land any further afield than the midland region of his birth and upbringing, or by sea beyond the Isle of Wight, he seems to have found pleasure in reading the literature of travel and exploration. Under the heading 'Peregrinationes' are listed over fifty publications. These include some of the classic accounts of early discovery: Hakluyt's *Principal Navigations*, Frobisher's *Three Voyages*, Willes's *History of Travel into the East and West Indies*—all published before the end of the Tudor era—and such seventeenth-century productions as Luke Fox's *Northwest Passage*, George Sandys's *Travels*, John Ray's similar *Collection* and Richard Whitbourne's *Discovery of Newfoundland*. But when we look for works

dealing with the developing polities and economies of the various plantations (which would seem to be of the greatest practical value for an English
statesman), we find almost nothing.[28]

Somers's collection of manuscripts was on the whole more indicative
of professional and political interests. In a sense they were the working
papers of the lawyer, judge and statesman. Some of the items, being copies,
had little value from the collector's point of view. In a catalogue running
to 177 folio pages, over half the entries relate to Parliament and the legislative process, the law, the administration of justice, and the conduct of
government generally. There are, for example, some twenty pages listing
parliamentary journals, acts and rolls; another eighteen enumerate collections of ancient statutes and old-time registers of writs, as well as treatises
on the canon law.[29]

But here, too, we are confronted with the roving character of Somer's
mind. As with the printed books, theology is substantially represented.
Among his interesting historical manuscripts were the Thurloe Papers,
which were found after the Interregnum concealed in the ceiling of a
Lincoln's Inn garret. These documents when bound formed sixty-seven
volumes; inherited by Joseph Jekyll, they ultimately passed into the keeping
of the Bodleian by way of Richard Rawlinson, who found in Somers's
library one of the principal sources of his acquisitions.[30] Other, smaller,
subdivisions of the catalogue relate to poetry, philosophy, rhetoric, meta-
physics, mathematics, astrology, and 'Medicinales Philosophici'. While the
manuscripts tend, much more than the books, to relate to England, there
is a notable sprinkling of items in foreign languages, particularly French,
Italian and Spanish. Of these manuscripts, enough to fill twenty volumes
were obtained for Somers by Joseph Addison during his travels in Italy.[31]

Here and there we catch a glimpse of Somers in quest of additional
treasures for his shelves and chests. He had regular dealings with Peter Le
Neve, the Norfolk antiquary and collector, who at twenty-six was a
Fellow of the Royal Society and later became Norroy King-at-Arms. Among
the Rawlinson Manuscripts is a copy of a letter from Le Neve to Somers,
apprising him of some manuscripts that had come on the market. Most
of the items were legal treatises, the prize of the lot being an early copy of
Bracton's 'De Legibus', but the list also included some theological and
political works, and what was advertised as Sir Philip Sidney's 'Arcadia'.
Somers bought the Bracton and Fitzherbert's 'Natura Brevium', along with
several other legal items; for the Bracton he paid five pounds. In 1697 he
acquired, apparently through Le Neve, twenty-seven manuscripts from Sir
William Hayward. Including Exchequer accounts, extracts from patent
rolls, chronicles, pedigrees, armorial and heraldic works, parliamentary
speeches, Leland's 'Itinerary' and Horne's 'Mirrour of Justices', the lot is
typical of Somers's manuscript collections as a whole. In all, it cost less than
nine pounds. On another occasion Le Neve made a memorandum to 'ask
Lord Somers what [he] will give for Bishop Worcesters Books'.[32] The
reference is to Stillingfleet's library, which was put up for sale upon his

death in 1699, having allegedly cost the bishop over £6000. If Somers bid
at all, he did not go high enough, for the manuscripts went to Harley and
the books to the Archbishop of Armagh. But he must have made substantial
cash outlays now and then. The principal part of his collection of medieval
historical and theological manuscripts is said to have belonged to Sir Henry
Langley, and he is supposed to have paid upwards of £500 to Thomas
Britton—the Clerkenwell coal-monger who formed a remarkable collection
of books relating, for the most part, to chemistry and the occult—for what
must have been (at that price) a very large number of choice pamphlets.[33]

In 1729, thirteen years after Somers's death, these holdings (of which
the printed books were appraised at £3144 16s 6d) were divided, in equal
lots, between his brother-in-law, Joseph Jekyll, and Philip Yorke, the husband of his niece, Margaret Cocks.[34] Both made their mark in the legal
profession: Jekyll became Master of the Rolls in 1717; Yorke would become
Lord Chancellor and be ennobled as the Earl of Hardwicke. With the passage
of time the collection was further dispersed. Jekyll's library was sold at
auction following his death in 1728.[35] Yorke's share remained longer intact,
but by the early years of the present century only a few of Somers's books
remained at Wimpole, and these not among the more valuable. Somers's
papers and correspondence, filling more than sixty quarto volumes, remained at his country residence, in the Jekylls' possession. Their value was
recognised by Charles Yorke who, along with his brother Philip and Thomas
Birch, appears to have projected an annotated selection, for which a rough
catalogue was drawn up. The collection was moved to Charles Yorke's
chambers in Lincoln's Inn, only to be almost completely destroyed by fire
in 1752.[36] It is lamentable that a collection which might have passed into
the public domain, as was the case with the Harley treasures or the
Cottonian library, was dispersed or obliterated. Only in so far as its contents
were drawn upon for the *Somers Tracts* was it preserved for posterity.
Fortunately, the first compilation of these valuable materials was completed in 1752, the very year of the disastrous fire.[37]

In addition to books and manuscripts Somers brought together an extensive collection of prints and drawings, and occasionally picked up a painting. One can picture a friendly rivalry with his colleague Halifax (whose
impressive holdings were not dispersed until 1740). Since he did not travel
abroad, he employed agents and friends to comb the markets of the continent, or at least those of Italy, the happy hunting ground of all seekers
of *objets d'art*. The Duke of Shrewsbury, sojourning in Rome for several
years, executed commissions for him, and Henry Newton, his friend from
Oxford days who was for five years envoy to Florence, was also useful.
But it seems that most of his prints were acquired through a certain Father
Resta, in Rome, 'a Person very well known among the Curious'.[38]

From the catalogue prepared for the auction of these effects in May 1717,
we can obtain a full and detailed picture of the extent of his holdings.[39]
In all there were about four thousand drawings and 'a much greater
Number of Prints', all 'very fair, and in good condition'. These were con-

tained in portfolios bound in 'Turkey and Morocco', finely gilt. Here too Somers's tastes were eclectic, and his collection embraced all the notable artists of the Italian, German, Dutch and Flemish schools. Italian works, however, heavily outweighed the others. He possessed drawings by Raphael, Michelangelo, Titian, Corregio, da Vinci, Vernonese, Bellini, Giorgione, Tintoretto and Bernini; and, among the non-Italians, Rubens, Van Dyke and Lely. There were prints of the work of most of these artists, and of del Sarto, Dürer, Hollar and the 'English Masters' as well. Unfortunately, the English contingent is not specifically identified—mute testimony, it would seem, of the inferior rank assigned to native talent. Whole books were filled with prints of Rubens, Loggan and Hollar, and Lucas Cranach and Guido Reni figured prominently among the woodcuts. In addition to these treasures, there was a large collection of medals, but no reference to other sculptured works. Paintings were not for sale on this occasion. But, while we have only fragmentary evidence, there is no doubt that from time to time he picked them up. The Rawlinson Manuscripts include a journal in an unidentified hand containing a sketch of a painting—possibly Mary Magdalene with angels—purchased for Somers in Italy in 1715, evidence that invalidism and senility had not extinguished his interest in works of art. There were also notations regarding two Albanos and a landscape of Paul Bril, which the unknown traveller appears to have brought to Somers's attention. His correspondence with Shrewsbury likewise reveals a persistent appetite for such works.[40]

In a few cases he had personal contacts with artists. His portrait was executed on several occasions, most notably by Godfrey Kneller, who painted all the Kit-Cats for Tonson's Gallery at Barn Elms, and who was almost an honorary member of the club.[41] Somers, when Lord Chancellor, also sat to Simon Dubois, an artist of Dutch origin who had migrated to London. He is said to have gone to Dubois incognito, paid him fifty guineas, and then to have revealed himself, sending him his robes of office and, upon completion of the portrait, another fifty guineas. Although Dubois had executed several commissions before the Revolution, including heads of the Whig lawyers Jones and Williams, he now, through Somers's recommendations, moved into more exalted circles and executed portraits of Rochester, Portland and Archbishop Tenison. He must have looked upon Somers as his patron, for upon his death in 1708 he left his pictures with him as executor, and bequeathed to him portraits of his parents by Van Dyke, and his books as well. A full length portrait of the painter was already in Somers's possession. This we learn from the engraver, George Vertue, who produced likenesses of Somers and his brother-in-law, Joseph Jekyll, and whom Somers commissioned to engrave a portrait of Tillotson, after Kneller. Somers, we are told, 'rewarded him nobly', though Vertue's great supporter was the Earl of Oxford.[42]

It was in the realm of literature that Somers became known as a patron, and this in an era which comes near to marking the zenith of such support. The writings of the Augustan age provide ample reference to his generosity and enlightenment. 'Arts he supports and learning is his care': so wrote Dr Garth; to him he was 'the matchless Atticus'.[43] Even Swift, whose friendship with Somers was clouded by disappointment over preferment and by his conversion to the Tory interest, in 1720 called him 'a great Patron of Learning, which induced many Learned men to dedicate their Works to him'.[44]

That a man of such prominence would attract dedications, regardless of his intellectual and artistic proclivities, was inevitable. Swift, dedicating his *Tale of a Tub* to Somers, declared that he would not 'desire any other Help, to grow an Alderman, than a Patent for the sole Privilege of Dedicating to your Lordship', adding that his name 'on the Front, in capital letters, will at any time get off one edition'.[45] Still, the variety and, in many cases, the eminence of those who laid their writings as tribute before Somers, reveal the scope of his interests and generosity. A partial list includes, besides Swift, such notables as Addison and Steele; the historians Madox, Rymer and Gibson; the philosopher Shaftesbury, and that virtuoso, best remembered as a diarist, John Evelyn. Among lesser lights are the poets Phillips, Dennis and Garth; John Ayliffe, author of *The Ancient and Present State of the University of Oxford*; and John Cary, merchant and writer on trade.[46] Most of these instances bespeak a consciousness of favours received. Some imply, at least, a desire for future interest and support. Such was certainly the case with John Dennis, though none would express himself as frankly as Guy Miege, who, in dedicating the third edition of his *New State of England* to Somers, remarked that 'as this Impression do's far exceed the former by its great Improvements, so I hope, my Lord, You will the more readily Countenance it, and become a Mecaenas to . . . Guy Miege'.[47]

Somers's first noteworthy venture as a patron occurred just before the Revolution. Milton, we are told, was his favourite poet. At this time his works were still looked upon with hostility or indifference by a large part of the reading public: the reaction of the Restoration years had not entirely passed away. It was Somers who encouraged Jacob Tonson to bring out a folio edition of 'Paradise Lost' in 1688. This bookseller had in 1683 purchased half the copyright of the work, but, though spurred on by Dryden, he was beset with misgivings, believing the times 'not propitious to blank verse upon a sacred subject'.[48] While Somers by no means stood alone in sponsoring the work—the subscribers listed at the end of the sumptuous folio number over five hundred members of the nobility and gentry, and Francis Atterbury, as well as Dryden himself, was active—there can be no doubt that he deserves the principal credit for promoting the undertaking. The most conclusive evidence comes from the publisher, who, in bringing out the second edition, dedicated it to Somers, remarking that 'his opinion and encouragement occasioned the first appearance of Milton, in the folio edition'.[49]

But Somers was not content to honour the works of the dead. He sought to encourage the talents of the living. Before the turn of the century he had discovered the most renowned of his protégés, Joseph Addison. According to Richard Steele, Congreve introduced Addison to Charles Montague, who in turn made him known to Somers.[50] However this may be, we know that Addison did not shun the direct approach. In 1695, when he was about twenty-four, he brought out *A Poem to His Majesty, Presented to the Lord Keeper*, appealing for support:

> On You, my lord, with anxious Fear I wait,
> And from Your Judgment must expect my Fate.

Somers is said to have made an encouraging response. Late in William's reign Somers and Montague, in the full tide of their political influence, co-operated to provide Addison with what in our day would be described as a government grant for travel and study abroad.[51] The result was a grand tour of the continent which lasted for over four years, and an abiding friendship and sense of gratitude on Addison's part. In 1696 he wrote from Paris:

I have now for some time liv'd on the Effects of your L^dp's patronage without presuming to return you my Most humble Thanks for it. But I find it no less difficult to suppress the sense I have of your L^dp's favour than I do to represent it as I ought. Gratitude for a kindness received is generally as troublesome to the Benefactor as the Importunity of soliciting it; and I hope your L^dp will pardon me if I offend in one of these respects who had never any occasion or pretence to do it on the other. The only Return I can make your Lo^dp will be to apply myself entirely to my Business and to take such a care of my Conversation that you^r favours may not seem misplaced.[52]

Not for six years was Addison ready to pay a more public tribute to his benefactor. Acknowledging that it was by Somers's means that he 'first of all obtained an opportunity of travelling', and that 'when the patrons worth is extraordinary 'tis generally expected there should be something answerable in the merits of those whom he encourages', he now produced his *Remarks on Several Parts of Italy*, with a dedication to Somers.[53] Addison's sojourn abroad had been designed to qualify him for the diplomatic service; he might otherwise have gone into the Church. Shortly after his return he was appointed under-secretary of state, and in 1709 secretary to the Lord Lieutenant of Ireland, Lord Wharton. Meanwhile he was hobnobbing with the leading Whigs in the Kit-Cat Club. Though specific evidence is lacking, it is only reasonable to suppose that Somers continued to support his protégé, and that he played a part in securing these preferments for him. Certainly the two men kept in touch, even after Addison's removal to Dublin, whence he corresponded with Somers on Irish and other political matters. In 1710 he was soliciting Somers's aid for Ambrose Philips, the poet, then secretary to the envoy to Denmark. The eulogy of Somers in *The Freeholder* is ample testimony that his regard for his benefactor never flagged.[54]

Addison was to become a leading journalistic spokesman for the Whigs. There can be no doubt that Somers and Halifax, whatever their regard for his literary ability, had an eye for his potential political usefulness. The great age of political pamphleteering was at hand, when both parties availed themselves of the pens of the leading writers. Steele was to be linked with Addison in this regard, but whereas Addison would regard Somers as the principal architect of his fortunes, it was to Halifax that Steele was primarily obliged. Apart from membership in the Kit-Cat Club, he does not appear to have been closely associated with Somers, although he held him in high regard.[55] It is true that he dedicated the first volume of the collected *Spectator* to him, but his remarks, though generous, lack some of the personal warmth of dedications to closer friends, such as Halifax. And it is noteworthy that Somers, upon the revival of his political fortunes in 1708, did not promote Steele's candidacy for the post of Gentleman Usher of the Privy Chamber.[56]

It appears that he was inclined to smile upon Jonathan Swift, rather than Steele, for the coveted ushership. Though Swift is today remembered as the Tory polemicist *par excellence*, Somers had known him for perhaps a decade, during which he had been of some use to the Whigs and certainly looked for favours and preferment at their hands.[57] In 1701 he came to the defence of the four impeached Lords in his *Discourse of the Contests and Dissensions Between the Nobles and the Commons in Athens and Rome.*[58] When it became known that Swift was the author, Somers and Halifax, as well as Bishop Burnet, 'with great marks of esteem and professions of kindness', sought his acquaintance, and, Swift goes on, 'were very liberal in promising me the greatest preferments I could hope for, if ever it came in their power'. He adds that he soon 'grew domestic' with Halifax, and was 'as often with Lord Somers as the formality of his nature (the only un-conversable fault he has) made it agreeable to me'.[59] Thus, though on a somewhat limited basis, an amicable association developed.

Yet the relationship bore little fruit. This was not entirely due to want of application on the part of the former Chancellor. There is no evidence that he was active on Swift's behalf until 1708, but these were years when he was out of office. Early in that year Swift is on record as valuing Somers's friendship, as well as his influence. Somers, in turn, gave him some assistance in connection with the claim of the Irish clergy to share in Queen Anne's Bounty.[60] He also supported his bid for the vacant bishopric of Waterford, though the prize fell to Dr Milles. About the same time there is reason to believe that he recommended him to serve as chaplain to Lord Wharton in his newly gained Irish post—against Swift's will, for he nursed an intense hatred for the rakish peer.[61] Somers's elevation to the Lord Presidency of the Council brought no advantage to Swift, though he was not without hope. Late in 1708 it was rumoured that he would be sent as Queen's Secretary to Vienna. Twice in 1709, in letters to Halifax, he speaks of the possibility of preferment.[62] Even in 1710, when rumours of the Lord President's ouster were circulating, Swift wrote Addison that 'if he were to continue, I might, perhaps, hope for some good offices'.[63] Somers sought to be of service regarding Queen Anne's Bounty as late as September of that year.[64] But the same month witnessed his dismissal. About all that Swift could chalk up to his association with the Whigs was a benefice for his 'little parson cousin', Thomas. It was 'a very good Benefice in one of the most Delicious Parts of one of the Pleasantest Counties of England', but it could carry with it no great obligation on the part of the disappointed satirist.[65]

By now Swift was ready to embrace the Tories, and before the year was out Harley, St John and Ormonde had taken the place of Somers and Halifax in his calculations.[66] Never truly a protégé of the Whigs, he had long before this been beset with misgivings over that party's attitude towards the Church. To be an effective cog in the Whig machine, with its broad-bottomed alliance with Nonconformity, and a self-respecting High Church-man were to Swift contradictions in terms. He had conversations with Somers on this subject, and found him not unsympathetic. But they did not share much common ground. To Swift the cry of 'the Church in danger' was to be taken seriously; to Somers it was merely a shibboleth.[67] And so Swift looked to the Tories. By 1711 he was not seeing his old Whig friends any more, except for Halifax; Somers—'a false deceitful rascal'—he never saw.[68] But the outburst should probably not be taken too seriously. When, in 1729, he listed his distinguished friends, Somers was placed second among 'Men famous for their learning, wit, or great employments or quality,' who were no longer living.[69]

With Alexander Pope Somers's connection was slight, the disparity in age precluding a long-enduring relationship. But the poet tells us that in 1706, when still in his teens, he 'had the honour' of knowing Somers. In a note to the 1736 edition of his *Pastorals*, Pope observes that these pieces, written at the age of sixteen, 'Past thro' the hands' of a number of con-noisseurs, all of whom gave the author 'the greatest encouragement'. Among them were Halifax and Somers, whom Pope in another place des-cribes as not only 'a consummate statesman' but 'a man of Learning and Politeness'.[70]

It has been said that Somers 'was not wont to take heed of the personal opinions of those whom he succoured or engaged'.[71] But while Pope includes him among the 'Patrons or Admirers' of Dryden, there is almost no evidence of patronage here.[72] One would hardly expect a Whig to embrace the author of *Absolom and Achitophel*. Dryden himself in 1699 referred to the Chancellor as his 'enemy', though Somers (to whom Dryden had once presented a pocket edition of Virgil) had recently contributed five guineas towards one of the illustrations for his translation of that poet, and the Kit-Cats would help pay for his obsequies in 1700.[73]

But Somers could be generous without regard for political implications or consequences. The most pointed instance of this is to be found in his good offices to George Hickes, the non-juring divine and Anglo-Saxon scholar. Somers could have felt little sympathy for the principles of this cleric, who had lost the deanery of Worcester and was forced into hiding for his refusal to recognise King William, and was known to be a link between the disaffected clergy and the exiled James. Yet he employed his influence as Lord Chancellor to set aside proceedings against him.[74] And his relations with the two major historians of the time, Madox and Rymer, were free from any discernible political orientation.

Thomas Madox is a somewhat elusive figure. Like Somers, he received a legal education at the Middle Temple. Unlike Somers, he was never called to the bar, but subsisted, after a fashion, in several clerkly assignments at the disposal of the government. He was 'first and foremost a student of records', and was called upon by the Lords to assist in the preservation and reordering of the public archives. In this connection he must have rubbed shoulders with Somers, though the two men were probably already acquainted. Of Somers's patronage there is no doubt. In 1702 Madox brought out his *Formulare Anglicanum, or a Collection of Ancient Charters and Instruments*. In his dedication to Somers he wrote:

The Patronage of It is devolved on Your Lordship by a Peculiar Right: Namely, As you are a great Lover of Ancient Monuments; And as Your Lordship's Approbation was the Principal Encouragement I had in the Beginning and Progress of this Undertaking.

Nine years later he published his *History and Antiquities of the Exchequer of the Kings of England*, for which Somers had lent him two copies of the 'Dialogus de Scaccario' from his own collection. This he dedicated to Queen Anne, but a long prefatory letter to Somers acknowledges his continuing relationship with the statesman. Madox was an isolated, sensitive and diffident man; Douglas suggests that 'the strongest personal connection which he formed may perhaps have been that with Lord Somers, whose patronage made possible his books'.[75] His efforts received further recognition in 1714, when he was made Historiographer Royal, but here there is no evidence that he was obliged to Somers.

Thomas Rymer was to leave as his enduring monument the multi-volume collection of British treaties, the *Foedera*. In the promotion of this work, Somers, along with other political magnates, played a prominent part. Though a persistent tradition ascribes the original scheme to Harley, it appears that Halifax and Somers did most to launch the undertaking. Certainly, it could not have been carried forward with any prospect of success by Rymer himself, whose social position and literary reputation were insufficient for the entrée which such a project required.[76] Madox, Kennett, Le Clerc and Des Maizeaux—all contemporaries of Rymer—alike concur in attributing the publication to the two Whig statesmen. Through their influence governmental support and publication was assured. In 1693, some eight months after Rymer had been appointed Historiographer Royal, he received a warrant authorising him to transcribe and publish 'all the leagues, treaties, alliances, capitulations and confederacies' that were relevant; further official approbation was forthcoming at a meeting of the Privy Council in April 1694, at which Somers was present.[77] When, beginning in 1704, the volumes began to appear, Halifax was presented with thirteen sets and Somers with one, an indication, perhaps, of their relative involvement in the project.[78] Apart from the *Foedera*—for Rymer also produced critical, dramatic and poetic works—there is no evidence of any connection with Somers, though Hardy suggests that Rymer wrote his *General Draught and Prospect of Government in Europe* (1681), a treatise which draws upon medieval chronicles to support the rights of parliaments against the royal prerogative, at his request.[79]

Mention may be made of one other figure who was linked with Somers, and, while lacking the distinction of Madox or Rymer, nevertheless left something of a mark in the field of antiquarian scholarship. This was Edmund Gibson. He had already attracted some attention, chiefly through his edition of the Anglo-Saxon Chronicle, when in 1695 he produced his translation of Camden's *Britannia*, which he dedicated to Somers. In his dedicatory remarks the youthful don—he was twenty-six at the time, and had just been made a Fellow of Queen's College, Oxford—noted the satisfaction which Somers's political advancement had produced among learned men; Britannia, he wrote, 'was pleased to hear them say that by such promotions they, as well as their neighbours, might at last have their Richelieus and Colberts'.[80] According to Basil Williams, Gibson, an 'irreproachable Whig' who climbed to the bishoprics of Lincoln and London, 'might not have risen above a college living had he not dedicated some of his works to Somers and Archbishop Tenison'.[81] If this be true, Tenison must have been far more instrumental than Somers, for the Lord Keeper appears to have offered him only a small benefice in the Isle of Thanet, worth £20 a year, which Gibson declined because of its unhealthy situation.[82]

In his dedication Gibson further noted how Somers had earned the nation's blessing for his 'defence of her distressed Prelates'. This sense of obligation, stemming from his contribution to the trial of the bishops, tapered off as he acquired the reputation of a latitudinarian, or perhaps even that of a freethinker or deist.[83] In the realms of theology and philosophy, he tended to favour the rational sceptical school. With the most notable of contemporary deists, John Toland, he does not appear to have associated, though a common interest in Milton may have drawn them together.[84] But he is said to have written the preface to Matthew Tindal's *Rights of the Christian Church Asserted Against the Romish and All Other Priests Who Claim an Independent Power Over It* (1706), a work which evoked more than a score of retorts from English clerics who objected to Tindal's contention that the Church had no rights of the kind claimed by the high church party. By this time Tindal had produced several treatises of a Whiggish or low church character; his best known work. *Christianity as Old as the Creation*, an effective statement of the rationalist approach, lay a quarter of a century ahead. He was something of an expert in the field of international law, and must have encountered Somers in Doctors Commons. It is noteworthy that a Whiggish House of Commons in 1710 ordered the *Rights* to be burned (apparently as a gesture against deism)—perhaps an indication that Somers's religious liberalism outstripped that of most of his colleagues.[85] According to tradition, his bounty extended to

Jean Le Clerc, the French Protestant theologian, whose exposition of the doctrine of the Trinity and of original sin were considerably in advance of conventional interpretations, and who argued against such conceptions as the Mosaic authorship of the Pentateuch.[86] Such support seems to have found little or no outlet in England, though in 1697 the Non-conformist minister, Walter Cross, sought his patronage for a work on the Bible.[87]

Among the philosophers Somers is linked in one way or another with Pierre Bayle, John Locke and the third Earl of Shaftesbury, but in none of these cases can he be described as a patron. In Bayle's case, it was not for want of trying, for Somers sought to assist in the publication of his *Dictionaire Historique et Critique*, which first appeared in 1697. The French sceptic had a few years earlier been deprived of his chair in philosophy and history at the University of Rotterdam, and was known to be in impoverished circumstances. Hearing of this, Somers wrote to a friend in Holland, suggesting that 'if Mr. Bayle would accept of his patronage for his Dictionary, he had 150 guineas at his service'. But Bayle refused the proffered support, allegedly because he was resentful towards King William, who had ordered the magistrates of Rotterdam to withdraw his pension and licence to teach, and could not bring himself to accept the generosity of a statesman who stood in so close a relationship to this prince.[88]

To Locke and Shaftesbury Somers was a close friend rather than a patron. As we have seen, Locke addressed his first published treatise in the field of economics to Somers, and the two men co-operated closely in some areas of government.[89] But Locke was the elder by some twenty years, with an established reputation before Somers gained any prominence. Locke certainly esteemed Somers as a man of parts and was mindful of his good offices. But, while there were undoubtedly many exchanges between the two, it does not appear that the philosopher was in any direct way obligated to the statesman in the production of such works as the *Essay Concerning Humane Understanding*, the *Letters on Toleration*, or *The Reasonableness of Christianity*, all of which appeared in the years of their association.

With Anthony Ashley Cooper, third Earl of Shaftesbury, Somers's relations were at least as close as those with Locke. The Earl was the grandson of the great Whig protagonist of Somers's youth. There was a strong political bond between them, involving co-operation on various issues. Early in Anne's reign, while Shaftesbury was on the continent, Somers held his proxy in the Lords.[90] As Shaftesbury remarked, in dedicating his *Letter Concerning Design* to Somers, he had often been disposed to act 'in concert' with him in public affairs, both holding 'the same views, on the interest of Europe and mankind'. But the association transcended politics; it involved close friendship and intellectual stimulation. Shaftesbury described the *Letter*, which had evolved from a conversation over newly acquired engravings, as a 'fresh instance' that he could never employ his thoughts 'with satisfaction on any subject' without making Somers a party.[91]

Shaftesbury also dedicated the six treatises which make up his *Character-*

istics to Somers. The collected work was published anonymously in 1711. Before that, however, the various essays appeared singly, and each was sent to him along with a dedicatory letter. The first of these presentations, as far as we know, was *The Sociable Enthusiast*, a precursor of *The Moralists*. It was proffered late in 1705, as a private communication. 'Nobody', wrote Shaftesbury, 'has sett their eyes on it, nor shall, besides your self.'[92] This reservation has been questioned in recent research, which suggests that an edition had appeared at least a year earlier.[93] But there can be no doubt that Somers was intimately connected with the philosopher's literary productions and, in general, had a prior view of them. When *The Moralists* appeared in 1708, Shaftesbury made haste to send him an unbound copy, 'lest it should be abroad anywhere' before he had it. In 1708 an indiscretion on Somers's part, which nearly led to the publication of a clandestine edition of the *Letter Concerning Enthusiasm*, prompted a word of warning from the author, who was hesitant to publish and clung to anonymity.[94]

Somers's interests were focused for the most part on the humanities. This is not to say that his mind was closed to scientific knowledge, the development of which was so remarkably accelerated in his own lifetime. From Leonard Plukenet, the Queen's Botanist, who presented him with a copy of his *Botany, or the Knowledge of Plants*, we learn that he planned to round out his library 'by a compleat Collection of Books in all Sciences'.[95] John Evelyn chose to dedicate his *Acetaria, a Discourse of Sallets* (a portion of a projected work on horticulture) to Somers, who, he tells us, received him 'with greate humanity and familiar kindnesse'.[96]

Evelyn was already acquainted with Somers, for both men were Fellows of the Royal Society. Somers, elected a Fellow in 1698, was simultaneously called upon to serve as President.[97] Prior to that time he does not appear to have shown any particular interest in the organisation, though he was acquainted with a number of Fellows, some of whom were or would become associates in the Kit-Cat Club.[98] It appears that he owed the office to his prominence in public affairs. His immediate predecessor was his political colleague, Montague, who must have played some part in his selection. Evelyn, who was one of the Councillors of the Society, was present when Somers was inducted into office; he reports that the Chancellor 'made a short compliment concerning the honour the Society had done him, and how ready he would be to promote so noble a design, and come himself among us as often as his attendance on the public would permit'.[99] The Society was in a flagging condition at the time; the number of Fellows had declined steadily for twenty years, and its financial arrangements were so informal that after 1677 no reports were made for nearly forty years. On the other hand, Somers could count on the experience and assistance of Sir Hans Sloane, for many years first Secretary, and of the two Vice-Presidents, Sir Robert Southwell and Sir John Hoskins, both of whom had formerly headed the Society.

There is no evidence that he showed more than a perfunctory concern for its affairs. He rarely attended its deliberations. Though he was present at a few of the ordinary meetings, he was never on hand for any of the more important sessions of the Council. When in 1698 Sloane arranged fifteen meetings for the purpose of discussing the worrisome financial condition of the Society, Somers attended none of them.[100] Nor did he make any contributions to the *Philosophical Transactions*. Perhaps, as he had warned the members, the pressure of official business was too intense; yet, when released from much of this, he does not seem to have become noticeably more active. It is not too much to say that he was President only in name, and that Southwell, Hoskins and Sloane provided such direction as was afforded. He remained in office until 1703. Perhaps he would have stepped down earlier had Sir Isaac Newton, who succeeded him, been willing to take over. He does not appear to have been, in any consequential way, a benefactor—we hear of no gifts except a Chinese chair—or to have bestirred himself with respect to membership, though he proposed Count Lorenzo Magalotti, a prominent Florentine statesman and 'accomplished universal Scholler'.[101] There is only a hint that his continental connections were of some use or that his official influence might be drawn upon, as in 1699, when he was asked to try to induce the King to purchase Stillingfleet's library.[102] Nevertheless, the Society thought well enough of him to issue three of the annual volumes of its *Philosophical Transactions* in his honour, and it has preserved his portrait to this day.[103]

NOTES

[1] *History*, III, 479. William Shippen, in *Faction Display'd*, calls Tonson the founder.

[2] Hist. MSS. Comm., *Bath MSS.* (London, 1904–8), III, 394.

[3] See Robert J. Allen, *Clubs of Augustan London* (Cambridge, 1933), 35–54; John Timbs, *Clubs and Life in London* (London, 1899), 47–53; *Portraits of Members of the Kit Cat Club* (National Portrait Gallery, London, n.d.).

[4] On Tonson, see Kathleen M. Lynch, *Jacob Tonson, Kit-Cat Publisher* (Knoxville, 1971).

[5] *Complete Works of Sir John Vanbrugh*, ed. Bonamy Dobrée and Geoffrey Webb (London, 1927–28), IV, 7.

[6] This when Tonson was nearly eighty. *Works of Alexander Pope*, ed. Whitwell Elwin (London, 1871–89), VIII, 279.

[7] See *Kit Cat Portraits*. The Kit-Kat Club's Ministers were Stanhope, Walpole, Thomas Pelham-Holles and Pulteney. On the club as representative of various sections of the Whig party, see Geoffrey Holmes, *British Politics in the Age of Anne* (London, 1967), 297.

[8] Lady Mary Wortley Montagu thought that many of the Kit-Cats were 'dupes to their leaders': Robert Halsband, *Life of Mary Wortley Montagu* (Oxford, 1956), 8; her remark probably dates from the 1750s.

[9] Holmes, 297–98 and notes 31–36.

[10] For a particularly sweeping castigation, see the ironic dedication to the Kit-Cats in Mary Astell's *Bart'lemy Fair* (1709).

[11] *Faction Display'd*, lines 391–94.

[12] Add. MSS. 40,060, f. 30v.; other toasts follow. See also *Private Correspondence of Sarah Duchess of Marlborough* (London, 1838), I, 159–60. The belles included Lady Essex, the Duchess of St Albans, Lady Hyde, the Duchess of Bolton, Mrs Brudenell, Mrs Spanheim and others.

[13] *Anguis in Herba* (London, 1701), sometimes ascribed to him is by Henry Maxwell. In 1702 *Several Orations ... English'd ...by Several Hands* was brought out under his direction. He may have written the preface for Tourreil's rendition of Demosthenes (1704). On *Jus Regium* (London, 1701), see above, p. 160; *Jura Populi Anglicani* (London, 1701), above, p. 180; *The Judgment of Whole Kingdoms and Nations* (London, 1710), below,

p. 295, n.71. Wing, but not the British Museum, credits him with A *Discourse concerning Generosity* (London, 1693), a lengthy work with a moral thrust. Laslett, *Locke Library*, 141, 236, appears to be uncertain. I have found no evidence for his authorship.

14 *Examiner*, No. 6.

15 *Bart'lemy Fair* (London, 1709), 12–13. Charles Leslie, in his *Rehearsal* (1705), speaks of the club as having 'Built a Temple for their Dagon, the new Play-House in the hay-Market,' with 'such Zeal shew'd, and all Purses open to carry on this Work, that it was almost as soon Finish'd as Begun.' See also Allardyce Nicoll, *History of Early Eighteenth Century Drama* (Cambridge, 1925), 271. See also Robert J. Allen, 'The Kit-Cat Club and the Theatre', *Review of English Studies*, VII (January 1931), 56–61.

16 *Works of John Dryden*, ed. Sir Walter Scott and George Saintsbury (London, 1882–93), XV, 192.

17 *Works*, ed. Scott, II, 19.

18 Edward Ward, *Secret History of Clubs* (London, 1709), ch. XXXI.

19 The former is Add. MSS. 40, 751–52; the latter Harl. MSS. 7191.

20 Francis Wormald and C. E. Wright, *The English Library before 1700* (London, 1958). Nor does Seymour de Ricci mention Somers's holdings in his *English Collectors of Books and Manuscripts* (Cambridge, 1930).

21 Burnet, IV, 187.

22 There are entries under 'Theologia' running from f. 39 to f. 181; the first thirty-eight folios are missing.

23 There are no entries. They may have been listed in the missing folios.

24 *Portland MSS.*, V, 611.

25 *Portledge Papers*, 256–57.

26 See below, pp. 243–48.

27 *A Consideration of Lowering Interest and Raising the Value of Money* (1692); *A Further Consideration concerning the Raising the Value of Money* (1695). See above, p. 106.

28 There are a few items of Americana under 'Historia Britannica'.

29 See Harl. MSS. 7191.

30 William D. Macray, *Annals of the Bodleian Library* (Oxford, 1866), 172.

31 Among them were collections on Venetian history, now in the King's Manuscripts, British Museum.

32 Bodleian Library, Rawlinson MSS. D. 888, ff. 29, 30v, 48v.

33 *The Library*, 4th ser., XXIII (June 1942), 3, 5; John Morgan, *Phoenix Britannicus* (London, 1732), I, 558.

34 Add. MSS. 36, 116, f. 72 ff. Some categories (Bibles, for example) were apparently not divided. There is evidence that others may have shared in the riches. On 29 September 1729, William Andrews wrote to 'My Lady'—probably Lady Jekyll—that M^r Jo: Cocks agrees that Mr Attorney may draw lots for him for the Books, as well as Mr James Cocks & Lady Williams': *ibid.*, f. 186. The three beneficiaries were all children of Charles and Mary Cocks. But erosion appears to have begun earlier. From Humphrey Wanley, the Harleys' librarian, we learn that the second Earl of Oxford had helped Nathaniel Noel, a London bookseller, 'to secure Lord Somers's books'. This could not have been later than 1726, when Wanley died: Arthur S. Turberville, *History of Welbeck Abbey and Its Owners* (London, 1938), I, 374.

35 See Rawlinson MSS. Catalogue, comp. William D. Macray, A. 146; also Rawlinson MSS. D. 716, ff. 44, 46v, *sub* Jekyll in index. A sale catalogue of the books was published in 1739. Some items remained unsold in 1740. See John Nichols, *Illustrations of the Literary History of the Eighteenth Century* (London, 1822), IV, 530; *Library*, 4th ser., XXIII (June 1942), 3, 5.

36 Hardwicke, *State Papers*, II, 399–481, where some of the surviving papers in the hands of the Earl of Hardwicke are published. See also New York Public Library, Hardwicke MSS., vol. XXXIII; Philip C. Yorke, *Life and Correspondence of Philip Yorke, Earl of Hardwicke* (Cambridge, 1913), I, 70n; II, 144, 179; Holmes, *British Politics*, 288.

37 Between 1748 and 1752 four collections were brought out, each comprising four volumes, by public subscription. Sixty years later Sir Walter Scott produced a better arranged edition in thirteen volumes.

38 Sloane MSS. 4223, f. 243, with reference to two cases of pictures shipped from Leghorn in 1707; Nicholson and Turberville, *Shrewsbury*, 149n; Coke, *Shrewsbury*, 642, 644.

39 *A Collection of Prints and Drawings, &c., of the Late Right Honourable John L^d*

Somers, to be Sold at Auction (London, 1717). The sale was at Motteaux's auction room in Covent Garden.

[40] Rawlinson MSS. D. 1162, f. 7v.

[41] Kneller painted several portraits of Somers. He was also painted by Richardson and possibly by Riley. There is a portrait of him as a boy at Eastnor Castle. See *Catalogue of Seventeenth-Century Portraits in the National Portrait Gallery, 1625–1714*, comp. by David Piper (Cambridge, 1963), 319–20 and 399–403 (for the Kit-Cat Club portraits); Freeman O'Donoghue, *Catalogue of Engraved British Portraits Preserved in the Department of Prints and Drawings in the British Museum* (London, 1908–25), IV, 141–42; D.N.B., John Somers. For engravings of groups (Lords Justices, Impeached Lords, Counsel for the Seven Bishops) in which he appears, see O'Donoghue, V, 71, 77.

[42] Horace Walpole, *Anecdotes of Painting in England* (London, World Library of Standard Books, n.d.), 289; *Works of Horatio Walpole* (London, 1798–1825), IV, 120, 133, 138; Joseph Strutt, *Biographical Dictionary Containing an Historical Account of All the Engravers* (London, 1785), II, 387.

[43] *The Dispensary*, canto VI.

[44] *Tale of a Tub*, ed. Guthkelch and Smith, 22n. Somers's reputation as a patron survived him, and seems even to have waxed with the passing years. The Earl of Orrery, in his *Remarks on the Life and Writings of Dr. Jonathan Swift* (London, 1752), 93, called him 'the general patron of the literati'. Oliver Goldsmith, lamenting that under Walpole the encouragement of learned men was neglected, recalled that 'when the great Somers was at the helm, patronage was fashionable among our nobility': *Enquiry into the Present State of Polite Learning in Europe* (London, 1759), ch. X.

[45] *Tale of a Tub*, 23.

[46] Phillips dedicated his *Vision of Mons. Chamillard Concerning the Battle of Ramillies* (1706) to Somers. Ayliffe was attacked by Bernard Gardiner, Vice-Chancellor of Oxford, for dedicating his work to Somers rather than to the Duke of Ormonde: William R. Ward, *Georgian Oxford* (Oxford, 1958), 110. John Hughes dedicated his edition of Spenser (1715) to Somers.

[47] See David H. Stevens, *Party Politics and English Journalism, 1702–42* (Menasha, 1916), 11.

[48] Maddock, 27; William Roberts, *Earlier History of English Bookselling* (London, 1889), 166.

[49] Maddock, 117; see also David Masson, *Life of John Milton* (New York, 1946), VI, 785.

[50] Steele's preface to Addison's comedy, *The Drummer* (2nd edn, London, 1722), xii.

[51] *Cal. Treas. Books, 1698–99*, 90. The grant was supposed to be an annuity, but only the single payment of £200 is recorded.

[52] See *Works of the Right Honourable Joseph Addison*, ed. Richard Hurd (London, 1872–1873), I, 3; *Letters of Joseph Addison*, ed. Walter J. Graham (London, 1941), 3 ff.

[53] *Ibid.*, 54 and n.

[54] *Ibid.*, 135 ff., 214 and n; *The Freeholder*, No. 39.

[55] In 1712 he spoke of Halifax and Somers as the 'wisest men': John Nichols, *Epistolary Correspondence of Sir Richard Steele* (London, 1787), 92. Professor Calhoun Winton is of the opinion that Steele probably had 'comparatively little contact with Somers beyond the ordinary relationship of being fellow-members of the Kit-Cat Club': personal letter, 31 October 1963.

[56] Willard Connely, *Sir Richard Steele* (London, 1934), 136–39.

[57] *Swift Correspondence*, ed. Harold Williams (Oxford, 1963–65), I, 57, 84, 144.

[58] See below, p. 211.

[59] Some said the *Discourse* was by Somers himself, or by Burnet: *Camb. Hist. Eng. Lit.*, IX, 94, 112–13; *Works*, ed. Scott, V, 379–80.

[60] *Swift Correspondence*, ed. Williams, I, 79–80; *Works*, ed. Scott, II, 8.

[61] Henry Craik, *Life of Swift* (2nd edn., London, 1894), I, 185–86, 197–200; and see *Works*, ed. Scott, V, 381.

[62] *Swift Correspondence*, ed. Williams, I, 104–5, 142, 159.

[63] *Addison Letters*, ed. Graham, 465.

[64] *Works*, ed. Scott, II, 8.

[65] *Tale of a Tub*, ed. Guthkelch and Smith, xviii–xix, quoting Wotton.

[66] *Works*, ed. Scott, V, 426, 430.

[67] *Ibid.*, V, 380.

68 *Ibid.*, II, 107; *Correspondence*, ed. Ball, V, 186 and n., for possible reference to Somers's lack of sincerity.

69 *Ibid.*, V, 466. Sir William Temple heads the list.

70 Cf. Malone, who believes that Pope's acquaintance with Somers could not have commenced until around 1711 or 1712: *Dryden*, I, pt. i, 165–66 and n. See also *Poems of Alexander Pope*, ed. E. Audra and Aubrey Williams (London, 1961), I, 59; *Poems of Alexander Pope*, ed. John Butt (London, 1961), IV, 317.

71 Alexandre Beljame, *Men of Letters and the English Public in the Eighteenth Century*, ed. Bonamy Dobrée (London, 1948), 318.

72 On early contact with Dryden, see above, p. 19.

73 *Poems*, ed. Butt, IV, 105–6 ('Epistle to Arbuthnot'), 386; George Harris, *Life of Lord Chancellor Hardwicke* (London, 1847), I, 57; *Letters of John Dryden*, 129.

74 David C. Douglas, *English Scholars* (London, 1939), 100, 340. Nash, *Collections*, II, appendix, clxvii.

75 Douglas, 302 ff.

76 In Le Clerc's words, 'Il vaut mieux avertir le public, qu'il a l'obligation du premier dessein de ce Recueil à my Lord Halifax et à my Lord Sommers, qui l'ont aussi soutenu depuis'; *Syllabus of Documents Contained in Rymer's Foedera*, ed. Thomas D. Hardy (London, 1869), I, xi and n. Des Maizeaux makes a similar remark in his unfinished life of Rymer: Add. MSS. 4223, f. 161. Calamy and Leibnitz do not exclude the possibility of Somers's co-operation with Halifax, though perhaps not at the earliest stages of the undertaking: *Syllabus*, I, vii–viii.

77 *Ibid.*, I, xxvi; P.C. 2/75, f. 395.

78 Lord Godolphin received eight sets, Lord Carleton six: *Syllabus*, I, appendix, xxv.

79 *Ibid.*, I, xxii.

80 On the difficulties of bringing out this edition of Camden, and of settling on the dedication, see Roberts, *Bookselling*, 112 and n.

81 *The Whig Supremacy* (Oxford, 1962), 77–78.

82 *Biographia Britannica* (London, 1747–66), supplement, Edmund Gibson.

83 I have found but one sermon dedicated to Somers; it is by John Bowler and was occasioned by the death of Queen Mary. See Anthony à Wood, *Athenae Oxonienses*, ed. Philip Bliss (London, 1813–20), IV, 742.

84 See *A Collection of Pieces by Mr. John Toland* (London, 1728), II, 337–51. For a reference by Swift to Somers's association with Toland, see below, pp. 301–2.

85 C.J., XVI, 385.

86 *Memoirs*, 48.

87 Somers MSS., Cross to Somers, 23 March 1697. The collection includes a letter from Bishop William Lloyd to Somers, dated 20 September 1703, discussing a work proving that Christ died in A.D. 33.

88 *Biographia Britannica*, 3749; Leo P. Courtines, *Bayles Relations with England and the English* (New York, 1938), 103–7. But neither the Courtines work nor Howard Robinson's *Bayle the Sceptic* (New York, 1931) makes any reference to the Somers offer.

89 See above, pp. 105–6.

90 See Robbins, *Eighteenth-century Commonwealthsman*, 128–29; Thomas Fowler, *Shaftesbury and Hutchinson* (New York, 1882), 25.

91 *Second Characters, or the Language of Form*, ed. Benjamin Rand (Cambridge, 1914), xxi, 19, 25–26; *Characteristics of Men, Manners, Opinions and Times*, ed. John M. Robertson (London, 1900), I, 8.

92 Rand, *Correspondence*, 236.

93 See S. F. Whitaker, 'The first edition of Shaftesbury's *Moralists*', *Library*, 5th ser., VII (December 1952), 235 ff.

94 Rand, *Correspondence*, xxv–xxvi, 386–87, 394; Whitaker, 235n. On background, see Fowler, 30.

95 Somers MSS., Plukenet to Somers, January 1698.

96 *Diary*, V, 361.

97 *Record of the Royal Society* (London, 1940), 335, 558.

98 For example, Lords Devonshire, Dorset and Halifax.

99 *Diary*, V, 304–5.

100 Lyon, 75, 112–13; cf. Charles R. Weld, *History of the Royal Society* (London, 1848), I, 345, who states that Somers regularly attended meetings.

101 *Travels of Zacharias Conrad von Uffenbach*, ed. W. H. Quarrell and Margaret Mare

(London, 1934), 100–1; Sloane MSS. 4061, f. 31. Counsellor to the Grand Duke of Tuscany, Magalotti translated *Paradise Lost* into Italian. He visited the Royal Society in April 1669, and was elected a Fellow in 1709: Weld, I, 218; *Record*, 391.

[102] In 1710 we hear of Somers receiving from his old friend, Henry Newton, English envoy to Tuscany, a book from Father Grando intended for the Society: Sloane MSS. 4042, f. 159; Evelyn, *Diary*, V, 324.

[103] Vols. xx–xxii; vol. xx was dedicated to the Council and Fellows as well as to Somers.

XI

The political wilderness, 1701–5

Somers had won a battle. But he still faced the possibility of arduous campaigning. The Lords' acquittal was no guarantee against further attacks; indeed, should the more rabid Tory element have its way, he might again be confronted with impeachment proceedings. The Commons, following his deliverance, had protested

that the Lords had refused them justice upon the impeachment against the Lord Somers, by denying them a Committee of both Houses, which was desired, as the only proper means of settling the necessary preliminaries, and afterwards by proceeding to a pretended trial of the said Lord, which could tend only to protect him from justice by colour of an illegal acquittal.

They went on to accuse the upper chamber of infringing upon their constitutional rights, and of further undermining responsible government by 'holding out a prospect of immunity to the greatest offenders'.[1] The Lords paid no heed; mincing no words, they replied that the Commons had shown by their actions that they never intended to go through with the impeachments, and wound up the proceedings forthwith. For the time being, at least, the lower House was stymied, for on 24 June the King prorogued the turbulent lawmakers. In another fortnight he had set out for the Lowlands, and the usual legislative interlude descended—mercifully, in the eyes of many—upon the nation.

Although the impeachment would never be revived, the next few years saw Somers's fortunes at a low ebb. He held no ministerial office. The Tories gained an unprecedented ascendancy in the Commons. A new and hostile sovereign ascended the throne. Amidst these disadvantages he was borne up by his primacy among the Whigs, and, briefly, while William lived, by some credit at Whitehall. The Junto could take comfort that William kept him on the Council. In the country at large there were some hopeful signs that the Tories had not only failed to discredit the Whig leaders, but had alienated public opinion by their rancorous manoeuvres. According to Burnet, the nation was in 'a great ferment', whipped up particularly by publications which dealt with the recent *causes célèbres*.[2] Most notable of these, from a literary point of view, was Jonathan Swift's *Discourse on the Contests and Dissensions between the Nobles and the Commons in Athens and Rome*. In this defence of the impeached magnates Somers appears as Aristides, 'the most renowned by the People themselves for his exact Justice, and Knowledge in the Law', unjustifiably attacked 'for a blind suspicion of his acting in an arbitrary Way'.[3] On the Tory side Sir Humphrey Mackworth produced a vindication of the late proceedings, and there were other pieces in which Somers was particularly singled out, as Vernon remarked, not only for his political sins but 'for adultery, socinianism, and I know not what besides'.[4]

Meanwhile, English foreign policy was entering a new phase. On 16 September 1701, James II died at St Germain. Despite the terms of the Treaty of Ryswick, Louis forthwith recognised his son, the 'Old Pretender', as King of Great Britain. English and Dutch envoys were recalled from France, and a new European war grew appreciably nearer—a war which, like that so recently concluded, would in due course redound to the advantage of the Whigs. Somers evidently envisaged more immediate gains. Among his papers are notes for arguments to induce the King to call a new Parliament. The existing one, in his opinion, was not fit to conduct a war. The Tories might now admit that it was unavoidable, but their hearts were not in it. Too many of them were 'engaged for the Prince of Wales'; neither their will nor their vigour could be relied on. What with their dilatory tactics it was 'no less than a miracle' that all had not already been lost. They were generally distrusted; a new Parliament would be 'more likely to dispose people toward a union'. Such a body would go far to assure England's friends abroad of the seriousness of her purpose, and, with luck, might wind up the war in the three years allotted to it.[5] He could have added that a new House of Commons might be less disposed to renew the impeachment proceedings against him.[6]

On 11 November he had the satisfaction of knowing that the old Parliament was no more. And with the resignation (in December) of Godolphin, who had returned to the Treasury only the year before, opportunity seemed to stand in the wings. The situation cried out for at least a caretaker head of the ministry, a position which might gain permanence and added stature once the electoral returns were in. With a view to gaining his assistance in the formation of a new government, he turned to Sunderland. A few months earlier the Earl again had given indications that he was willing to lend a hand. He had reappeared in London late in June, and, though he remained but a fortnight, had 'conversed with chiefs of all sorts', and certainly with Somers. The former Chancellor was willing to let bygones be bygones, and, now that Shrewsbury had deserted the Whigs and was far away in Rome, even to accept Sunderland as the Duke's successor. The two men saw eye to eye in the matter of foreign policy, both regarding Parliament as negligent and short-sighted in this department.[7]

Meanwhile the King, abroad at Loo, had been turning over in his mind the pros and cons of continuing to deal with the existing Parliament. He was dissatisfied with the Tories, but lacked confidence that the Whigs could do his business. In August he sought Sunderland's advice. The old politician was aware of the stresses and strains that were affecting the fabric of government. The Tories, he observed, 'will not be satisfied without ruining my Lord Somers, nor the Whigs without undoing the ministers'. He advised William to return to England as soon as possible, and to send for

Somers: 'He is the life, the soul, and the spirit of his party, and can answer for it; not like the present ministers, who have no credit with theirs, any further than they can persuade the King to be undone.' William should deal frankly with the ex-Chancellor; he should 'ask him plainly, what he and his friends can do, and will do, and what they expect, and the methods they would propose'. He assured the King that Somers would seek nothing for himself nor for his impeached colleagues, and that, even if he were unable to give satisfaction he would nonetheless 'remain still zealous and affectionate' to the royal person and government. He acquainted Somers with this interchange by sending him copies of the correspondence.[8]

Replying at once, Somers signified his appreciation of Sunderland's vote of confidence, but disavowed his ability to lead the government. He urged, rather, that Sunderland himself should undertake this assignment, provided a new Parliament could be convened. There was, he said, 'a very general good disposition' among the Whigs to unite behind Sunderland; at least he could count on the Junto. He further suggested that the 'Association' (which had proved such a useful partisan instrument in the past) might well be revived. But the Earl did not want to take responsibility; he did not flourish in the limelight, and was now elderly and ailing. He would, he said, continue in his resolution of 'not meddling, or doing anything that can look like it'—an extraordinary rejoinder, considering its source. The renewing of the 'Association', he agreed, was necessary. As for a dissolution, which Somers regarded as all-important—'the great point is a new Parliament, or not'—he was evasive. But his representations to the King were not without effect. On 10 October William, still at Loo, sent Somers a short note accrediting Lord Galway as his confidential agent; Somers was asked to show no reserve in dealing with him and was assured of the continuation of the royal friendship.[9]

But when, following the dissolution in November, Somers invited Sunderland to come up to London he found that it was to no purpose: the doughty veteran had really retired. The best he could do was to provide a lengthy memorandum in which the principles and techniques of 1693—which at the time had proved so successful—were dusted off and applied to the new conditions. He dealt specifically with certain issues that would have to be faced, calling for an act of grace on behalf of the impeached Whigs and others who had incurred the hostility of the legislators, and for an abjuration of the Prince of Wales. As for appointments, he made few suggestions apart from advocating a cabinet restricted to those possessing 'a right to enter there by their employment'.[10] But the memorandum was not to be put to the test. Neither before nor after the general election would the King make sweeping changes in the ministry, and certainly none involving the restoration of Somers.

Meanwhile the attention of the nation was focused on the elections. The resignation of Godolphin and the subsequent dismissal of Secretary Hedges deprived Tory elements of the crown support that was always so important in determining victory at the polls.[11] The anti-Tory elements made much of the alleged influence of Poussin, the French ambassador, with the 'New Country' members, a number of whom, including Charles Davenant, were reported to have dined with the diplomat. Black-listed as 'Poussineers', most of this group were defeated, in some cases by Junto candidates.[12] In his *True Picture of a Modern Whig*, Davenant accused the Whigs of constantly harping on the dangers of French pensioners and Jacobitism, so that the electorate would believe that 'the French and popery were coming in if all our bribed Ban of my Lord S---r's and my Lord H-----x's Tools and Flatterers were not elected'.[13] The impeached lords, it was said, were trying to 're-establish the old gang that has brought us into debt and made themselves by the nation's ruin'.[14]

In the end the 'old gang' enjoyed considerable success. Altogether the Junto 'Connexion', representing the combined interests of Wharton, Somers, Halifax, Orford, Lord Spencer and the Duke of Bolton, managed to seat sixty-four Members, twenty-five of them nominees of the redoubtable Wharton.[15] Except for Walsh, the Members particularly identified with Somers were all re-elected, but he gained no recruits.[16] The returns from the greater London area were also gratifying. Elsewhere things had not gone so well. Vernon complained that 'many of the old members and some of the hottest' had retained their seats.[17] And, in the over-all count, the Tories emerged with a majority of sixty-five.[18] But if the new House was not Whiggish enough it was overwhelmingly anti-French: on foreign and military policy, at least, a broadly based consensus could be expected.

With such a Parliament Somers and his Junto colleagues had worked effectively in the past, and, if William were spared, they might count on repeating their earlier successes. The new legislature sat for the first time on 30 December 1701, and on the following day listened to the speech from the throne. This proved to be the longest and most eloquent of William's communications to his English subjects. It was composed by Somers[19]— evidence of the extent to which the ex-minister continued to serve as aide and counsellor, though, apart from his seat on the Privy Council, still offi- cially outside the pale. The speech was widely hailed at the time. Oldmixon describes it as the 'most memorable that ever came from the Throne'.[20] Printed copies appeared, in Dutch and French as well as English; they were even framed to hang upon walls. And, indeed, as a charge to a nation on the brink of war, and so much a prey of partisan bickering and division, it was frank, reasonable and inspiriting. After noting the dangers to Europe as well as to the political and economic well-being of England that could be expected to flow from the actions of King Louis, and calling upon the legislators to secure without question the Protestant succession in England, the King moved to his exhortation:

It is fit I should tell you the eyes of all Europe are upon this Parliament; all matters are at a stand till your resolutions are known, and therefore no time ought to be lost. You have yet an opportunity, by God's blessing, to secure to you and your posterity the quiet enjoyment of your religion and liberties, if you are not wanting to yourselves, but will exert the ancient vigour of the English nation; but I will tell you plainly, my opinion is, if you do not lay hold of this occasion; you have no reason to hope for another.

In conclusion, he urged Parliament-men to lay aside the animosities which divided and weakened them: 'to disappoint the only hopes of our enemies by your unanimity'. They could count upon him to be a 'common father' to his people, and to forgive and forget even the most flagrant offences of the past.[21]

The two Houses lost no time in replying in kind, and in backing their words with deeds. Addresses were unanimously passed inveighing against Louis's conduct in 'owning and setting up the pretended Prince of Wales'. The Commons agreed to provide 40,000 men for the navy, as well as the 40,000 soldiers which the King, in the Grand Alliance of the previous summer, had stipulated as England's share in the joint operations.[22] Soon the King was signing commissions at the rate of two hundred a day, and from Vienna Stepney wrote: 'You will easily guess what a favourite I am grown since his Majesty's Speech has reached us and the noble resolutions of the Commons.'[23]

The unanimity with which the nation girded for war, combined with Whig gains in the Commons, must have been read as hopeful signs by the Junto. Under its direction the recent war with France had been brought to at least an honourable conclusion: might not these veterans reasonably expect to provide leadership in the rekindled conflict? Might not Somers, especially, capitalise on his predominance, now that Sunderland and Shrewsbury were both on the shelf, and Halifax and Orford in semi-retirement? But these things were not to be. The balance in the lower house was too precarious, and the royal inclinations averse. The friends of Littleton, the Junto's man, failed by four votes to elect him Speaker, Harley continuing in this assignment. Nor was the new legislature ready to take the King's advice and forgive the impeached Whigs, an attempt to revive the attacks being defeated by only fourteen votes. In other ways, too, it was made apparent that old animosities and partisan zeal had not cooled— witness the revival of proceedings against the Kentish Petition, which was once more branded as 'scandalous, insolent, and seditious', and the acrimonious reviewing of election returns.[24]

As for William, he had never been a man for new ministries at one fell swoop. By nature he was pragmatic and deliberate. His concept of the relations between monarch and ministers continued essentially along traditional lines. And now his military and foreign policy was bolstered by bi-partisan support. Some changes were made. By the end of December the Earl of Carlisle, who frequently worked hand in glove with Wharton, had been named First Commissioner of the Treasury in place of Godolphin. Before the session was a month old Rochester was recalled from Dublin Castle[25] and the Earl of Manchester, a stepson of Halifax, had replaced Hedges as Secretary of State. The Earls of Radnor and Burlington were given places in the Council. Such alterations tended to advance the

Whig interest.[26] But Somers, despite Wright's shortcomings, was not called upon to take the Great Seal, or any other office; neither Orford nor Halifax were brought back into harness; and Wharton, despite Sunderland's change of heart—he had finally recommended that he be given a secretaryship—still held only his court post.[27]

Had William lived longer, the government would probably have assumed a more Whiggish aspect, and Somers's fortunes might have risen to something like their earlier peaks. On the other hand, the last weeks of William's life afford little basis for such a prognostication. However much the King may have turned to him, he was no latter-day Sunderland. And there was a rising star on the horizon—Marlborough—with whom William had finally buried the hatchet, and whom he described as 'the one man fit to subordinate the English factions to the terrible necessity of saving Europe'.[28] In the Lords Somers appears to have left but a slight mark on the more important transactions of these days, though he attended with considerable regularity. He signed an address against Louis's recognition of the Prince of Wales, and was named to a conference with the Commons over amendments to the bill for his attainder.[29] The Whigs followed up his suggestion that a clause remodelling the Association be tacked to the Abjuration Bill.[30] Apart from these matters his attention seems to have been largely devoted to private acts—one of them involving the establishment of Worcester College.[31]

Late in February the King suffered a broken collar-bone in a fall from his horse. Complications set in and within a fortnight he was dead. In some ways the accession of Anne was less of a break with the preceding reign than had ever been the case. By virtue of legislation passed several years earlier, Parliament was authorised to sit for six months after that event. The great programme designed by William was carried forward. War was formally declared. Marlborough departed for the field, and Parliament arranged for necessary supply. But, in another sense, a deep gulf separated the regimes, for towards the Whigs who had played so important a part in William's administration Anne was cool, if not positively hostile. In part her attitude stemmed from a revulsion from William, with whom her relations had been at best only correct; in part it represented an aversion to a party identified with the curtailment of personal royalty and the broadening out of the religious settlement.

Under the circumstances Somers found himself in the political wilderness. As the most prominent survivor of the Whigs he was bound to be *persona non grata* at Kensington. Anne could not have forgotten his opposition towards the more liberal schedule for her support, a dozen years before; moreover, he was suspected of having acted against her inclusion in a council of regency and was disliked by Prince George. Apart from these grudges, his religious views were reputedly far too latitudinarian for Anne's tastes. It is not surprising that—along with Halifax and Orford—he was forthwith dropped from the Privy Council. For years Anne would refuse even to admit him to her presence.[32]

Although the ex-Chancellor now stood outside the administration, and headed a party[33] (or a powerful segment of one) suspect in Anne's eyes, he should not be regarded as joining an organised opposition. Neither in March nor the following autumn, when a general election produced a Commons of a more Tory complexion, was this the case. The chief reason was the war, which Somers, along with his Junto associates and the rest of the Whigs, would conscientiously support. On the other hand, there was room for some opposition manoeuvres. As mentor of the Junto interest, he could take the field on behalf of religious liberty, tied as it was to Whig fortunes; he could champion the rights of constituents when trenched upon by Tory politicians; he could work to insure the Protestant succession against legitimist coups. And, while the Tories enjoyed a new ascendancy linked with royal favour, the Whigs could still point to a more integrated party, and to their majority in the upper house. There Somers and his Junto colleagues welcomed a recruit, Charles Spencer, who succeeded his father as Earl of Sunderland in September 1702.

William's last Parliament sat until 25 May, Somers continuing to attend conscientiously under the new regime. He helped frame an address of thanks for the royal declaration of war, as well as another calling upon the Queen to do everything possible to prevent 'Correspondence' between France and England's allies.[34] In these undertakings he was in a goodly company, not only of Whigs but of moderate Tories. But he had to contend with the vengeful tendencies of the higher flying Tories, who looked for opportunities to discredit the late regime and to undermine such influence as the Whigs still retained.

There was, for one thing, a report that among William's papers had been found a proposal to bring in the house of Hanover immediately upon his death, eliminating Anne altogether. This was so widely circulated that the Lords ordered an investigation, and when it became apparent that it was without foundation a handful of peers, including Somers and Halifax, pressed for a resolution that the Queen should undertake to prosecute whoever had been responsible.[35] This was duly framed. The Lords also took exception to Dr James Drake's *History of the Last Parliament* (that which had first met in February 1701), in which William's aides were accused of complicity in such a design. Brought before the house, Drake cited, among other pamphlets, Somers's *Jura Populi Anglicani*, but when pressed could not give chapter and verse. The Lords thereupon declared his expressions in this regard to be 'Groundless, False and Scandalous', and again called for prosecution. Somers himself was named to a committee to determine how extensively these proceedings should be published.[36] In the end Drake was tried, but acquitted.

It was not easy to restrain the Tories. To them, the 'sunshine day' of Anne's accession brought visions of the spoils of office. No time had been lost in reshaping the ministry. At Marlborough's insistence Godolphin returned to the Treasury; Nottingham and Hedges replaced Manchester and Vernon as Secretaries; Wharton lost his Comptrollership to Seymour.

Harcourt, so prominent in Somers's impeachment, was now Solicitor-General. Such set-backs were to be expected. It was not a clean sweep. Boyle remained Chancellor of the Exchequer, and Devonshire and Somerset kept their court posts, minor positions, to be sure, but not without some weight. But these were 'Court Whigs', not disposed to accept Junto domination.

With Marlborough and Godolphin, neither of them strong party men, Whigs might accommodate themselves, provided that hungry subordinates, with Anne's tacit or overt consent, did not push them too far. But many a Tory was in a pushing mood: not many might climb to the top of the greasy pole, but there was kudos, influence and profit in lesser appointments to which the Whig incumbents naturally clung. Particularly did they eye the commissions of the peace. Somers himself had demonstrated how these could be tailored to suit the political occasion, and the lesson was not lost upon his successor. With an election in the offing—at the latest the existing Parliament must die in September—and with the influence of the local magistracy an electoral factor of consequence, Lord Keeper Wright, a keen partisan, proceeded to undo Somers's appointment of 'dependable' men to the commissions. Between 1700 and 1704 several hundred magistrates gave way to new men. Among them was Somers, who, despite his reputation and experience, was not even allowed to serve his native county.[37] Save for his two recorderships, he was now without any public office.

The parliamentary elections resulted in substantial gains for the Tory elements: their majority came to 133, double that of the last Parliament.[38] They benefited from the Queen's influence and that of the clergy, and, in Burnet's words, 'the conceit, which had been infused and propagated with much industry, that the Whigs had charged the nation with great taxes, of which a large share had been devoured by themselves'.[39] The Junto connection, which in the late Parliament had commanded sixty-four seats, could now count on but forty-nine. But the six 'Somers men' of the previous Parliament were all re-elected, and William Walsh now sat again for Worcestershire.[40] Wharton deserved part of the credit for Walsh's victory; elsewhere he was less successful, ten of his nominees failing in their bids. At Reigate Harvey again shared the honours with Parsons, Somers's other candidate, Haestrict James, bringing up the rear.[41]

Although Somers was lord of the manor at Reigate, he did not make it his residence. About this time he was settling himself at Brookmans, destined to be the most permanent of his abodes. He had also exchanged the St James's Square house for another in Leicester Square.[42] This had long been a fashionable residential section. It was dominated by Leicester House, where Peter the Great was entertained in 1698 and where George II, when Prince of Wales, would hold his court. It was still relatively green and open; on occasion the older name of Leicester Fields was applied. Perhaps its only drawback was its attractiveness to duellists. Here Somers maintained town quarters until his death.[43] But he desired a country place: one near enough to London to be conveniently accessible, yet far enough away to be free from the smoke and noise of the metropolis. From time to time he had sought refuge at Mortlake, Clapham and Tunbridge Wells. In 1701 he acquired the manor of Brookmans. Located in the hamlet of Belbar, in the Hertfordshire parish of North Mimms, it was seventeen miles from the city, near the road from Hatfield. The estate was purchased from Andrew Fountaine. The manor house had been built about 1680; it was handsome and well situated, commanding a 'delightful prospect' of the surrounding countryside. We may picture the new owner, in his months of freedom from parliamentary duties, without official tasks at Whitehall or entrée at Kensington, arranging his books and *objets d'art*, familiarising himself with his rights (which included the jurisdiction of a court baron), and getting to know his tenants. The arrangements apparently satisfied him, for it was in this house that he died in 1716.[44]

The new Parliament convened late in October and sat through most of the winter. The improved position of the Tories made it unlikely that the relations between the two houses would be more amicable. Apart from general agreement on the prosecution of the war—and even here the Tories were divided as to the extent to which England should participate—there were few major issues which did not evoke friction. Entrenched in the Lords, the Junto magnates were for the most part active, not least of them Somers, who was on hand pretty regularly until late in January.[45]

Any possibility that his reputation in the eyes of the Queen would be rehabilitated during these months was shattered by his determined opposition to two projects which she sought to drive on. One involved the status and endowment of the Prince Consort; the other was the first of several attempts to outlaw the practice of occasional conformity. Towards her amiable but ineffective spouse, Anne's affection was deep and abiding, and her political resentments can to some degree be measured by the slights which others, and particularly her brother-in-law, put upon him. She had hoped, upon her accession, to draw him up to the rank of King Consort, but this project was still-born. Nor was she able to secure for him the command of the Allied forces. Baulked in these designs, she fell back on providing him with what she regarded as an appropriate income, and on insuring that the offices held by him during her lifetime would remain in his hands thereafter. The latter guarantee would require exempting him from the provision of the Act of Settlement whereby foreigners were to be excluded from national offices upon the accession of the Hanoverian line.

Though legislation to this effect was passed in the Commons, it ran into strong opposition in the Lords. The trouble did not arise from the size of the annual grant, though at £100,000 it had created adverse comment even in the Commons. It stemmed rather from the fear that the bill might jeopardise the rights of individuals—particularly those peers of foreign origin who had received their rewards in William's day—by implying a retroactive application of the Act of Settlement, and from the Lords' increasing opposition to the practice of tacking.[46] Seymour was already baying for the resumption of all crown grants made under William; he was restrained by Robert Walpole, who was duly rewarded through Junto influence. As for tacking, there could be no question that this was a money bill; nor was there any doubt among the peers that the practice, if not restrained, might lead to the extinction of their legislative independence.

On 9 December Somers was among those who signed a resolution that they would pass no money bill to which the Commons had tacked any clause regarded as extraneous.[47] All the Junto lords, save Orford, had registered like misgivings; young Sunderland was particularly identified with the opposition, despite the fact that his in-laws, the Marlboroughs, strongly supported the Queen. Only when the judges had given assurances that foreign peers could not be dispossessed of their rights did the Lords comply, and then only by the narrowest of majorities.[48] Somers could not be induced to accept the exempting clause. He was one of nine peers (though the only Junto man) who signed a protest against it, arguing that it was not only an unwarrantable instance of tacking but that in making 'no Provisions for other Peers under the same Circumstances' it might prejudice their interests.[49]

Meanwhile the Commons had passed an Occasional Conformity Bill by a large majority, and the measure came before the Lords on 2 December. It was designed to prevent the abuse by Nonconformists of those provisions of the Corporation and Test Acts which stipulated communication with the Church of England as a *sine qua non* for officeholding. The measure had the advantage of combining zeal for the Church, a recognised Tory attribute, with an attack on Whiggish elements. The net, moreover, was finer than that woven by Restoration legislators; inferior officers and even freemen of corporations, as well as the more important magistrates, were now to be marked men. A slip, and they were to be heavily fined; worse still, they were to lose their places and the parliamentary franchise that went with them. As Burnet, who was active in opposing the bill, remarked, 'the intent of it was believed to be the modelling of elections, and by consequence of the house of commons'.[50]

By the time the Lords took up the measure, the issue had created something like a frenzy throughout the realm. London mobs attacked meeting houses. Pamphleteers and preachers fanned the flames of bigotry and partisanship. Under the circumstances, and with the Queen determined to secure the passage of the bill, the Whig majority in the Lords, though naturally opposed to it, did not dare to reject it out of hand. Instead they sought to side-track it with amendments. On the one hand they insisted that it should be inapplicable to the officers of corporations; on the other, knowing that the Commons would not even consider such an emasculation of the measure, they raised a constitutional issue by amending the schedule of fines. Even as the Peers were resolved to limit the Commons in tacking, so the lower House had recently 'set it up for a maxim that the lords could not alter the fines that they should fix in a bill, this being a meddling with money'.[51] The result was an impasse which, despite several conferences between the Houses, could not be resolved. On 17 December Somers, who had been active in debate, was named one of the managers for the Lords, along with the rest of the Junto leaders.[52] The following day he was placed on a committee to search the records of the House for precedents regarding the thorny issue of altering fines, a piece of research which resulted in incontestable proof that the Lords had for centuries time and time again engaged in the practice.[53]

In the eyes of more unbending Tories, Somers was running true to form. As the leading Whig he could be expected to do what lay in his power to counteract a measure so unpalatable to his own party. But, apart from this, he was widely regarded as the embodiment of those latitudinarian and even free-thinking proclivities in which Nottingham and Sacheverell saw the destruction of the historic Church. Such a man could be expected to deny the Church for political advantage: he was not a true churchman but looked upon the institution as an adjunct to governmental power—a point of view in itself highly distasteful to its more ardent supporters, wherever they were to be found. Such views were not without some grains of truth. Yet, while the political philosophy of the rank and file of the Anglican clergy, as well as the religious views and practices of its more extreme element, tended to run counter to his own, he could, at least, sympathise with those in straitened circumstances. Before William's reign was over he, along with Bishop Burnet, had concerted the relief which took effect in the next, as Queen Anne's Bounty.[54]

The show-down on the first occasional conformity bill came at a free conference on 16 January 1703. As managers for the Lords, Somers, along with the Duke of Devonshire, the Earl of Peterborough, Lord Halifax and Bishop Burnet, supported the alterations which had been made by their chamber. As principal manager, Somers argued that the Lords did not consider attendance at dissenting meetings to be *malum in se*. The Dissenters, he pointed out, were Protestants, differing from the Church of England only in 'some little forms'. He depicted them as 'well affected to the present constitution, and hearty enemies to the Queen's and kingdom's enemies', noting that they had demonstrated their loyalty in the crucial days of 1688. The Toleration Act deserved to be upheld; it had not only produced a good 'temper' among the Dissenters, but also enhanced the security and reputation of the Church. It was enough that occasional conformists should forfeit office and be subjected to reasonable fines, without eroding the revolutionary settlement by excessive disqualification.[55] The Lords admitted that no subject could claim an office by birth-right; yet they conceived 'that giving a vote for a representative in parliament is the essential privilege whereby every Englishman preserves his property; and that whatsoever deprives him of such vote, deprives him of his birth-right'.[56]

Such was the gist of Somers's remarks. Since it was the object of the Whig Lords to take a line which would insure a stalemate, and hence prevent any legislation at all, these points should not all be taken at face value. The Whigs could not cheerfully entertain the prospect that any occasional conformist might lose office, and consequently political usefulness. On the other hand, this was not merely an exercise in shadow-boxing: Somers's confidence in the Dissenters, his regard for the benign influence of the revolutionary settlement, his equation of political activity and property rights—all these bespeak Whig convictions which he fully shared and publicised. As the Whig Lords had hoped, no agreement could be reached. The bill consequently fell to the ground, and a serious threat to Whig influence was for the time averted.[57]

In the course of the session the Tories launched other offensives, which met with varying degrees of success. Of these the scrutiny of ministerial conduct during the last years of King William was perhaps the most worrisome. The Commons still refused to regard the investigations of 1701 as a closed book. Their interest was focused particularly on the use of public moneys, and as the session opened Halifax, the Earl of Ranelagh (William's Paymaster-General), and others found themselves the objects of close inquiry on the part of seven Tory commissioners.[58] As usual, in matters of this kind, the Lords applied a brake on the extravagance of the Commons. Particularly did they rally to support Halifax, for a successful prosecution of this prominent statesman would have been a serious body blow to the Whig interest. When the Commons, despite the fact that their commissioners could not nail down any specific charge of malfeasance, ordered the Attorney-General to prosecute, the Lords embarked upon an investigation of their own. Somers was one of the committee selected to consider the commissioners' report on 2 February. There can be no doubt that he was deeply concerned with this issue, affecting not only the reputation of his old friend and colleague but the fortunes of the Junto. But once more illness plagued him; while he may have helped to shape the report, it was the Duke of Somerset who brought it before the house on 5 February, Somers being absent on that occasion.[59] The relations between the two chambers were now so heated that, with supplies voted and the Lords threatening to launch counter-attacks against certain Tory officials (especially Seymour), the Queen brought the session to an end on 28 February. Parliament did not meet again until 9 November.

As the new session approached, Somers must have found it difficult to assess political prospects. The High Tory Rochester had finally resigned.[60] Godolphin and Marlborough, it was rumoured, were of a mind to oust other extreme Tories and, in the interest of the war effort, effect some kind of an accommodation with the Whigs. Godolphin had already used his influence, in January, to prevent the removal of Whig officials from the treasury. But he was not strong enough to avert a purge of the commissions of the peace; nor could the Queen be prevailed upon at this time to remove Nottingham. Although Marlborough and Godolphin threatened to resign rather than contend with so incompatible a colleague, High Churchmen were predicting that before Christmas he would be installed as Lord Treasurer. Also on the debit side was the creation of four Tory peers by the Queen, with but one Whig so honoured—a threat to the partisan balance in the upper house.[61] With the future so uncertain, Somers, like others at the time, may have sought to insure himself against the eventuality of a prolonged Tory ascendancy, and one that might culminate in the restoration of the St Germain Stuarts. According to one account he made overtures in the spring of 1703 to that court, tendering his services by way of the French Foreign Minister, Torcy.[62] Just what (if anything) was involved remains a mystery; if there was such a flirtation it was ephemeral.

Though Anne urged in her autumn speech that the legislators 'carefully avoid any Heats and Divisions' that might serve to encourage 'the common Enemies of our Church and State', the relations between the chambers were even more inflamed than had been the case in the previous session. Indeed, the Prussian envoy saw in such chronic incompatibility an opportunity for a reassertion of royal authority.[63] Somers continued to play an important part in Whig tactics, but in the more important issues, at least, they more often resulted in deadlocks than in victories. Though involved in a wide variety of business (he served as chairman of no less than eight select committees), he was most prominently identified with the Scottish Plot and the case of Ashby *v.* White, both of which produced acrimonious constitutional repercussions.

On 17 December Queen Anne informed the Lords that she had 'unquestionable information', obtained from her Commissioner, the Duke of Queensbury, of Jacobite machinations in Scotland. Sir John Maclean and other Jacobite agents had already been arrested. The country was a prey to rumours and counter-rumours. Though Nottingham had undertaken the investigation of the Maclean case, the Whigs of the upper House suspected that the Tory ministers would not choose to dig very deep. They proceeded to set up their own committee of investigation, electing by ballot seven of their members. Somers came third with fifty votes. The Junto was well represented, Sunderland and Wharton also being chosen. The committee lost no time: by 21 December Devonshire, who had topped the poll, was ready to report. As a result the House voted an address to the Queen that James Boucher, an aide-de-camp to the Duke of Berwick (who was supposed to lead an expedition from France) be prosecuted for high treason.[64]

These proceedings greatly offended the Commons, and at a time when they were still smarting from the Lords' rejection, 71–59, of their second occasional conformity bill.[65] They at once complained to the Queen that the peers, in defiance of customary legal procedure, had 'wrested the persons in custody out of your Majesty's hands, and without your Majesty's leave or knowledge.'[66] Thus the incident took on the proportions of a constitutional issue. Actually, the Lords at the Queen's request had backed down with regard to Maclean, but the High Tories could not overlook what they regarded as a censure of Nottingham.

In justifying its actions the upper House leaned heavily upon Somers. He was placed upon a select committee charged with drawing up a statement of its rights in examining conspirators, and the ensuing document, though reported by Somerset, came from Somers's pen. This was submitted to the Queen; and when the Commons raised objections to certain points, the Lords fired another salvo (also prepared by Somers), substantiating their position with numerous precedents from the journals of both houses. These addresses gained a wider audience than was customarily the case, for the Lords saw that they were committed to the press.[67]

While this was going on, the case of Ashby v. White served to exacerbate inter-cameral relations still further. Here attention was focused upon the rights of electors vis-à-vis the privileges of the Commons. On 6 December a writ of error in the case was brought before the peers.[68] Matthew Ashby, an Aylesbury burgess, had brought an action for damages against William White, as well as other returning officers, for disallowing his vote in the parliamentary election of 1702. Ashby was successful at the assizes, but this decision was not upheld by the Court of Queen's Bench. The Lords, with its substantial Whig contingent, could be expected to look sympathetically upon Ashby's plight, for the Tory majority in the Commons had handled the contested returns of the last election with more than the usual partisan prejudice. But the judges who attended were almost in a deadlock —five for affirming and four for reversing the order of the Queen's Bench. Lord Keeper Wright, not being a peer, had no voice, but his predecessor, the only law lord of the time, could and did make his influence felt.

The gist of Somers's argument was that, inasmuch as the plaintiff had been deprived of the exercise of his franchise by the malicious act of the defendants, who were to be regarded as having rejected the vote while knowing it to be good, he was entitled to legal redress. The objection that this infringed upon the privileges of the Commons was invalid; for while that House by itself could rightfully determine electoral results, 'the elective franchise was a common law right regulated by statute, on which a court of common law was competent to determine'. The judgement was reversed, fifty to sixteen, on 14 January 1704.[69] But this by no means terminated the controversy. By a vote of 215 to 97 the Commons returned to the charge, resolving that the qualifications of electors were cognisable only before their own body; that Ashby, in undertaking his action, was guilty of a breach of privilege; and that anyone following his example was to be regarded in the same light.[70]

The Lords now appointed a committee to consider their position, and again Somers was the guiding spirit, composing the report which was brought before the House late in March. In it the veteran jurist described at considerable length the English representative system and the electoral function. The latter he described as 'a legal Right'. In county elections it was 'inherent in the Freehold'; in boroughs it belonged to 'the real Estates of the Inhabitants' or was 'vested in the Corporation, for the Benefit of the particular Members, who are the Electors'. It followed, then, that the possessors must have a legal remedy to maintain such a right: 'if the Law doth not allow an Action to the Party injured, it tolerates the Injury, which is absurd to say is tolerable in any Government'. After demonstrating that Ashby was protected by both common law and statutory provisions, and consequently had access to a remedy, Somers turned to the question of whether the one employed in this case was 'the proper Remedy allowed by the Antient Law of England'. He concluded that it was the *only* one available to the plaintiff. The novelty of the action was irrelevant, provided it could be 'supported by the old Grounds and Principles of Law', as was here unquestionably the case. As for the contention that the Commons, by virtue of their privileges, had the right to determine such an issue, Somers again took pains to differentiate between their role in resolving contested elections and the individual rights of the voters: 'there is a great Difference between the Right of the Electors, and the Right of the Elected; the one is a temporary Right to a Place in Parliament, *pro hac vice*, the other is a Freehold, or a Franchise: Who has a Right to sit in the House of Commons may be properly cognisable there; but who has a Right to chuse, is a Matter originally established, even before there is a Parliament: A Man has Right to his Freehold by the Common Law, and the Law having annexed his Right of voting to his Freehold, it is of the Nature of his Freehold, and must depend upon it'. It was absurd to say that the elector's right was founded upon the law and custom of Parliament: 'it is an original Right, part of the Constitution of the Kingdom, as much as a Parliament is'. To deny this action, then, was to 'deny the Benefit of the Law in a Matter of the most tender Concern to an Englishman'. It was to deny his property rights.[71]

On 27 March the Lords approved this report and drafted a set of resolutions derived from its arguments. In particular they recorded their opposition to the Commons' position, as 'a manifest assuming a Power to controul the Law, to hinder the Course of Justice, and subject the Property of Englishmen, to the arbitrary Votes of the House of Commons'.[72] These resolutions, along with Somers's report, were ordered to be printed. According to the partisan Burnet, 'the lords got great credit by the judgment they gave, which let the people of England see how they might be redressed for the future, if they should meet with the injustice, partiality, and other ill practices that had appeared of late'.[73] But the Commons were far from convinced, and so hot had the relations between the two chambers become that the Queen was induced to order a prorogation a few days later, leaving the matter unresolved.

As for other business, he undoubtedly exerted himself in defence of the Earl of Orford, whose alleged financial misdeeds, regarded as a typical example of Junto corruption, were being investigated.[74] He served as chairman of a committee to investigate the Irish linen industry, his report serving as the basis, in the following session, of legislative provision for the export of the commodity to the colonies.[75] His later activity regarding the care of public documents suggests that he took seriously his appointment to a committee set up for this purpose.[76] And the large number of private bill committees to which he was named is mute testimony of the many hours devoted by legislators to such proceedings; during this session he served as chairman of at least seven.[77]

Before the session ended he twice voiced protests on legislative provisions.

On 21 March he objected to certain features of an 'Act for raising recruits for the land forces and marines', which empowered magistrates to conscript the unemployed.[78] This device was regarded by many as an infringement upon the liberties of Englishmen (though the press gang had long been an indispensable adjunct to the naval establishment); it became a partisan issue because of the drastic reshaping of the commissions of the peace by Lord Keeper Wright. In this connection the Lords ordered a perusal of the lists of justices of the peace who had been removed from office, and Somers could take satisfaction in hearing his ouster described as a particularly flagrant example of petty partisan politics.[79] The other protest arose in connection with the Maclean case. Maclean having been released from custody, in view of the disclosures he had made, the Lords proceeded to petition the Queen for 'as full and complete a pardon as may consist with the safety of herself and her people'. But Somers and some twenty other peers (including the entire Junto leadership) continued to hammer away at Nottingham as luke-warm, at least, in prosecuting Jacobites, and when their claim that the account of Maclean's examination was defective went unheeded, they recorded their dissatisfaction.[80] Both protests must be regarded as representing political manoeuvres rather than convictions based upon political principles.

Actually, Nottingham's days were numbered. For months Godolphin and Marlborough had been handicapped by his resistance to their programme for an all-out war. In the spring of 1704 a showdown came when he called for the dismissal of Somerset and Devonshire in the interest of an all-Tory administration, and threatened to resign unless his representations were heeded. The ultimatum backfired. Though the Queen saw eye to eye with him in many respects, she was prevailed upon to support the Godolphin-Marlborough interest. Somers's role, if any, in this business is not apparent. But we may be sure that the Junto did what it could to prevent a clean sweep for Nottingham. The upshot was that Somerset and Devonshire both remained, but Jersey, who was suspected of Jacobitism, and Seymour, a prominent aide of Nottingham who had been particularly zealous in the dismissal of Whig J.P.s, were dismissed. Upon this Nottingham resigned.[81]

The new appointments, however, could have brought little comfort to the Whigs. Only one, the insignificant Earl of Kent (who replaced Jersey) was associated with their party. And in Henry St John, who took the War Office in place of the rather colourless Blathwayt, and Sir Thomas Mansell, the new Comptroller, the Tory influence was strongly maintained. As for Robert Harley, who took over Nottingham's duties, though he was associated with the middle ground in politics, which encouraged the hope of effective coalition with the Whigs, he was already known as 'Robin the Trickster' for his devious tactics. Somers described him in 1704 as a knave.[82] If he had hopes for his own political future, he did not reveal them. Writing to Shrewsbury about this time, he complained that the nation's 'present humour' afforded 'few pleasant subjects' for correspondence, and in an uncharacteristic outburst added: 'Never man was wearier of a place, than I have been of this country, for many years.' His weariness, however, did not prevent him from importuning the expatriate to return to the lists.[83]

When the final session of Anne's first Parliament met late in October, the reconstituted ministry might count on Marlborough's great victory at Blenheim to shore it up. Not since the days of Cromwell had England's military reputation stood so high on the continent; not since the repulse of the Armada had her people, despite the grudging attitude of High Tories, engaged in such rejoicing and thanksgiving. Yet the ministry was far from secure, and was subject to attacks from both Tories and Whigs.

Apart from the assurance of supply, which was effected in the early weeks of the session, it was principally concerned with Anglo-Scottish relations. However Englishmen in the past had ignored—or, even worse, condescended to—the Scots, passage of the Scottish Act of Security now brought their affairs to the foreground. By this Act, which the Queen had been forced to accept under threat of refusal of supply, the Scottish estates were empowered to provide for the descent of the crown of Scotland as they saw fit, regardless of who ruled south of the Tweed, unless 'there be such conditions of Government settled and enacted as may secure the honour and sovereignty of this Crown and Kingdom, the freedom, frequency, and power of Parliaments, the religion, liberty, and trade of the Nation, from English or any foreigne influence'.[84] Here was a sticky business: while many Englishmen were disposed towards reprisals, they could not afford to throw the Scots into the arms of the French, or to encourage the ties with St Germain. As for the ministry under which such a perilous situation had come into being, it was clearly embarrassed; a vote of censure against Godolphin seemed in the offing.

Somers's experience with Scottish affairs had been hitherto virtually confined to the investigation of the recent conspiracy and, in William's reign, of the Darien debacle. His eclipse in the first year of Anne's reign had precluded his appointment to an Anglo-Scottish commission for the discussion of a union of the two kingdoms, which had deliberated in a desultory way. Now, however, he played an important part in shaping the English retort to the Act of Security. The peers set aside 29 November for a consideration of the measure.[85] The Queen was present as on other occasions that winter; it was hoped that her attendance might moderate the heat of debate. Rochester and Nottingham were particularly vociferous in denouncing the pernicious consequences of the Scottish Act; Godolphin could only defend its passage as the lesser of two evils. The debate ranged rather far afield. When Nottingham cast aspersions on the late King for his partition treaty dealings, Somers seized the opportunity to demonstrate his constancy while rebuking political foes. It was 'unbecoming', he said, for a fellow peer 'to sully the Memory of so great a Prince', adding (doubtless with a glance in Anne's direction) that he did not doubt that 'a man, who could reflect on King William, before his Successor, would do the same by her present Majesty, when she was gone'. He also got in a blow at the

expense of the Earl of Jersey, 'who was the principal Agent and Plenipotentiary in that treaty, and whose duty, as well as interest, it was to vindicate
both the memory of his late most gracious Master and his own conduct'.
As for Scottish affairs, he was critical of the way the government had
handled them, protesting in particular against the opening of any Scottish
trade with France. But he advised against hasty action, moving an adjournment to permit a cooler consideration of the problem.[86]

A week later the Lords returned to the Scottish problem, Somers leading
off in debate. The Scots, he observed, were unreasonable in their complaints
of hardships since the union of the crowns. Noting the commercial advantages they enjoyed (specifically in traffic in sheep, black cattle and linen
cloth), he proposed that, should the succession to the Scottish throne
not be satisfactorily arranged within a suitable time, the Scots should be
declared aliens and economic sanctions launched against them. By February
1705, legislation to this effect (the Aliens Act) had been passed, though it
was not to be operative until the following December. The importation
of Scottish linen, coal and cattle, as well as the export to Scotland of wool,
horses and arms, were enjoined. But there was also a recommendation that
new commissioners work towards a union of the kingdoms.[87]

During the last days of the session the Aylesbury election case again
troubled the relations between the two houses. Emboldened by Ashby's
success in securing damages, five other Aylesbury burgesses, with like
grievances, had brought similar actions since the previous spring. The
Commons retorted by committing them to Newgate for breach of privilege.
The old impasse stood, blocking the burgesses in their appeal to justice
and fanning the smouldering animosities between the chambers. When the
suitors failed in an attempt to obtain writs of *habeas corpus,* they sought to
bring their case before the Lords by a writ of error, petitioning both the
Crown and the peers to that effect. Once more the Lords were in the thick
of the fray.

Although Somers is credited with prominent services on behalf of the
embattled burgesses, he could not have been active on the floor of the
Lords.[88] After 3 February he was absent for the rest of the session, incapacitated by illness, and was forced to rely upon his colleagues. The Junto
responded in full measure, Sunderland, Halifax and Wharton managing
conferences with the Commons, Wharton supplying the needs of the five
prisoners.[89] But it is virtually certain that Somers's counsel was sought, and
that the proceedings of the Lords reflected his understanding of the law
and his opinion as to the tactics. And it is highly probable that he was
responsible for the address to the throne, justifying these proceedings, and,
in particular, supporting the contention that a writ of error must be regarded as a writ of right, and not of grace—a crucial point in the dispute.[90]
Its effect, however, was blunted when Anne, caught in a cross-fire between
the chambers, extricated herself by first proroguing and then, three weeks
later, dissolving Parliament. And so the contest was again interrupted. It
was to remain unresolved, for it was never taken up again, nor was any

similar case put to the test. But whatever its value as a precedent in English constitutional development, the stand taken by Somers and his fellow Whigs enhanced the popularity of that party and contributed to the revival of its fortunes in the ensuing elections.

Somers had anticipated an early end to the session. Writing to Shrewsbury late in February, he exhibited some impatience: had it 'desired to dispatch, it might have been over before this time'. His thoughts naturally turned towards the forthcoming contests:

As soon as the session is over, the kingdom will be in the wonted ferment, upon the account of elections, and there is much expectation, how the weight of the court will be turned upon that occasion. They have felt, severely enough, what it is to have one party so great an overbalance for the other (though it was their own party), and would have felt it much more, without the assistance of the House of Lords, to stem some of their extravagancies.[91]

A couple of months later he could be somewhat optimistic about the 'weight of the court', which in the course of the spring would tilt the balance towards the Whig side in various appointments. As for the 'wonted ferment', few elections have been more bitterly contested. The Tories lifted aloft the banner of the Church; with occasional conformity now thrice upheld, the battle cry that it was imperilled had considerable appeal.[92] 'The danger of the Church of England', wrote Burnet, 'grew to be the word as given in an army. Men were known as they answered it.'[93] On the other hand, the Whigs could pose as unwavering prosecutors of the war, and they could cite the recent tacking operation and the Aylesbury case as evidences of the illiberality of a Tory-dominated chamber.

From bits and pieces we can see that Somers played his part in securing a favourable outcome. His efforts were needed, for though Godolphin and Marlborough had for some time been steadily drawing nearer the Whigs, the Queen (however disappointed High Tories might be in her abandonment of the crusade against occasional conformity) remained most at home with their party. The court, as Tindal pointed out, 'acted with such caution and coldness, that the Whigs had very little strength given them by the Ministers in managing the elections'.[94] In his February letter to Shrewsbury, Somers had warned the absentee peer that his interest might 'go wrong now, as it did in the last elections'; he also called upon Lord Herbert to lend his assistance on behalf of Wharton. That politico, along with the Duke of Somerset, was particularly important in an election whose outcome depended perhaps more than ever on the activities of the peers.[95]

For the Junto the results were gratifying. The scope of the High Tory retreat may be measured by the losses suffered by the 'Tackers', who were particularly singled out for denunciation. According to one report, the Whigs could claim 240 seats for themselves, allowing 200 to the Tories and 73 Members who would 'act for the Court' and hold the balance. But Godolphin chalked up the score as 160 Whigs, 190 Tories and a hundred 'Queen's servants'.[96] A present-day scholar finds the Tory majority reduced from 133 to 21.[97] Regardless of tallies, it was clear that the Whigs had made substantial gains, and that the character of the new house would be materially different, a prognostication borne out by the choice of a Whig Speaker the following autumn. As for Somers's 'interest', it weathered the storm very well. Although Walsh failed to be re-elected for Worcestershire, he came in for Richmond in a by-election. The rest of his acknowledged followers retained their seats, including the relatively inexperienced Thomas Wylde. Reigate witnessed the customary sharing of the spoil between Harvey and Parsons.[98]

The Whigs' improved parliamentary fortunes were to a degree reflected in administrative changes. Not that Anne subscribed to the modern concept that the complexion of parliaments and ministries must be of the same hue, or that the election marks a sharp break in the position of the Whigs. But Marlborough and Godolphin, to offset extremist disaffection in the ranks of the Tories, had during the past winter drawn nearer the Junto, which continued to direct the fortunes of a comparatively well-knit party. Godolphin had relied upon the Junto lords to exert their influence against a proposal to invite Sophia of Hanover to take up residence in England—a project offensive to the Queen—and a similar manoeuvre had been employed against a place bill.[99] Negotiations obviously went on. The Tory chiefs, of course, had no intention of surrendering to Whig domination. What they had in mind was a coalition of moderate men, who looked upon victory over France as the most important task on the agenda, and who underwrote without reservations the Hanoverian succession. But, as they became more useful and even indispensable, the Whigs could not be expected to be content with virtual exclusion from the seats of power. By April the signs were clearly in the wind. Anne was persuaded to dismiss the caballing, half-Jacobite Buckingham as Lord Privy Seal and put in his place the Duke of Newcastle, whose house was a social centre for the Whigs. Her aversion to the Junto, deep-seated as it was, appeared to be cooling. At least she was willing to dine with Lord Orford. It is also worthy of note that upon her visit to Cambridge about this time three of the Junto magnates—Orford, Wharton and Sunderland—received honorary degrees. Somers was not included—an indication, perhaps, of the Queen's continuing aversion, though both Wharton and Sunderland seem to have been regarded with at least equal disfavour.

The election results brought further concessions. Somers may have dared to hope that he would again be entrusted with the Great Seal, for the general dissatisfaction with Lord Keeper Wright marked him as the most likely sacrifice.[100] But, though Wright was removed in October, the Queen did not call upon Somers. She wanted 'a moderate Tory' for the position, fearing that concessions already made to the Whigs would put her 'insensibly into their power'. There is almost a pathetic note and surely a tacit reference to Somers in her plea to Godolphin that she might be delivered from 'the merciless men of both parties'.[101] Her predilections apart, Somers's unpopularity with at least the more conservative Tories militated against his appointment. The honour went to William Cowper, a Whig of moderate and somewhat independent tendencies.

Somers had at first given some support to the Duke of Newcastle's nominee, Chief Justice Trevor, once regarded as his own protégé.[102] But he preferred Cowper as more dependable from the Junto's point of view. When Trevor declined, Somers worked closely with Godolphin and Halifax to assure Cowper's appointment.[103] Ten years earlier, impressed by Cowper's skill in Chancery, he had urged him to go into Parliament. He had no cause to regret it, for Cowper had supported him at the time of his impeachment. The new Lord Keeper would maintain a close association with Somers, and clearly held him in high regard. He turned to him in the matter of Chancery reform, chose three of his secretaries as assistants, and commissioned Kneller to execute his portrait.[104]

With Kent, Newcastle and Cowper occupying significant offices; with the chief command of the navy firmly in Whig hands; and with the rising Walpole attached to Prince George's Council, Somers, who the previous December had found little cause, under any circumstances, 'to envy any one who has a share of the ministry in England', must have been in a more optimistic frame of mind.[105] He could take satisfaction, too, in seeing his protégé Addison an under-secretary of state. Nor could he any longer be denied some recognition of his service and influence. Before the summer was over the Privy Council had been somewhat revamped, several High Church members being dismissed. He now regained the seat he had lost at the outset of the reign, and his name was restored to the commissions of the peace.[106] He still stood outside the ministerial ranks. But he had emerged from the political wilderness, and the coming years would witness some of his most constructive and significant accomplishments.

NOTES

[1] C. J., XIII, 639. In September 1701, Sunderland warned that 'the Tories will not be satisfied without ruining my Lord Somers': Hardwicke, *State Papers*, II, 446. Vernon echoes this: Add. MSS. 40,775, f. 116. And cf. Daniel Defoe, *A New Satyr on the Parliament* (London, 1701), lines 66–70.

[2] Burnet, IV, 523.

[3] See the edition by Frank H. Ellis (Oxford, 1967), 98.

[4] Humphrey Mackworth, *Vindication of the Rights of the Commons of England* (London, 1701); *Vernon Letters*, III, 156.

[5] Hardwicke, *State Papers*, II, 453–56.

[6] Burnet, IV, 531, notes that some M.P.s were clamouring for this.

[7] *Vernon Letters*, III, 150; Kenyon, *Sunderland*, 321.

[8] Hardwicke, *State Papers*, II, 443–46.

[9] *Ibid.*, II, 448–52.

[10] *Ibid.*, II, 457–61.

[11] Walcott, *English Politics*, 90. But see George M. Trevelyan, *England under Queen Anne* (London, 1936), I, 153–54, who takes the view that, since William did not change the Tory ministry before the dissolution this influence was not 'thrown decisively on the side of the Whig candidates'. Hedges was dismissed 29 December 1701; Rochester was to be dismissed, early in 1702, but remained in office until 1703.

[12] Feiling, 353–54; Walcott, *English Politics*, 90n.

[13] *A True Picture of a Modern Whig* (London, 1701), 9.

[14] Feiling, 356, citing Add. MSS. 22,851, H. Whistler to Gov. Thomas Pitt of Madras, 20 December 1701.

[15] On Wharton's electoral influence see Walcott, *English Politics*, 200–2; Holmes, *British Politics*, 240; John Carswell, *The Old Cause: Three Biographical Studies in Whiggism* (London, 1954), 74–76, 90–91.

[16] See Walcott, *English Politics*, 202, and above, p. 175. A discussion of the electoral prospects of Somers's 'men' may be found in Somers MSS., William Walsh to Somers, 26 October and 15 December 1701.

[17] *Vernon Letters*, III, 162. Several Junto stalwarts died about this time: Sir James Houblon (1700); Sir George Treby (1700); Sir Charles Sedley (1701); Thomas Papillon (1702).

[18] Speck, *Tory and Whig*, 123.

[19] C.J., XIII, 646–47; Hardwicke's note in Burnet, IV, 546.

[20] Oldmixon, 253.

[21] L.J., XVII, 6.

[22] Ibid., XVII, 7; C.J., XIII, 647, 665; Ogg, *James II and William III*, 483–84.

[23] Trevelyan, *Anne*, I, 156.

[24] C.J., XIII, 645, 648 ff.; *Parliamentary History*, V, 1339; Luttrell, *Relation*, V, 147; Feiling, 356.

[25] In March, with Anne on the throne, he was reinstated.

[26] See Burnet, IV, 531n.

[27] He was Comptroller of the Household.

[28] Feiling, 358.

[29] L.J., XVII, 7–8, 28. The *Lords MSS.*, 1699–1702, has only two references to participation by Somers in the work of the Lords between 30 December 1701 and the death of William early in the following March.

[30] Feiling, 358; also L.J., XVII, 119.

[31] Ibid., XVIII, 42, 48, 95; *Lords MSS.*, 1699–1702, 466–67; ibid., 1702–04, 16–22. His experience on the equity side must have been a factor in his association with a bill designed to prevent the defrauding of the poor: L.J., XVII, 17.

[32] As late as 1708 Somerset could speak of an 'aversion . . . that was personal' to Somers: Blenheim MSS. E. 25, Mainwaring to the Duchess of Marlborough, 28 (?) June 1708.

[33] Burnet, II, 241; Holmes, *British Politics*, 262.

[34] L.J., XVII, 113, 129, 140.

[35] Ibid., XVII, 114–15; Burnet, V, 14–15; Boyer, *Annals*, I, 33–34.

[36] L.J., XVII, 122, 143; Boyer, *Annals*, I, 34–36.

[37] *Vernon Letters*, III, 257; Add. MSS. 29,579, f. 400.

[38] Speck, *Tory and Whig*, 123.

[39] Burnet, V, 45.

[40] Walsh relied heavily on Somers's influence, as is shown in his letter to him in the Somers MSS., 22 July 1702.

[41] Walcott, *English Politics*, 229–32.

[42] The Somers MSS. indicate that he was living in Leicester Square in 1701. According to Dasent, p. 244, Lord Conway did not occupy No. 21 St James's Square until 1702.

[43] According to the *Daily Courant*, 1 August 1716, Somers's house in Leicester Fields was to be 'disposed of'.

[44] Henry Chauncy, *Historical Antiquities of Hertfordshire* (London, 1700), 530–31; Nathaniel Salmon, *History of Hertfordshire* (London, 1728), 64; Robert Clutterbuck, *History of Hertfordshire* (London, 1728), 64; Robert Clutterbuck, *History of Hertfordshire* (London, 1815–27), I, 453 ff.; V.C.H.: *Hertfordshire* (London, 1902–12), II, 256. The house was destroyed by fire in 1892. There are various items relating to Somers's possession of this property in Herts. County Records, Manorial Documents, Brookmans Park Collection, No. 23,813 *et seq.*

[45] Thereafter, it appears, ill health plagued him again; he was never present in this session after 4 February.

[46] See Burnet, V, 54–56 .

[47] L.J., XVII, 185; for foreigners in the Lords, see Leadam, *History*, 28.

[48] L.J., XVII, 240–41.

[49] Ibid., XVII, 247; Rogers, *Protests*, I, 163–64.

[50] Burnet, V, 50.

[51] Ibid., V, 52.

[52] See Nicolson MS. Diary, 3, 7 and 9 December 1702, where Nicolson describes him as

'more passionate than usual' in debate. The committee, numbering twenty-six, included Sunderland, Orford, Wharton and Halifax, as well as Bolton and Townshend: *L.J.*, XVII, 192.

⁵³ *Ibid.*, XVII, 192, 195, 206-30. Nicolson, who served on the committee, tells us that the search covered reigns from Henry VII's: MS. Diary, 23 December 1702; 8 January 1703.

⁵⁴ On plans for Queen Anne's Bounty, see Burnet, V, 117 ff.

⁵⁵ This reference was primarily to the Commons' provision that in addition to being ousted occasional conformists should be barred from any other employment until a year's conformity had been demonstrated.

⁵⁶ *L.J.*, XVII, 306-14; *Parliamentary History*, VI, 59-92. See also Abel Boyer, *Impartial History of the Occasional Conformity and Schism Bills* (London, 1717), 19-38. According to Boyer, Somers and other managers 'own'd it to be a scandal to Religion, that Persons should conform only for a Place'. On subsequent occasional conformity activity, see below, pp. 304-5.

⁵⁷ For the Lords' division list on the 'penalties amendment', see *Parliamentary History*, VI, 170-71.

⁵⁸ *C.J.*, XIV, 140, 143; *Parliamentary History*, VI, 97 ff.

⁵⁹ *L.J.*, XVII, 266, 269-71; *Parliamentary History*, VI, 129-30; Boyer, *Annals*, I, 213-15. On Somers's illness, see Holmes, *British Politics*, 236.

⁶⁰ On 4 February 1703.

⁶¹ Burnet, V, 66.

⁶² *Correspondence of Nathaniel Hooke*, ed. W. D. Macray (Roxburghe Club, 1870-71), I, 13-14; Trevelyan, *Anne*, I, 174. Somers was not among those excepted from James II's pardon in 1692: Oldmixon, *History*, 72.

⁶³ *L.J.*, XVII, 331-32.

⁶⁴ *Ibid.*, XVII, 353-54; *Cal. S. P. Dom.*, 1703-4, 238. On 18 December six of the committee-men, including Somers, sought to be excused, but to no avail: *Lords MSS.*, 1702-4, 301n.

⁶⁵ Campbell, V, 152, states that Somers secured its defeat. *Parliamentary History*, VI, 171, merely lists Somers as one of the seventy-one. The Lords denied the Commons' bill a second reading on 14 December 1703: *L.J.*, XVII, 348.

⁶⁶ *C.J.*, XIV, 259-60.

⁶⁷ *L.J.*, XVII, 371-74, 506, 554; *Somers Tracts*, ed. Scott, XII, 423-29; Burnet, V, 133-34; Horwitz, *Revolution Politicks*, 191-96.

⁶⁸ *L.J.*, XVII, 341.

⁶⁹ Campbell, V, 153-54; *L.J.*, XVII, 369; *State Trials*, XIV, 645-887.

⁷⁰ *C.J.*, XIV, 308.

⁷¹ *L.J.*, XVII, 527-34.

⁷² *Ibid.*, XVII, 534-35.

⁷³ Burnet, V, 116.

⁷⁴ Holmes, *British Politics*, 137.

⁷⁵ *L.J.*, XVII, 378, 485-87, 507; *Lords MSS.*, 1702-4, 344; 3 and 4 Anne, c. 7.

⁷⁶ *L.J.*, XVII, 345.

⁷⁷ They dealt with: Grey's Estate, Jarman's Estate, Frampton Estate, Gresham College, Grainge Estate, Worcester Workhouse, and Brisco's Estate: House of Lords MSS., Committee Minutes.

⁷⁸ *L.J.*, XVII, 503.

⁷⁹ *Ibid.*, XVII, 483; *Vernon Letters*, III, 257; Burnet, V, 135-36.

⁸⁰ *L.J.*, XVII, 523-24.

⁸¹ According to D.N.B., *sub* John Somers, he and his friends 'effected the elimination from the ministry of the high tory element'. Horwitz, in *Revolution Politicks*, 197-98, makes no mention of Devonshire and notes that Anne warmly pressed Nottingham to reconsider.

⁸² *Cal. S. P. Dom.*, 1700-02, 486.

⁸³ Coxe, *Shrewsbury*, 640-44.

⁸⁴ *Acts of the Parliament of Scotland*, XI, 137.

⁸⁵ See *L.J.*, XVII, 586 ff.

⁸⁶ James Mackinnon, *Union of England and Scotland* (London, 1896), 182 ff.; Tindal, XXI, 113; Abel Boyer, *The History of Queen Anne* (London, 1735), 165; *Correspondence of George Baillie of Jerviswood* (Bannatyne Club, Edinburgh, 1842), 12, 15; Marchmont MSS., 156. The Scottish Parliament had recently permitted the importation of foreign wines and liquors.

⁸⁷ *L.J.*, XVII, 602 ff.; *C.J.*, XIV, 514. The Commons bill was entitled 'An Act for the

effectual securing the Kingdom of England from the apparent Dangers that may arise from several Acts lately passed in the Parliament of Scotland'. The minatory provisions of the Act never took effect.

88 Onslow's note in Burnet, V, 191; Campbell, V, 155–57.

89 L.J., XVII, 677–79; *Parliamentary History*, VI, 387–436.

90 L.J., XVII, 698–715.

91 Coxe, *Shrewsbury*, 647.

92 A third occasional conformity bill, sent up by the Commons, was rejected on 15 December 1704; L.J., XVII, 600.

93 Burnet, V, 218.

94 Tindal, XXI, 273. For a contrary view, see Morgan, *Political Parties*, 119–20, 122.

95 Coxe, *Shrewsbury*, 647–48; Rebecca Warner, *Epistolary Curiosities* (2nd ser., London, 1818), 29; Morgan, *Political Parties*, 111.

96 Portland MSS., IV, 291. Only 80 of the 134 'Tackers' sat in the new Parliament: Trevelyan, *Anne*, II, 31; Burnet, V, 178.

97 Speck, *Tory and Whig*, 123.

98 Harvey died in 1707; his seat was taken by Somers's nephew, James Cocks.

99 Portland MSS., IV, 154; Trevelyan, *Anne*, II, 18.

100 Tindal, XXI, 275.

101 B. Curtis Brown. *Letters and Diplomatic Instructions of Queen Anne* (London, 1935), 172.

102 Portland MSS., II, 190, and see above, p. 93.

103 Ellis, 'Junto', 534, citing Somers to Cowper, undated letter [1705] in Cowper MSS.

104 Campbell, V, 227; *Downshire MSS.*, I, pt. ii, 843; Somers MSS., Cowper to Somers, 14 July 1708.

105 Coxe, *Shrewsbury*, 647.

106 Campbell, V, 158.

XII

Influence without office, 1705-7

Anne's second Parliament, which first met on 25 October 1705, was launched with an extraordinary turn-out of the Commons—the largest, we are told, in half a century.[1] Even in the Lords, where in recent years the early meetings had been somewhat scantily attended, fifty-nine peers showed up. There can be little doubt that the gains made by the Whigs in the spring elections provided the principal stimulus, at least in the lower house, where the first business was, as usual, the election of a Speaker. Harley, as Secretary of State, put himself out of the running. The contest lay between John Smith, who had been associated with the Junto during most of William's reign as a Commissioner of the Treasury, but had been out of office for several years, and William Bromley, who was to serve for thirty years as a Member for Oxford University.

One can imagine the efforts made by the Junto lords.[2] Not that there was much chance of any Whig giving his vote to Bromley, for he was regarded as 'a violent Tory, and as a great favourer of Jacobites'.[3] But there was always the uncommitted element, whose votes might go in either direction. The court, however, was for Smith, and he emerged the victor, by a close vote. It was a step up for the Junto. They could also take some satisfaction that Sunderland, though denied ministerial preferment, had in June been sent off as envoy to Vienna, where the recent death of the Emperor Leopold called for a reconfirmation of the alliance. Though Somers expressed doubt 'that any good can be done at that Court', it was at least further evidence that the Junto was not to be ignored in the principal deliberations of the government.[4]

The session was to be a busy one for Somers. Though five years had passed since he had been forced to relinquish the Seal, and a new and highly capable Lord Keeper presided on the woolsack, he was still not only a power to be reckoned with in the upper chamber but its acknowledged mentor in matters relating to the law and constitution of the realm. Never before had he been active on so many select committees. Between 14 December and 12 March he served as chairman (or temporary chairman) of thirteen such bodies, most of them, of course, concerned with private bills, and meeting but once or twice, but two—those dealing with law reform and the preservation of the national archives—of more general importance.[5] Apart from this tangible evidence that he was not merely called upon to act but did so, the Journals of the House give ample proof that he provided counsel and leadership in all the more important issues before the Lords: the state of the Church, Anglo-Scottish relations, the problem of arranging for the succession and the improvement of legal procedures. His efforts, moreover, were crowned with considerable success: it is noteworthy that he did not feel impelled to voice a formal protest on any legislative measure before the Lords between 1704 and 1711.

On 15 November the peers took time to consider the state of the nation, the Queen being present at the debate. Anne, in her opening speech, had called for a continuation of the war until the balance of power was restored, with the French dislodged from Spain and British trade insured against the exercise of a French monopoly. She also indicated that she would continue her moderate position in church affairs, stating categorically that she would 'inviolably maintain the toleration'.[6] Her remarks revealed her concern that the Grand Alliance was losing its solidity, not without justification, for the French had already made overtures to Pensionary Heinsius, who had wavered enough to make Marlborough uneasy. As for the Church, she had been stung by the outspoken attacks of pamphleteers, who had gone so far as to depict her as a betrayer of its interests.

Debate was led off by Lord Haversham, renowned for his interminable speeches.[7] As Sir John Thompson he had been one of the earliest supporters of King William, who had made him a baron and a Lord of the Admiralty. But though, in the late reign, he had worked closely with the Junto and been highly esteemed by Somers, the days of his Whiggery were over. He who had supported Somers at the time of his impeachment had parted from the Whigs, resigning his Admiralty post in 1701, and now sought to lead the Tories in the upper House. An impulsive and somewhat undisciplined man, he had broken with Somers in 1703, apparently taking offence at words used by his old colleague in the debate occasioned by the Scottish conspiracy.[8]

In his speech Haversham began by commenting adversely on the conduct of the war, particularly with regard to the part played by Britain's allies. What with English subsidies, he could not see how the Dutch had been 'out of pocket one Shilling'. But this was merely introductory: his real objective was to revive the project to bring Sophia of Hanover to England, in order that she could be on hand to assume the government in the event of Anne's death.[9] It was argued that such a course was necessary to insure the Protestant succession: the Stuart Pretender was nearer London than the Electress, and might win the race to the throne. Whatever merit there might be in this project, there is no doubt that the manoeuvre was a partisan one, designed to embarrass the ministry and its Whig aides. If they supported it they would mortally offend Anne, who was irrevocably opposed to a rival court in England (and perhaps conscious that the lively Electress, despite her advanced years, could cut a better figure than herself); on the other hand, if they opposed Haversham's motion their attachment to the House of Hanover would naturally be questioned, perhaps with disastrous political consequences. That the Tories, too, could be injured by playing with this double-edged sword does not seem to have occurred to the quixotic Haversham, who must have known that Anne (who had of late made a point of attending the more crucial debates in the Lords) might well be present to mark what was said and who said it. At any rate, it was a risk he took.

But news of Haversham's proposal had leaked through to Godolphin. He proceeded at once to sound the alarm, calling upon Newcastle, the Lord Privy Seal, and the Duke of Bolton, who was closely associated with the Junto chiefs, 'to send to such lords as you and he shall think proper' to meet at Bolton's house to consider what steps should be taken. As a result the Whig peers were alerted and were able to respond effectively, first with delaying tactics and then with a regency bill. Somers contributed materially to both. With Anne looking on, it was he who, after Nottingham, Rochester and Buckingham had supported Haversham's motion, moved the previous question. As a result the proposal was rejected by a considerable majority.[10]

The Whigs gained credit in Anne's eyes. 'I am sensible', she wrote to the Duchess of Marlborough, 'of the services those people have done me that you have a good opinion of, and will countenance them.' According to the Duchess this was the first sign of a reconciliation between the Queen and the Whigs, Anne going so far as to instruct Godolphin to assure the Junto that 'she would be served only by men of whom they would approve'.[11] While this is hardly credible, from Somers himself comes evidence that an alliance between the court and the Junto was, at least to some extent, undertaken. Among the Hardwicke Manuscripts is a fire-damaged fragment, endorsed by Lord Hardwicke as 'A sketch for the conduct of the Whigs, by Lord Somers, and some Rules for their conjunction with Lord Godolphin', composed in 1708. The ministers, he wrote, had seen that

difficulties were likely to arise to themselves unless they took in [the Whigs] and they seemed desirous to engage the Whigs whose [conduct in] publick matters they then declared the Queen approved. [It was agreed, therefore] to concert measures with them for carrying on the publick [business] and preventing or obviating what they apprehended.[12]

Not for a couple of years, however, would the Junto be able to hold the ministers to any such agreement.[13]

Although Haversham had been rebuffed it was recognised that an inter-regnum might endanger the Protestant succession. The Lords set about to insure the orderly transmission of the crown by further legislation. In mid-November Wharton introduced a proposal for a regency bill, conceived, it appears, mainly by Somers. Supported almost unanimously by the Whig peers, it was so well received that within a week the judges were ordered to frame such a measure, as well as one naturalising the Electress and her issue.[14] By 3 December the Lords had passed both of them; thereafter Somers (along with other Junto lords) laboured to convert the Commons, serving as a manager for three conferences in February.[15] Progress was held up by controversy over whether the provision in the Act of Settlement, excluding those holding office under the Crown from parliamentary seats, should be repealed. Both Whigs and Tories were divided in this matter, but the Junto supported the government, which advocated repeal. Somers urged such a course, claiming general agreement that the existing law was 'unreasonable'.[16] In the ensuing compromise this was done, but, by subsequent legislation, holders of offices created since 1705 were excluded.[17]

There is evidence apart from parliamentary archives of Somers's involvement in the regency legislation. In April 1706 Lord Halifax was deputed to carry formal tidings of these proceedings to Herrenhausen. With him he took a letter from Somers to the Elector, the future George I.[18] After referring to Halifax as 'a witness, above exception' of his conduct, he goes on to say:

I confess I always depended upon it, that my public behaviour should be an abundant testimony for me as to my zeal for the Protestant succession, and for promoting the war in order to reduce the power of France, which I take to be the most effectual security to that succession.

Mindful that the Whig opposition to Haversham's proposal might have had 'a strange appearance', he took pains to point out that such an arrangement might later have 'pressed very inconveniently' upon the Elector, who could hardly be expected to leave a domain where he was sovereign to reside in a land where he was but heir apparent. But the strongest objection to the proposal lay in its presentation:

The turn of it was to show, first, that we could go on no further with the Dutch (which was, in effect, to say we must make peace); and next to say, the Queen's administration was hardly sufficient to keep us in peace at home, unless the next heir came over. The Queen was present at this discourse, and none can judge so well as your Electoral Highness whether this was a compliment proper to engage her Majesty to enter willingly into the invitation; and if it had been assented to with reluctance, whether it might not have given rise to unkindnesses which might in the end have proven very fatal.

He concluded by scotching the contention that the Naturalisation Act was 'unnecessary, if not a diminution, to your most Serene Family'. It was, on the contrary, the 'one complete and perfect' way of assuring aliens of English inheritances, honours or offices.[19]

The answer of the Elector reveals an awareness of Somers's services, and must have encouraged him in the hope of future rewards:

The Lord Halifax delivered to me the letter which you was at the trouble of writing to me. I am much obliged to you for the light it gives concerning the affairs of England, but especially for the part which you have had in all that has been done there in favour of my family. The testimony of my Lord Halifax was not necessary to inform me of this. He could give you no other in this respect, but that which is due to you by all good Englishmen who love their religion and their country. I am not ignorant of what influence you may have amongst them, nor of the manner in which you have employed it. Nothing can give me a better opinion of the English nation than the justice they do your merit.

His sentiments, he added, regarding the invitation of the successor were in complete harmony with those of Somers.[20] But it would be nine years before George as King of England would summon him with other Whig leaders to his presence.

A few days after Haversham's speech, Somers lent a hand as the Whigs sought to lay low the 'Church in danger' bogey, which was not only stalking through the halls of Parliament but was abroad in the land in the form of countless outpourings from the press, Drake's *Memorial of the Church of England* being the most noteworthy of such productions. At the instance of Halifax a day was set aside for debate. Again the Queen was present and, to the discomfiture of the moderate Tories and delight of the Whigs, listened to such irreconcilables as Rochester, who opened the debate, maintain that the institution which Anne cherished so deeply and for which she had recently made generous provision was indeed in danger, what with Presbyterians arming in Scotland, the Protestant heir hundreds of miles away and occasional conformity successfully defended from legislative restraint. The Tories, for the most part, had little stomach for the encounter, as is seen from the awkward silence while the House waited for someone to second Rochester. Halifax then spoke in rebuttal, and others entered the debate, most of them bishops, though the irrepressible Wharton had some fun at the expense of the 'High Flyers'.

Somers came last. After recapitulating the arguments of both sides, and expressing confidence regarding the state of ecclesiastical affairs, he ended on the broader note of support for the administration and all its works. The nation, he said, was happy under a government 'wherein the Public Money was justly applied, the Treasury kept in a most regular Method, and thereby the Public Credit in the highest Esteem'. With the armed forces well supplied, and the successes gained in the theatre of war, England's military reputation had reached an unprecedented level, and there was 'a fair Prospect of bringing the War to a happy Conclusion'. He concluded with a shot at the Tory malcontents: 'Wherefore for Men to raise groundless Jealousies at this time of day, it could mean no less, than an Intention to embroil us at Home, and to defeat all those glorious designs abroad.'[21] By a vote of two to one the Church was found not to be in danger; indeed, by a further resolution it was declared to be 'in a most safe and flourishing Condition', and whoever intimated the contrary 'an Enemy to the Queen, the Church, and the Kingdom'. A committee, including Somers, was appointed to map strategy in presenting the resolution to the Commons. A few days later he was named to another to prepare an address to the Queen.[22]

Meanwhile, he was busy with another problem, of marked interest to him personally and to which he brought an unrivalled specialised knowledge. This was law reform. On 15 December he moved the House to 'inquire, what Defects there are in the Laws relating to the Administration of Justice, and to consider of proper Methods to prevent expensive Suits'. As a result, a large committee was set up for this purpose; it was to 'have Power to send for Persons, Papers, and Records' and to report to the house from time to time. The membership included three other Junto leaders (Wharton, Halifax and Orford) besides Somers. Except for him, only the Lord Keeper, who was authorised to assist the committee, had professional legal experience. In mid-January Somers brought in the report.[23]

Dissatisfaction with outmoded procedures and legal devices was not new; it had smouldered in the early Stuart era, as is seen by the reforms projected by the Barebones Parliament. The crisis of 1688 afforded an opportunity for renewed discussion, at least, of major grievances. But as already noted, when Somers and his colleagues framed the Bill of Rights they included only a few guarantees of a very general nature regarding courts and procedures. Under William III the legislators turned their attention to the problem in piecemeal fashion. In statutes that came to be regarded as constitutional landmarks treason trial procedure was reformed and judges assured of continuance in office during good behaviour. There were other forward steps: benefit of clergy was redefined, juries were regulated and frivolous suits discouraged. Altogether the reign produced about a dozen enactments of this kind. Apart from the Treason Trial Procedure Act of 1696 Somers's contributions are not apparent. But it is inconceivable that one who during these years served as Crown lawyer, judge, lawmaker and minister could have had no share in such legislation, most of which was of a highly technical nature.[24]

Somers's report was readily accepted by the Lords, who called upon the judges to prepare a bill, first read on 25 January, entitled 'An Act for the Amendment of the Law, and for the better Advancement of Justice'. Burnet gives Somers high marks for his handling of the business:

The Lord Somers made a motion in the house of lords to correct some of the proceedings in the common law and in chancery, that were both dilatory and very chargeable. He began the motion with some instances that were more conspicuous and gross; and he managed the matter so, that both the lord keeper and judges concurred with him: though it passes generally for a maxim, that judges ought rather to enlarge than contract their jurisdiction.[25]

At no stage did the measure encounter serious obstacles in the Lords. But the project involved much close work: there were numerous meetings of the committee and frequent consultations with the judges.[26] Within ten days the bill was given its third reading and sent to Commons. Within a month that chamber had agreed to accept it, in the main, but various amendments necessitated further deliberations, and it was not until 19 March that it was given the royal assent.[27]

In the final enactment there were twenty-seven clauses.[28] Most of them amended common law and equity systems of procedure and pleading. In the field of procedure the clauses applying to the common law courts considerably outnumber those affecting Chancery. A party seeking to rely upon any errors of form in the conduct of an action was now compelled to make specific reference to them, that they might be corrected. Dilatory pleas were not to be received unless verified by affidavit. A party was no longer to be prevented from pleading payment of money after the due date. Persons overseas when a cause against them became enforceable might be sued during a year after their return—a timely reform in view of the increasingly far-flung operations of Englishmen. Juries were henceforth to be drawn from the bodies of counties, where civil actions were involved; no longer were challenges for want of hundreders to be permitted.[29] The position of the defendant was strengthened in that he might now avail himself of several defences: no longer did his fate hang upon a single thread.

On the equity side, no subpoena or other process for the enforcement of appearance was, as a rule, to issue until after the bill was filed. The concern over vexatious suits is particularly reflected in the provision that where the plaintiff dismissed his own suit, or where it was otherwise thrown out for want of prosecution, the dependant was entitled to full costs. By way of reducing expense, the measure eliminated the copy or abstract of the bill which had been required in connection with the defendant's answer, the clerks being compensated for their loss of fees. Other clauses effected some changes in the land law. The attornment of tenants, upon the grant of manors, rents, and the like, which could be time-consuming and expensive and was certainly a nuisance, was abolished;[30] and the law was clarified with regard to such matters as declarations of use, entries and warranties. The statute also defined the competency of witnesses for nuncupative wills, and (in a clause added by the Commons) extended the scope of the action of account.[31]

Although the finished product has been described as the only eighteenth-century enactment 'in which any attempt was made to survey the field of law, and to remedy some of the many defects of its adjective and substantive rules', it cannot be said to have effected sweeping reforms.[32] But its limitations cannot be entirely laid at Somers's door. As usual, it was difficult if not impossible to make consequential alterations if they threatened the vested interests of the legal confraternity, from the most august judges to the lowliest clerks. Burnet attributes the opposition of the Commons, which resulted in the exclusion of certain provisions, to their concern in this regard:

when this [bill] went through the house of commons, it was visible that the interest of under-officers, clerks, and attorneys, whose gains were to be lessened by this bill, was more considered than the interest of the nation itself.[33]

It would appear that this had some bearing on the action of the lower House in striking out a clause to prevent frivolous writs of error, another for shortening decrees and orders in equity by forbidding recitals, and still another for taking a bill in equity *pro confesso* for want of appearance.[34] This is not to say that the House of Commons was motivated entirely by a concern for the perquisites of the legal establishment. One of the provisions rejected would have allowed a person, unable because of illness or absence to give evidence at a trial, to be interrogated by plaintiff or defendant, and permitted the introduction of his deposition. The Lords strongly defended the proposal, as preventing delay and needless and tedious suits in equity; but the Commons were distrustful of written evidence not taken in open court, and fearful of abuses, especially perjury.[35] We may conclude that the measure went as far as possible under the conditions of the time. What it did effect was of extraordinary permanence. Two hundred years later, after the extensive and varied reforms of the Victorian age, a legal historian could still describe much of it as 'live law'.[36]

The session of 1705–6 reveals an interest in reforming legislative as well as judicial procedure. Attention was focused on private bills. The pages of the Lords' Journal introduce us to committee after committee set up to consider such measures. Even though these bodies were deliberately made large, and their quorums kept small, the inroads on the energies of individual members and on the agenda of the House itself were considerable. During this session Somers was appointed to more than thirty, reporting from five.[37]

In mid-February, 1706, the Lords met in committee of the whole to wrestle with the problem. They had already relieved the pressure somewhat by prohibiting the reading of private bills on a cause day (that is, when judicial cases were heard), and had resolved that no further private measures would be entertained during the session.[38] Their discussion now bore fruit in standing orders, issued the following day. Proposals advanced by Somers appear to have formed the basis of these orders.[39] Here again vested interests of individuals made sweeping reform impossible: the processing of bills was accompanied by fees to the speakers and clerks of both houses, inclining them 'to favour and promote them'. On the other hand, the new Lord Keeper, unlike his predecessor, was disposed to curtail private bills; this must have provided crucial support for Somers and his allies.[40]

About this time another project in which Somers was involved began to bear fruit. Late in 1703 he had been appointed to a committee 'to consider the method of keeping records in Offices', with a view to remedying what might be found amiss.[41] Largely owing to the confusion of the Civil War and the neglect of Interregnum officials, the national archives had fallen into a sorry state.[42] When William Prynne was made Keeper of the Records in 1661 he discovered that an enormous mass of valuable documents 'through negligence, nescience, and sloathfullness had for many years then past layen buried together in one confused chaos under corroding putrifying cobwebs, dust and filth in the darkest corners of Caesar's Chapel in the White Tower.'[43] He laboured manfully to improve these conditions, but was forced to confess that his efforts did not 'conquer a tenth part of the work'. In 1703 Caesar's Chapel still presented a scene of decay and disarray, with 'Multitudes of Records . . . laid in confus'd Heaps . . . in great Danger of utter perishing.'[44]

Although Halifax served as chairman of the committee set up in 1703 (and for some years annually renewed), Somers was his close associate in various efforts to provide suitable accommodations and supervision for the public records. In January 1704 he was among those ordered by the Lords to investigate conditions in the Tower. A similar order was issued in November of that year, with a view to ascertain what improvements had been effected by William Petyt, for many years Keeper of the Records.[45] Something was being accomplished, for about that time Nicolson observed 'the new-appointed clerks sorting the long neglected and confused records into Baskets'; and a few years later Thoresby professed himself to be 'mightily pleased' with the results.[46] The committee continued its labours in Anne's second Parliament, Halifax reporting on three occasions. In January, following a petition to the Queen to reform the State Paper Office, he advanced various proposals on this score, and two months later reported the committee's recommendation to purchase the house and grounds of Sir John Cotton, which adjoined the Houses of Parliament, and where the Cottonian library, transferred to the nation in 1702, was still located. Somers was present, along with Halifax and Rochester, for negotiations with the trustees of the library; it was a collection that must have made his mouth water.[47] The committee had ambitious plans for the development of this property, involving additional space for the Houses of Parliament and, in addition, a 'noble structure' which would house not only the Cottonian collections (which at the time were almost shut off from public use), but the libraries of the Queen and the Royal Society as well—an Augustan version of the British Museum. But, though the property was acquired, these plans came to nought.[48]

Parliament was prorogued on 19 March, but springtime did not bring its customary leisure. From April to July Somers was engaged in helping to hammer out the arrangements for a union between England and Scotland. Despite doubts of the ministry's sincerity, a pathway had been cleared to some extent.[49] The Scots had broken the log-jam the previous September by empowering Queen Anne to appoint their commissioners. By 12 November Somers was taking a leading part in undoing what he had done so much to effect in the previous session.[50] Later that month, upon his motion, the Lords undertook to revoke the Aliens Act. 'Our affairs went in the House of Peers as we could have wished,' wrote Loudon, and it was not long before the lower House, led by Harley, had added its seal of approval.[51] The Earl of Marchmont, one-time Lord Chancellor of Scotland, a strong protagonist of union with whom Somers corresponded during the months of planning and negotiations, gave him full honours in these transactions, and urged him on:

I could very easily trace your Lordship's hand in what has passed there of late, because I am so well acquainted with your principles; and I must acknowledge, it is to me a principal ground of hope, that a treaty of union will now be brought to a happy issue, that your Lordship's influence and interest will be at hand to promote it; and I must say it, though to yourself, I am convinced, that more depends upon you than upon any other man.[52]

Late in February Anne appointed the commissioners to represent the Scottish Parliament at Westminster. Somers was undoubtedly consulted in these appointments; at least Marchmont assumed that this was the case, for he appealed to Somers, as well as to the Queen and Wharton, on behalf of a mixed commission including various shades of opinion.[53] The thirty-one English commissioners were appointed in April. There was a full representation of the Junto—Somers, Sunderland, Orford, Wharton and Halifax; among the others were the archbishops, various ministers, judges and other legal luminaries.[54] The jurists included Lord Keeper Cowper and Trevor, now presiding over Common Pleas. The involvement of the Junto is a far cry from their detachment, and even hostility, towards the court's Scottish policy a few years before.[55] The commissioners got down to work on 16 April, meeting in separate rooms at the Cockpit, except on a few occasions, as when the Queen put in an appearance. Virtually all business was furthered by written minutes communicated from one body to the other.

Among the English commissioners Somers played the leading part.[56] His opposite on the Scottish side appears to have been Lord Chancellor Seafield.[57] Of the forty-five meetings, Somers attended forty. It was he who drafted the basic premises of an 'incorporating' union, rather than a federal alliance, to the effect

That the two Kingdoms of England and Scotland be for ever United into one Kingdom by the name of Great Britain. That the United Kingdom of Great Britain be represented by one and the same Parliament, and that the Succession to the Monarchy of the United Kingdom of Great Britain in case of failure of heirs of her Majesty's body, be according to the limitations mentioned in an Act of Parliament made in England in the 12th and 13th years of the Reign of the late King William.[58]

Though most Scots favoured a federal union, they did not persist. They knew that, with the English, provision for one king and one parliament was fundamental, even as the English were aware that no settlement without assurance for the independence of Scottish religious arrangements could prevail. When the English thought of federalism the United Provinces came to mind—scarcely an example of effective central government, especially in time of war. There was general agreement that there should be uniformity of taxation and trade regulations, Somers being among the eleven commissioners called upon to investigate attendant problems.[59] He and Halifax agreed that the former was subject to such alterations that particulars should not be defined in the treaty, but be left to subsequent legislative action by the reconstituted Parliament. This was the course taken.[60] On the whole, negotiations proceeded amiably enough, great precautions being taken—even to the extent of avoiding social contacts— to prevent any charges of undue influence on the part of the English. Late in April the Earl of Mar could write: 'The English appear very reasonable, so far as we have gone; and I really believe they are hearty in it, as I hope we all are too.'[61] But progress was rather slow, and Anne twice intervened to speed things up. At the thirty-fifth meeting, on 28 June, four commissioners from each camp were appointed to put the articles of the treaty into form, but here Somers is not in evidence.[62] A few weeks later all but a few of the sixty commissioners affixed their signatures, and the following day, walking two by two—Scot with Englishman—they proceeded to St James's Palace and delivered their handiwork to the Queen.

With another session of Parliament at an end, the Whigs, conscious of the services they had rendered the government, pressed for a larger share of the political plums. Godolphin and Marlborough's dependence upon them was undeniable, however much they, particularly the Duke, might resent their importunities. With the war and the Scottish question still unresolved, an alliance was invaluable, and Marlborough had assured his colleague that he would, with all his heart 'live friendly with those that have shown so much friendship to you and service to the Queen'.[63] Early in January Harley gave a dinner at which Godolphin and Marlborough, as well as St John, broke bread with the leading Whigs. Sunderland, Halifax and Cowper were there. Somers was invited, but did not attend. He had gone to Brookmans; according to Cowper he sent 'a kind letter to excuse his absence'. The Lord Keeper suspected that the occasion was for the purpose of reconciling Somers and Halifax with Harley; and this, he wrote, 'was confirmed to me, when, after L^d. T^r was gone, (who first went), S^y. Harley took a Glass, & drank to Love & Friendship & everlasting Union'.[64] More than a year earlier, when the Whigs had been in a much less advantageous position, Defoe had urged Harley to wean Somers from them, in order to 'weaken and Distract the Party'.[65] What his precise motives were at the moment is hard to say, but for a time the relations between the two men appear to have taken a turn for the better.

During the latter part of the year the Junto, bent on representation in the ministry, manoeuvred to effect the ouster of Secretary Hedges and replace him, not with Somers but the young Earl of Sunderland. They were, they believed, 'driving the nail that would go'.[66] But it proved to be no easy task to install him in office. Dubbed republican and atheist, he was at least as unacceptable to Anne as was Somers. His own father-in-law, Marlborough, did not regard him as the right man for the post.[67] Godolphin, however, was keenly aware of the need to placate the Junto. Beset with the obstinacy of Anne, who waxed almost profane in her resentment of being made a tool of party, the jealousy of the High Tories whose interest Hedges supported, and the misgivings of Marlborough, he was in a most uncomfortable position, and even threatened to resign. Ultimately, with Marlborough's somewhat reluctant support, he carried the day, and early in December Sunderland took over Hedges' duties. Godolphin had no choice: it was either that or face the loss of Junto support, with all that it meant for his programme. For Somers and Halifax made it clear that they would not be satisfied with half-measures, and threatened a complete break with the Treasurer. As early as September Sunderland wrote:

Lord Somers, Lord Halifax, and I, have talked very fully over all this matter, and we are come to our last resolution in it, that this and what other things have been promised must be done, or we and the lord treasurer must have nothing more to do together about business; and that we must let all our friends know just how the matter stands between us and the lord treasurer, whatever is the consequence of it.

Somers and Halifax were to acquaint Godolphin with this resolution 'in the plainest words, and in the fullest manner they can'.[68] Once more Somers had stood aside, as far as personal preferment went, and had worked effectively to advance the fortunes of another, and of his party. But Godolphin and Marlborough grumbled at the 'tyranny' of the Junto.[69]

Sunderland's appointment was announced on 3 December, the day on which the new session of Parliament convened. It heralded a few additional honours and advantages for the Whigs. The Lord Keeper and Thomas Pelham, an influential Sussex magnate, were made barons; Wharton and Cholmondeley, along with Godolphin, were raised to earldoms. Halifax's brother, Sir James Montague, became Solicitor-General, and among the new Commissioners for Trade was the Whig stalwart, Lord Stamford. The Privy Council was virtually stripped of prominent Tories; Nottingham, Rochester, Jersey and Sir George Rooke were all removed, though Harley and St John remained. Not that Anne had delivered herself, body and soul, into the hands of the 'merciless' men: the forthcoming appointment of Tory bishops would be evidence of this.[70]

In her opening speech the Queen noted that the treaty of Union was under consideration by the Scottish Parliament; she hoped that 'the mutual advantages of an intire Union of the two Kingdoms' would be so apparent that she could shortly acquaint her English lawmakers with its acceptance in the north.[71] Somers was appointed to a committee to signify the Lords' gratitude for the royal endeavours in this direction.[72] The early weeks of the session were placid enough, with little business of any consequence; but the Tories were restive, and by mid-January their patience was exhausted. Learning that supplementary legislation provided for the perpetual recognition of the Scottish Presbyterian system, Nottingham (though long an advocate of union) raised once more the well-worn banner of the Church in danger, and called for a review of the proceedings in Edinburgh. Anxious to avoid any activity that might rock the boat, Godolphin opposed this motion, Somers, Wharton and Halifax standing behind him. It would be 'an honour to this Nation', they argued, 'that the Treaty of Union should first come ratified from the Parliament of Scotland'; not before then should the Lords take it into consideration.[73]

Somers was kept abreast of developments north of the Tweed by the Earl of Marchmont, whose esteem continued unabated. In March he would write: 'Give me leave once more to tell your Lordship, that I have greater confidence of both your wisdom, honesty, and hearty concern in this matter, than of any other.'[74] But Somers was not content merely to observe what was transpiring in Scotland, where the outcome was far from certain. There is evidence that John Shute, later Viscount Barrington, whose versatility embraced the law, polemics and Christian apologetics, and who served for a time as Wharton's secretary, was at the instance of Somers commissioned to gain Presbyterian support there. According to Swift, Shute, despite his youth, was 'reckoned the shrewdest Head in England', and the man in whom the Presbyterians chiefly confided.[75] In addition, Somers—along with Harley, Halifax and Marlborough—sent letter after letter to their adjutants in the Parliament House in Edinburgh, urging them on and rebutting the arguments of dissentients.[76] Though not blind to certain Scottish objections, as those directed towards economic arrangements, he pressed for confirmation of the treaty as drafted by the commissioners. But involvement, if any, in the purchase of support cannot be traced.

Late in January the Queen notified the Lords that the Scots had ratified the Treaty, though in a form that differed somewhat from the commissioners' draft. The document was forthwith presented at Westminster. The Lords sat four times in committee of the whole house to discuss the articles, Somers being present on all but one occasion.[77] The responsibility of reporting the various resolutions of this body was entrusted to Bishop Burnet. In his *History of His Own Time* he remarks that 'the matter was argued for the union by Oxford, Norwich, and my self, by the lord treasurer, the earls of Sunderland and Wharton, and the lords Townshend and Halifax, but above all by the lord Somers'.[78] The Bishop of Bath and Wells raised objections to the admission of the sixteen Scottish peers to the Lords, arguing that, since 'they could no ways be supposed to be well affected', they should be barred from voting on Church of England matters. But both Somers and Halifax rose in rebuttal.[79] Somers had already been sounded out by Archbishop Tenison in connection with a bill for securing the Church of England—a measure now introduced and speedily approved, confirming all previous acts passed for its establishment. This, along with a similar guarantee for the Kirk, was recognised in the Treaty of Union as a fundamental condition.[80]

These efforts were finally crowned with success, and on 6 March Anne gave the royal assent. The great merger, unresolved over the course of more than a century, was an accomplished fact. For over a year it had absorbed much of Somers's time, not so much on the floor of the Lords as in negotiations, both formal and behind the scenes. These were so ticklish and many-sided that he had at times despaired of success.[81] Its evident unpopularity in Scotland must have been disheartening. His conviction, however, did not flag. Two years earlier he had written to the Earl of Marchmont:

I have been always desirous of an entire union between the two kingdoms, without which I have always feared it might be in the power of a designing and enterprising prince of our own, or in our neighbourhood, by taking advantage of opportunities to make either kingdom the means of ruining both.[82]

The larger aspects of the settlement have naturally received most attention from historians. This has obscured, to some degree, lesser matters of political immediacy and expediency.[83] According to Swift, Somers told him that 'the union was of no other service to the nation, than by giving remedy to that evil which my Lord Godolphin had brought upon us, by persuading the Queen to pass the Scotch act of security'.[84] And he appears to have at least countenanced an attack upon it in 1713.[85] Yet these suggestions of political opportunism, even if authentic, are light in weight when balanced against tangible contributions and unequivocal pronouncements. His belief in the importance of the great concordat, as it was being worked out, is manifest. He linked it, in importance, with the revolutionary settlement itself:

The establishing the Protestant religion, the setling the succession, the fixing the monarchy, the securing the liberties of the people and setling peace throughout the Island, are matters of such moment as I hope will never be thrown away for a humour or upon any private consideration. I have had time during the progress of this treaty to consider very throughly the state of both kingdoms and to be convinced of the absolute necessity of a union; we cannot stand where wee are. In my opinion if wee do not now become better freinds than ever, wee shall soon be lesse so. This is the only juncture which has offered in an age past, and which no man living can hope ever to see again. God grant it be not neglected, but that amongst the many wonderfull blessings of this year [1706] the union of Great Brittain may not be the least.[86]

NOTES

[1] Tindal, XXI, 277.

[2] See W. A. Speck, 'The choice of a Speaker in 1705', *Bulletin of the Institute of Historical Research*, XXXVII (May 1964), 20–35. Orford promised Somers that 'our Country Members will be early in Town': Hardwicke MSS., XXXIII, f. 101. Two months before Parliament assembled Somers was urging the Duke of Newcastle to require his 'friends' to be present for the choice of the Speaker: B.M. Portland Loan 29/237. 18 August [1705].

[3] Tindal, XXI, 278.

[4] Nottingham Portland papers, Somers to Portland, 21 June and 2 August 1705.

[5] House of Lords MSS., Committee Minutes.

[6] L.J., XVIII, 7–8; Tindal, XXI, 279–83.

[7] The speech was published: *The Lord Haversham's Speech in the House of Peers, November 15, 1705* (London, 1705). Haversham followed it up with *The Lord Haversham's Vindication of his Speech in Parliament, November 15, 1705* [against the reflections of Defoe] (London, 1705).

[8] Somers attempted to make amends, and in a conciliatory letter referred to his continuing appreciation of Haversham's 'generous behaviour at the time of the impeachments', but apparently to no avail: Hardwicke, *State Papers*, II, 464–65.

[9] L.J., XVIII, 19; Timberland, II, 148–51. See also below, pp. 266, 309–11.

[10] Trevelyan, *Anne*, II, 91–92; Arthur S. Turberville, *House of Lords in the Eighteenth Century* (Oxford, 1927), 73; *Account of the Conduct of the ... Duchess of Marlborough* (London, 1742), 159.

[11] *Ibid.*, 154, 159–60; cf. Lord Cowper, *Diary*, 1–2.

[12] Ellis, 'Junto', 554; Hardwicke MSS., XXXIII, f. 125. The reconstruction of the document, here and elsewhere, is from Ellis, 555–56, who refers to it as 'Lord Somers's Rules'.

[13] Somers admitted, referring to the ministers' promises, that 'all that tended towards them was obtained with great effort and never conceded without the utmost Reluctance': Hardwicke MSS., XXXIII, ff. 125–26.

[14] It was designed, according to Cowper, to put the succession 'in such a method as was not to be resisted but by open force of arms and a public declaration for the Pretender': 'An impartial history of parties', in Campbell, *Lives of the Chancellors* (London, 1845–47, 1869), IV, 426. On Somers as its author, see notes of Onslow and Hardwicke in Burnet, V, 229. Nicolson, in his MS. Diary (20 November 1705), notes that Somers suggested particular

Lords Justices to be appointed upon the death of the Queen, the Archbishop of Canterbury to have preeminence.

15 L.J., XVIII, 20 (where Stamford is referred to in connection with the 19 November motion), 39–40, 96, 111; Burnet, V, 228–32; Tindal, XXI, 291 ff.; *Parliamentary History*, VI, 470–75. See also Holmes, *British Politics*, 84 and n; Angus McInnes, *Robert Harley, Puritan Politician* (London, 1970), 66 and n.

16 Panshanger (Cowper) MSS., box 33, shelf 231; L.J., XVIII, 83–85. He also advised the Lords to repeal the clause providing that important public business was to be transacted by the Privy Council, as an unreasonable limitation upon efficient administration.

17 L.J., XVIII, 83–85. On the Commons' reaction to the bill, and the fierce court–country struggle over the place clause, see Holmes, *British Politics*, 132–34. He notes that the deadlock 'was only broken through the efforts of the Junto lords and their friends in the Upper House', and refers to 'crucial conversions' among country Whig leaders effected by Halifax and Somers.

18 As Holmes remarks, the initial reaction at Herrenhausen to the Regency Act had not been as favourable as the Whigs had hoped: *ibid.*, 471, n. 6.

19 Stowe MSS. 222, ff. 286–89v, 12 April 1706; Campbell, V, 159–61.

20 Stowe MSS. 222, f. 442, in French, 20 June 1706; English translation, Campbell, V, 161–62.

21 Timberland, II, 154–60. According to Nicolson, Somers concluded that the gist of the dispute was 'Whether it was necessary, for the preservation of yᵉ Church, that three or four particular Lords should be in the Ministry. If so, he thought there ought to be a Bill brought in, not only for yᵉ restoring of yᵐ, but for the continueing them there for ever, and makeing them *Immortal*'. MS. Diary, 6 December 1705.

22 L.J., XVIII, 44, 49.

23 *Ibid.*, XVIII, 52, 55, 69–70; 77; Nicolson, in his MS. Diary, 15 December 1705, notes that Somers instanced several laws relating to wills, fraud, perjury, recovery of debts, etc., 'which he thought capable of Amendment'.

24 3 and 4 W. and M., c. 9; 7 Wm. III, c. 32; 8 and 9 Wm. III, c. 11.

25 Burnet, V, 242. Burnet believed that Somers should effect a codification of English law: Thomas E. S. Clarke and Helen C. Foxcroft, *Life of Gilbert Burnet* (Cambridge, 1907), 435.

26 *Lords MSS.*, 1704–06, 355–57.

27 L.J., XVIII, 87, 123, 136, 145, 160–62; C.J., XV, 191–93, 196–99.

28 See Holdsworth, XI, 519 ff., for a detailed analysis.

29 Hundreder: one eligible to serve on a jury in controversies over land in the hundred to which he belongs.

30 Attornment: the agreement of a tenant to acknowledge one claiming to be his landlord.

31 Account: a writ or action against someone who, by reason of office or business, should render account, but refuses to do so.

32 Holdsworth, XI, 519, 527. See also Campbell, V, 164–65.

33 Burnet, V, 243.

34 See Campbell, V, 166n.

35 Holdsworth, XI, 522–23. In general, the lower House was sceptical of the system of written evidence employed by the Court of Chancery, which this seemed to approximate.

36 Edward Jenks, *Short History of English Law* (London, 1912), 210n.

37 L.J., XVIII, 43–165 passim. His reports were in connection with the relief of Evance and Cornish, the tithes of St Bride's, and Williams's, Lord Coleraine's and Deane's bills: see *ibid.*, XVIII, 88, 114, 122, 124, 147.

38 *Ibid.*, XVIII, 65, 70, 76, 104–6.

39 Burnet, V, 243. For the recommendations of the committee, see L.J., XVIII, 105. On 21 January 1706 Somers seconded a motion of Rochester dispensing with a standing order allowing fourteen days leeway after the commitment of a private bill. Wharton and Halifax were opposed, an example of Junto disunity. Nicolson's MS Diary.

40 Burnet, V, 243, notes that Cowper 'did indeed very generously obstruct those private bills, as much as his predecessor had promoted them'. I have uncovered no evidence regarding Somers's own policy in this regard when he held the Seal.

41 L.J., XVIII, 345.

42 See Douglas, *English Scholars*, 347.

43 Sir Joseph Ayloffe, *Calendars of the Ancient Charters* (London, 1774), xxxvi.

44 Nicolson's MS. Diary, 13 November 1704.

45 Halifax reported on 30 March 1704; L.J., XVII, 555. Lords MSS., 1704–06, 36–37; House of Lords MSS., Committee Minutes, 1704–10, p. 2.

46 *Transactions of the Cumberland and Westmorland Antiquarian and Archaeological Society*, n.s., II, 214; see also *ibid.*, III, 30, on discussion between Nicolson and Somers about records late in 1705: *Diary of Ralph Thoresby*, ed. Joseph Hunter (London, 1830), II, 26. In 1706 Nicolson found Rochester, Grey, Somers and Halifax at the 'Paper office', which he found 'in better Order than I ever saw it': MS. Diary, 14 January 1706.

47 Burnet, VI, 2.

48 *Ibid.*, V, 245–46. Nicolson refers to King William's 'good Designe' for consolidating London libraries, as told to him by Somers: MS. Diary, 10 November 1704. The Cottonian Library was in 1712 removed to Essex House and, after several other migrations, reached the British Museum in 1753.

49 See *Portland MSS.*, IV, 250, for the opinion that 'the managing Whigs such as Lord Wharton, Lord Somers and Halifax, and even Mr. Harley, whatever they may pretend, are really the greatest enemies to the Union, and will indirectly yet effectually obstruct it, because it is by the present confusions and differences that they make themselves necessary to a Court that in their heart hates them" (1 October 1705).

50 L.J., XVIII, 16. Two months earlier Halifax had been in consultation with him over questions raised by Godolphin on this thorny subject: Peter Hume Brown, *Letters relating to Scotland in the Reign of Queen Anne* (Scottish Historical Society, Edinburgh, 1915), 160–163.

51 Joseph McCormick, *State Papers and Letters Addressed to William Carstares* (Edinburgh, 1774), 740; L.J., XVIII, 27; Nicolson's MS. Diary, 23 November 1705.

52 *Marchmont Papers*, III, 290.

53 See Mackinnon, 221; *Marchmont Papers*, III, 283 ff.

54 Acts Parl. Scot., XI, appendix, 146. The Junto magnates, except Halifax, who was in Hanover, attended sedulously.

55 See P. W. J. Riley, 'The Union of 1707 as an episode in English politics', *Eng. Hist. Rev.*, LXXXIV (July 1969), 503, 514.

56 Burnet declared that Somers's was 'the chief hand in projecting the scheme', a statement supported by Hardwicke: *History*, V, 274, 276, 287. Addison described him as the 'chief conductor' of the project: *The Freeholder*, No. 39. See also McInnes, *Harley*, 96 and n.; Holmes, *British Politics*, 85; *Conduct of the Duchess*, 260; Riley, 'Union of 1707', 514. For the proceedings see Acts Parl. Scot., XI, appendix, 162 ff.; *Memoirs of the Life of Sir John Clerk*, ed. John M. Gray, Publications, Scottish Historical Society, 1892.

57 Brown, *Letters*, 126.

58 Acts Parl. Scot., XI, appendix, 165; the reference is to the Act of Settlement. See Trevelyan, *Anne*, II, 265; cf. Tindal, XXI, 359–60, who states that the Lord Keeper 'delivered' these preliminaries.

59 Acts Parl. Scot., XI, appendix, 167.

60 William Fraser, *The Melvilles, Earls of Melville, and the Leslies, Earls of Leven* (Edinburgh, 1890), II (correspondence), 208–9.

61 *Carstares Papers*, 753.

62 The English were here served by the two law officers of the Crown, Edward Northey and Simon Harcourt, and by two experts in civil law, Cooke and Waller.

63 Coxe, *Marlborough*, I, 376.

64 Lord Cowper, *Diary*, 33.

65 *Letters of Daniel Defoe*, ed. George H. Healey (London, 1955), 69.

66 *Conduct of the Duchess*, 160–61.

67 For the Duchess of Marlborough's adverse opinion see her *Correspondence*, II, 194.

68 Coxe, *Marlborough*, II, 4–5; *Conduct of the Duchess*, 161–65.

69 Coxe, *Shrewsbury*, 661.

70 *Conduct of the Duchess*, 174. The bishops were Offspring Blackall and Sir William Dawes; see below, p. 252.

71 L.J., XVIII, 174–75.

72 *Ibid.*, XVIII, 175; Timberland, II, 165.

73 Tindal, XXII, 143; Luttrell, *Relation*, VI, 127.

74 *Marchmont Papers*, III, 303 ff., especially 309, 321, 325.

75 *Swift's Correspondence*, ed. Williams, 115n. His successful execution of this mission gained him a commissionership of the customs. See *Portland MSS.*, VIII, 243, for a reference

to Somers's desire that William Paterson be sent to Scotland to promote the Union. On Harley's agents in Scotland, including Paterson, see McInnes, *Harley*, 79–84.

[76] Fraser, *Melvilles*, II, 206; Mackinnon, 319; and see Hardwicke, *State Papers*, II, 465–66; Hist. MSS. Comm., *Report on the Manuscripts of the Earl of Mar and Kellie* (1904), 332.

[77] L.J., XVIII, 207, 239 ff.

[78] Burnet, V, 287. Nicolson attests to Somers's activity in his MS. Diary, 15 and 24 February 1707.

[79] Timberland, II, 175; Tindal, XXII, 163–64.

[80] Somers MSS., Tenison to Somers, 23 and 27 January 1707. On 3 February Nicolson notes that Somers supported the bill, without amendments: MS Diary. Trevelyan, *Anne*, II, 284, observes that this measure 'gave to existing Acts, which protected the Church of England in her rights and monopolies, the character of essential parts of the constitution of Great Britain'. Tenison asked Somers, in his letter of 27 January, to clarify and amend, as he thought necessary, the rough draft which he sent. Writing to Marchmont in February 1707, Somers notes: 'The method taken in Scotland made it inevitable to have such an act here, but I hope you will find it conceived in such cautious and moderate terms as not to give any just occasion of offence in Scotland'; *Marchmont Papers*, III, 159. It received the royal assent 13 February 1707: L.J., XVIII, 236.

[81] *Jerviswood Corr,*. 156–57, 171, 174.

[82] *Marchmont Papers*, III, 156.

[83] See *Jerviswood Corr.*, 171, 180. Somers was concerned over the effects of Scottish representation on the Westminster parliament. In January 1707, Baillie reported that Somers was convinced that, without the 'New Party', the Whigs would not be gainers from the Union.

[84] *Works*, ed. Scott, V, 372.

[85] See below, p. 309.

[86] Somers to Lord Marchmont, 23 July 1706, in Marchmont MSS., Hist. MSS. Comm., *14th Rept.*, iii (London, 1894), 157; see also *ibid.*, 158–59.

XIII
Grand strategy, 1707–8

Early in 1707 Somers appeared fairly confident that the Queen would reward those who had contributed to the creation of the Union: at least he wrote in this vein to Lord Marchmont.[1] But the immediate gains of the Junto were, to say the least, disappointing. Within a year he was complaining to Jonathan Swift of the ingratitude of Godolphin and Marlborough: these men, 'after the service he and his friends had done them in making the Union, would hardly treat him with common civility'.[2] True, most of the Junto leaders obtained seats in the new Privy Council of Great Britain. But in the reshuffling of other posts, save for the solicitor-generalship, they were by-passed. The Junto girded its loins. Measures were set in train that would culminate in the capitulation of Godolphin and Marlborough, and the resignation of Harley, early in the following year.

More and more was Harley regarded as an evil genius, responsible for every obstructive move of the Queen. A reversal in the area of episcopal preferment pointed this up, and rubbed salt in Junto wounds. The bishoprics of Exeter and Chester became vacant; the Junto sought to fill them with Whigs. But Anne, without consulting her chief ministers, bestowed the posts on Tory divines. The Junto attributed her action to the machinations of Harley and his new found ally, Abigail Masham. Marlborough and Godolphin, resentful over being ignored, joined in accusing Harley of underhanded dealings. Something of a ministerial crisis occurred. Harley disavowed the charge, and had the Queen's backing, but his colleagues were not convinced, and the episode contributed to the growing tension in his relations with them.[3]

Somers, whose advice Godolphin had sought, was keenly aware of the importance of advancing Whigs to the episcopal bench. In June he wrote Archbishop Tenison, his Whiggish friend and colleague of many years (but *person non grata* to Anne), urging him to be more assertive in recommending candidates for bishoprics, making particular reference to the opening at Exeter and to still another at Norwich. He confessed to being vexed upon being told that 'the Archbishop is principally in fault, who does not speak plainly & and fully to the Queen, wⁿ the Archbishop of York never suffers her to rest'. He should, at all costs, strive to counter such High Church influence.[4] Though obviously disappointed over the outcome at Exeter and Chester, Somers could take satisfaction (after a six-months campaign in which the Junto joined with the chief ministers) in seeing Dr Trimnell, a thorough-going Whig and one-time tutor of Lord Sunderland, installed at Norwich. He could be counted on to vote the right way in the Lords—and this, of course, was the crux of the matter. It was also some comfort that the Queen agreed to appoint Dr Potter to the Oxford Regis Professorship of Divinity, since this was a stepping stone to the episcopal bench and Potter, a protégé of Marlborough, was not tarred with the High Tory brush.[5]

As Whig bishops were useful to the Junto, so support could be expected to flow the other way. In dealing with the ills of an Establishment torn by conflict between Low Church prelates and a predominantly High Church (and Tory) parish priesthood, the Whigs, despite their sympathy for Dissent, would generally favour the enhancement of episcopal authority. The Carlisle Cathedral Bill of 1708 is an example of this. The measure was the outgrowth of a quarrel between the Whig Bishop of Carlisle, William Nicolson, and his Dean, an arch-Tory and future Jacobite, Francis Atterbury. The contest became so fierce that Nicolson sought the aid of Somers and his allies; the resultant bill, introduced by Somers, served to confirm episcopal control over cathedral personnel. In this dispute, according to Addison, he exerted himself 'more than he had ever done before'.[6]

The new Parliament met in late October—called 'new' because, even thought it followed upon no general election in England, it was the first Parliament of Great Britain, seating the Scottish representatives under the Act of Union. The glow of victory which had warmed the opening weeks of the last session had now given way to a chill produced by military frustration and defeat, for the year had brought catastrophe at Almanza, naval disaster off the Lizard, failure before Toulon and a blank sheet in the Netherlands. Such a record played into the hands of those, whether among High Tories or Whigs, who sought to attack the administration. The attack came at once, and in the Lords. While the Commons were proceeding with remarkable alacrity and unanimity to vote something like six million pounds for the war, the Lords were reproaching the ministers for its mismanagement. A few days after the royal address Wharton rose to expatiate on the decay of trade and the scarcity of money, which was being drained from the realm to satisfy the accounts of war; farmers, he claimed, were unable to pay their rents. He was seconded by Somers, who held forth on the ill condition and maladministration of the navy, and on the serious losses sustained at sea by the merchants during the past summer. The House then beheld an extraordinary scene, as Rochester and Buckingham joined with the Junto peers. Godolphin was unable to divert the attack, with the result that the address of thanks was postponed and a day appointed for a full discussion of the state of the nation.[7]

Wharton had moved that the Lords should go into a committee of the whole 'to consider of the State of the Nation, in relation to the Fleet and Trade', the Commissioners of Trade being charged to bring the House up to date. A committee was set up to hear merchants' complaints. A full-scale attack on the admiralty ensued, for the second time in three years, climaxed by an address to the throne.[8] That the merchant shippers had real grievances cannot be doubted. Memorial after memorial came in from the City of London, castigating naval commanders for the damage inflicted by the press-gangs in draining off the supply of able-bodied seamen, and for the inadequacy of convoy arrangements, with consequent delays in sailing and depredations by Dunkirk and West Indian privateers. Worse still, there were accusations that at least one naval commander had withheld protection from the ships of merchants who could not, or would not, pay for it. Even apart from mismanagement and peculation, the merchants and their skippers were in a mood to protest, for these central years of the war saw French privateering in full flower. Since the spring of 1702 no less than 1,146 merchantmen had been lost, though 300 were retaken.[9]

The investigation was justifiable, but it was obviously undertaken as much for the sake of political leverage as in the interest of national security and well-being.[10] While the Admiralty was formally governed by Prince George, it was actually administered by Admiral Churchill, Marlborough's brother and a strong Tory. The Prince, because of his royal station, could hardly be arraigned; Wharton and Somers must have found it awkward enough to take the lead in censuring his department, for Anne was once more attending the sessions of the Lords 'incognito'[11]—that is, without royal state or attendance—and she continued to be extremely sensitive towards any criticism which reflected even indirectly upon her consort. But it was another matter with George Churchill: he was fair game. Too long had he depended on the support of fellow Tories to assure his ascendancy. Here was an opportunity to oust him, or, relying on Marlborough's loyalty to his brother, to call off the hunt only if the General showed himself willing to make terms. And the opportunity was heightened by the disunity of the Tories; the old support could not be expected, what with Rochester and Haversham standing forth to denounce the cabinet. Between the Whigs, dissatisfied with their winnings, and the disgruntled High Tories an accommodation of sorts had come into being.

But the immediate Junto objective was not the overthrow of Godolphin, and certainly not the pillorying of Marlborough. What they wanted was greater influence in the existing government. Fearful that debate might get out of hand, they raised technical objections to any indictment of the ministry and worked to focus attention on the encouragement of trade and on privateering in the West Indies. But all without any profit for the Junto. Though the House sat twice more in committee on the state of trade and the fleet, Churchill remained at the Admiralty and the Whigs obtained no preferment.[12] In these manoeuvres Somers does not appear to have played a prominent part beyond the initial stages; it was Lord Herbert who reported the resolutions to the Lords in mid-December. Yet there can be no doubt that the Queen, though she responded favourably to the Lords' plea that sea affairs should be her 'first and most peculiar care', looked upon this episode as another reason for distrusting Somers.

In the meantime the conduct of the war as a whole was occasioning increasing comment and controversy. The route of the allied forces under Galway at Almanza, in April, had focused attention on the Spanish theatre. The recall of the Earl of Peterborough injected notes of personal and partisan rivalry.[13] Once supreme commander in the Spanish theatre, he had been removed early in 1707, upon the recommendations of Marl-borough, Godolphin and Sunderland. Back in England—to which he returned in leisurely fashion—he was barred from court pending an explanation of his conduct both before and after his recall. A resourceful and persistent man, he did not stand mute. The Tories were ever ready to clasp to their bosoms any reasonably heroic figure who might serve to counteract the political weight of the Whiggish Galway and the ambivalent Marlborough. On 19 December, Rochester rose in the Lords, which was sitting in committee of the whole, to champion the fallen Earl, and a debate was launched which went far beyond the behaviour of the ex-commander.[14] For it led to a review of the progress of the war in Spain, so unfavourable compared to the results in the Lowlands and Germany, and to an attack on general strategy. This in turn provided an opportunity to sound the war cry of 'No peace without Spain', which was given its most uncompromising and definitive form by Somers.

From the days of King William's campaigns Somers had embodied the stereotype of the war-minded Whig, unshakeably determined to counteract the imperialism of the Sun King. As Addison remarked, in Protestant countries 'their hopes or fears for the common cause rose or fell' with Somers's political influence.[15] For a couple of years, at least, he had coun-selled against a disadvantageous peace. There was, from time to time, sharp criticism of the Dutch on the ground that their prosecution of the war was too limited and overly influenced by domestic considerations. Such had been the case in 1705, when their refusal to sanction Marlborough's pro-posed attack on Overyssche evoked widespread expressions of indignation. Even the Whigs had joined in the outcry. But they changed their tune when Somers warned that the incident might be used to effect a speedy peace with France. 'You know', Somers wrote to the Duke of Portland, 'wee have too many in England that despair of obtaining their wicked designs but by an abrupt putting an end to this warr and leaving France in a condition to oppress their neighbours.' Such men, he went on, argued that the Germans were in no condition to fight, and that the Dutch, too, were averse and influenced by a great party 'earnest for a peace'. It was ridicu-lous to imagine that a settlement could be made at that time which would not leave Louis master of the Indies and able to dictate to Holland and the rest of Europe, once he gained 'a little time to recover himself'. He urged Portland 'to keep all things right on his side', prior to the convening of a new Parliament, that autumn, which could be counted on to support the war.[16]

The following year, in justifying Whig opposition to inviting Sophia of Hanover to England, he told her grandson, the future George II, that one of the strongest objections arose from the implication 'that we could not go on no farther with the Dutch (wch. was in effect to say we must make Peace)'.[17] A few months later, when the English were engaged in consulta-tions with the Dutch over treaties guaranteeing the Protestant succession and the Dutch barrier, Somers, serving as an unofficial adviser to the ministry, warned Lord Halifax, one of the negotiators, against putting too

much power in the hands of the Dutch as long as the 'evil spirit' of accommodation with France was to be reckoned with. Though he professed
himself anxious to see 'the foundations of such a peace as may be lasting',
study and experience made him suspicious of French intentions:

I have always had a great dread of the beginning a treaty with France. I am in
some degree versed in treaties of the last age. The French, as soon as it is once
entered into, will transact with particular plenipotentiaries, and are more busy
in shewing them their respective particular interests, than in convincing the
several commissions: I could enumerate instances of this kind, from the treaty
of Vervins downward.[18]

Halifax would have to be the judge if there was danger of this sort under
existing circumstances. There can be little doubt that painful memories
of the Partition Treaties crowded in on Somers, making him cautious and
even fearful. Though the Barrier Treaty failed to materialise at this time,
he remained alert for signs of Dutch independence. When, in the summer
of 1707, Godolphin took the line, under Marlborough's influence, that the
Grand Alliance should be strengthened and broadened, and 'that the
foundation of the whole should be, never to admit the inclination of the
States to peace', save in accordance with the preliminaries, he was seconded
by Somers, along with Halifax.[19]

By December 1707, the question of grand strategy had been brought into
the open by the Earl of Rochester. Recalling Schomberg's remark that to
attack France in the Netherlands 'is like taking a bull by the horns', he
urged that 'we should stand on the defensive in Flanders, and send from
thence 15 or 20,000 men into Catalonia'. Marlborough was in the House.
With some warmth he spoke against the reduction of the Lowlands forces:
their presence was required to safeguard the strategic points already won in
Brabant, and to insure the belligerency of the Dutch, whose peace party
could be expected to take advantage of any gains made by Louis's forces.
But Rochester still insisted on the 'absolute necessity' of English assistance
for King Charles, and before the House rose he had gained satisfaction.
Though doubting (as well he might) the propriety of revealing military
designs in so public a manner, the Duke assured the noble lords that
'measures had been already concerted' with the Emperor for forming an
army of 40,000 men under the Duke of Savoy, and for sending powerful
reinforcements to Spain. It was hoped that Prince Eugene could be
prevailed upon to assume command there.[20]

Committed as they were to the pattern, established in the past reign, of
close alliance with the Dutch and of joint responsibility for the security of
their territory, Somers and the Junto could not be expected to support
Rochester's original proposal. On the other hand, Marlborough's disclosures appeared to remove the necessity of choice. The Dutch Netherlands
could be safeguarded, France menaced on her Lowlands frontier, and the
unfavourable situation in Spain given proper attention: all might be done.
There should be, indeed, no peace without Spain. Somers lost no time in

securing from the House its formal approval of this grand objective. Before Lord Herbert left the chair, he rose to move that 'it is the Opinion of this Committee, That no Peace can be honourable or safe, for Her Majesty and Her Allies, if Spain and the Spanish West Indies be suffered to continue in the Power of the House of Bourbon'. The resolution was agreed to with only the Earl of Scarborough dissenting.[21]

At the close of debate Somers was named to the select committee called upon to cast his resolution, along with two further motions, in a form suitable for presentation to the Queen. Save for Rochester, it was almost solidly Whig in composition, but this does not appear to have occasioned protest.[22] At its meeting the following day in Prince George's chambers, Somers was called to the chair. He now proceeded to extend even further the national commitment to oppose the Bourbons, by requiring their exclusion, not only from Spain and the West Indies, but from 'any part of the Spanish monarchy'. The revised resolution met with the committee's approval, and was reported by its author to the Lords on 22 December. He then moved that a message be sent to the lower House requesting their concurrence, and the Lords, after a few minor amendments, complied. Before the day was over the Commons had voiced their agreement, and the address was forwarded to the Queen as a joint recommendation. In due course the royal answer, framed by Godolphin and Marlborough, gave full approval to the project.[23]

In conducting this business, Somers had showed marked skill and vigour. The episode goes far to account for his continuing leadership of the Whigs, despite ill health and exclusion from office. He was aided by the general prevalence of war-mindedness: not for another year or so can a marked turn in the tide of public opinion be discerned. It is, nonetheless, remarkable that in both Houses the Tory element, long critical of the war effort and to some extent opposed to English involvement on the continent, either lent support to Somers's motion or were passive. But, having of late made capital of alleged ministerial indifference to French commercial advantages in the Mediterranean and in Spanish America, they were in a poor position to question, much less denounce, the Somers resolution. Indeed, the principle of 'No Peace without Spain' had been enunciated four years earlier by the Tory Nottingham, who now seconded Rochester's proposal.

Whether Somers fully appreciated the difficulty of implementing his resolution is hard to say. At the time he was without doubt encouraged by Marlborough's hopeful remarks. But it is not clear that he realised the need for massive manpower and close Allied co-operation. During the debate the question of putting pressure on the Allies to fulfil their quotas was raised. Somers argued that only the Emperor should be pressed in the matter, inasmuch as he 'had the greatest stake in the war and was most defective in his quotas'. Pressure on the other allies, he contended, might do more harm than good. Here, too, he had his way, and the Commons concurred, without amendment.[24] On the other hand, it is unlikely that he counted upon half-measures to do the business. He knew something of

Spanish conditions, partly through correspondence with Galway.[25] One may conclude that, like Marlborough, he looked for adequate support from Austria and feared military deployments which might reduce pressure on the French position in the Netherlands and arouse the Dutch peacemakers. If we may take Addison's *Present State of the War*, which appeared in 1708, as substantially representing Somers's point of view, this conclusion is reinforced. Essentially an argument for no peace without Spain, this treatise developed the argument that even if England could hold what she had hitherto gained she would suffer irreparable harm by conceding Spanish naval power and New World treasure to France. But Addison opposed the notion that the war could be won by banking on the eventual exhaustion of French financial resources, even should the West Indies be captured: a despotism could always find means of raising additional funds. The allies, rather, must substantially augment their forces and thus over-whelm the French army.[26]

Meanwhile, Somers was busy with matters closer to home. Most impor-tant was putting the finishing touches on the Act of Union. These involved the reconstitution of an Exchequer Court for Scotland and the abolition of her Privy Council. It was generally assumed, by Scots, that the courts of Scotland, markedly different from those of England, would remain unchanged, though the Act of Union provided for future regulation and alteration by the united Parliament.[27] It was realised that to keep the old courts functioning at Edinburgh would preserve something of its character as a capital city, and thus make the union more palatable. But, in the interest of fiscal integration, the Act of Union provided for a jurisdiction in Edin-burgh identical to that exercised by the English Court of Exchequer, and a select committee to draw up a bill for this purpose was named before the Christmas holidays. Somers served as chairman; it was no easy assignment, for the body deliberated in upwards of twenty meetings, from late December to early March. The Lords passed the bill on 27 March.[28]

Somers also contributed significantly to the passage of the Act 'for rendering the Union of the two kingdoms more entire and complete'. This measure, adumbrated in the Treaty of Union and the recent speech from the throne, abolished the separate Scottish Council and provided for Scottish justices of the peace having the same jurisdiction as their English counterparts.[29] Here we are able to reconstruct a powerful speech in the Lords on 28 January, when, along with Halifax, Sunderland and Cowper, Somers led a successful fight to extinguish a body which, since the union of the British crowns, had been 'the catspaw of the English Court'.[30] Unlike the Edinburgh Parliament, the Council had little claim on Scottish affec-tions, particularly among those old enough to remember its ruthless treat-ment of Presbyterians in pre-revolutionary years. Nonetheless, it was not without its defenders, chiefly among the 'Old Party' of Queensberry, which had dominated it for years. Some saw in this project the realisation of fears that Union would mean utter domination by Englishmen and English institutions. The interests of Scottish families, influential under the old dispensation, were thrown on to the scale, as was that of Godolphin and his aides, who feared the loss of political leverage afforded by an agency lying beyond the control of Parliament.[31]

In calling for abolition Somers argued that there could be no perfect union with two administrations in being: 'the true argument for the Union was the danger to both kingdoms from a divided state'. It was in Scotland's interest 'to be under the immediate personal care of the Prince', without relying on a subordinate institution. This had been his contention before the Union was framed. But a distinct administration would be even worse now, inasmuch as the Scots had no Parliament of their own to resort to. As for the argument that a separate Council was necessary to preserve the public peace, Somers, while disavowing expert knowledge of Scotland and confessing that he had heard much of the suitability of such an arrangement, dwelt at some length on England's unsatisfactory experience with 'courts that are mixed of state and justice'. The Privy Council, the Star Chamber, and the Councils set up for the control of the north and the west (which were particularly relevant to the discussion, since they were designed to facilitate the governing of remote regions) had all proved to be afflictions, in that policy had got the better of justice. England had found it necessary to abolish such jurisdictions; they should not now be perpetuated in Scotland: 'I should think the true way to make the union well relished, is to let the country see plainly, that England means no otherwise than fairly by them, and desires they should be in the very same circumstances they are themselves.'

To Somers the argument that sudden alterations were dangerous and that, in any case, they should not be effected in time of war, was outweighed by the importance of implementing a well-integrated nation. He cited Poland and Lithuania as unhappy examples of the perils of an imperfect union, where the advantages of a general legislature were offset by the retention of 'their distinct great offices of state, and their distinct diets'. He called for confidence in the Queen and a British Council as keepers of the peace throughout the entire island. Should the forces of Louis have to be reckoned with north of the Tweed, Britons must rely not 'upon the orders or advices of the privy council in Scotland, but on the troops'. He rejected temporary extention of the *status quo* by way of compromise. He knew, of course, that the government was fighting a rearguard action to move the Council's expiration date ahead five months, to 1 October, after the elections.[32] In the end the government was defeated, by only five votes in the Lords but by a sizeable majority in the Commons.[33] The Council ceased to be, certain of its powers passing to the justices. Scottish opposition continued, in some quarters, but the new arrangements were on the whole introduced without serious resistance.[34]

The passage of the Council Act was but another thrust at Godolphin's government. Indeed, the Lord Treasurer scarcely knew where to turn. Tories and Whigs alike had joined in castigating naval administration and in damming a channel of political influence. It was difficult to say who was hungrier for power: the Junto, ever more resentful that, except for Sunderland, they still remained outside the magic circle of government; or Robert Harley, Secretary of State since 1704, who was negotiating with Tory politicians in order to end the ascendancy of the Godolphin-Marlborough duumvirate. It was clearer by the day that the coalition, which with considerable success had conducted the government for several years, was on its last legs. There is reason to believe that by the end of 1707 the two chiefs had resolved to seek support from the Whigs.[35] It was easier said than done, for the Queen looked upon Harley as a deliverer and supported him with rock-like determination. But in the end fortune favoured the Whigs.

The Junto had trained its guns on Harley since at least the previous summer.[36] It was given ammunition that autumn by William Greg. A clerk in Harley's office, Greg succumbed to the temptation of enriching himself by providing official information for the French War Minister, Chamillart. He was in a favourable position to forward such intelligence because of the way in which official papers were handled under the Secretary's lax management.[37] In due course his sins came to light and on 19 January he was found guilty on his own confession at the Old Bailey and condemned to a traitor's death. To make matters worse for Harley, two smugglers whom the Secretary had employed as spies were at this time detected in counter espionage.

Greg's acknowledgement of guilt at his trial made short work of the proceedings, but provided no evidence that Harley was implicated. He was reported as saying that 'the devil and his necessities were his prompters'.[38] The Lords therefore took upon themselves the responsibility of eliciting further information about Greg's activities and the conditions that had made them possible. On 9 February they resolved to elect by ballot a committee of seven peers for the purpose of examining him. The result was a septet of zealous Whigs. Three—Somers, Wharton and Halifax—were acknowledged Junto leaders. Devonshire, Bolton and Townshend were in one way or another associates of the Junto, Townshend being known as Somers's 'creature'. Only the Duke of Somerset may be said to have moved in an orbit of his own. All could be expected to exploit any possible case against Harley.[39]

Over the next three weeks this committee heard Greg's testimony and that of other persons brought before it. Somers's role cannot be distinguished from that of his colleagues; he did not serve as chairman of the committee, Somerset delivering the report on 1 March.[40] Diligent and suspicious as they were, they could uncover no evidence that the Secretary had been a party to his clerk's crime. Slothful and unsystematic he had been, traitorous he was not, as Greg never failed to point out. So the Lords called off their dogs. But if Harley had saved his neck, his reputation did not emerge unscathed. The committee's report was published on 18 March.[41] Despite its negative findings it reinforced the suspicion that hung about him and that went so far as to link him with the French invasion even then in the making. On the other hand, there were some—Swift, for example

—who looked upon the methods of Somers and his associates as inquisitorial in the worst sense of the word. It seems likely that Greg might have saved his life had he betrayed Harley. Though there is no conclusive evidence, the Whig chiefs may have descended to such machinations.[42]

In the meantime, Harley had fallen.[43] Godolphin had already broken with him. On the day before the Greg Committee was created he was sharply rebuffed when he attempted to transact cabinet business relating to the war without the presence of Marlborough. Led by Somerset, the cabinet refused to deliberate. The end was near. First the Lord Treasurer, then the Generalissimo, believing that the Secretary was plotting to 'form a scheme of government in which the first proposition was to remove my Lord Godolphin', had thrown down the gauntlet: they would no longer serve with him. Anne must choose between them. For a time she hoped that she might be able to retain Marlborough—Godolphin could go, for all she cared. But the duumvirate stood firm, backed by the court party and the Whigs. It was Harley who broke the deadlock, resigning on 11 February. It was probably just in time. At least Bishop Burnet's wife thought so:

Had this affair hung longer in suspense, most, if not all the Whigs of considera-tion would have laid down their places; and not only the Bishop of Salisbury, but most of the other bishops, would have come and offered lord treasurer and the Duke of Marlborough all the service in their power, and have been ready to join in any thing to show their regard to the duke and lord treasurer.[44]

One can imagine Somers's satisfaction. For though Harley, for all his anti-pathy towards the Junto lords, was not completely opposed to their aims—he had supported Somers's 'No Peace Without Spain' resolution in the lower House and worked for the Union—there was no doubt that his ascendancy would block their advance. Nor can personal sentiments be over-looked. According to Edward Harley, as far back as the 1690s his father's opposition to heavy war expenditures and the suspension of habeas corpus had drawn upon him and his family 'the implacable rage of the Lord Wharton, Lord Somers, and the other Whigs of their party'.[45] Nor could Somers forget Harley's role in the Kidd affair, and his belligerency in the impeachments of 1701. For this the Whigs never forgave him.[46]

Harley's resignation was accompanied by that of Thomas Mansell, the Comptroller. Within a couple of days Henry St John, Secretary at War, and Simon Harcourt followed suit. Junto hopes were high. But in large measure they were disappointed. Henry Boyle received Harley's post, giving up the office of Chancellor of the Exchequer to John Smith, who for the remainder of the parliamentary session held it concurrently with the Speakership. The future disposition of power was presaged by the appoint-ment of Robert Walpole as Secretary at War. All were Whigs, but not Junto men. They were court Whigs, 'more "Court" than Whig'; earlier in the session they had stood against the Junto, though Walpole (who was indebted to Orford for preferment) and his small group of followers almost always could be counted on for support. In addition, Anne's refusal to expedite the appointment of James Montague, Halifax's brother, as Attorney-General, was annoying. But what particularly rankled was Somers's continued unemployment.

As early as April 1707, when Pembroke was made Lord Lieutenant of Ireland, it was rumoured that Somers would succeed him as Lord President of the Council.[47] But more than a year and a half would pass before Anne could be persuaded to bring into her cabinet a man so unacceptable to her. In March 1708 she told the Lords: 'I must always place my chief dependence upon those who have given such repeated proofs of their warmth and concern for the support of the Revolution, Security of my person and the Protestant Succession.'[48] Yet notwithstanding Somers's signal services, not only in these matters, but in connection with the Union, he remained *persona non grata* at Kensington. He was, in Anne's eyes, 'the first promoter of Whiggism as a political faith', a Whiggism which in Junto hands was insupportably aggressive.[49]

Against Anne's monumental resistance Somers's supporters for months strove in vain. But strive they did. As early as March, Whigs of various complexions, from the obstreperous Sunderland to the moderate Devonshire, began to apply pressure. The same month saw the descent of the Pretender upon the coast of Scotland. It proved to be abortive, but it was not without unsettling effects in England. In an atmosphere of rumour and of real or fancied Jacobite intrigue, the funds fell 15 per cent, and a run on the Bank of England—perhaps deliberately organised—was narrowly averted.[50] In the end it had little effect save to revive suspicions of Tory disloyalty to the Revolutionary settlement. With Harley's departure the ministry lost the support of his personal adherents among the moderate Tories. The government was virtually defenceless at the hands of the Whigs, who were cheerfully prognosticating an even more complete control, once the forthcoming elections were over. Under such circumstances Godolphin and Marlborough had no other practicable course but to placate the clamorous Whigs by bringing Somers into the government in one capacity or another.

In mid-April Jonathan Swift wrote: 'I was told in confidence three weeks ago by a Friend in Business, that the chief Whig Lords resolved to apply in a Body to the Queen, for my Lord Sommers to be made President.' But, he added, 'the Ministry would not joyn, and the Qu. was resolute, and so it miscarried'.[51] Such ill success was not for want of efforts on the part of Godolphin, who urged the Queen to accept the former Chancellor's services, and called upon Marlborough, who was once more on the continent, to bring his influence to bear. It would be best if he could find time to return to England in order to grapple at first hand with the knotty problem.[52] This the General could not or would not do. But he was well aware of the seriousness of the situation. 'The queen's inclinations', he wrote the Duchess, 'are such, that the Whigs must be angry, and, consequently, the lord treasurer and I not only uneasy, but unsafe.'[53]

The great Whig Dukes of Newcastle and Devonshire did what they could to overcome Anne's obduracy. When Anne pleaded that dismissal would prove a great hardship for Lord Pembroke, the incumbent President, the Dukes proposed that Somers be given membership in the Cabinet Council without portfolio. This, too, was to no avail. When her objections to the strangeness of such procedure were countered by a recital of precedents, she replied that the Cabinet was already full enough. The Dukes left empty-handed 'in much discontent'. The following day, when she consulted with her Treasurer, the proposal was strongly supported by that bedevilled statesman. In a letter to Marlborough, he reported that he had told her

that the matter was much changed by this proposall, & that he could not but think it entirely for her service to accept of it, that it was a very small condescension, if they would bee satisfied with it, that it gained her poynt absolutely in relation to Lord P[embroke], that it would make all her affairs easy at once, & that if Mr. Freeman were in town he was sure it would bee his mind as much as it was Mr. Montgomerys.[54]

But, as she confided to Marlborough, she was unconvinced. As for employing Somers, that would be 'utter destruction' as far as she was concerned. She hoped he would not press his solicitations, 'for it is what I can never consent to'.[55]

The Junto, aware that Godolphin's influence was on the wane, had already sought Marlborough's aid.[56] He was by now deeply concerned. The Queen's letter, he wrote Godolphin, was 'a plain declaration to all the world that you and I have no credit', and that all was 'governed underhand' by Harley and Abigail Masham.[57] As for Anne, he took pains to disabuse her of any idea that the Tories would be victorious in the forthcoming election. What with their link to the Pretender, and the recent invasion attempt, it was out of the question. Such being the circumstances, he came to the point:

If what I have the honour to write to your majesty be the truth, for God's sake consider what may be the consequences of refusing the request of the dukes of Newcastle and Devonshire; since it will be a demonstration not only to them, but to everybody, that lord treasurer and I have no credit with your majesty, but that you are guided by the insinuation of Mr. Harley.[58]

But it was all for nought. In mid-February Somers, writing to Portland of the ministerial changes, had noted that he was not 'let into any secrets'.[59] Three months later he was still on the outside looking in, and so it was to be until November. Anne could not be moved: when Marlborough's reply was delivered she would not even open it in Godolphin's presence, nor did another lengthy conversation with the Treasurer have any beneficial effect.[60] Marlborough's representations went unanswered. Late in May he was still hopeful.[61] But, for all his familiarity with the Queen's prejudices and principles, he appears to have underestimated her aversion to Somers and the Junto machine. Several months later, after marked Whig successes at the polls and when both her Treasurer and Generalissimo were talking of resigning, she put the matter in a nutshell:

There is nobody more desirous than I to encourage those Whig friends that behave themselves well; but I do not care to have anything to do with those that have shown themselves to be of so tyrannizing a temper; and not to run on farther on these subjects, to be short, I think things are come to whether I shall submit to the five tyrannizing lords, or they to me.[62]

As for the 'tyrannizing lords', their frustration and anger grew by leaps and bounds. In their denunciations Godolphin and Marlborough did not escape. When Godolphin proffered the olive branch Somers composed an indictment of ministerial deceit, charging the duumvirate with supporting projects to divide the Whigs and with labelling Junto projects as designs to diminish the royal authority—all this while the Junto's aims, 'without the least thought of Advantage for themselves, are as forward as ever to follow the best measures for obtaining a conjunction with their Friends'. But, before any 'New Steps' were taken in this direction, he set forth a bill of particulars ('Lord Somers's Rules') for which the Court should give satisfaction:

2. Considering the late attempt upon Scotland and all that has been done and not done in relation to that Affair, what shall be done for quieting People's minds, without further securing the Protestant Succession.
3. What is thought fit to be done towards putting the sea administration on a better Foot.
4. What kind of Behaviour is it which shall entitle persons to Favour and Countenance with regard to Employments in Church and State.
5. What provision shall be made for securing our constitution and Liberties and restoring and enlarging Trade in case God shall grant us a peace.[63]

Parliament was prorogued on 1 April and dissolved two weeks later. The ensuing election has been called 'as much a contest between Godolphin and the Junto as it was between Court and Country or between Tory and Whig'.[64] Impelled by their grievances and scenting victory within their grasp, the 'tyrannizing lords' put their shoulders to the wheel. A pamphlet, *Advice to the Electors*, described by an Anglican clergyman as laying 'the whole blame of the late invasion at the poor T--y's' door', was attributed to Somers 'or some eminent member of the Kit Cat'.[65] As predicted, the returns showed marked gains for the Whigs, who chalked up a majority of sixty-nine. Sunderland thought it would be 'the most Wig Parliament since the Revolution'.[66] Somers could take satisfaction in that Jekyll, Clarke, Dowdeswell and Wylde were re-elected in their old constituencies. His influence at Reigate was again demonstrated, not in the reelection of Stephen Harvey (who had represented the borough for a decade) but in the success of his nephew, James Cocks, who now embarked upon a parliamentary career that would last, almost without a break, until 1747. But Charles Cocks was a casualty, beat out at Worcester by Samuel Swift. As for the Junto as a whole, it failed to maintain the English seats garnered in 1705.[67]

In view of this, the returns from Scotland were consequential. There the

Junto leaders had joined forces wtih the group of politicians known as the *Squadrone Volante*. Sunderland in particular, though serving as Secretary of State, directly opposed the court north of the Tweed, conduct which understandably raised Anne's resentment to the boiling point. The Junto-*Squadrone* alliance contributed to the election of about a third of the Scottish M.P.s and more than that proportion of the representative peers. What the Junto had lost in the south it had gained, or more than gained, in the north, though the government won a majority of the shire and burgh elections, and counted on ten of the sixteen representative peers.[68]

'If our friends will stick together and act like men, I am sure the court must, whither they will or no, come into such measures as may preserve both us and themselves': so Sunderland had prohesied late in May.[69] In the event he proved to be correct, at least in part. But the months following the election gave little comfort to the Whigs, and showed no abatement of the Queen's resistance to the pressures of the 'tyrannizing lords'. That Anne was blind to the need to make concessions is scarcely credible. That she was further antagonised by the methods of the Junto, and continued to fear she would become a captive of a party machine, is clear. Under the circumstances she saw no cause for haste: the new Parliament would not meet until the autumn. But as weeks and then months passed without the slightest nod in Somers's direction, or any other assurances that might salve Junto ambitions, the magnates became increasingly restive and disgruntled, and cast about ever more recklessly in their efforts to secure preferment.

Under the stress and strain of this deadlock, mistrust and suspicion continued to grow. What, exactly, was Godolphin up to? In the spring Arthur Maynwaring, the Duchess of Marlborough's secretary and M.P. for Preston, had regarded him and Somers as 'so perfectly agreeing' that, if only the latter were brought into the ministry, there need be no fears of what Harley might do with 'his woman'.[70] But now, with the passing of summer, the Junto charged Godolphin with giving false assurances of support while actually arranging for a government depending on 'Treasurer's Whigs'.[71] These, it was noted, had obtained some tokens of court favour. Early in August, Robert Pringle, Under-Secretary for Scotland, revealed his perplexity:

The present situation of the court appears pretty odd. The Treasurer, who has the sole management, seems to have little deference for the Whig lords, of which they seem themselves very sensible; and at the same time it is hard to imagine, how he shall be able to support himself without them.

There was talk, Pringle added, of an accommodation with the Tories, 'which still seems more odd, that he should take a party by the hand, that seems weaker this, than they were the last session of parliament'.[72]

Actually, the Tory threat was slight compared to the possibility of a serious split in Whig ranks. Maynwaring believed that a breach was inevitable should Somers not gain a place in the government.[73] But the Duke of Somerset now viewed his preferment as politically impractical, because of Anne's aversion. Somerset entertained the idea that he might provide acceptable leadership for the reconstruction of the ministry, and even sought to draw Wharton away from the rest of the Junto. But Somers's long-time ally refused to take the bait; he would not act apart from the former Chancellor. The 'proud duke' could not pull it off.[74]

But neither could the Junto. Anne was adamant, and the Junto's attempt to exercise pressure by a proposal to invite a member of the house of Hanover (in this case the Electoral Prince) to come to England merely intensified her resistance. Such a project, which but a few years back in Tory hands had provided political capital for the Whigs, was still a thing she could not bear, 'though but for a week'. This to Marlborough, to whom, a little later, she again underscored the depth of her distrust of Somers and his coterie. They were men

whom I can never be satisfied mean well to my service till they behave themselves better than they did in the last parliament, and have done ever since the rising of it: for from that minute they have been disputing my authority, and are certainly designing, when the new one meets, to tear what little prerogative the crown has to pieces.[75]

In the end they took a course even more intolerable, from Anne's point of view: an attack upon the Admiralty, involving the ouster of her beloved consort. To retire the Prince would be the key move on the political chessboard. The pieces could then fall into place: Pembroke could have the Admiralty in lieu of his Presidency and Irish Lieutenancy, and these offices could pass to Somers and Wharton. Such drastic tactics were not unopposed. Marlborough, for one, had grave doubts. He fully recognised the importance of making room for Somers. But the fruitlessness of his representations had bred pessimism; by the autumn he appears to have lost hope that Somers could gain the Presidency unless Mrs Masham were removed. He sought, rather, to avoid a head-on collision with the Queen, and yet placate the Whigs, by sacrificing his brother, George, whom he called upon to resign.[76] But the Junto was in full cry. Half measures would not do. Around the middle of October they delivered an ultimatum to the Lord Treasurer. The scene was Sunderland's country seat at Althorp. The Junto leaders were present in force, along with Dorchester, Devonshire and Bolton.

From Sunderland himself comes an account of these proceedings. His colleagues, he wrote Newcastle on 19 October,

have upon the best consideration among themselves come to this resolution & opinion, that it was impossible for them with any reputation to themselves, or safety to the publick, to go on any longer with the Court, upon the foot things are at present, for that if one looks round every part of the administration, the management of the fleet, the condition of Ireland, the Procedings in Scotland, the management of the late Invasion, the disposall of Church Preferments, &c; they are all of a Piece, as much Tory, & as wrong, as if Ld. Rochester & Ld. Nottingham were at the head of every thing, under the disguise of some considerable wigs [Whigs], in some considerable places, but with so little credit or to so little purpose, that they can neither obtain any right thing to be done, nor prevent any wrong one.

They found the fleet to be 'under the most scandalous management of all', a condition not to be remedied save by the retirement of the Prince, for only in this way could the malign influence of George Churchill be removed. The Lord Treasurer was informed that if this were not done 'they must lett the world & their friends see that they have nothing more to do with the Court'. They concluded by proposing that Pembroke should be Lord High Admiral, and—that which 'is much desir'd by all honest people'— that Somers should succeed him as Lord President. If they did not obtain immediate satisfaction they would launch their obstructive tactics by opposing the court in the choice of a Speaker for the forthcoming Parliament.[77] It is noteworthy that the Junto's programme closely parallels Somers's "Rules" for an accommodation with the government.[78]

Even as the Junto was laying down the law at Althorp the sands of Prince George's life were running out. Had the magnates been able to restrain their impatience but for a fortnight their attack would have been unnecessary. But the end of his precarious life could not be forecast; he had rallied during the summer under the effects of Bath waters, and the Junto probably did not realise that his chronic ailments had entered their terminal phase. Their intransigence, callous though it was, wrung some concessions from the distracted Queen. On 19 October, the very day that Sunderland reported the Whig ultimatum to Newcastle, he was able to add tidings that a log-jam over the law officers of the crown had been broken:

I must nott forgett telling you that this day, unexpectedly without any body knowing any thing of it, Sr James Mountague has been made Attorney Generall, & Mr Eyres Sollicitour, which I believe, has been owing to the vigour, with which those Lords spoke to Ld. Treasurer, & confirms them in their opinion, that if they go on in their resolution & stand together, the other more essentiall things will be also done.[79]

Three days later Godolphin could tell Marlborough of the royal retreat: '42 (the Queen) is at last come to allow 38 (Godolphin) to make such condescentions, which if done in time, would have been sufficient to have eased most of our difficultys'.[80] With the Prince's death what was left of her resolution crumbled quite away.[81] On 4 November Sunderland could report to Newcastle that she had agreed to make Pembroke Lord High Admiral, Somers Lord President and Wharton Lord Lieutenant of Ireland. Things, he crowed, could be now put 'upon a thorough right foot'.[82]

Up to this point there had been no inkling that Somers might not accept the office which had been demanded for him for the past six months or more. But now Sunderland expressed a shadow of a doubt. 'Ld. Sommers is out of Town,' he wrote, 'so that whither he will be perswaded to accept of it, or no, I can't tell, but he would be so much in the wrong, if he should nott, that I won't doubt, but he will.'[83] What gave rise to the

Secretary's misgivings is not apparent. But there is evidence that at least two former Presidents, Halifax and Danby, had been more than a little disappointed with their appointments.[84] Could it have been that the head of the Junto had given some sign that he looked upon the office of Lord President as beneath the dignity and attainments of a man who had once held the Great seal? Did he hope to dispossess Cowper of this prize? Or was he ambitious for the prime position held by Godolphin himself? Neither hypothesis seems to provide the key to Sunderland's uneasiness. Cowper was a staunch Whig, who had conducted his official duties capably and with whom Somers was on excellent terms. Somers was well acquainted with the arduous responsibilities of the office; at fifty-seven, with indifferent health,[85] he was probably quite willing to leave the Seal in younger hands. As for the treasurership, the Junto had never during the long months of agitation suggested that their continued support required Godolphin's removal, even though he at times seemed ready enough to lay down the burdens of office. The Godolphin-Marlborough combination had been a winning one for many years. It was not lightly to be set aside, certainly not from the standpoint of practical politics.

In any case, Sunderland's underlying conviction that Somers could be counted upon turned out to be justified. Within a couple of days Vernon could report that it was common talk that the cabinet changes projected by the Junto would take place.[86] By 12 November Jonathan Swift was writing that Somers would be made Lord President; four days later Luttrell was aware of it. At last, on 25 November, it was official.[87] After more than eight years out of office, he had returned to the ministry.

NOTES

[1] Marchmont MSS., 159.

[2] *Works*, ed. Scott, V, 372.

[3] See Walcott, *English Politics*, 121–24; McInnes, *Harley*, 97–98; Norman Sykes, 'Queen Anne and the Episcopate', *Eng. Hist. Rev.*, L, (July 1935), 433–64. The Junto's candidates were Dr Charles Trimmell and Dr White Kennett; Anne appointed Offspring Blackall and Sir William Dawes, later Archbishop of York, both High Churchmen. Cf. G. S. Holmes and W. A. Speck, 'The fall of Harley in 1708 reconsidered', *Eng. Hist. Rev.*, LXX (October 1965), 673–74, who assert that this contretemps, along with the Greg case, 'no longer warrant detailed consideration as major factors' in Harley's downfall.

[4] Lambeth Palace MSS., Misc. 1133, f. 55, 3 June 1707; and see Arthur T. Hart, *Life and Times of John Sharp* (London, 1949), 228.

[5] See *Conduct of the Duchess*, 175; Potter (later Archbishop of Canterbury) served as domestic chaplain to Archbishop Tenison.

[6] It was, wrote Vernon, 'a party cause', with all the Whigs on the Bishop's side: *Letters*, III, 358. Nicolson consulted Archbishop Tenison as well as Somers, while Atterbury turned to Harley and Archbishop Sharp. In his diary Nicolson described the bill as providing for 'the security of our Chapter Statutes; and empowering Her Majesty to appoint Commissioners (of Bishops) to inspect and correct those we have': *Transactions of the Cumberland and Westmorland Antiquarian and Archaeological Society* (new ser., IV, 1904), 18. The bill encountered little opposition in the Lords, passing by sixty-five to three; the going was rougher in Commons, but Somers obtained a promise from Joseph Jekyll to fight for it, and it received its third reading 17 March: *ibid.*, IV, 20, 23; *L.J.*, XVIII, 478; *C.J.*, XV, 614; *Addison Letters*, ed. Graham, 92.

[7] *L.J.*, XVIII, 338, *Parliamentary History*, VI, 597–600; Tindal, XXII, 341–42.

8 L.J., XVIII, 341–42, 482–83; *Parliamentary History*, VI, 618–62.

9 See Ralph Davis, *Rise of the English Shipping Industry in the Seventeenth and Eighteenth Centuries* (London, 1962); *Lords MSS.*, 1706–08, 99–334; L.J., XVIII, 366–92, 405–23, 466–72; Burnet, V, 323–24.

10 But see Holmes, *British Politics*, III, who observes that while the Junto hoped to see Orford, their own man, in charge, they were genuinely interested in eliminating mismanagement, and were ready to accept any interim settlement that would have this effect.

11 Burnet, V, 182.

12 L.J., XVIII, 351, 359.

13 So had the appearance of Earl Rivers, who returned to England after quarrelling with and attempting to supersede Galway. Somers vainly attempted to persuade Rivers to work with Galway. See *Bath MSS.*, I, 138–9, 160–61, 23 December 1706, 17 February 1707).

14 L.J., XVIII, 395.

15 Dedication to *Remarks on Several Parts of Italy*, *Works*, ed. Hurd, 356.

16 Add. MSS. 34, 515, ff. 206–07v.

17 Stowe MSS. 241, 12 April 1706.

18 Hardwicke, *State Papers*, II, 470–1.

19 Douglas Coombs, *Conduct of the Dutch* (The Hague, 1958), 164–65; Coxe, *Marlborough*, II, 117.

20 *Parliamentary History*, VI, 607.

21 L.J., XVIII, 395. Halifax reminded the Lords of Somers's 'sense of the partition treaty, for which he was so violently persecuted some years ago'; Hist. MSS. Comm., *Egmont MSS.* (London, 1920–23), II, 221. See also Holmes, *British Politics*, 77–78, and cf. Addison's remark that the resolution carried 'nemine contradicente': *Letters*, ed. Graham, 85.

22 L.J., XVIII, 395.

23 *Ibid.*, XVIII, 398–401, 403; C.J., XV, 481–82.

24 *Addison letters*, ed. Graham, 85.

25 See, for example, Egerton MSS. 891, ff. 6v–7, 22 February 1707. Somers had also been in touch with Earl Rivers (the commander of a force that joined Galway in Valencia early in 1707). See *Bath MSS.*, I, 138–39, 160–61 (23 December 1706, 17 February 1707).

26 Addison was an under-secretary. The piece 'would be taken as a statement of government and party policy': Peter Smithers, *Life of Joseph Addison* (Oxford, 1954), 125,

27 6 Anne, c. 11, article XIX.

28 L.J., XVIII, 397, 503, 554; the bill passed in Commons 1 April 1708: C.J., XV, 648. Somers appears to have instructed his colleagues on the merits of the rival schemes of the Earl of Seafield and Lord Chief Baron Ward: *Lords MSS.*, 1706–08, 576–77; L.J., XVIII, 397. For Somers's interest in reforming the Scottish judiciary, see *Jerviswood Papers*, 192–95.

29 L.J., XVIII, 334.

30 Trevelyan, *Anne*, II, 336; Hardwicke, *State Papers*, II, 473–78. According to Vernon, the Council Bill was argued chiefly by Godolphin and Somers: *Letters*, III, 341.

31 Burnet, V, 349–50; *Addison Letters*, ed. Graham, 90.

32 *Ibid.*, 89.

33 L.J., XVIII, 450, and see Holmes, *British Politics*, 341.

34 Burnet, V, 350–51. On the co-operation of the Junto and the Scottish *Squadrone*, see below, pp. 274–75; Holmes, *British Politics*, 243.

35 See Feiling, 399. On the other hand, according to Holmes and Speck, by mid-January 1708, 'mounting parliamentary pressure from both High Church and Junto flanks had at last persuaded the duke and lord treasurer to listen more attentively to Harley's project for an accommodation with the tories': 'Fall of Harley', 609.

36 See Henry L. Snyder, 'Godolphin and Harley: a study of their partnership in politics.' *Huntington Lib. Quar.*, XXX (May 1967), 260.

37 But see McInnes, *Harley*, 76–77.

38 *Vernon Letters*, III, 362.

39 L.J., XVIII, 452–53; Luttrell, *Relation*, VI, 266; Nicolson MS. Diary, 9 February 1708. On the vote, see *Lords MSS.*, 1706–08, 548. Somers was fourth, with fifty-seven votes. For Edward Harley's remark on the Junto's determination to ruin Robert Harley, see *Portland MSS.*, V, 647–48. James Ralph found it 'remarkable, that they were all of one Side': *The Other Side of the Question* (London, 1742), 344. See also Holmes, *British Politics*, 241–42.

40 L.J., XVIII, 489.

41 As digested in an address to the Queen; and see *ibid.*, XVIII, 516–42.

42 Burnet, V, 346–48; *Portland MSS.*, IV, 484; Trevelyan, *Anne*, II, 332 and n. For Swift's

remarks, see *Works*, ed. Scott, V, 33; *Correspondence*, ed. Ball, I, 78. McInnes states that Greg might have saved his life by implicating Harley, but gives no source: *Harley*, 76. On the importuning of Greg and the 'many artifices' employed to induce Valière, one of the smugglers, to accuse Harley, see Elizabeth Hamilton, *The Backstairs Dragon; a Life of Robert Harley, Earl of Oxford* (London, 1969), 115–16.

[43] On Harley's resignation, see (in addition to the articles by Holmes and Speck and by Snyder, cited above) Godfrey Davies, 'The fall of Harley in 1708', *Eng. Hist. Rev.*, LXVI (April 1951); Walcott, *English Politics*, 153–54; McInnes, *Harley*, ch. v. Somers professed not to have known what caused Harley's resignation, but was 'persuaded the carrying of the Bill for taking away the Scottish Privy Council was no little ingredient towards making the changes which have since happened': Nottingham Portland papers, Somers to Portland, 14 February 1708; see also Holmes and Speck, 'Fall of Harley', 674n.

[44] Coxe, *Marlborough*, II, 195.

[45] Portland MSS., V, 645. McInnes refers to Harley's hatred of the Junto, in William's reign: *Harley*, 33.

[46] See McInnes, *Harley*, 60 and n.

[47] Luttrell, *Relation*, VI, 159; *Remarks and Collections of Thomas Hearne*, ed. C. E. Doble (Oxford Historical Society, 1885–1921), II, 5.

[48] *Parliamentary History*, VI, 729.

[49] *Letters and Diplomatic Instructions of Queen Anne*, ed. B. Curtis Brown (London, 1935), 258; Neville Connell, *Anne. the Last Stuart Monarch* (London, 1937), 193; Marie R. Hopkinson, *Anne of England* (London, 1934), 272, 279–80; David Green, *Queen Anne* (London, 1970), 195.

[50] Boyer, *Anne*, 331. Charles Davenant called it the 'Pannick Terror': Blenheim MSS. B.I, 7, Davenant to Marlborough, 16 July 1708.

[51] *Correspondence*, ed. Williams, I, 79. On 9 March 1708 Addison wrote to the Duke of Manchester of rumours that Somers was to be made Lord President; see also letter of S. Edwin to the Duke, 18 May 1708: Hist. MSS. Comm., *Eighth Rept.*, pt. ii (re-issue 1910), Duke of Manchester's MSS., 96b, 99b.

[52] *Anne's Letters*, ed. Brown, 246; Coxe, *Marlborough*, II, 209–10.

[53] *Ibid.*, II, 214.

[54] Blenheim MSS., A. II, 38, wrongly dated 22 April in Tresham Lever, *Godolphin, his Life and Times* (London, 1952), 199.

[55] Blenheim MSS. B. II, 32, in Lever, 199.

[56] Coxe, *Marlborough*, II, 210.

[57] Blenheim MSS. B. II, 32, in Lever, 199.

[58] Coxe, *Marlborough*, II, 221.

[59] Add MSS. 34, 515, f. 208.

[60] Blenheim MSS. A. II, 38, in Lever, 200.

[61] *Corr. Duch. Marl.*, I, 121.

[62] *Anne's Letters*, ed. Brown, 257–58.

[63] 'Lord Somers's Rules', Hardwicke MSS., XXXIII, ff. 125–26; Ellis, 'Junto', 608–9. See also Blenheim MSS. B. I, 7, Halifax to Marlborough, 10 June 1708

[64] Walcott, *English Politics*, 150.

[65] *Downshire MSS.*, I, pt. ii. 858. The clergyman was Ralph Bridges.

[66] Sunderland to Newcastle, 27 May 1708, in Trevelyan, *Anne*, II, 413; Speck, *Tory and Whig*, 123. On contemporary estimates of returns, see Holmes, *British Politics*, 18, who notes, p. 219, that the Whigs had built up a small majority in the expiring Parliament.

[67] Cussans, *Hertfordshire*, III, 285; James O. Richards, *Party Propaganda under Queen Anne: the General Elections of 1702–1713* (Athens, Georgia, 1972), 100–2. Somers's protégé, Joseph Addison, would make his parliamentary debut at this time as M.P. for Lostwithiel; the following year he was to gain a Malmesbury seat, which he held until his death.

[68] See Walcott, *English Politics*, 150–51; Brown, *History of Scotland*, III, 139–41; Holmes, *British Politics*, 243–45; Patrick W. J. Riley, *The English Ministers and Scotland, 1707–1727* (London, 1964), 105. For Somers's restraining influence regarding subsequent Junto–Squadrone plans to increase their strength by contesting elections, see *ibid.*, 114; *Marchmont Papers*, III, 331–33.

[69] Sunderland to Newcastle, 27 May 1708, in Trevelyan, *Anne*, II, 413.

[70] *Corr. Duch. Marl.*, I, 113.

[71] See Walcott, *English Politics*, 151 and n. That Godolphin was disposed to accommodate the Junto, within reason, is revealed in a draft, in his own hand, of a communication to

the Queen: Blenheim MSS. B. I, 13, in Lever, 208–9. Somers once remarked that a 'cautious and prudent management between parties' was Godolphin's 'ordinary road': *Marchmont Papers*, III, 332.

72 *Marchmont Papers*, III, 335–36.
73 *Corr. Duch. Marl.*, I, 105.
74 *Ibid.*, I, 141–43; Coxe, *Marlborough*, II, 279.
75 Hopkinson, *Anne*, 282. It was on this occasion that she referred to the Junto as the 'five tyrannizing lords'.
76 Morgan, *Political Parties*, 350, citing Add. MSS., Coxe Papers, XXV, 156.
77 Trevelyan, *Anne*, II, 414.
78 See above, p. 264.
79 Trevelyan, *Anne*, II, 415.
80 Blenheim MSS. A. II, 38, in Lever, 212; and see *Portland MSS.*, IV, 509–10, for new rumours that Somers was to be Lord President.
81 Prince George died on 28 October.
82 Trevelyan, *Anne*, II, 416. According to Lever, 213, Somers was made Lord President 'at Marlborough's especial request'.
83 Sunderland to Newcastle, 4 November 1708, in Trevelyan, *Anne*, II, 416.
84 The latter accepted it in 1689 with some reluctance, hoping that William would reward him with the more important post of Treasurer: Browning, *Danby*, I, 439.
85 Somers had been so ill that summer that he was forced to forego a visit to Welbeck: B.M. Portland Loan 29/238, Somers to Newcastle, 31 July 1708.
86 *Vernon Letters*, III, 369–70 (6 November 1708).
87 *Correspondence*, ed. Williams, I, 109; Luttrell, VI, 373; P.C. 2/82, f. 205; *Cal. Treas. Books*, 1708, XXII, pt. ii, 454.

XIV
My Lord President, 1708-10

The office of Lord President was relatively new to the English constitution. Instituted under the Tories, it was not regularly filled until the later Stuart era. But after the appointment of Shaftesbury, in 1679, incumbents appear to have succeeded one another without a break.[1] The position was honorific enough; as chairman, under the sovereign, of the Privy Council, it was invariably held by a peer of the realm, and usually by one of the degree of earl or better. In precedence it ranked high. When the ruler formally attended the House of Lords, places were provided on his left for the Chancellor, Treasurer, President of the Council and Lord Privy Seal, in that order. The post carried a salary of £1500—£1000 'in lieu of ten Dishes every Meal' and the rest 'as of her Majesties Bounty'.[2] And there were the customary opportunities for patronage.

In 1701, to subject the activities of royal aides to greater publicity, a provision had been inserted in the Act of Settlement that all matters 'properly cognizable in the privy council by the laws and customs of this realm' should be transacted there.[3] But it was a dead letter and was repealed in 1705. The venerable agency remained what it had been when Somers first joined its ranks, more than a decade earlier, an increasingly formal body, too unwieldy for the efficient conduct of business. In 1708 its roster numbered fifty-five persons.[4] As under William, administrative power was lodged in the 'Cabinet Council'. Here the Lord President had a seat, but did not enjoy primacy.[5] On the other hand, Anne's increasing inattendance at Council meetings tended to augment the directive power of the President. While the Council's work was largely routine, it retained importance as an authenticating agency, and a wide variety of public business continued to come before it. Its agenda to some extent reflects the crucial problems of the day. Thus in 1709 it was deemed necessary to impose an embargo on continental shipping to prevent the spread of the plague, and considerable time was devoted to the problem of Protestant refugees crowding into the realm. Its minutes also reveal an increasing preoccupation with burgeoning colonial possessions and overseas commercial interests.[6] As President, Somers attended to his duties conscientiously. This was recognised even by hostile observers:

> The President, as usual, fill'd the Chair
> With serious Aspect, the malignant Air.[7]

When the new Parliament came together in mid-November the Whigs had ample reason to believe that, after a weary pilgrimage, they had once more entered the promised land. Their superiority in the Lords was a constant factor. The elections of the previous spring had improved their advantage in the Commons. As for ministerial offices, they had now virtually swept the board. Only Godolphin, continuing at the Treasury, and Pembroke at the Admiralty represented, among major officials, the Tory interest. And it was, essentially, a triumph for the Junto. Sunderland continued as Secretary for the South; in December Wharton obtained long-deferred recognition as Lord Lieutenant of Ireland. Lord Chancellor Cowper was closely aligned with the Junto. Newcastle, Lord Privy Seal since 1705, had given valuable support in its bid for power.[8] Halifax and Orford, it is true, had received no plums of office, but Halifax's brother had gained the attorney-generalship. Additional fruits might be expected. A control comparable to that of the mid-1690s seemed possible.

Yet these bright prospects were to prove largely illusory. For all his prestige as mentor of the Whigs and unquestioned leader of the Junto, Somers lacked several advantages he had enjoyed in the previous reign. Though Anne would mellow towards him, she could not overcome her aversion to the Junto; she would never bestow her confidence as William had done. There had been no Harley, no Abigail Masham in William's time. And for all Marlborough's good qualities things had been simpler, in a way, when the sovereign himself had served as generalissimo. Apart from these personal considerations, currents of opinion and even acts of nature contributed to the difficulties of the Junto. Long years of unremitting conflict, even great victories (which seemed to bring peace no nearer) had produced an inevitable war-weariness boding ill for a party that clung to the policy of 'No Peace without Spain'. And the oncoming winter would prove to be one of the bitterest in living memory, bringing in its train puny harvests and popular distress—less disastrous than on the continent, but nonetheless damaging to national morale and well-being. Meanwhile the Tories, nursing their grievances, drew together in opposition and awaited the opportunity for a restored ascendancy. It would come soon enough: the new reign of the Junto would last less than two years.

The contest for the speakership showed that the Junto lords were determined that this official (unlike John Smith, who now became Chancellor of the Exchequer) should not be drawn into the orbit of the court. For weeks they opposed the nomination of Sir Richard Onslow, whom (though a Whig) they regarded as a court candidate, and rallied support for Sir Peter King as a party nominee. But in the end, assuaged by the admission of Somers and Wharton to the inner circles of government, and concerned that the Tory Bromley might carry off the spoils, they accepted Onslow.[9]

At the outset parliamentary business went well enough in Junto eyes. Financial support for the war effort was forthcoming on the usual scale. The Commons' address to the Queen, requesting that she urge the allies to make their contributions proportionally large, reflected some dissatisfaction, but in the Lords the Whig superiority was manifested in a restatement of the resolution 'that no peace can be safe and honourable, until the whole Monarchy of Spain be restored to the House of Austria'.[10] It was

not a session productive of great measures, and Somers's ministerial responsibilities relieved him from routine work. Of the various committees to
which he was named only two may be described as dealing with national
issues. In January he was called upon to assist in an investigation of the
election of Scottish peers; two months later he was on a committee entrusted
with framing an address to the Queen on peace terms.[11] Yet his attendance
in the Lords was, save for a week in February, regular. Writing in January,
Jonathan Swift noted that Somers and Halifax were 'as well as busy
statesmen can be in Parliament time'.[12]

After the Christmas recess, when the legislators really got down to
business, an investigation was launched into the abortive Jacobite invasion
of the preceding spring. Why, Haversham asked, had the late ministry not
pursued those Scots who had at least encouraged the treasonable enterprise?
He suggested that Godolphin was guilty of complicity: 'even among the
Apostles themselves, he that bore the bag proved the traitor'.[13] The Whigs,
though far from satisfied with their relations with the Treasurer, nevertheless stood by him and the attack collapsed. But the Scottish law of treason
came in for sharp criticism. A number of Stirlingshire gentlemen, known
to have been 'out' with horses and men, had to all practical purposes been
acquitted in Scotland.[14] The new government now proceeded to introduce
a bill providing one law of treason—the English law—for the entire island.
This proposal was indignantly opposed by the Scots (particularly in the
Commons), who denounced what they regarded as an infringement of
Scottish judicial autonomy, and who upheld their arrangements as more
favourable to the rights of defendants than those of England.[15] But, after
some concessions to Scottish sensibilities, the government was able to push
its bill through both houses.

Somers wielded some influence in framing this measure. In particular he
worked to blunt the force of an amendment that no estate in land was to
be forfeited upon a judgement of high treason. Arguing that since the
Pretender had 'assumed the title of king of Great Britain, and had so lately
attempted to invade us, it was not reasonable to lessen the punishment and
the dread of treason as long as he lived', he moved that the amendment
should not take effect until the death of that prince.[16] Aware as he was of
Scottish opinion, and of the premises of the Act of Union, his attachment
to the English system and his concern for the security of the regime outweighed other considerations. But he was ready to join with the other
ministers in carrying through an Act of Grace and Free Pardon, sent down
by the Queen, granting amnesty for virtually all treasons hitherto committed. It was the broadest measure of this kind since the Revolution,
though insufficient to allay the fears and disillusionment that were mounting in Scotland.[17]

Somers fully realised the importance of cultivating as close an attachment as possible between the Junto and influential Scottish politicians. For
immediate purposes such a policy was important in counteracting the
manoeuvres of Godolphin. The Junto had allies in the 'New Party' or

Squadrone Volante, in which the Dukes of Montrose and Roxburghe were particularly prominent. The Junto-*Squadrone* had contributed to the forming of the Union; it was further cemented in the session of 1707–8 by common opposition to the Edinburgh Privy Council, a body controlled by the Duke of Queensberry and his adherents, bitter rivals of the *Squadrone.* The Junto now sought to block the growing influence of Queensberry, who in 1708 was created Duke of Dover in the English peerage. In the autumn of that year his claim to participate in the election of the sixteen Scottish representative peers was contested, Somers and Sunderland successfully leading the attack. For the newly created third secretaryship, designed to deal primarily with Scottish affairs, they worked to promote the interests of Roxburghe or Montrose (Somers's candidate for the post), and even of the Duke of Hamilton, who, though tarred with Jacobitism, was a foe of Queensberry and had been elected in 1708 on the so-called *Squadrone* 'list'. But here they failed. Queensberry's credit with Godolphin was high; in February 1709 he was appointed to the new secretaryship. According to Burnet, 'all the posts in Scotland were given to persons recommended by him'.[18] A breach with Godolphin seemed imminent.

The Junto lords had grievances closer to home. Two of them, Halifax and Orford, remained without preferment. Halifax wished to be a joint plenipotentiary at the forthcoming peace negotiations; Orford was a natural choice for the Admiralty. Godolphin might well agree with Swift that the Whigs, 'as they "waxed the fatter", did but "kick the more" '.[19] He unburdened himself to Marlborough: 'The life of a slave in the galleys is paradise in comparison with mine'.[20] Amidst these bickerings and distractions Somers gave some stability to the ministry. He was able to assert an influence comparable to that of Godolphin and Marlborough, with whom he remained, during these days, on good terms. Even Anne began to be won over by his ceremonious demeanour and impressed by his good judgement. Unlike Halifax and Sunderland, he was able to cloak animosity towards the Tories, which they showed so openly; indeed, there were rumours that he was paying court to Abigail Masham, though actually he does not seem to have turned to the new favourite before 1710.[21] As his reputation rose with Anne it declined with the Duchess of Marlborough, who took credit for Somers's restoration.[22]

But he still managed to retain Marlborough's confidence. Over the years the relations between the two had been on the whole co-operative. Towards the end of William's reign Somers, along with other Whigs, had shown some ill will, occasioned by his role in political affairs, and in 1708, as already noted, he had voiced suspicion of his good faith and serviceability. But the Junto had not yet ranged itself against his bid for a life-long captain-generalship, and memories of mutual support counted for something. In 1706 Somers and Sunderland had both joined with Anne in approving the Emperor's offer to make Marlborough Governor of the Spanish Netherlands. Two years later, on the eve of the Greg investigation, the Whigs saw fit to give him personal assurance of unanimous, thorough-going support.[23]

And Somers frankly acknowledged his obligation to Marlborough in connection with his return to office. 'I am well assured', he wrote, 'without your Grace's concurrence nothing of that nature had been done.'[24] Sarah, in the frustration and irritation of visible decline, might describe Somers as ungrateful and disrespectful, but her husband, though he inveighed against Halifax. Sunderland and Orford, recognised the Lord President's sound judgement. His only concern was that he sometimes gave way to the 'violence' of his Junto colleagues. 'I do, with all my heart', he wrote Sarah, 'wish that Lord Somers would always follow his own good sense, by which he would serve both his queen and country.' As for the Whigs in general, their principles were 'for the good of England'; the Tories 'would not only destroy England, but also the liberties of Europe'.[25]

So matters stood at the beginning of 1709. But in the course of the year the relationship cooled. The General, who over the years had owed so much to the unvarying Whig support of the war effort, would disagree with the Junto prescription of 'No Peace without Spain', and be resentful of its failure to support him in his bid to insure his military supremacy.[26] Meanwhile the tide of peace sentiment throughout the nation had risen further. Louis, the archfoe, had been thoroughly beaten, and was believed to be ready for a settlement at almost any price. The stumbling block was the Spanish commitment. To the cry 'For God's sake let us be at once out of Spain!' many a Tory would say amen. But not Lord Somers, or his Junto colleagues, or the Whigs as a whole, if this would involve admission of failure regarding the disposition of the Spanish Empire. It was the Spanish commitment, rather than the importance of ending the interminable war, that held priority in their counsels. And it was this pre-condition that, more than any other issue, contributed to their downfall the following year.

Bishop Burnet, applauding the restoration of Somers to public office, makes special reference to the beneficent influence that he could be expected to exert at the peace table:

The great capacity and inflexible integrity of this lord, would have made his promotion to this post very acceptable to the whigs at any juncture, but it was most particularly so at this time: for it was expected, that propositions for a general peace would be quickly made; and so they reckoned, that the management of that, upon which not only the safety of the nation, but of all Europe, depended, was in sure hands, when he was set at the head of the councils, upon whom neither ill practices nor false colours were like to make any impression.[27]

But Somers appears to have found it difficult to believe that the French were ready to act in good faith. Writing to Marlborough late in 1708, he could only hope that 'the circumstances of France are such at present, that it will be her interest to make an end of the whole & to avoid all those Chicanes and prevarications which are so natural to the French Genius'.[28] As has been noted, the Lords had reiterated the principle of victory in Madrid as well as Paris, and in December Godolphin and Somers worked out some preliminary proposals which involved an uncompromising application of that premise.[29] Both men were concerned over the strength of peace sentiment among the Dutch, ever a disconcerting factor with those who championed a fight to the finish. As Godolphin wrote:

Somers and I seem entirely to agree that the chief motive at this time with the States for pushing the War, is because no other way appears at coming at peace in such a manner as will be pleasing in any degree to England, but that in the bottom the States have the same kindness for peace and perhaps more than ever; and considering that the King of France may in all probability incline to leave that matter very much in the disposition of the States, that there may be no room for nor pretence for mistaking the opinion of England, we have resolved some heads relating to this business.[30]

Here was the inception of the Barrier Treaty, by which the English government purchased the continued support of the weakened and war-weary Dutch. When finalised the following autumn it extended handsome concessions in the Spanish Netherlands, regardless of the interests of Austria and Charles III, and in the Latin-American trade.

In the meantime, Marlborough, who was in The Hague seeking to induce the Dutch to augment their forces in proportion to those of England, was notified of French peace proposals involving the partitioning of the Spanish domains. These he forwarded to London. In their reply, Godolphin and Somers adhered to the position, laid down as early as 1706, that no steps should be taken towards general peace negotiations until England and the States had settled the 'preliminaries'. In other words, they closed the door to any immediate conversations with France. Marlborough was further informed of ministerial concern over a report from the Duke of Portland that the General's reluctance to discuss the Barrier Treaty had caused 'uneasiness' among Dutch authorities.[31] Already the General was revealing his dissatisfaction with such arrangements, and he sailed for home some six weeks later without having promoted the negotiations so important in Junto eyes.

But the Junto pressed on, with Parliament the forum. On 2 March the two Houses presented a joint and unanimous address to the Queen, to the effect that no peace was to be regarded as honourable which did not provide for the restitution of the Spanish monarchy, Louis's recognition of the Protestant succession and deportation of the Pretender, the destruction of Dunkirk harbour, and barriers for both Savoy and the Dutch. The address was first proposed in the Lords by Halifax, but Somers appears to have made the motion with regard to the succession and the Pretender, and was placed on the committee entrusted with its composition.[32]

The co-operation of the Commons and concurrence of the Queen was all to the good, but the possibility that the Dutch might be won over by French representations continued to worry the Junto. Louis was extending peace feelers through his emissary, Rouillé. Somers, along with Godolphin and the Queen, was appraised of these through a letter from Heinsius to Marlborough. Although Heinsius had urged secrecy, the General had in-

sisted that all such communications should be read by the other three.[33]
The Junto was now all the more desirous of forestalling the French by
pressing on with the Barrier Treaty. Despite their awareness of Marlborough's reluctance, he was now given the necessary powers to negotiate
both the barrier arrangements and an agreement over peace preliminaries.
By 9 April he was back in The Hague. But he was determined to avoid
responsibility for the kind of barrier treaty the Dutch were bargaining
for, and before the month was over wrote to Godolphin asking for the
appointment of an associate plenipotentiary.[34] There was, of course, the
further consideration that negotiations might drag on for some time, and
he could scarcely be expected to direct his armies and sit at the council table
at the same time.

The ministry responded favourably, though it is likely that they would
have preferred to have had Marlborough, obedient to their will, bear
full responsibility.[35] They cast about for an emissary who could be expected
to do their bidding. Halifax, disgruntled at being left out of public employment, was the Junto's choice, but Marlborough and Godolphin were
opposed.[36] The impulsive Sunderland was out of the question. In the end
they fastened upon Lord Townshend, a personable and amiable man, and
a student of foreign affairs. He was a friend and protégé of Somers; a fellow
Kit-Cat, he had voted against his impeachment, and in other ways had
manifested his support of the Junto. His diplomatic career would not long
survive the new ascendancy of his mentor, but in the spring of 1709
Somers must have been fully satisfied that in Townshend he would have
at The Hague an agent entirely faithful and compliant, though without
experience in diplomacy apart from negotiations over the Treaty of Union.[37]

By the middle of May Townshend was at the Dutch capital by the side
of the Duke. Within a fortnight the two plenipotentiaries, along with those
of the Emperor and the States General, had put their signatures to forty
articles, which were presented to the principal French emissary, De Torcy,
as preliminaries to a peace settlement. These terms comprehended and went
beyond those called for in the address to Queen Anne. Hopes for peace ran
high.[38] Somers was kept abreast of the proceedings, and his advice sought.
On 31 May Marlborough wrote to Sarah: 'We have settled everything that
England could wish, except what concerns the Pretender': here the plenipotentiaries would require assistance from the Lord President, as well as
Godolphin and Sunderland.[39]

But Marlborough had reckoned too soon. Louis XIV would agree to the
surrender of the Spanish Empire, intact save for such portions as were
reserved for Britain or Holland, to Charles. He was ready to cede or relinquish one base after another in the Netherlands or in France itself. He
would abandon rights in Alsace, destroy the fortifications and Dunkirk
and recognise the British claim to Newfoundland. Portuguese and Savoyard
boundaries were to be adjusted. He was even ready to co-operate with the
Allies in coercing his grandson to abandon Spain. But he baulked at the
thirty-seventh article, which called for a termination of the armistice if

the entire Spanish monarchy should not be delivered to Charles within two months. He regarded the consequences as too dangerous for France, which, weakened in its defences, would be exposed to invasion from Strasbourg, Tournai and other bases surrendered by the terms of the treaty. The negotiations were broken off; the troops, already marching again, headed for the carnage of Malplaquet, and attention was focused once more on the Barrier Treaty.

There is no evidence that Somers—or any other English minister—took any steps to save the abortive preliminaries. But the Barrier Treaty was another matter, as Marlborough noted with misgivings. 'I know', he wrote Godolphin, 'that Lord Townshend and Lord president are very fond of having the treaty for the barrier settled.' By August he was clearly disturbed by the Somers-Townshend connection. Townshend he regarded as 'a very honest man'. On the other hand he complained that he did not understand the temper of the Dutch, and would probably mislead Somers. But the General's influence on diplomacy was ebbing, and the Whigs pressed on, carrying with them the beleaguered Godolphin.[40] That autumn, at Malplaquet, Marlborough could claim another victory. But it had been costlier to the allies than to the French, whose armies were still in being and whose morale had improved. Peace, it seemed, was no nearer. And when Somers, in a letter of congratulations, voiced his hopes for 'a happy and lasting peace', the General was not sanguine. He could only express his confidence that Somers believed that he was doing his utmost to promote it through his efforts to 'improve our advantages'.[41]

With such a reaction from the great Marshal, so soon after a major victory, it is not strange that Somers remained determined to insure the continuance of the Anglo-Dutch military effort. Peace was desirable, but further hostilities must be prepared for. Writing to Marlborough on 14 October, he confided:

If you will please to allow me to tell my wish it should be that before the meeting of the Parliament we may be in possession of good terms of Peace or firmly agreed upon the necessity of carrying on the War for another year.

It was plain that the French would not agree to a 'reasonable' peace until compelled by 'downright necessity'. It could not be hastened 'by that eagerness to be treating of Peace which is always shewing itself at the Hague'.[42] And, he might have added, in England, where Shrewsbury now estimated that 'the generality of the nation', and even most members of Parliament, were united in their longing for peace. The Junto, however, could take comfort in assurances, arising out of a conversation between Godolphin and the Governor of the Bank of England, that the Whig financial and commercial interests fully supported its demand for the 'Spanish Monarchy entire' and its rejection of a settlement, such as Marlborough contemplated, leaving the recovery of Spain as 'an after game'.

Thus fortified, the ministry moved ahead with the Barrier Treaty, and on 18 October Townshend was able to forward the document to London. Great as had been the desire of the Junto lords to close the negotiations, they were nonetheless appalled by the advantages which the Dutch had wrung from their plenipotentiary. Since Marlborough had refused to sign, their complaints had to be countered by the amiable Viscount, whom they criticised for having exceeded instructions in the matter of the barrier fortresses. But they were forced to accept his argument that 'there was no other way left to keep this people firm to the Common Interest against France'.[43] Somers must have supported his protégé; certainly he regarded the completion of the treaty as the greater good, and wrote at once to tell the Duke of Newcastle the tidings. He added, however, that the treaty should be kept secret, if possible.[44]

Despite his preoccupation with the complexities of international affairs he could not, from the very nature of his position, escape involvement in other matters. Of particular concern were the problems created by the migration of the Palatines to England.[45] 'The case of the Palatine is all our domestic talk,' wrote a Londoner in August.[46] They were, for the most part, religious refugees who began to descend upon England in May of 1709, encouraged by a naturalisation act pushed through by the Junto two months earlier. It was not enacted without a struggle, drawing opposition from High Church elements who feared the strengthening of Nonconformity, as well as from those worried over economic competition.[47] Somers, absent from the Lords, does not figure as a protagonist. But he was involved with the fate of the immigrants. These came in unexpected numbers, no less than 8400 from Rotterdam alone reaching England between May and July. An encampment of 6500, provided with tents from the Board of Ordnance, was formed on Blackheath.[48] The problem was the more serious in that the rigours of the past winter had adversely affected the national economy.

To deal with the crisis a board of trustees was set up, its principal responsibility being to supervise the collection and disbursement of funds raised to assist the immigrants.[49] Somers served on this body, showing a genuine concern over the plight of so many uprooted men and women, faced with an uncertain if not forbidding future in a strange land. A correspondent at the time speaks of his 'conspicuous' compassion. The Somers Manuscripts include a number of proposals forwarded for his consideration. An anonymous correspondent asked for his blessing on a proposal to build houses and workshops for the Palatines at a low cost, and to employ them. Another envisaged a colony of ten thousand to be settled at Cobham Park, which might be purchased. When this proved abortive, Nasborough Forest was proposed as an alternative. Others advanced projects for American settlements. Colonel Robert Hunter, soon to be Governor of New York, offered to transport Palatines to that colony; they were to be armed and enlisted in his regiment for the defence of the frontier. John Chamberlayne, the miscellaneous writer who in the past had been indebted to Somers as a patron, now exercised official responsibilities in connection with the refugees. He sought Somers's protection against the Duke of Somerset, who claimed that Chamberlayne had been neglecting his duties, and his support for the settlement of six hundred Palatines in North Carolina.[50] In the end more than that number were shipped to the southern province, and three thousand to New York. Over eight hundred families were sent to Ireland, where Wharton, Somers's old associate, was active in providing for their settlement. Another three thousand were absorbed into military service.

By the time Parliament assembled in mid-November, the stresses and strains that from the outset had wrenched the fabric of the government had become painfully apparent. In one respect the Junto had made a concrete gain. Orford was once more at the Admiralty—not as Lord High Admiral but as First Lord, presiding over a three-man commission. It had taken a bit of doing to bring this off. The Queen deeply resented the part that he had played in the attack on her late consort's administration. In June the Duke of Marlborough had doubted if anyone could prevail upon her to give her consent; he himself was at first opposed to it, as was Godolphin, both being averse to seeing so influential a post pass into Junto control.[51] Somers drove hard towards the objective. By August he appears to have been ready to make it a condition of his continued association with the government. According to Halifax, Somers, having been 'at the head of all the complaints' about the Admiralty, could not 'with any decency, nor without losing quite his interest,' continue in office with the faults of that department unamended.[52] Sunderland lent support, yet tried to restrain him. 'I am sorry,' he wrote, 'to see you have such a fit of the spleen upon you; for though there is but too much reason for it upon the whole, yet if you will give me leave to say so, I think you push it a little too far.' He went on to assure him that, if the project continued to be 'pressed by all of us', the opposition forces would capitulate, though probably not until shortly before the assembling of Parliament. If, on the other hand, they would refuse to do what was 'so necessary and reasonable', then

I think we have nothing to do, but to continue, as we have done, to press as far as possible towards this point, that we may discharge ourselves to the public, to our friends, and indeed to ourselves; and when that is done, and the proper time come, which I cannot but think is just before the meeting of the parliament, to take our leave of them, by quitting, and have nothing more to do with them.

But for the present he thought it desirable 'to keep fair with them, and not seem to distrust them too much'.[53] In the end Sunderland's prognostication proved to be correct. Godolphin and Marlborough found that they were supported only by Boyle; and the General was importuned by his tireless wife to use his influence to persuade the Queen to do the business. They now beat a retreat, and the appointment was formalised early in November.[54]

It was a victory for the Junto. Save for Halifax they were now all holding high offices.[55] But it had its price. Once more the Queen had been forced to yield to the 'tyrannizing lords'; would she never escape their machinations? She could take comfort only in her successful blocking of the appointment of Sir John Jennings (a good Junto man) as one of the naval commissioners. Another Jennings—Sarah, Duchess of Marlborough— was, in her credit with Anne, close to the point of no return, if she had not already reached it. The publication of Mary Manley's *New Atalantis*, slandering without restraint the Duchess and various Whig leaders, and extolling the new favourite and Harley, elicited no overt sign of displeasure from the Queen.[56] Marlborough, at least, had no illusions. When informed that Anne had smiled upon Sunderland he was unimpressed. In his opinion her 'easiness' arose from continued dependence on the Whigs; he warned the Duchess that 'Mrs. Masham and Mr. Harley will, underhand, do every thing that can make the business uneasy, and particularly to you, the lord treasurer, and me.'[57] Events would prove him correct.

Even as the Junto had needed Marlborough to secure Orford's preferment, the General now required its support to preserve his military supremacy. In one respect they had already proved unreliable. As early as May his trusted aide, James Craggs, was at work in London seeking precedents whereby he might obtain a life appointment as Captain-General, and thus maintain his influence regardless of political vicissitudes. But neither Craggs nor Lord Chancellor Cowper could (or would) come up with the evidence he sought, and the Junto magnates, doubtless out of respect for Cowper's expert knowledge, did not support the project.[58] The Duke's direct appeal to the Queen was no more successful, its only effect being to provide ammunition for those who sought to convince her that she was being made a tool of the insatiable Churchill interest.

Anne now took the initiative, with Harley by her side. In January 1710, she bestowed the constableship of the Tower of London upon Lord Rivers. Once a leading Whig, he was now closely associated with Harley. He bore a grudge against Marlborough, who had refused to appoint him Commander-in-Chief in Spain in place of the beleaguered Galway. The Duke protested, but to no avail. On the very same day the Queen called upon him to give the Oxford Regiment, vacant from the death of Lord Essex, to Colonel Hill. The Colonel was Abigail Masham's brother. To Marlborough these manoeuvres were blows threatening his command. It was, in his words, 'to set up a standard of disaffection to rally all the malcontent officers in the army'.[59] To the Junto they revealed the growing strength and boldness of the Harley-Masham combination. Somers had for some months been conscious of the dangers that Harley's ambitions and influence posed for the ministry. As early as July 1709 he had passed on to Godolphin what he knew of Harley's 'schemes and designs'. Since, with the country at war, there could be 'no attacking of Ministers, nor no naming maladministrations of any kind', Harley's strategy was supposedly to induce the Queen to wave the olive branch while he linked the continuation of the war with Godolphin and, particularly, Marlborough, and counted upon peace sentiment for the withholding of supply.[60]

When Marlborough found that his representations to the Queen were without effect, he turned to the Whig leaders to see what support he could muster in that quarter. This time he was more successful. Sunderland assured him of the co-operation of Somers, who stood ready to remonstrate with the Queen against Hill's appointment, either in company with the Duke or by himself. Emboldened, Marlborough sought another audience, but to no avail. It was now high time to bring Somers's influence to bear. A meeting was arranged, in which, to use Somers's words, he was to receive the Duke's commands. But the Lord President was prevented by illness from attending. Marlborough, refusing to temporise further, withdrew to Windsor Lodge; there he drew up a statement of his grievances, particularly those against Mrs Masham, and in conclusion threw down the gauntlet with the words: 'I hope your majesty will either dismiss her or myself.' This manifesto was laid before Godolphin and the Whig leaders.[61]

The Junto was far from decisive at this juncture.[62] Godolphin was torn with doubts and fearful of pressing the Queen further after the Orford incident. But he arranged that Somers should go to the Queen for the purpose of dissuading her from her resolution. On 16 January he secured an audience. After referring to Marlborough's apprehensions and the 'fatal effects' to be expected from the circumvention of his military authority, he turned to the matter of international implications:

And may I take the liberty to observe, that the Duke of Marlborough is not to be considered merely as a private subject, because all the eyes of Europe are fixed upon him, and business is transacted with him, under the notion of one who is honoured with your majesty's entire trust and favour; and as men depend on all which he says, it gives full force and effect to all which he does. The army also unanimously obeys him, because the soldiers look up to him for advancement. Nor can I conceal from your majesty the unspeakable inconveniences which must ensue, should any thing be done which may induce ill-intentioned persons to conceive that there is any alteration in this matter, or which might excite jealousy in him, and diminish his zeal and spirit at so critical a period.

But the Queen appeared little affected. She was, she replied, fully cognisant of the Duke's long and distinguished service, but she trusted that, 'after mature reflection', he would not find her proposal unreasonable. Since she was 'very reserved, and not willing to enter into any farther explanation', Somers saw no point in pressing her further.[63]

It is clear that he realised the need for restraint in dealing with Anne on this issue. This is further indicated by the position he took with regard to a proposal, advanced by Sunderland and seconded by Robert Walpole, that Parliament should frame an address calling for the removal of Mrs Masham. This went beyond Marlborough's intentions. He wished to handle the matter by way of a private remonstrance; even the implacable Sarah apparently shrunk from such a public censure of the Queen.[64] According to Coningsby, Maynwaring (the Duchess's principal source of political information) suggested to her that if Somers could be brought to promote such a measure in the Lords, and Coningsby in the Commons, and if Sarah would use her influence with Godolphin to line up Secretary Boyle and the Speaker, 'it was not possible it could miscarry in either House'. Maynwaring would undertake to see that Marlborough received assurances from Somers himself.[65] But Somers, along with Godolphin and Cowper, favoured less drastic tactics, and the project was stillborn.[66]

Instead he turned again to the task of persuading the Queen, and a second audience found her in a more receptive mood. Expressing surprise at the offence taken by Marlborough because of her recommendation, she assured the Lord President that, when the Duke came to town, she would attempt to convince him that her friendship for him was 'as entire as he can desire'.[67] Though Marlborough appeared fixed in his resolution, Somers advised him to put in an appearance in order to take advantage of the rising barometer, and Godolphin persuaded him to delete from his letter of protest the ultimatum regarding Mrs Masham. Except for Sunderland, the Junto appears to have been in accord. The Queen now gave way, informing Marlborough that she would not insist upon Hill's commission. Thus the crisis passed. Marlborough's military prerogative was in part upheld.

But Abigail was still at the Queen's side, and Anne was well aware of the General's hostility towards her favourite. The ministry, too, bore scars from this episode. The views of Godolphin and the moderate Whigs headed by Somers had clashed with those of the aggressive Sunderland and his coterie. Violent altercations had occurred, leading Secretary Boyle to warn Walpole: 'Take care what you do, or the remedy will be worse than the disease.'[68] Somers was alarmed by Sunderland's intransigence; in turn, his caution and moderation were construed as evidence of jealousy and even disloyalty to the Marlborough interest, and even of an attachment to Harley.[69] But he could take satisfaction that he had done yeoman service in helping to bring about a solution which vindicated the General, while avoiding a head-on collision with the Queen and the adverse effects of a parliamentary issue.

Before the smoke of the Hill-Masham incident had cleared, a *cause célèbre* was in the making, in which Somers's counsels went largely unheeded and which was to pave the way for the downfall of the ministry. On 5 November 1709, Dr Henry Sacheverell, Fellow of Magdalen and Chaplain of St Saviour's, Southwark, had preached the usual Guy Fawkes Day sermon before the Mayor and Aldermen of London. Entitling it *The Perils of False Brethren both in Church and State*, he vigorously denied the lawfulness of resistance, no matter what the provocation, and expressed his detestation of those who embraced comprehension and toleration in religion as political expedients. Sacheverell had already acquired some fame for his inflammatory preaching in the High Church cause.[70] The ministry was disposed to take him seriously, particularly when his sermon appeared in print, to the number of 40,000 copies.[71] For it appeared not only to undermine the arrangements flowing from the Revolution, such as the Act of Settlement and the Hanoverian succession, but it struck at the ministers, and particularly Godolphin, as enemies of the Church. Personal resentment as well as political principles contributed to their determination to proceed against the Doctor, and they decided to impeach him.

Impeachment was pressed chiefly by Wharton and Sunderland. Godolphin, resentful of a thinly veiled attack in the sermon, also supported it, despite the further damage (on which the Junto promoters were counting) that this would do to his credit with High Tories. Marlborough, somewhat hesitant at first, came round.[72] According to the Duchess of Marlborough, the Lord President 'to my knowledge and to my hearing pressed all the Ministry to have Sacheverell prosecuted', declaring that, if it were not done, 'the clergy would take the Crown from the Queen by preaching'.[73] But it was one thing to prosecute, another to impeach. Somers advised his colleagues to be cautious. 'Order a charge to be drawn up against the offender,' he advised his colleagues; 'but still take care not to consult your passions or affections more than your own dignity and usage.' He looked upon the injuries done by Sacheverell to the ministry as 'very great', but warned them not to make him a martyr:

Let no hatred, revenge, anger or passions interpose; for where these take place, the mind does not easily discern the truth; or if it does discern it, it is not apt to embrace it; and that which would pass among others as anger only, our people would call cruelty in the government, which is odious to all men.

Impeachment he clearly regarded as dangerous: 'as to the great number of noble lords, if they should absent themselves, or the members of parliament should revolt to the other party, ye will certainly find it too late, and to no purpose now to have judiciary proceedings'. The circumstances of the case should be given careful consideration; if, he counselled

a condign punishment can be found out for this man's offence, and suitable to the greatness of the danger, I approve of the extraordinary method of proceeding; but if the greatness of the offence exceeds the constitutions of our ancestors, and the conceptions of men, I think it best to make use of that method of process which our laws have provided.[74]

There can be little doubt that Somers favoured the latter alternative, that is, resort to the regular procedure of the courts. Swift, who attributed the impeachment to 'a foolish, passionate pique' of Godolphin, reports that, a few months later, Somers told him that 'he had earnestly, and in vain endeavoured, to dissuade the Earl from that attempt', and foretold that it was likely to end in the ruin of the ministry.[75] But he was overborne by his colleagues. Too many Whigs were determined to 'roast the priest'.[76] Under impeachment a mere majority would secure conviction. With a jury, unanimity was mandatory, and the law officers had raised doubts regarding successful prosecution in the Queen's Bench. Sir Christopher Wren was therefore called upon to arrange facilities in Westminster Hall—no easy task, considering the universal interest in the spectacle—and on 27 February the trial got under way.

While ticket-holders crowded in and the mob surged outside Somers joined his fellow peers in the proceedings.[77] Despite his earlier opposition, now that the impeachment was launched he worked to insure its effectiveness. As early as 15 December he had been named to a committee on procedural methods.[78] He could have no formal influence in shaping the articles, for this was a function of the Commons. But they were drafted at the house of his brother-in-law and political associate, Sir Joseph Jekyll, a manager of the trial, who undoubtedly relied upon his counsel.[79] According to Coningsby, Somers, along with Halifax and Sunderland, insisted that Sacheverell's preaching of passive obedience and non-resistance be included in the articles.[80]

By the middle of March the Lords were considering their verdict. Somers was less prominent in debate than one might expect, perhaps from ill health. But he supported the motion that the Commons had 'made good the first article' against the embattled Doctor. This accused him of falsely maintaining

That the necessary means used to bring about the said Happy Revolution, were odious and unjustifiable: That his late majesty, in his Declaration, disclaimed the least imputation of Resistance; And that to impute Resistance to the said Revolution, is to cast black and odious colours upon his late majesty and the said Revolution.[81]

Along with a bevy of Whig peers, including Halifax, Cowper, Wharton and Sunderland, he spoke in vindication of the Revolution, maintaining that extraordinary circumstances may render resistance necessary and lawful.[82] He also strove, with Cowper, to counter objections that the charge had not specifically identified the obnoxious passages in the sermon. These were raised primarily by Nottingham and Guernsey, and supported by the judges; but the two ministers, with assistance from Halifax, argued that their Lordships were not to be 'tied up to the forms of the inferior courts': the usage of Parliament, and not of Westminster Hall, must prevail. Their decision, they pointed out, should not be taken merely on narrow, legalistic grounds; they should have regard for 'what is equity, and what the public good, the common safety and the constitution of the kingdom necessarily require.'[83] Peter Wentworth, who was present in the chamber, was impressed by their powers of persuasion; according to him they

answered all th' other lords objections so clearly that Mr. Lechmore and Sr. Joseph Jekel that were next me concluded the Drs. business done[84]

And indeed it was. After considerable debate the House carried a resolution that 'by the Law and Usage of Parliament, in Prosecutions by Impeachments for high Crimes and Misdemeanours, by writing or speaking, the particular Words supposed to be criminal are not necessary to be expressly specified in such Impeachments'. By 17 March the Lords found that the Commons had 'made good' the four articles of impeachment.[85] But a substantial number had protested, and the question was raised as to whether a vote should be taken on each of the four articles of the impeachment, as opposed to a single vote on the impeachment as a whole. To the former course Somers raised strong objections. The Lords were both judge and jury; he assured them, therefore

That, as Jury, they might, in conscience, pronounce the Doctor guilty, though they thought him guilty only of one article: But that the Lords, who did not think him guilty of all the four articles, might, afterwards, as Judges, moderate the punishment.[86]

He secured the necessary support, and the final vote was taken on the question: 'Is Doctor Henry Sacheverell guilty of high Crimes and Misdemeanours, charged upon him by the Impeachment of the House of Commons?' Voting, in accordance with official precedence, third from the last, Somers adjudged him guilty. By a vote of 69 to 52 the Doctor was condemned.[87]

Somers had stood with the Whig magnates, and had, as usual, been serviceable. But his political instinct had been sound. Prosecution had been, technically speaking, successful; the Whig lines had not been breached, the vote in the Lords falling essentially into the usual partisan pattern. Yet the victory brought no gain; on the contrary, the case provided a golden opportunity for a manifestation of Tory sentiment on a nation-wide basis, and this in turn encouraged the Queen to hearken even more carefully to the counsels of Harley and to rid herself of the 'tyrannizing lords'. As one Tory put it, 'it happily ended in the Removal of the Arbitrary Junto, and the Dissolution of a Parliament that was entirely at their Devotion', a sentiment echoed by Swift.[88]

In the months that followed, while Sacheverell was widely acclaimed as a national hero, the Lord President witnessed, but could do little to prevent, the progressive disintegration of the ministry. At the prorogation of Parliament on 5 April it stood intact; five months later it was wrecked. Anne moved warily to effect this transformation. Neither she nor Harley wished to exchange what they regarded as a captivity at the hands of the Whigs for a similar bondage to the Tories, however attractive and useful their rising reputation. The Queen was not unaware of dangerous repercussions that might follow any sweeping changes. She knew how sensitive the London money market was to any rise or fall in Whig fortunes, and how closely the Allies and Louis himself kept themselves informed of projects that might effect the British war involvement.

She began by ousting the Lord Chamberlain, the Marquess of Kent, calling upon him to deliver his key of office to the Duke of Shrewsbury. Though the change was effected without reference to the Lord Treasurer, who had withdrawn to Newmarket, or the other ministers, the news, after the initial shock wore off, appears to have been accepted by the Whig leaders without undue alarm. Kent, a court Whig, was a man of little consequence; as for Shrewsbury, the Junto had worked with him in the past, and might do so again. In a letter acquainting Marlborough with these developments, Somers showed little concern. Godolphin, however, remonstrated with considerable firmness over what he naturally regarded as a withholding of confidence; he believed both Somers and Sunderland to be as much 'mortified' as himself, though disposed to dissemble.[89] It is likely that the Junto leaders took the position that the issue, for all its implications of back-stairs counsel, was hardly worth a head-on collision that might provoke what they were determined to postpone as best they could—the dissolution of the Whiggish Commons. And even Godolphin came round, telling Marlborough that though the Whigs were 'mightily mortified and dejected' at Shrewsbury's appointment, 'I find most people are of opinion that he will like very well to live easily with us, and I am not unapt to think so too.'[90]

Meanwhile, the Whigs could take comfort from reassuring tidings from their hero. He had forced the lines before Douai, and he was as loyal, it seemed, as he was invincible. On 5 May he wrote his duchess: 'You may be assured, and pray assure Lord Somers, Lord Sunderland, and whom they shall think proper, that I am determined to do just as they would have me, not only now, but in all the actions of my life.' The utmost care should be taken to keep Parliament in being, and the Whigs must stand united: 'Of all things, the Whigs must be sure to be of one mind, and then all things, sooner or later, must come right.'[91]

But the Whigs were not of one mind, and within a month the ranks of the Junto itself had been broken. The first blow fell upon Sunderland, almost inevitably, for the intractable Secretary continued to be held in particular detestation by the Queen, and had not shown much ability in his department. He was, moreover, the junior member of the Junto, still in his mid-thirties, and his rash and autocratic temperament had alienated many of his colleagues. By the latter part of May, at the latest, rumours of the manoeuvre began to circulate. The Junto, beset with uncertainties, concerned on the one hand with the sensibilities of Marlborough and on the other with the ever-present threat of a dissolution, were off balance and chose to play a defensive role:

Lord Halifax, lord president, Lord Sunderland, and generally the rest of the Whigs, are so uneasy, that they are ready to make their court to Mr. Harley, who appears as ready to receive it, and is making advances and professions almost to every one that he thinks our friends.[92]

This Godolphin wrote to Marlborough on 29 May. In vain did the Duke call for unanimous support of his son-in-law. He was dismissed on 13 June, without any accompanying resignations.

Somers had been no more effective than the rest of his colleagues. This is not to say that he had been inactive. Whatever his concern for Sunderland and the domestic implications of his ouster, he could not ignore the unsettling military effects. He wrote to Viscount Townshend, urging him to exhort the Dutch and the Emperor to exercise their influence and to make sure that they understood that a new Parliament and a drive for peace must be reckoned as consequences of the Secretary's dismissal.[93] Beyond this the record offers little. Illness may have been in part to blame, for he was confined during these crucial weeks. In any case, by early June he was in a discouraged and defeatist mood. 'Our enemies', he wrote Marlborough, 'will not be in good earnest for peace, when they see us so busy in doing their business for them; and our friends can never think it reasonable to depend on so wild a people.' But he urged the Duke not to allow personal feelings to interfere with his continued direction of the war effort:

I have, I must confess, but little to say for myself, unless it be the owning, as I have done already, that I can see no reasonable ground of hopes, but from what your grace is able to perform this summer; and, therefore, to beg that you will have that just regard to the glory you are possessed of, as not to let any resentment, or any contrivance, how artful soever, put you out of the way of carrying it on, to all the perfection it is capable of receiving.[94]

A few days later he had an opportunity to dissuade the Queen, who called him into her presence to discuss the impending change. On this occasion she assured him of her unshakeable resolution, but added that she was 'entirely for moderation' and did not plan to make 'any farther alterations'. Somers made only mild protestations regarding the political consequences of Sunderland's deposition, but remonstrated against the dissolution of Parliament, as something to be avoided at all costs.[95]

Whatever Somers's ambitions for himself, whatever ministerial sacrifices might have to be made, it is clear that two conditions—the preservation of Marlborough's command and the continuance of the existing Parliament— were to him fundamental.[96] They were, moreover, intertwined. He had not flagged in his zeal for total victory. As late as March 1710 he even toyed with the idea of a new Edict of Nantes as a condition of peace.[97] During the spring fresh peace negotiations at Gertruydenberg had raised the hopes of the war-weary, but, like those of the previous year, had ended in failure. Somers, along with his Whig colleagues, had been unsympathetic. In the Council he insisted that the French were 'encouraged' by events in England, and tried vainly to rekindle a war-mindedness in Shrewsbury and Somerset.[98] Writing to Wharton, absent in Ireland, he remarked:

The French ambassadors at Gertruydenberg have sent a very insolent letter, or rather manifesto, to the Pensioner in order to justify their breaking off the negotiation. I hope so unnecessary and so insolent a provocation will give the Dutch courage enough to resent it as they ought; but I have not the resolution taken upon it. It breaks my heart to think what a noble game we are unnecessarily throwing away.[99]

The old doubts of Dutch constancy, despite the bribe of the Barrier Treaty, still remained. In April both Somers and Devonshire had privately expressed fears to their colleagues that Dutch impatience for peace would preclude much support for demands not included in the preliminaries, such as those for Newfoundland and Hudson Bay.[100]

The great asset was still the military reputation of Marlborough. Somers, not content, with his personal plea of 6 June, joined with his colleagues on the morrow of Sunderland's fall in exhorting him to hold fast. After expressing sympathy for the 'mortification' he had suffered through his son-in-law's dismissal, they underscored his importance both to 'the fate of Europe' and Whig political fortunes:

We must therefore conjure you by the glory you have already obtained, by the many services you have done your Queen and country, by the expectation you have justly raised in all Europe, and by all that is dear and tender to you at home, whose chief dependence is upon your success, that you would not leave this great work unfinished, but continue at the head of the Army. This we look upon as the most necessary step that can be taken to prevent the dissolution of this Parliament. Your grace's compliance with this our earnest request would be the greatest obligation to us, and all that wish well to our country. And you may depend upon it, that the contrary will be the greatest satisfaction to your enemies.[101]

Marlborough did not disappoint them. Though he had toyed with resignation, he was at heart—and in his purse—not disposed to lay down so consequential an authority; nor, in the middle of a campaign, and with the political groundwork at home not fully prepared, were his enemies quite ready to cashier him. But his regard for the Junto, including Somers, was cooling. By the summer of 1710 he was beset with suspicions and mistrust.[102]

It is likely that the representations of his Duchess had much to do with this. Her final break with Anne had occurred in April; in her eclipse, she was more than ever consumed with strong resentments and prejudices. Her comment, written years later on the cover of Somers's letter of 6 June, is revealing. It was, she believed, sincere enough, in so far as it wished the Duke 'good success'.[103] Nonetheless, she was certain that the Lord President, concerned with his own political future, had betrayed him. He had 'made his court' both to Anne and to Abigail about the time of the dispute over Lord Essex's regiment; thereafter he had 'passed many hours' with the Queen 'without ever saying the least word to make her uneasy, but put the task upon the Duke of Marlborough and the Earl of Godolphin', in the expectation that 'he should be the chief and govern all things in a little time.' Personal pique looms large, despite the passage of years. Whatever the Lord President's relations with Abigail,

this I am sure of, that after he knew I had lost the Queen's favour, which I showed him myself in a month after he came into the Court, he left off visiting me, and after I was removed out of my employments he never came near my house, no more than if I had had the plague, tho' I had been a master for him and his friends, and we never had any quarrel or the least difference; but when he saw I could do him no more services he thought it righter to court those that had the power.[104]

Marlborough had suspicions of his own. 'I have had an information concerning Lord Somers,' he wrote Sarah, 'which I would trust nobody but yourself with, and that can't be till we meet. Be upon your guard as to what you say to him, and let nobody know that I have given you caution.'[105]

What the 'information' was is not revealed. But there were rumours that the Lord President was ready to come to terms, and he may have thought he had at least a reasonable chance of remaining afloat in the troubled political seas, provided he did not head into the wind. Six weeks after Sunderland's fall, and only a matter of days before the dismissal of Godolphin, he was seemingly unaware of the relentless current, in both court and country, that would carry the Tories into office with unprecedented force. ''Tis a strange uncertain state we are in,' he confided to Wharton, '& perhaps wee may have this good effect of the present irresolution, as not to be without hopes of a good Parliament in case they will put us upon a new election.' For, he added, 'there is no certainty what the complection of the new Parlt. will be ... since they are not Whigs only who will be affected by the Dissolution.'[106]

From other sources come intimations, at least, that he was prepared to negotiate with Harley,[107] who continued his efforts to undermine the solidarity of the Whigs. Others, too, were hoping and scheming. Wharton, we are told, had long been 'nibbling' with Mrs Masham; Orford looked for the Garter, through the influence of Shrewsbury; Newcastle, the Lord Privy Seal, was on friendly terms with Harley and Shrewsbury, and hoped this might insure his continuance in office.[108] As for Somers, not only does the Duchess of Marlborough accuse him of 'double-proceedings' with Godolphin, and repeat a story to the effect that an intimate of the Masham clique thought he might serve the Queen 'tho' the others were out', but Harley himself describes him as working against the Treasurer. On 5 August Harley wrote Newcastle that Somers was seeking help from him and Dartmouth, who had taken over Sunderland's duties, in gaining 'revenge' on Godolphin. The details of the project are not divulged; Harley regarded it as 'chimerical'.[109] From Speaker Onslow comes another report of this kind: Jekyll had told him of negotiations carried on with Harley by Somers, Halifax and Cowper, in response to assurances that they might count on keeping their places if they would consent to Harley's taking over Godolphin's post. Wharton's opposition had made this project abortive.[110]

Nothing from Somers's pen has come to light to confirm or deny these manoeuvres. But it is clear that he was not disposed to write off his political future. As recently as 24 June he had received another grant of £1000 from the secret service moneys, a fund set apart for special contingencies. Twice before, in April and October 1709, his salary as Lord President had been augmented by payments in the like amount[111] The June grant, coming after two blows at the Whig organisation, suggests that he was, at least, still a figure to be reckoned with, and possibly to be passed. Following hard upon the Queen's assurance, given to Somers himself, that she did not 'intend to make any further alteration', it must have served to shore up his confidence. But the *douceur*, as Feiling calls it, was not the only encouraging sign. He had made considerable progress in overcoming Anne's long-standing aversion. Their relationship, ostensibly at least, had mellowed. According to Swift, not given at this time to kind words for Somers, the Queen showed him, and to a less extent Cowper, 'as great a Personall Regard and Esteem as her Nature was capable of admitting'.[112] As we have seen, the Duchess of Marlborough bore witness to *tête-à-têtes* between the sovereign and the minister, while Dartmouth noted that 'she thought herself very much obliged to him, and that he was a man that had never deceived her'.[113]

But, while he enjoyed better relations with the Queen, his situation was precarious. As Addison concluded, he could only stand in the wings 'in expectation of proper opportunities'.[114] All might come right in the end; on the other hand, the ground swell of Toryism was mounting. And while Harley would encourage him (along with Cowper, Walpole and Boyle) to regard himself as a necessary cog in a broad-bottomed administration that he hoped to create, his design was essentially to divide and rule. For the moment his principal objective was the isolation and routing of Godolphin. He sought to detach the Lord President from that veteran. In this he had the support of the Queen; her new-found amiability towards Somers was, in the Duchess of Marlborough's opinion, merely play-acting to lull him into a sense of false security.[115]

On 8 August the Queen dropped the pilot. After eight years of service Godolphin was tersely commanded to break the White Staff. The Treasury was placed in the hands of a five-man commission. In addition, John Smith surrendered his post as Chancellor of the Exchequer to Harley. Once again the surviving members of the Junto stood by, showing no inclination to accompany the fallen ministers. Halifax went so far as to congratulate Harley as he took over the nation's finances.[116] Somers appears to have been, at best, neutral. Harley was not asking for a show-down. Once more he undertook to soothe the Whigs. In a letter to the Duke of Newcastle he assured him that the policy of the remodelled government would be 'directed to the sole aime of making an honorable and safe peace, securing her [the Queen's] allys, reserving [preserving?] the liberty and property of the subject in general, and the indulgence to dissenters in particular, and to perpetuate this by really securing the succession of the House of Hanover'.[117] And as late as 18 September Cowper could report that Harley, in urging him to remain in office, had assured him that a 'whig game' was intended at bottom.[118]

Meanwhile rumours and counter rumours were flying. Marlborough had heard that the Whigs would not quit even upon a dissolution.[119] Tories were grumbling. Why was the old Parliament still in being? Why had so few Whigs been ousted? Much as Harley was drawn towards moderation and compromise, the Tory tide was too strong. Rochester insisted that a ministry cutting across party lines was impracticable. Somers could now have had few illusions. On the day of Godolphin's dismissal, in a letter urging Newcastle to return to the capital, he complained that 'matters have grown worse and worse, and that sort of intercourse which your Grace's weight and credit gave some life to, has insensibly dwindled to nothing'. Godolphin's fall, he added, was 'as considerable a step as can well be made'.[120] In August, Swift looked momentarily for Somers's dismissal; the following month he noted that he expected 'every day to be out, and has done so these two months'.[121] Yet Harley, in mid-September, describing Somers as angry with colleagues (even Cowper) and inconsistent in his actions, attributed his conduct to his rage to be chief minister.[122] Somers used what influence he had to defer the dissolution of Parliament, but this was a fond hope. Harley, though uneasy at the prospect of a Tory landslide and its effects on his programme of moderation, could not stand in the way of an election. Early in September the first changes in the roster of Lords Lieutenant showed that it could not be far off.

Before the month was out the Junto had been routed. At a Council meeting on 21 September the Queen ordered Sir Simon Harcourt to present a proclamation for dissolving Parliament. Cowper attempted to remonstrate, on the grounds that it had sat but two years and that an untimely dissolution of a legislature that had energetically supported the war effort would have unfavourable military and diplomatic repercussions. But this was in vain. Anne would permit no debate. She then announced the appointment of her uncle, Rochester, as Lord President. Somers had already been notified of his dismissal. Unlike Sunderland and Godolphin, he did not depart alone: with him went Wharton, Orford, Devonshire and Boyle. Burnet might well complain that 'so sudden and so entire a change of the ministry is scarce to be found in our history'. Not since the Revolution has so clean a sweep been effected.[123]

NOTES

[1] Of any length, at least; see Turner, *Privy Council*, I, 6, 71 ff.

[2] Harl. MSS. 2263, f. 284; *Cal. Treas. Books*, 1708, XXII, pt. ii, 454.

[3] S.R., VII, 636.

[4] Two years later it had risen to sixty-two; in 1712 it reached a high, for Anne's reign, of eighty-two: Turner, *Privy Council*, II, 20.

[5] See J. H. Plumb, 'The organization of the Cabinet in the reign of Queen Anne', *Transactions*, Royal Hist. Soc., 5th ser., VII (1957), 137–57.

[6] For these instances from the summer and autumn of 1709, see P.C. 2/82, *passim*.

[7] 'The Junto', in *Tory Pills to Purge Whig Melancholy*, 22.

[8] Walcott, *English Politics*, 151–52.

[9] *Vernon Letters*, III, 366, 368; Tindal, XXIII, 153; Trevelyan, *Anne*, II, 416; Holmes, *British Politics*, 41.

[10] Richard Chandler, *History and Proceedings of the House of Commons* (London, 1742–1744), IV, 106; L.J., XVIII, 583.

[11] Lords MSS., Committee Minutes, *passim*; L.J., XVIII, 580 ff., especially pp. 600, 651.

[12] *Correspondence*, ed. Williams, 121.

[13] *Harl. Misc.*, XI, 66–76; *Parliamentary History*, VI, 764.

[14] By the verdict of 'not proven': see Trevelyan, *Anne*, II, 347–49; Lords MSS., 1708–10, iii–xv, 32–264.

[15] The former Lord Chancellor, Marchmont, was not of this view. In July he wrote to Somers: 'I have ever been of opinion that the laws and trials relating to treason were safer in England than in Scotland. I mean that innocent persons were more safe and the guilty as obnoxious": *Marchmont Papers*, III, 354.

[16] Burnet, V, 396; *Parliamentary History*, VI, 794–98; Lord Stanhope, *History of England Comprising the Reign of Queen Anne* (London, 1870), 376–77; Brown, *History of Scotland*, III, 142–45.

[17] L.J., XVIII, 717. It was introduced in the Lords by Sunderland, and took its place in the statute books as 7 Anne, c. 21.

[18] Burnet, V, 388–89; Trevelyan, *Anne*, II, 412–13.

[19] *Works*, ed. Scott, V, 101.

[20] Coxe, *Marlborough*, II, 379 (10 January 1709).

[21] So Trevelyan believed: *Anne*, II, 390–91.

[22] See below, p. 290.

[23] Coombs, 137; Coxe, *Marlborough*, II, 191.

[24] Add. MSS. 34, 518, f. 40v (30 November 1708).

[25] Coxe, *Marlborough*, II, 384 (4 February 1709).

[26] Daniel Defoe, in his *Conduct of Parties in England* (1712), maintained that the Junto undermined Marlborough, that Godolphin was timid, and that the Tories took advantage of this to overthrow the ministry.

[27] Burnet, V, 381.

[28] Add. MSS. 34, 518, f. 40 (30 November 1708).

[29] Coombs, 189.

[30] Roderick Geikie and Isabel A. Montgomery, *The Dutch Barrier, 1705–19* (Cambridge, 1930), 100–1.

[31] *Ibid.*, 101–2; Coombs, 190.

[32] Tindal, XXIII, 193; *Parliamentary History*, VI, 788; L.J., XVIII, 651.

[33] Bert Van 'T Hoff, ed., *Correspondence, 1701–1711, of John Churchill . . . and Anthonie Heinsius* (The Hague, 1951), 429–31.

[34] Late in May, however, Marlborough wrote to Godolphin that proceedings were so far along that it appeared unnecessary to send another plenipotentiary: Churchill, *Marlborough*, VI, 78, citing Blenheim MSS.

[35] Churchill suggests this: *Marlborough*, VI, 65.

[36] Geikie, 121–22, citing letter from Halifax to Marlborough, 24 April 1709, Blenheim MSS., and L'Hermitage's and Hoffman's dispatches.

[37] Burnet, V, 404; *Wentworth Papers*, 154.

[38] Cowper, in his *Diary*, 44 (12 April 1709), notes that the Lords of the Council 'did ever seem confident'.

[39] *Corr. Duch. Marl.*, I, 173–74.

[40] Coxe, *Marlborough*, 412, 414–15. Marlborough allowed that Townshend was 'a very good fellow', but he was 'a Whig party man': Churchill, *Marlborough*, VI, 70, citing Marquis de Torcy *Memoires* (ed. Michaud and Poujoulat, 1850), 606.

[41] Hardwicke, *State Papers*, II, 480–81 (30 September 1709).

[42] Blenheim MSS., B. I, 23.

[43] Coombs, 210.

[44] Portland MSS., II, 209 (29 October 1709).

[45] See H. T. Dickinson, 'The poor Palatines and the parties', *Eng. Hist. Rev.*, LXXXII (July 1967), 464–85; Burnet, V, 398–99.

[46] Hist. MSS. Comm., *Seventh Rept.*, appendix, Verney MSS., 507. See also *Memoirs*, 113–14.

[47] Holmes, *British Politics*, 69, 105–6. Joseph Trapp spoke of the Whigs 'bringing over so many thousand beggarly Palatines, in order to starve the same number of Britons': *The Character and Principles of the Present Set of Whigs* (London, 1711), 16.

[48] Leadam, *History*, 141, citing P.R.O., Treasury Papers, Anne, 1709, vol. CXIX. Dickinson, 'Poor Palatines', 468, notes that probably as many as 13,000 came in the summer of 1709.

[49] See *Cal. Treas. Books, 1709*, XXII, pt. ii, *passim*; Daniel Defoe, *Brief History of the Poor Palatines* (Augustan Reprint Soc., 1964), 35.

[50] Somers MSS., various letters between 19 June 1709 and 21 October 1709. See also B.M. Portland Loan 29/238, Somers to Duke of Newcastle, 18 August 1709.

[51] *Corr. Duch. Marl.*, I, 175 (4 June 1709).

[52] *Ibid.*, I, 241–42. But see *ibid.*, I, 233, for Somers's protestation, on the eve of Orford's appointment, that he would continue 'as far as he could', to support Godolphin and Marlborough, 'because he was convinced that if they were ever removed from the Queen, worse men in every respect would have all the power, who would bring in the Prince of Wales and popery'.

[53] Hardwicke, *State Papers*, II, 479 (8 August 1709); see also *Corr. Duch. Marl.* I, 194–95, 197.

[54] Ibid., I, 196, 241–42; Coxe, *Marlborough*, II, 483–84.

[55] Even Halifax secured some recognition as Keeper of Bushey Park and Hampton Court, in June 1709. But he was evidently disgruntled; according to Maynwaring, writing late in 1709, he was 'highly dissatisfied with Somers': *Corr. Duch. Marl*, II, 264 (Maynwaring to the Duchess).

[56] Leadam, *History*, 162. The first volume was published in May 1709.

[57] Coxe, *Marlborough*, II, 484.

[58] On the part played by Somers and Cowper in opposing Marlborough's first attempt to obtain life tenure as Captain-General, see H. L. Snyder, 'The Duke of Marlborough's request of his Captain-Generalcy for life: a reexamination', *Journal of the Society of Army Historical Research*, XLV (1967), 67–83.

[59] Coxe, *Marlborough*, III, 7. It was also a blow at his patronage, under which, from 1704 to 1710, 'Whig officers had carried off the bulk of the most coveted prizes in the army': Holmes, *British Politics*, 27.

[60] Blenheim MSS. B. I, 22b (26 July 1709), in Lever, 216–17.

[61] Coxe, *Marlborough*, III, 7–8.

[62] According to Lord Coningsby, Somers was involved in a proposal of Harley's that the regiment should be given to Sir Richard Temple, an intimate of the Junto: 'Political parties during the reign of Queen Anne', *Archaeologia*, XXXVIII (1860), 11. But this is not substantiated elsewhere.

[63] Coxe, *Marlborough*, III, 10.

[64] Ibid., III, 11; Geoffrey Holmes, *The Trial of Doctor Sacheverell* (London, 1973), 115–16.

[65] *Archaeologia*, XXXVIII, 10.

[66] Trevelyan, *Anne*, III, 43; Feiling, 416.

[67] Coxe, *Marlborough*, III, 13.

[68] Ibid., III, 16.

[69] *Archaeologia*, XXXVIII, 9–10. Trevelyan, *Anne*, III, 346, n. 39, discounts this.

[70] *Hearn's Collections*, II, 320. On Sacheverell, see Holmes, *Sacheverell*.

[71] Burnet, V, 422. Sacheverell's assertions provoked many rejoinders, including *Vox Populi, Vox Dei* (London, 1709), in 1710 re-entitled *The Judgment of Whole Kingdoms and Nations*, which went through many editions. This has been attributed to Somers, Defoe and others; see Morgan, *Bibliography*, No. L, 105; Robbins, *Commonwealthsman*, 79; British Museum *Catalogue*; D.N.B., John Somers. In my opinion evidence of Somers's authorship is lacking. The description of the author, on the title page, does not fit him. John R. Moore does not include it in his check-list of Defoe's writings.

[72] Burnet, V, 422n; Lever, 228; Holmes, *Sacheverell*, 84. Plumb refers to rumours that Wharton urged Godolphin on 'in the hope that he might disgrace himself': Walpole, I, 147.

[73] Trevelyan, *Anne*, III, 49, citing her letter to Mallet, 24 September 1744, in Althorp MSS. Cf. Somers's comment that 'by addresses and counter-addresses [to the crown] there seems to be a kind of listing of men for and against' the Pretender: Blenheim MSS. B, II, 5, Somers to Marlborough, 14 [April] 1710; Speck, *Tory and Whig*, 30.

[74] Cunningham, II, 277–78. According to Swift, Somers was opposed to 'engaging in that foolish prosecution as what he foresaw was likely to end in their [the Whig ministry's] ruin': *Works*, ed. Scott, IX, 143.

[75] *Prose Works of Jonathan Swift*, ed. Herbert Davis and Irvin Ehrenpreis (Oxford, 1939–68), VIII: *Political Tracts, 1713–1719*, 115.

[76] *Ailesbury Memoirs*, II, 620.

[77] He is said to have been absent towards the end of the trial because of the death of his mother: *Corr. Duch. Marl.*, II, 152.

[78] L.J. XIX, 21; also 86, 103, for other committee assignments.

[79] Tindal, XXIII, 333; Burnet, V, 426. See also L.J., XIX, 32ff; *Parliamentary History*, VI, 831–36; Boyer, *Anne*, 410–11.

[80] Holmes, *Sacheverell*, 98–99.

[81] *State Trials*, XV, 38.

[82] Tindal, XXIII, 354.

[83] Cunningham, II, 297.

[84] *Wentworth Papers*, 115.

[85] L.J., XIX, 107, 110–11.

[86] Tindal, XXIII, 362.

[87] L.J., XIX, 115–16. The four other Junto lords helped to swell the majority: Tindal, XXIII, 358n. Somers, because of illness, was not present the following day, when a proposal to bar Sacheverell from preferment during his suspension was defeated by one vote. See Holmes, *Sacheverell*, 229, 283–85.

[88] *An Essay toward the History of the Late Ministry and Parliament* (London, 1710), 17. Swift's *Works*, ed. Scott, V, 438.

[89] Somerville, *Anne*, 262; Coxe, *Marlborough*, III, 64n, 65.

[90] *Ibid.*, III, 66.

[91] *Ibid.*, III, 68.

[92] Leadam, *History*, 171; Coxe, *Marlborough*, III, 79.

[93] Plumb, *Walpole*, I, 156; and see Coombs, 222. On Vryberg's memorial, to deter Anne from dismissing her Whig ministers, see Holmes, *British Politics*, 70. It was presented 30 June 1710.

[94] Coxe, *Marlborough*, III, 84–85.

[95] *Ibid.*, III, 88, citing letter from Godolphin to Marlborough, 24 June 1710.

[96] Swift noted that when Sunderland was dismissed the Junto hoped that the other ministers would be retained, and had the 'insolence' to convey this sentiment to foreign ambassadors: *Examiner*, No. 25, 18 January 1711.

[97] Somers MSS., Portland to Somers, 11 March 1710.

[98] See Hardwicke MSS., XXXIII, f. 231 (note in Hardwicke's hand). On 19 August 1710 Somers wrote Newcastle: 'We are utterly undone and must not think of a peace with France but upon terms France will give': *Portland MSS.*, II, 217.

[99] Campbell, V, 173–74.

[100] Coombs, 222.

[101] *Conduct of the Duchess*, 258–59.

[102] In general, over the years, Marlborough had held Somers in greater esteem than the other veterans of the Junto, and Somers, while he came to regard the perquisites and honors of the Churchill family as excessive, had as a rule supported the Duke. See Coxe, *Marlborough*, III, 111; cf. Lord Coningsby's comment, *Archaeologia*, XXXVIII, 7.

[103] The Duchess adds: 'I cannot doubt but he would have joyned with Abigail to put him out when that service was completed, as he did contribute to bring her into full glory': Trevelyan, *Anne*, III, 327.

[104] Hist. MSS. Comm., *Eighth Rep.*, appendix, Marlborough MSS., 38b–39a. 'Master' may be a misreading for 'martyr'. For the Duke of Manchester's suggestion that Somers was as little a favourite with the Duchess as with the Queen, see *Court and Society*, ed. Montagu, II, 377.

[105] Coxe, *Marlborough*, III, 93.

[106] *European Magazine*, XXIII (1793), 5.

[107] Perhaps by early June: B.M. Portland Loan 29/156, Somers to Harley, 6 June [1710?].

[108] Coxe, *Marlborough*, III, 108; Plumb, *Walpole*, I, 158. Halifax had at last obtained appointment as joint plenipotentiary to The Hague, from which he had hitherto been excluded by Marlborough. Newcastle retained the Privy Seal until 1711.

[109] *Portland MSS.*, II, 213 (5 August 1710); Hist. MSS. Comm., *Eighth Rept.*, appendix, pt. i, 38b–39a.

[110] Burnet, VI, 11–12n.

[111] On the nature of 'secret services', see J. Y. Ackerman, *Moneys Received and Paid for Secret Services of Charles II and James II*, Camden Soc., LII (1851), v. Henry M. Imbert-Terry, in *A Constitutional King: George I* (London, 1927), 93, claims that Somers agreed to the dismissal of Godolphin for a £3,000 bribe. Leadam, *History*, 171, says that Somers was 'tranquillised' by the June grant. See also *ibid.*, 160n; Trevelyan, *Anne*, III, 40; Feiling, 407, 418.

[112] *An Enquiry into the Behaviour of the Queen's Last Ministry*, ed. Irvin Ehrenpreis (Indiana University Pub., Humanities Series, No. 36, 1956), 23.

[113] *Court and Society*, ed. Montagu, II, 376; *Corr. Duch. Marl.*, I, 226.

[114] *Letters*, ed. Graham, 233.

[115] The Duchess had written Somers off by June: *Corr. Duch. Marl.*, I, 226, 342.

[116] *Portland MSS.*, IV, 560.

[117] *Ibid.*, II, 213

[118] *Diary*, 18 September 1710.

[119] *Corr., Duch. Marl.*, I, 375.

[120] *Portland MSS.*, II, 213–14.

121 *Addison Letters*, ed. Graham, 465; *Swift Works*, ed. Scott, II, 8. But Halifax, as late as 16 September, was not sure that Somers would shortly be dismissed: *Portland MSS.*, II, 220.

122 *Ibid.*, II, 218–19, Harley to Newcastle, 12 September 1710.

123 Burnet, VI, 10–11, where the date is wrongly given as October. Somers, Devonshire and Boyle were dismissed on 20 September; Wharton and Cowper resigned on the 22nd; see Clayton Roberts, *Growth of Responsible Government in Stuart England* (Cambridge, 1966), 352. *Cal. Treas. Books*, 1710, XXIV, pt. ii, 480, shows salary payment to Somers to 20 September; see also Swift, *Works*, ed. Scott, II, 12; Luttrell, *Relation*, VI, 632.

XV
Recessional, 1710-16

Once more Somers was without office. For nearly four years his lot would again be cast with the opposition. His personal fortunes had come full circle, back a decade to the opening years of the century. In some ways the reversal would be less drastic; this time there would be no impeachment, though men might talk of it. His credit with the Queen stood higher than had been the case when William died.[1] But in other respects his liabilities were greater. Politically he was more isolated. In the early years of the reign the issue of the war had provided something of a common denominator, high as the Tories might fly. Now they drove on to wind up the proceedings, regardless of past commitments. They were unrestrained by considerations for their Dutch allies. 'No peace without Spain', which Somers continued to uphold as all-important, was anathema to them. A clear-cut parliamentary ascendancy lay ahead. They would see no need to compromise. Men like St John and Harcourt would prove to be much more difficult to deal with than Godolphin, and it was small comfort that the more tractable element was represented by Harley.

Even more serious was the physical wear and tear of the passing years. Somers was now approaching sixty. This was a weighty burden of years in Stuart times, especially for one who seems never to have been robust. Periodic absences from bench or Lords attest to the ravages of various ailments—bouts of fever, colds, rheumatism, jaundice, kidney stones, gout. In 1710 he could still rally from the sickbed. But he might be on the sidelines for several weeks, and he was obviously less effective than of old. Indeed, time was rapidly running out. Though he would live until 1716, his activities during his last four years would be progressively curtailed by physical and mental deterioration.

Unlike some inveterate bachelors, Somers did not take a wife in his declining years. He continued to maintain his establishment at Brookmans, ministered to by Margaret Cocks, his niece, as well as Mrs Blount.[2] One sister, Lady Jekyll, was close at hand, with a residence in Lincoln's Inn Fields. His other sister, Mary, and his mother lived in Worcestershire, the one in the cathedral city, the other at Severn Stoke.[3] The Jekylls were childless, but the Cockses had four children, two boys and two girls, now growing to maturity. At least three of them were to make advantageous matches. Margaret Cocks first married into the Lygon family; then, in 1719, she was wed to Philip Yorke, later first Earl of Hardwicke and Lord Chancellor of England. Her sister Mary became Lady Williams. James Cocks, for so many years M.P. for Reigate, linked himself with two aristocratic families by marrying daughters of the Earl of Bradford and of William Lord Berkeley.[4]

Thus, though Somer's celibacy brought an end to the direct line and blocked the advantages which a good match might have provided, the family as a whole moved to a socially and economically higher plane.

Catherine Somers did not live to see her son's dismissal as Lord President. She died in March 1710, in her eighty-sixth year, and was buried by her husband's side in Severn Stoke church. Here Somers erected a marble tablet to his parents' memory, with an inscription of his own composition.[5] Of the relations between mother and son we know little. The few surviving fragments of correspondence give glimpses of a country-woman seemingly untouched by her son's success. We see her on occasion sending him a lamphrey pie or flitches of bacon, complaining of her financial condition or offering hard-headed advice on the value of land in which he was interested.[6] The old lady's will apart from a variety of bequests to her daughters, their husbands and children, and the poor, left the remainder of her property, real and personal, to her son, who was named executor.[7] In this way, nearly thirty years after his father's death, Somers came into the Worcestershire and other family holdings. That he sought to improve upon them is revealed in a letter to Charles Cocks, dated a week after the probate of the will, indicating his intention to buy land at Clifton.[8]

But he showed no inclination to exchange the adventures of politics for the pursuits of a landlord. He was not yet ready to retire. He was still dean of the Whigs, though younger men—particularly Robert Walpole—were gaining stature. The more amiable attitude of the court had netted him nothing, but there might be a further thaw.[9] And perhaps the electorate would not prove to be as Tory-minded as prognosticated. The Junto must put its shoulder to the wheel. In July he had reminded Wharton that its fortunes depended in the main upon his generalship. In August he wrote in like vein to Newcastle, stressing the interrelationship of election returns and a satisfactory peace settlement; a month later he was soliciting his support for General Stanhope, as a candidate for Westminster.[10]

Though as late as September Sunderland could write that 'by all the accounts from the counties there is like to be a good election', such hopes were ill-founded.[11] Parliament was dissolved at the end of the month, and the electoral contests were held at once. When the returns were in it was found that the new Commons would be a very different body; controlling about 350 seats, Tories outnumbered Whigs almost two to one.[12] Even such influential Whig politicos as Wharton and Somerset saw their candidates go down to defeat, though Whig magnates had some success in northern England. As for veteran 'Somers men', only two, Jekyll and Wylde, would have seats, although Rudge again represented Evesham, and a Dowdeswell (not Richard, but his son, William) got a Tewkesbury seat in a by-election in 1712.[13]

With such results there could be no doubt that for the immediate future Somers must make the most of his seat in the Lords. According to the Duchess of Marlborough he 'came often to wait on the Queen at Kensington, after his party was destroyed'; from this she was convinced that he was still hopeful, 'by some accident or other', of winning her favour. But if this be true, he was to be disappointed.[14] Although not removed from the Council, he appears to have discontinued attendance until August 1714, when the Queen lay upon her deathbed.[15] In the Lords the Whigs, along with a moderate element, could still impede the progress of Commons' measures that lacked full ministerial support, but they were at times hard pressed. Regular attendance was essential. During the first two-thirds of the session Somers was usually present, but after mid-March he was absent half the time.[16]

His activities were centred almost exclusively on the conduct of the war in Spain; he was to sign no fewer than five protests involving its ramifications—testimony to the diminished influence of his party, for not since 1704 had he found it necessary to resort to this device. His almost proprietary interest in the war, as the Junto wished to conduct it, now perhaps depended less on reason than on ingrained prejudice. According to Oxford he was unable to present a rational defence of the war, contenting himself with saying that he had been 'bred up in a hatred of France'.[17] But his activity at the beginning of 1711 did not hinge primarily on the pros and cons of the war as such, but on the attack launched by the Tories against the late ministry's methods in conducting that conflict. The Queen had referred, in her speech from the throne, to its prosecution, 'with the utmost vigour in all its Parts, particularly in Spain', as the likeliest road to 'a safe and honourable peace'.[18] Campaigns in Spain had obviously gone badly. Here was an opportunity for revenge on the part of those who, either from partisan zeal or personal grudges, were ready to stand up and be counted in an indictment of Marlborough, the Junto and its political associates, and the Whig generals, Galway and Stanhope.

When Parliament reconvened after the Christmas holidays the peers learned, through a message from the Queen, of Stanhope's defeat at Brihuega, involving the capture of some 4,000 British troops. The fat was now in the fire. On 4 January the Duke of Beaufort moved for an investigation.[19] Peterborough, whom Marlborough and the Junto had recalled in 1706, and Argyle, ever hostile to the Duke, led the attack. Stanhope, a prisoner of war, could not be present to defend himself; but the battle-scarred Galway was arraigned before their lordships. On 11 January they formally declared that the strategy insisted upon by Galway and his second-in-command, Baron Tyrawley, had been 'the unhappy occasion of the battle of Almanza, and a great cause of our misfortune in Spain'. The two generals petitioned that they should be heard further in their defence, but the Lords were opposed, 57 to 46.[20]

Somers entered the lists, arguing that a man had a right to defend himself before being censured. Upon the adverse vote he was one of the thirty-six peers to sign a protest; it was, they insisted, 'the rule of natural justice, that every one should have an opportunity of answering for themselves, at least upon their humble petitions, before what we take to be a public censure should pass upon them'.[21] On the same day he was among those who protested against the censure itself, as based on insufficient proofs, and likely to limit the effectiveness of commanders in the future. The late ministers' turn came next; Sunderland in particular was subjected to denunciation, since as Secretary of State he had ordered a vigorous offensive. On the 12th the Lords carried a resolution blaming the ministers for having contributed 'to all our misfortunes in Spain, and to the disappointment of the expedition against Toulon'. Somers, of course, opposed it, and joined with those who protested that they saw no reason to change their opinion that 'an offensive war was then fittest for those in her Majesty's service to advise'.[22]

It was a difficult week for the Junto lords. They were ineffective in stemming the tide, and could only sling together in registering their opposition.[23] But their troubles were not over. Early in February the Tories returned to the charge, framing no less than nine resolutions regarding deficiencies in the military contingents approved by Parliament for the Spanish theatre. Two of these, the eighth and ninth, constituted censures of the late ministry. The former referred to two regiments, 'twice demanded, and provided for by Parliament', but not supplied; while the latter affirmed, in a sweeping indictment, that the ministers, in not supplying the full quota as approved by Parliament, had 'greatly neglected that service, which was of the greatest importance'. Once more Somers and the rest of the Junto joined the protesting peers. Their rejoinder to the eighth resolution was largely a matter of bookkeeping. In the final protest the adherents of the pilloried ministry maintained that the evidence did not justify a censure, and defended its conduct in supplying funds and troops. In conclusion they submitted that

the Ministers cannot be justly charged with having neglected the war in Spain, when by the treaties concluded with the allies there was a great army agreed to be furnished for the service, and the execution of these treaties was pressed from time to time in the most earnest manner, and the part of Great Britain was so amply supplied, as enabled Her Majesty's generals to march twice to Madrid, and be in full possession of the capital city of Spain.[24]

The Lords took exception to these particulars, ordering them to be expunged, despite opposition from the embattled minority. According to Luttrell, Somers was among those who spoke against the abridgement of the protestation. But 'the Scotch lords, being all of a side, over-balanced the rest', and he had to content himself with signing three protests.[25] Meanwhile he had been named to a committee to draw up an address on the Spanish war to the Queen, but its contents were so unacceptable to him that on 8 February he supported two more protests.[26] His parliamentary influence was in almost total eclipse.[27]

Though here and there men talked of impeachment, the fallen ministers were chiefly bedevilled with attacks in the press. In saluting the new Lord President, Jonathan Swift took pains to castigate his predecessor. Rochester's best friends, he jibed, had to admit that he 'is neither deist nor socinian; he has never conversed with Toland, to open and enlarge his thoughts, and dispel the prejudices of education; nor was he ever able to arrive at that perfection of gallantry, to ruin and imprison the husband, in order to keep the wife without disturbance'.[28] Despite Swift's venom this was old stuff, and a far cry from the articles of 1701. But among the Tories there was a corps of violent partisans, who consorted in the October Club. Altogether they numbered around 150 Members of Parliament. According to Swift, they were determined to 'drive things on to extremes against the Whigs, to call the old ministry to account, and to get off five or six heads'.[29] Harley's moderation was not proof against the importunities of this group. By January Walpole, who showed no signs that he could be won from the Whigs, was dismissed from his treasurership of the navy. A fortnight later an investigation of public accounts was launched, in an attempt to reveal malversation. But the inquisitors were unable to sustain their claim that, of some £35,000,000 granted by Parliament, a large part remained unaccounted for.

They were forced to fall back on another device, more limited in scope, but with which they were more familiar. A hue and cry was again raised with regard to the grants made by the late King. This, as Burnet noted, was the method that had succeeded before, in connection with Ireland. The bringing in a bill to resume William's grants 'was looked on, as a sure step, for carrying the resumption of all the grants that they had a mind to make void'.[30] It was introduced in the Commons at the end of March. Ostensibly it was to serve as a means to raise money for the war, and pious professions were made to this effect. But some regarded it as a Tory design to blacken the memory of King William, while Somers's earliest biographer supposed it to have been directed as much against the ex-President as anyone. In the end it came to nothing; though passed by the Commons, the Lords, with Somers's help, threw it out on 3 May.[31]

In the course of the year there were short-lived flurries of hope among the Whigs. The death of the Earl of Rochester in May weakened the intransigent Tories and strengthened the position of the moderate Harley, who now became Earl of Oxford.[32] His popularity had already benefited from a wound at the hands of a would-be assassin. Might he not seek to placate the opposition at this juncture?[33] Maynwaring threw cold water on the idea. Harley, so he advised the Duchess of Marlborough, had no more intention of dealing with Junto Whigs than with High Tories like Nottingham: 'although Lord Halifax, Lord Somers, and Lord Sunderland had endeavoured to be well with him, he certainly fooled them who were the last men in the nation that he would have anything to do with'.[34] By the end of the month Swift could report the dashing of Whig hopes: 'You hear no more of Addison, Steele, Henley, Lady Lucy, Mrs. Finch, Lord Somers, Lord Halifax, &c.'[35] The presidency went to Buckingham in June. The following month a fall from a horse proved fatal to the Duke of Newcastle, Lord Privy Seal, the sole survivor of Whiggish days. Somers was regarded as a possible successor. He had strong backing from the Duke and

Duchess of Somerset, now enjoying considerable influence at court, and his admission to the ministry could be expected to insure the support of Godolphin and Marlborough, as well as the Whig contingent.[36] But if Somers saw opportunity within his grasp, he was to be disappointed. The Earl of Jersey was designated for the post, and when death intervened before he could take office, John Robinson, Bishop of Bristol, was appointed.

Parliament continued to sit until mid-June, the Commons being engaged for the most part in seeking out evidence of misconduct on Godolphin's part. In its last weeks Somers was apparently inactive. The new session did not convene until December, although the date had been fixed for 13 November. The great issue was the peace. The Tory ministers had in October worked out the preliminaries with France; the next step was to secure acceptance, both from Parliament and from the Allies, of this basis for a formal treaty. It proved to be no mean undertaking. The Dutch, indignant at being deprived of commercial advantages earlier assured them, dug in their heels and concerted measures with the Austrians and the Whigs.[37] The Whigs were still a power to be reckoned with in the upper house. But whether they would prove as adamant as ever on the question of war aims remained to be seen. The death of the Emperor without issue, the previous spring, had brought the Austrian inheritance to the Archduke Charles. In October he obtained the imperial crown. The possibility of a vastly extended Bourbon influence, on which the war-hawks had constantly harped, was now offset by visions of an all-embracing Hapsburg sway, unprecedented since the time of Charles V. These implications and their bearing on Junto strategy did not escape Somers.[38]

The government proceeded cautiously. Late in November Swift had looked for another prorogation.[39] As the Members prepared to reassemble, the atmosphere was feverish. Tories were ready to believe that Somers, as well as Somerset, Wharton and other Whigs, had been involved in a project to raise the mob against the government on 17 November (the anniversary of Elizabeth's accession), by taking advantage of anti-Catholic processions and gatherings long associated with that holiday.[40] From the press poured a torrent of opinion, for and against the peace. Late in October Swift wrote: 'The Whig party are furious against a peace, and every day some ballad comes out reflecting on the ministry on that account.'[41] There were, of course, more substantial productions, and none as trenchant as Swift's own *Conduct of the Allies*, which appeared on the eve of the new session, and sold 11,000 copies in a month. It was a masterful, and of course thoroughly biased, justification of the current peace project: Oxford's brother was assured that it would 'put the country gentlemen in the temper you desire'.[42] Swift was not so sure, and in the following month came close to abandoning all hope of success. For the Tories were by no means united, either in the ministry or the Commons. The antagonism between Oxford and St John was sharpening, as the former continued to follow a comparatively moderate course: he would not, for example, go along with a general purge of Whigs from all offices, for which the High Tories were clamouring.

The situation presented the best opportunity for Whig fortunes since the debacle of 1710. Both Somers and Halifax continued to hope that they might make a deal with Oxford. For some time they had believed that he could be separated from St John. Might he not be induced to break with the October Club and then, with the help of the Duchess of Somerset, prevail upon the Queen to call another election and revive coalition government? They went so far as to discuss these tactics with the Hanoverian agents, as the best way to guarantee the Protestant succession. But the plan was put aside on the grounds that public opinion was still too strongly anti-Whig to yield the desired results at the polls.[43]

Shortly before Parliament convened, the Whig leaders approached Oxford on another tack. The Tories were clamouring for an Occasional Conformity Bill.[44] The Whigs would undertake to help him pass it in the upper House, where its chances of success were regarded as unlikely, if in return he would reconstitute the ministry and revise the Preliminaries. But Oxford could not be won over; he stood firmly behind his government's peace policy.[45] Frustrated on this front, the Whigs fell back on Nottingham, out of office since 1704 and reported to be 'as sour and fiercely wild as you can imagine anything to be that has lived long in the desert'.[46] If he would take the lead in pledging the Lords against a peace without Spain, the Whigs would support his restrictive religious measure. Swift voiced fears which were shared by the ministry:

The Whig lords are doing their utmost for a majority against Friday, and design, if they can, to address the Queen against the peace. Lord Nottingham . . . is gone over to the Whig side: they toast hm daily, and Lord Wharton says, It is Dismal (so they call him for his looks) will save England at last.[47]

At this point Anne's services were recruited. She had interviews with Somers, as well as Marlborough, Grafton, Cowper and other Whig notables, in an attempt to gain their support for the peace policy.[48] But her efforts were fruitless.

On 9 December, in her speech from the throne, Anne informed the legislators that, 'notwithstanding the Arts of those who delight in War', and with the concurrence of the allies, arrangements had been made for a general peace settlement.[49] In the Lords the customary address of thanks was moved, but it was no sooner endorsed by a knot of Tory peers than Nottingham was on his feet with his anticipated amendment. No peace, he contended, could be 'safe and honorable', either to Britain or Europe, if any branch of the House of Bourbon should be allowed to hold sway over Spain and the West Indies. Though the debate lasted for several hours, and virtually every peer of note participated, Somers appears to have remained silent. Did he deem it advisable to let Wharton, Cowper, Halifax and Sunderland speak for him, as one whose responsibility for 'No Peace without Spain' would tend to place his remarks at a discount? Probably not: the others were tarred with much the same brush. The answer probably lies in physical disability, for he did not attend again until January. But he was certainly present, contributing to the majority of six by which Notting-ham's amendment was inserted in the address.[50]

Though the Commons rejected a similar provision by an overwhelming majority, the Tories were disturbed by the failure of their administration to muster the necessary support in the Lords. The coffee-houses continued to buzz with rumours of ministerial changes. Oxford's secretary anticipated retirement in Wales; Dartmouth spoke of resignation. The Whigs began to smack their lips. Dissolution seemed imminent. Swift was beset by anxiety and mistrust:

The Whigs are all in triumph; they foretold how all this would be, but we thought it boasting. Nay, they said the Parliament should be dissolved before Christmas and perhaps it may.

He inveighed against the influence of the Duchess of Somerset, Anne's trusted friend, whose husband, though a Whig, continued to serve as Master of the Horse. Both were allies of Somers. Obviously the Duchess should be removed from the court, but the cure might be worse than the disease: some even thought that the Queen, rather than dismiss the Duchess, would dissolve Parliament and 'get a Whiggish one', by managing elections.[51]

With the government off balance, the Whigs made the most of their opportunity. They paid their debt to Nottingham. At long last occasional conformity was outlawed in a measure which moved through the Lords with unwonted speed. Somers had no part in these proceedings; it was Wharton who led the Whigs.[52] But he was undoubtedly involved in the preliminaries. Christmas was now approaching, and on 22 December the Commons adjourned until 14 January. The Whiggish lords, seeking to drive all before them, wanted no such interim, and resolved to return twelve days earlier.[53]

But it was all for nought. The Queen, despite Swift's fears, was not 'false'. She was as committed to the peace project as ever. In two sharp blows she first undermined and then utterly destroyed the budding Whig revival. Before the Lords returned Marlborough was cashiered and twelve peerages were created to reinforce the Tory phalanx. Somers, with the rest of the Whigs, was powerless against this exercise of the prerogative, though even Bolingbroke was later to write, with reference to the wholesale creation, that it was 'unprecedented and invidious, to be excused by nothing but necessity and hardly by that'.[54]

The new balance of power was discernible at once. On 2 January, the day appointed by the Lords for the resumption of business, Anne sent them a message commanding their adjournment until the reassembling of the lower House. To this Somers strongly objected, as unprecedented: 'in all his reading he cou'd never find that any such command ever came singly to either house from the Crown'. He urged the Lords to appoint a committee to search their records. Should no example be found he believed 'her majesty wou'd thank them for doing their duty to her and themselves in endeavour-ing to be rightly inform'd, and did not doubt but they wou'd find her majesty wou'd readily recall her command'. But even as he was speaking, Lord Rivers was going about 'from one t'other of the Court sides', lining up the vote against further debate of the issue, and the Queen's command was carried by a majority of thirteen.[55] The only comfort for the Whigs came when Wharton asked one of the fledgling peers if they would vote by their foreman.

Somers could now, at best, do no more than fight a rear-guard action against the peace manoeuvres. But his name was still prominently associated with the old war aims. In February it was linked with rumours that Prince Eugene (then visiting England) and Marlborough had concocted a plot to seize the Queen, force a dissolution of Parliament, and call a new one, which would inquire into the 'clandestine correspondence with France'. Besides Somers, Cowper and Halifax were supposed to have been consulted, but, after some hesitation, to have refused to become embroiled in the project. Actually there was no such plot, but Oxford's government, seeking to discredit the war-minded generals, is said to have given the tale some encouragement, and (however out of character) it was widely believed to be true: Swift, for one, refers to it.[56] Prince Eugene himself describes Somers as considering less violent, but still drastic methods, of blocking the peace: along with Halifax and Cowper he was for 'winning over the Treasurer to their interest and reducing all things again into a right channel, or in case of necessity to invite over the Duke of Hanover to dissolve the new ministry'.[57] The Prince may have assumed that a man who had supported the intervention of William of Orange might be expected to resort to such a *coup d'état*. But Anne's regime was a far cry from that of James II, and it is inconceivable that Somers would have countenanced an attack of this sort on her authority.

In any case, he was becoming increasingly incapable of attending to business of any kind, much less such conspiratorial designs. His health was clearly failing. Beginning in mid-February he was absent for two months, as he was again in June, during the last weeks of the session. About this time he was incapacitated by a severe paralytic stroke. His mental and physical powers were permanently impaired. In July a Jacobite referred cryptically to 'poor Sanders who cannot live long, and is already dead in effect'.[58] There would be ups and downs; he would live for several years, but he was at best a shrunken figure, a shadow of his former self.

Meanwhile news of the terms presented by the French at Utrecht, calling for the restoration of a long list of fortresses and allocating the Spanish Netherlands to the Elector of Bavaria, gave leverage to those opposed to the negotiations. Had Somers been attending the Lords at this time he would certainly have ranged himself on the side of those who, like Halifax, branded them as 'trifling, arrogant, and injurious to her Majesty and her allies'.[59] As it was, Halifax's motion against them passed; on this occasion, as Swift pointed out, the upper House was 'too strong in Whigs, notwithstanding the new Creations'.[60] The administration now decided to let negotiations in Holland sleep, while St John and Torcy addressed themselves, in secrecy, to the concerns of the allies. In May St John called upon Ormonde (who had succeeded Marlborough late in 1711 as commander-in-chief) to 'avoid engaging in any siege, or hazarding a battle, till you have farther orders from her Majesty'.[61] This step was taken without the knowledge of the rest of the cabinet, but it was impossible to conceal it for long, and on 28 May both Houses engaged in debate on the so-called 'restraining orders'. Once more Halifax led the opposition in the Lords, supported by Wharton, Cowper and Marlborough. But this time the government, after Oxford had assured the House that necessary siege operations were not to be prescribed and that a separate peace with France was not projected, prevailed by 68 votes against 40.[62] Somers was able to join in the protest, signed by twenty-seven peers, including all the Junto lords save Sunderland. The purport of this statement, which was so vigorously expressed as to provoke its erasure from the record, is most succinctly set forth in the second article. Here the restraining policy is stigmatised as

derogatory to her Majesty's honour, to public faith, and that justice which was due to her Majesty's allies; and that it was a sort of imposing upon our allies a cessation of arms, without their consent, and in the most prejudicial manner, because they were not so much as acquainted with it, and so might have been led into great difficulties; besides that, it frustrated all essential advantages against the common enemy, which might be of fatal consequence to this nation and all Europe.[63]

Ten days later the Queen informed Parliament of the principal provisions for the peace. Again there was heated debate in the Lords, Marlborough denouncing the proceedings of the past year as 'directly contrary to her majesty's engagements with the allies'.[64] Somers did not participate in the debate, nor was he among the twenty-six lords who entered a protest against the peace terms, as based on separate negotiations with France without consultation with the principal allies, and hence contrary to the framework of the Grand Alliance.[65] The Junto lords may have decided that such opposition was fruitless, for only Wharton joined the protesters. Indeed, as far as Parliament was concerned, this was virtually the case. Two weeks later it was prorogued, not to assemble again until the following April. By then the peace was a *fait accompli*.

Although the Junto chiefs had suffered defeat on the peace they did not abandon hope of a coalition. When, in the spring of 1713, the definitive treaties were at last signed, they were again in the news. Late in March, as these formalities were getting under way, Wentworth described the Tories as 'jealous and angry' upon hearing that Oxford had met at Halifax's house with Somers, Orford, Wharton, Cowper and others.[66] This was interpreted as a sign that

the Peace is not so good as to stand the test of nice inquiry, and they are to be hust [hushed?], or that 'twas to compound with them not to produce some letters that have been intercepted to encourage the Dutch to hold out, if they will promise to approve of all that's been laid before them.

Or perhaps the Whigs, 'cunning men', seeing that peace was inevitable, were ready to 'agree to anything, so that they may come in again'.[67] Such speculation was not entirely idle. Oxford had reportedly told the Elector that he was 'content to have the late chancellor Cowper, and some of that stamp in', but not personal enemies like Wharton. It was bruited abroad that Somers, Halifax and Cowper were pressing Netterville daily 'to use his interest with Mr. Harley, to bring them and their Friends into business'.[68] As for 'agreeing to anything', Halifax, for one, had assured the Treasurer of support in whatever measures he desired.[69] Jonathan Swift could only regret that Oxford had allowed himself 'to converse with his greatest enemies'.[70]

On 9 April, at the opening of the new session, Anne announced the signing of the treaties. Parliament had been eleven times prorogued, pending the working out of details. Not since the Revolution had a winter passed without debate at Westminster. Members' nerves were on edge and feuding within the ministry had reached dangerous proportions. Even now the terms of the treaties were not disclosed; not until 9 May was Parliament formally acquainted with them. Although the proclamation of peace evoked unmistakable signs of joy among the people, the trading interests were at once in arms over the commercial treaty, by which a substantial step was taken in the direction of free trade between Britain and France. Here the Whigs, acknowledged patrons of the moneyed men and supported by economists who argued that commercial relations with France had always been detrimental in producing an adverse balance of trade, had a wieldy club with which to beat their opponents. Somers now emerged from semi-retirement, returning to the Lords on 4 May. In somewhat better health, he joined Halifax, Cowper, and the maverick Nottingham in leading the opposition.[71] This time Whig efforts were crowned with success. But the effective repudiation of the capital articles of the treaty came not in the Lords but in the lower House, where the Tory, Thomas Hanmer—'the most considerable man in the House of Commons', in Swift's opinion—defected with his following.[72]

In the meantime an attack had been launched by the Scots upon the very structure of the nation, as guaranteed by the Act of Union. The merger of the two kingdoms had always had its enemies, but a series of measures had served to alienate even those who were disposed to forget the past. The Scottish Treason Act and the abolition of the Edinburgh Council were both sore points, as was the restoration of lay patronage and the toleration of Anglican rites. The vote in the Hamilton peerage case, denying to those who were Scottish peers at the time of the union, and were subsequently made peers of Great Britain, the right to sit in the latter capacity, also rankled.[73] The crowning grievance was economic: the imposition of a malt duty, widely regarded as inequitable. Some of the Whigs sought to make political capital out of this discontent. According to Lockhart they promised to support a dissolution of the union, provided the Scots 'wou'd join heartily with them against the ministry in all things'.[74]

He mentions no names. But at least one of the Junto, Wharton, strongly supported the project, and Sunderland may have done so; Halifax and Townshend drew back only when the terms proved to be unsatisfactory.[75] Somers's role is less clear. As one of the principal architects of the union, he must have hesitated to endorse any manoeuvre which would threaten it. Yet we are told that at a meeting held at his house he urged, beyond all others, that the motion be made.[76] Apart from the political pressure that these machinations might apply, the Whigs may have doubted that the union could be depended upon to serve its most important purpose in their eyes—a guarantee of the Protestant succession.[77] They now insisted that any enactment providing for the divorce of the two kingdoms should not only safeguard Anne's authority in each, but should effectually guarantee 'the succession in the Protestant line in the illustrious House of Hanover, as the same stands limited and secured'. We are told that because the bill, as introduced by the Earl of Findlater (the former Seafield, Somers's close associate in creating the union) did not satisfy these conditions, they drew back and by their negative votes contributed to the defeat of the measure.[78]

The most credible aspect of this strange business, as far as Somers's connection goes, is the caveat regarding the Hanoverian succession. The Whigs were ever ready to convey the impression that the government was at least faint-hearted in its support of this project. Somers continued to be prominently identified with it; his name appears on a list of peers 'For the Family of Hanover', prepared for Herrenhausen a few years before Anne's death, and Addison would emphasise the importance of his role.[79] What with the Queen's indifferent health and rumours of schemes for bringing about the succession of the Pretender, it is not surprising that the Whigs considered again the advantages of having at least one member of the Hanoverian house in England. In April 1711 the Dowager Electress had remarked that she was entirely uncertain of what would transpire upon Anne's death: 'what Parliament does one day, it undoes the next'. To secure the presence of the Elector himself (at least for any length of time) was hardly practical, but Sophia or the Electoral Prince, who held an English peerage as Duke of Cambridge, might serve the purpose. Somers appears to have seriously considered such a project, for when Count von Bothmar, the Hanoverian agent, decided against it as impolitic, it was to him, Sunderland and Godolphin that he turned. Upon Bothmar's representations—he feared that such a move would only unite Jacobite and Harleian Tories and antagonise the Queen—the three agreed early in 1712 not to proceed in the matter without the Elector's consent.[80] But Somers's further involvement may be traced in discussions over a pension for the Electress and in the drafting of a memorandum on what was to be done when Anne should die.[81]

In her speech opening the April session Anne pointedly linked her announcement of the peace with a reference to her concern for securing the Protestant succession, and for 'the perfect Friendship there is between Me and the House of Hanover'.[82] But the Whig leaders were unwilling to take this at face value. It was, they maintained, but another manoeuvre of the devious Treasurer. 'He has gained the people by the artifice of the Queen's speech. He will also succeed in the approaching elections; and establish the Pretender in the kingdom, as the eventual successor to the throne.'[83] For two days Somers and the other Junto lords (save Orford) conferred; Townshend, Cowper and Lord Chief Justice Parker were also on hand. Appealing to Kreienberg, co-resident with Bothmar, they entreated the Elector to send over his son. The Prince should take advantage of the Queen's declaration, and come under pretence of expressing his gratitude. Halifax and Townshend went twice to Kreienberg, emphasising the need for a decisive step. But, as always with intrigues of this sort, to no purpose: the Elector was not disposed to take any step which might excite Anne's resentment, nor was he inclined to push into the limelight a son of whom he was already jealous. The most he would do was to agree to send his brother, Duke Ernest. The Whigs now fell back on a request for financial support, by which the Hanoverian interest might be advanced, particularly in the forthcoming general election. Here, too, they came away empty-handed, the Elector maintaining that, even if he could spare the funds, he could not bring himself to engage in activities so likely to give offence to the British people. But the Junto, too, showed some caution. When, early in 1713, the Hanoverian ministers raised various questions with regard to preparing the way for the German regime, Somers, along with Cowper and Halifax, made it clear that no commission from either Sophia or the Elector could be valid if executed during Anne's lifetime.[84]

Parliament was dissolved in August and the elections followed immediately. Whig partisans marched about wearing locks of wool in their hats and wooden shoes, symbolising the damaging commercial treaties of the Tories and their betrayal of the country to France. They hammered away at the charge that their opponents would upset the Protestant succession. But the opposition of the court was in full measure directed against them, and to some extent they were handicapped by the Property Qualifications Act of 1711, by which a substantial income from real estate was required for both county and borough Members.[85] When the results were tabulated the Tories found that they had a majority of 213 seats, outnumbering the Whigs more than two to one, and there was reason to fear that many Whigs would be disqualified once the session got under way.[86] Yet Somers's comparatively small coterie weathered the storm better than in 1710. James Cocks again sat for Reigate. Joseph Jekyll was returned for New Lymington. Thomas Wylde and two Dowdeswells, William and Charles, would also have seats, as would John Rudge.

Once more the ministry delayed for months in calling Parliament together, the session not opening until 16 February 1714, and again Somers's waning powers are revealed by the record. Though present on 2 March for the Queen's speech, and on the following day, he was absent for the rest of the month and for all meetings save three between 14 April and 27 May.[87] But he was on hand for debates early in April, relating to the peace treaties and the succession, in the course of which Halifax called for the exclusion of the Pretender from Lorraine, and Wharton moved that a price be set on his head. Nearly a year earlier a committee with a similar purpose had included Somers, and he must have backed, to the extent of his ability, the address embodying these recommendations which was submitted to Anne on 14 April.[88] But the Queen held back. In response to the Halifax motion (as well as a request that the Emperor and other princes be asked to guarantee the Hanoverian succession), she went no further than to declare that she would 'give proper Directions therein'. But she appealed to the Duke of Lorraine on 30 April.[89] Late in June the Lords returned to the charge, Somers being among those instructed to urge her to take action as proposed, as well as to enforce more rigidly the penal laws against Catholic recusants. Again she contended herself with general assurances, but already, on 21 June, a proclamation offering a reward of £5,000 for the head of James Stuart had gone forth.[90]

The coolness of the Queen could be—and was—interpreted as partiality to the Jacobite cause, and kept alive the desire to have a member of the House of Hanover within the realm. The Electoral Prince, it was suggested, should be issued a writ of summons to take his seat in the Lords. After all, he was not only Duke of Cambridge, but since 1712 had been recognised as first peer of the realm. The project was driven on by Schütz, recently installed as Hanoverian agent; he was abetted by the Dowager Electress Sophia, who though an octogenarian retained a keen interest in English affairs. Baron Schütz turned for advice to the 'Hanoverian party', and once more Somers—along with seven other Whig magnates and a few Tories—gave his support. The agent was entreated to demand the writ and to bring the Prince to England forthwith. The writ was obtained, but to no effect: Anne's angry opposition was made known at Herrenhausen, and the Elector (who had not been consulted in the affair) ignored it. He was willing to bide his time. Not so Somers and Wharton, who were reported in mid-May to be urging the Prince's removal to London as 'absolutely necessary, otherwise they could hold out no longer'.[91]

As spring slipped into summer Somers reappeared in the Lords, and attended with some regularity. But his assignments were few, mostly committee appointments of little consequence.[92] About this time, however, he was regarded in at least one quarter as capable of transacting more important business. Writing on 29 June, Peter Wentworth noted that 'warm work' was expected in the Lords on the morrow. 'Some tells me'tis to be open'd by Lord Nottingham, others by Lord Somers; if by the latter 'tis look't upon as a matter of more weight.'[93] This had to do with Spanish trade; as it turned out, Nottingham led off, Somers apparently not participating. Before the month was over he found himself in the unusual position of supporting St John, now Viscount Bolingbroke.[94] The Viscount was advocating a bill subjecting anyone who enlisted in the Pretender's service to the penalties of high treason. The debate in committee of the whole seems to have been largely a Junto show; we are told that it was

Halifax, Townshend, Cowper, Somers and Wharton who 'spoke most in this Committee', and extended the scope of the measure to service under 'any foreign Prince, State or Potentate'.[95] The Lords passed the bill, as did the Commons, and it became law for three years.[96]

Two weeks earlier Somers had taken part in the protest over the Schism Act, likewise introduced by Bolingbroke. It aimed at the suppression of dissenting schools, by making it illegal for anyone to teach without a licence from a bishop. It excited violent debate, particularly in the Lords. When Bolingbroke moved the second reading Cowper, Wharton, Halifax and Townshend were among those who voiced their opposition, as did Nottingham, who declared himself 'in conscience obliged to oppose so barbarous a law'.[97] Somers appears to have remained silent, but when the bill was finally carried, by the narrow majority of five, he joined thirty-two other peers (including all the Junto lords) in protest.[98] He had participated in the manoeuvres more than two years earlier by which occasional conformity had been banned; but now he joined with those who argued that the Dissenters were not a danger to Church or State, and that in any case 'severity is not so proper and effectual a method to reduce them to the Church, as a charitable indulgence'. The former action had been patently a political deal, in which the Dissenters were the victims of Whig war-mindedness. It had brought little or no profit, and was over and done with. Now the Whigs could resume their traditional role as patrons of nonconformity, at the same time striking what blows they could against the increasingly influential Bolingbroke.

On 9 July Anne prorogued her last Parliament. Three weeks later she was dead, and the dynastic transference was in process. According to Campbell Somers was 'constantly consulted' by the Hanoverian minister in this matter, and, along with Sunderland, Cowper and Chief Justice Parker, 'gave minute instructions as to all the steps to be taken on the expected demise of the Crown'.[99] But it is not until 31 July, the day before that event, that he emerges from the shadows to assist the Council in the all-important business of insuring the inheritance of the German house. When on 30 July the news went forth that Anne's death was imminent, and the Council was hastily called together, Somers, Sunderland and Cowper, though their names were on the Council list, remained absent. Somerset, Shrewsbury and Argylle, middle-of-the-road men, were assigned the responsibility of weighting the balance for the Protestant succession The dying Queen placed the Treasurer's staff, surrendered three days before by Oxford, in Shrewsbury's hands. It was now resolved that all Privy Councillors, regardless of political alignment, should attend, and the following day Somers took his place at a table where he had not sat for nearly four years.[100]

So it was at the eleventh hour that the veteran Whig, whose career was in so many ways intertwined with the principles and the designs of the Revolution, was able to participate directly and officially in the dynastic change so important to their continuance. With the other Councillors Somers listened to the reports of the Queen's physicians, explained to

Bothmar the steps that had been taken to secure the Elector's succession, and dispatched a letter to that prince apprising him of Anne's condition and urging him to come to England at once. Another letter went forth to the States General, reminding them of their obligation, by treaty, to provide armed support for the Protestant succession in England, if the need should arise.[101] When this and other business had been accomplished, adjournment was ordered until the following morning. It was to be Anne's last Council; before it could reassemble the Queen's life was over. George of Hanover was King.

The Council turned at once to the proclamation of the new monarch and the swearing in of the Regents appointed to rule until George could reach his island realm.[102] By the terms of the Regency Act they were to consist of seven notable officers of state and eighteen other persons named by the Elector. Bothmar and Kreienberg produced three sealed documents, which were duly opened, compared, and found to correspond. The Regents were for the most part moderate Whigs, with a sprinkling of Hanoverian Tories. Somers was not included, nor was Sunderland. Wharton, Orford and Halifax were on the list, however, as were Cowper and Townshend. Thus, while it can be said that 'George was not in the pocket of the Junto', the old party machine was far from ignored.[103] Somers could take further satisfaction that Archbishop Tenison was an ex officio member, and that George had chosen Somerset as one of the eighteen peers.

The omission of Somers is said to have caused some surprise. Did the new King shy away from the oracle of the Whigs as representing too militant a partisan leadership, too liberal a political philosophy? George, with his autocratic sensibilities, could easily believe the worst of the extreme Whigs, whom High Tories were still ready to depict as despoilers of kings. Or could the Elector have learned of the old statesman's alleged dalliance with St Germain? Possibly, yet it seems inconceivable that he could have doubted Somers's rooted commitment to the Hanoverian cause. There was certainly some sense of obligation: Bothmar, for one, recommended that something be done for the Whig mentor.[104] The explanation probably lies not in any personal mistrust or political aversion, but rather in the increasing invalidism and even senility of a veteran in his grand climacteric. Of this there was no doubt: Bothmar had apprised his master of the old Whig's 'bodily and mental ills'.[105]

Honours and emoluments, however, were not withheld. He was voted a yearly pension of £2000, and was appointed *custos rotulorum* of Worcestershire and commissioner of coronation claims. He was continued on the Privy Council, being sworn anew on 1 October.[106] He was also tendered a place in the cabinet, as were Halifax, Wharton, Orford and Sunderland. But whereas they obtained official posts— Halifax as First Lord of the Treasury, Wharton as Lord Privy Seal, Orford as first Admiralty Commissioner, and Sunderland as Lord Lieutenant of Ireland—Somers held his cabinet seat without portfolio.[107] Except for Sunderland, however, the future belonged to none of these men. Wharton and Halifax would both die in 1715, and Orford would resign two years later. Time had set the stage for younger leaders, and especially for Stanhope and Walpole.

Since the cabinet kept no minutes it is impossible to ascertain how often Somers occupied his seat in that body. But the Privy Council registers show that, of the forty-one meetings held between 1 October 1714, when he was sworn, and 6 April 1716 (the last meeting during his lifetime), he was present at twenty-two. The Council met irregularly—meetings might be a day or a month apart—but only in the late summer of 1715, when it was occupied with the Jacobite rebellion, did he attend more than twice consecutively.[108] The sands were running out. But he strove to keep in touch, not finally withdrawing until mid-December 1715. His attendance in the Lords was also irregular, though he managed in 1715 to be present about two-thirds of the time. His last appearance was on 27 January 1716, three months before his death.

The old Parliament was dissolved early in January 1715. The ensuing elections restored the Whig ascendancy with a comfortable majority of 119 seats.[109] The Commons' roster bore the names of Cocks, Jekyll, Wylde, Rudge and Dowdeswell, but the enforced retirement of their old patron was bound to reduce his effectiveness as an electioneer and weaken their ties with him. He was definitely on the sidelines. With one exception his parliamentary assignments involved routine measures and a handful of private bills. Only the committee ordered to seek out precedents for the impeachment proceedings against Oxford and other victims of Whig vengeance was in any sense consequential.[110] This was a subject on which Somers was an expert, but the extent of his labours (if any) cannot be determined, and there is no evidence that he participated in any debates after the summer of 1714. But we are told that he advised the Whigs against pursuing vindictive measures against Bolingbroke and Oxford, and that when Lord Townshend—who kept in touch with his old mentor—acquainted him with the prosecutions that were afoot, 'the old peer asked what he meant, and shed tears on the foresight of measures like those of the Roman Triumvirate'.[111] With the Sacheverell debacle so fresh in mind he must have looked upon the weapon of impeachment as a double-edged sword.

But he favoured extending the life of Parliament—including the existing one—for four years beyond its allotted time. This measure, the Septennial Act, which gained support because of 'The 'Fifteen' and a consequent fear that, should elections be held in the near future, Jacobitism might imperil the new dynasty, was debated during the last weeks of his life. He was now confined to Brookmans, broken and sometimes insensible. During the debate Townshend, one of the principal authors of the bill, learned that he had rallied: a fit of gout, supposedly, had lessened the grip of paralysis and revived his faculties. He paid a call on his old patron. The conversation turned to the Septennial Bill, and Somers is reported to have said: 'I have just heard of the work in which you are engaged and congratulate you upon it; I never approved the triennial bill, and always considered it in effect, the reverse of what it was intended', adding that in his opinion the new measure would provide 'the greatest support possible to the liberty of the country.'[112] Townshend, no doubt, made good use of the 'response of the Oracle', but we are left in doubt as to the reasons for his support. Despite the revival of Whig fortunes, he may well have been disenchanted with frequent elections, usually producing Tory majorities, and have embraced the measure as contributing to increased control by the more Whiggish upper chamber. But it seems likely that he was primarily concerned with insuring the stability of the new regime. The Lords passed the bill on 18 April.

Eight days later Somers was dead, carried off by a final onslaught of his crippling disease.[113] His death occurred at Brookmans, and he was buried in the nearby parish church of North Mimms. No account of his obsequies appears to have survived. His sister, Lady Jekyll, provided for the erection of a monument. Installed in the chancel, where it is still to be seen, it features a figure of Justice holding a pair of scales in one hand and a scroll in the other. It bears a simple inscription:

The Rt. Honble. John Lord Somers
Baron of Evesham
Lord High Chancellor of England in the Reign of King William III
To whose Memory this Monument was erected by Dame Elizabeth Jekyll.[114]

The great lawyer left no will.[115] Letters of administration were granted to his two sisters, and his estate was divided between the Cocks and Jekyll households.[116] The Reigate manor and Brookmans were acquired by the Jekylls. The Worcestershire properties went to the Cockses, but Mary Cocks did not long enjoy the inheritance, following her brother in death late in 1717. Under the circumstances no provision could be made for specific bequests, but it is likely that arrangements had been worked out *inter vivos*; we know that shortly before his death he conveyed a field in North Mimms to trustees for the use of the poor.[117] His title, of course, expired with him, as did his pensions. His valuable collections were divided and dispersed by his heirs.[118] For one who rose to such heights and wielded influence for so long, his personnal arrangements were singularly impermanent. His abiding monument would rest on the broader foundations of statesmanship.

NOTES

[1] According to Swift, Anne regretted the 'resignations' of Cowper and Somers, for whom she had a great 'personal regard and esteem': *Works*, ed. Scott, V, 438. Somers apparently continued to enjoy improved relations with the Queen. He was present, in February 1713, at her birthday celebration; hardly any other Whig was there: *Wentworth Papers*, 318. See also below, n. 9.

[2] Somers MSS., Margaret Cocks to Katherine Somers, 16 February [1716?], and see above, p. 68.

[3] Nash, *Collections*, II, 345; Somers MSS., John Cocks to Charles Cocks, April 1711.

[4] Cussans, *Hertfordshire*, III, 285.

[5] Nash, *Collections*, II, 345; V.C.H. *Worcestershire*, IV, 196.

[6] Somers MSS., January 1695.

[7] P.C.C. Proved, 16 February 1711, Reg. Young, f. 37.

[8] Somers MSS., 22 February 1711.

[9] See Burnet, VI, 10, Dartmouth's note regarding Anne's assurances that, despite his dismissal, 'she had not lessened her esteem for him, and designed to continue his pension, and should be glad if he came often to her'.

[10] Sloane MSS. 4223, f. 215, July 1710; B.M. Portland Loan 29/238, 19 August 1710.

[11] Coxe, *Marlborough*, III, 137.

[12] Speck, *Tory and Whig*, 123, puts the Tory majority at 151 (332 Tories, 181 Whigs). See also Mary C. Ransome, 'The general election in 1710', *Bull. Inst. Hist. Res.*, XVII (November 1939), 95–97, and William T. Morgan, 'An eighteenth-century election in England', *Pol. Sci. Quar.*, XXXVII (December 1922), 585–604. Morgan contends that the Tory margin of victory has been exaggerated.

[13] In Wylde's case there was complaint of undue return: Oldfield, V, 242. Dowdeswell's son, William, was returned in a by-election in 1712. On James Cocks, see Speck, *Tory and Whig*, 22.

[14] *Corr. Duch. Marl.*, II, 153.

[15] *Memoirs*, 117. Abel Boyer did not include Somers in his list of councillors in June 1711, but he appears in the list for July 1712: *Political State of Great Britain*, I, 375–76; IV, 52.

[16] He was absent 25–29 November 1710, 17 March–16 April and 9–18 May 1711. He drew something like the usual number of committee assignments, but served as chairman only twice, for the Isaac Estate Act and the Lady Clarges Estate Act, both on 3 March 1711: Lords MSS., Committee Minutes.

[17] *Works of Lord Bolingbroke* (Philadelphia, 1841), II, 312 ('Letters on the study and use of history').

[18] L.J., XIX, 166.

[19] *Ibid.*, XIX, 184; *Parliamentary History*, VI, 936ff.

[20] L.J., XIX, 190.

[21] *Ibid.*, XIX, 190–91; Rogers, *Protests*, I, 199–201.

[22] L.J., XIX, 192–93; Rogers, *Protests*, I, 201–2. Somers argued that military failures did not in themselves justify opposition to offensive warfare; if military opinion and advice were to be judged by future events 'no man could be safe': *Parliamentary History*, VI, 979.

[23] All five Junto lords signed the first two protests; all but Halifax the third.

[24] L.J., XIX, 212–13; Rogers, *Protests*, 203–5.

[25] Luttrell, *Relation*, VI., 689; Burnet, VI, 25–26; L.J., XIX, 221.

[26] *Ibid.*, XIX, 213, 218.

[27] His discomfiture was heightened, a fortnight later, by the Lords' passage of the Property Qualification Bill (*ibid.*, XIX, 233), only three days after it was brought before them. Presumably his position on measures of this kind had not changed over the years; see above, p. 134.

[28] *Examiner*, No. 27, 1 February, 1711.

[29] *Works*, ed. Scott, II, 123.

[30] Burnet, VI, 40.

[31] C.J., XVI, 567, 611; L.J., XIX, 287; *Memoirs*, 116–17; Tindal, XXIV, 240. A similar bill was rejected by the Lords in 1712: L.J., XIX, 453–54.

[32] On 24 May 1710.

[33] A rumour was abroad that Somers and Cowper would be restored to the Council: Holmes, *British Politics*, 49.

[34] *Corr. Duch. Marl.*, II, 69.

[35] *Works*, ed. Scott, II, 186. Catherine Lucy was the wife of Sir Berkeley Lucy and the aunt of 'Moll Stanhope'; her Whiggery produced quarrels, and ultimately a break, with Swift. Anne Finch was the wife of Heneage Finch, who became fourth Earl of Winchilsea.

[36] Coxe, *Marlborough*, III, 215. The Duke of Somerset, though a Whig, continued as Master of the Horse.

[37] Geyl, 26–29; Geikie and Montgomery, 187–238.

[38] Somers MSS., Somers to Mrs Cocks, n.d. [April 1711].

[39] The Whigs, Swift remarked, were 'too strong in the House of Lords': *Works*, ed. Scott, II, 287.

[40] *Post Boy*, 17 and 22 November 1711. Members of the Kit-Cat Club were in particular held responsible: Oldmixon, *History*, 478–79.

41 *Works*, ed. Scott, II, 267–68.

42 *Portland MSS.* VII, 79. To Robert Walpole *The Conduct* was a 'Masterpiece, fill'd with Falsitys and Misrepresentations': *A Short History of the Parliament* (London, 1713), 13.

43 Trevelyan, *Anne*, III, 189, and see *Portland MSS.*, V, 108; Onno Klopp, *Der Fall des Hauses Stuart* (Vienna, 1875–88), XIV, 672–77.

44 See Holmes, *British Politics*, 104.

45 Trevelyan, *Anne*, III, 194, citing *Portland MSS.*, V, 120. But according to Feiling, 444, it was Oxford who opened conversations with Halifax and Somers; Oxford was willing to offer assurances against the introduction of an occasional conformity bill, but Somers and Halifax wanted concessions on peace negotiations.

46 *Portland MSS.*, V, 119. Horwitz, *Revolution Politicks*, 230–32.

47 *Works*, ed. Scott, II, 294.

48 Turberville, *Lords in Eighteenth Century*, 111.

49 *L.J.*, XIX, 335.

50 *Ibid.*, XIX, 336, 339. For the debate, see *Parliamentary History*, VI, 1036 ff. Somers was absent 10–21 December. On his ill health, see B.M. Portland Loan 29/198. Halifax to Harley, 25 November, 2 December 1711.

51 *Works*, ed. Scott, II, 296–97; *Correspondence*, ed. Ball, I, 312–14. On Somers's relations with the Duke and Duchess of Somerset, see A. A. Locke, *They Seymour Family* (Boston, 1914), 169–71, 298. Somers and Halifax had been anxious to have Somerset continue in his household office, as one who had the Queen's ear. But he was not regarded as entirely trustworthy, Cowper describing him as 'a false, mean-spirited knave': Hardwicke MSS., XXXIII, ff. 72–74, Somers to Halifax, autumn, 1710; *Cowper Diary*, 50.

52 Turberville, *Lords in Eighteenth Century*, 114; *Wentworth Papers*, 224; *Memoirs of … Wharton* (London, 1715), 93. Somers was, however, characterised as Habakkuk Slyboots in John Arbuthnot's *History of John Bull* (London, 1712). See also Holmes, *British Politics*, 113, who declares it to be 'almost certainly true that the Junto believed the ministry to be on the point of bringing in its own far tougher bill to appease the High Church Tories in the Commons', citing Auchmar MSS., George Baillie to Montrose, 13 December 1711. On Wharton's supposed continuing lack of sympathy which the Church of England, see *The Dissenting Teachers Address to the J-to* (London, 1711), 12–13, where, in connection with a project for building more Anglican churches, he is made to say, 'let them build Churches if they will, and be damn'd; the more they build, the more we shall have to Plunder, when we get uppermost again, and let that Glorious Prospect content you'. On a proposed meeting at Somers's house, on occasional conformity, see B.M. Portland Loan 29/198, Halifax to Harley, 2 December 1711.

53 *C.J.*, XVII, 25; *L.J.*, XIX, 352.

54 See Leadam, *History*, 193.

55 *Wentworth Papers*, 238–39.

56 See James Macpherson, *History of Great Britain from the Restoration* (London, 1775), II, 531; *Memoires de Monsieur de Torcy* (London, 1757), III, 166. Nicholas Henderson, *Prince Eugen of Savoy* (London, 1964), 200–1, dismisses the plot as a pure fabrication, to which currency was given by the Harley government in its desire to discredit Eugene and Marlborough. Swift, for one, accepted it: *Works*, ed. Scott, II, 301.

57 *Portland MSS.*, V, 158.

58 James Macpherson, *Original Papers Containing the Secret History of Great Britain* (London, 1785), II, 332. In July 1712 Somers was described as 'dangerously ill' and not likely to recover: *ibid.*, II, 334.

59 *L.J.*, XIX, 379; *Parliamentary History*, VI, 1108–9.

60 *Works*, ed. Scott, II, 338.

61 Trevelyan, *Anne*, III, 216–17.

62 *L.J.*, XIX, 460–61.

63 Rogers, *Protests*, I, 211.

64 *L.J.*, XIX, 471–72; *Parliamentary History*, VI, 1145–47.

65 Rogers, *Protests*, I, 213–17. The argument of the protest was obliterated from the journal (XIX, 474).

66 Cf. Hist. MSS. Comm., *Seventh Rept.*, appendix, Verney MSS., 508, to the effect that Oxford had dined with Halifax, but that the other leaders of the Junto had declined.

67 *Wentworth Papers*, 324.

68 Macpherson, *Original Papers*, II, 380, 390.

[69] Portland MSS., v, 271.

[70] Correspondence, ed. Ball, II, 15.

[71] Turberville, Lords in Eighteenth Century, 123–24; L.J., XIX, 512.

[72] Works, ed. Scott, II, 432; McInnes, Harley, 156 and n.

[73] The case involved the ennoblement of the Duke of Hamilton as Duke of Brandon. The Whigs, who regarded the Scottish peers as wholly subservient to the Crown, succeeded in carrying the measure. The principal opposition came from Oxford. Somers was absent during these proceedings. The Scottish Duke of Queensberry, created Duke of Dover, was also excluded. See L.J., XIX, 346–47; Timberland, II, 351–52, 357; G. S. Holmes, 'The Hamilton affair of 1711–1712: a crisis in Anglo-Scottish relations', Eng. Hist. Rev., LXXVII (April 1962), 257–82.

[74] Memoirs and Commentaries upon the Affairs of Scotland, 1702–15, by George Lockhart, ed. Anthony Aufrere (London, 1817), I, 434; Mackinnon, 428.

[75] Riley, 'English Ministers', 243; Parliamentary History, VI, 1216–20. Holmes, British Politics, 113, finds no convincing evidence that any leading Whig, except Wharton and possibly Sunderland, was prepared to wreck the Union.

[76] Onslow's note in Burnet, VI, 150.

[77] See Brown, History of Scotland, III, 152.

[78] More Culloden Papers, ed. Duncan Warrand (Inverness, 1923–30), II, 34–35. Though present at the bill's introduction, Somers does not appear to have spoken: L.J. XIX, 556.

[79] Macpherson, Original Papers, II, 643 and n., and see ibid., II, 202–3, for representations on the Whig position addressed to the Hanoverian resident, which Campbell, v, 176, attributes to Somers; The Freeholder, No. 39.

[80] Adolphus W. Ward, The Electress Sophia and the Hanoverian Succession (London, 1903), 401–2.

[81] John Robethon, the Elector's secretary, advised Otto von Grote, Hanoverian statesman, that 'all our ministers' believed that he should conform, in the matter of the pension, 'to the sentiments of lord Somers': Macpherson Original Papers, II, 467. Chief Justice Parker was principally responsible for the memorandum; Somers and Cowper assisted him: ibid., II, 475, 481.

[82] L.J., XIX, 512.

[83] Macpherson, History, II, 597.

[84] Ibid., II, 596–97, 609–11. As much as £100,000 was sought from Herrenhausen, but George refused even £2000 to influence common council elections: Lewis Melville, The First George in Hanover and England (London, 1908), I, 155–56.

[85] On the effects of this Act, see Holmes, British Politics, 179–82.

[86] General Cadogan estimated that 160 Whigs were returned: Stowe MSS. 225, f. 208, Baron Schütz to Robethon, 29 September 1713. Speck, Tory and Whig, 123, has 150 Whigs, 363 Tories.

[87] L.J., XIX, 626 ff. The Lords recessed for the Easter holidays between 19 and 31 March. In June and July Somers's attendance was fairly regular.

[88] Ibid., XIX, 591; Timberland, II, 412–13, 416–17. Somers had advised an address to the Queen to 'set a Reward' on the Pretender's head, upon his landing in England: Sloane MSS. 4223, f. 213–13v.

[89] Feiling, 468; Ward, Electress, 423 ff.

[90] L.J., XIX, 728; Oldmixon, History, 555; Steele, Proclamations, I, 537 (No. 4545).

[91] Macpherson, Original Papers, II, 592; Trevelyan, Anne, III, 277–79.

[92] On 17 June he reported in connection with a private bill: L.J., XIX, 702, 720. He had not served as committee chairman since 30 May 1713.

[93] Wentworth Papers, 394.

[94] St John had been created Viscount Bolingbroke on 7 July 1712.

[95] Timberland, II, 432–33; Oldmixon, History, 555.

[96] It was entitled 'An Act to prevent the listing of Her Majesty's Subjects to serve as Soldiers, without Her Majesty's Authority'. It passed the Lords 24 June: L.J., XIX, 734.

[97] Timberland, II, 420 ff; Portland MSS., v, 322.

[98] L.J., XIX, 716–17.

[99] Campbell, v, 182.

[100] Trevelyan, Anne, III, 302 ff.; P.C. 2/84, ff. 371, 375.

[101] Ibid., ff. 385–89.

[102] Somers signed the proclamation; for the list, see Oldmixon, History, 564.

[103] Trevelyan, Anne, III, 311 and n, where there is a list of the regents.

104 Leadam, *History*, 223, referring to secret service money; Macpherson, *Original Papers*, II, 640.

105 Stowe MSS. 227, f. 292.

106 *Cal. Treas. Books*, 1714–15, XXIX, pt. ii, 250; *D.N.B.*, John Somers; Oldmixon, *History*, 576, for a list of Privy Councillors.

107 E. T. Williams, 'The Cabinet in the eighteenth century', *History*, XXII, n.s. (December 1937), 247.

108 See Campbell, V, 184–85n. Between 31 August and 23 September 1715, he sat in five successive meetings.

109 Speck, *Tory and Whig*, 123.

110 *L.J.*, XX, 222.

111 Walter S. Sichel, *Bolingbroke and His Times* (New York, 1901), 505–6, citing a letter of Bolingbroke to Wyndham.

112 William Coxe, *Memoirs of the Life and Administration of Sir Robert Walpole* (London, 1800), I, 130. Coxe obtained this account from Townshend's grandsons, Lord Sydney and Charles Townshend. See also Wolfgang Michael, *England under George I: the Beginnings of the Hanoverian Dynasty* (London, 1936), 219. Turberville, *Lords in Eighteenth Century*, 165, observes that 'the best opinion of the time seems to have been in favour of the Septennial Act upon one ground or another'. The Triennial Act was blamed for sowing 'the Seeds of Corruption': see Timberland, III, 29.

113 *Memoirs*, 118.

114 There are descriptions in Clutterbuck, *Hertfordshire*, I, 464; *V.C.H. Hertfordshire*, II, 258; Nikolaus Pevsner, *Buildings of England* (London, 1951–74), VII: *Hertfordshire*, 179. Canaletto painted a capricio or fantasy of the tomb, which, with other similar representations, adorned the country house of the Duke of Richmond. See illustration in *Time*, 16 October 1964; Eugene MacSwiny, *Tombeaux des Princes* (London, 1741).

115 Lady Mary Wortley Montagu remarked, 'I have heard he is dead without a Will, and I have heard he has made young Mr. Cox his Heir; I cannot tell which account is the truest': *Letters*, ed. Halsband, I, 247–48 and n. 'Young Mr. Cox' was James Cocks, the elder of Somers's nephews.

116 Acts of Administration, 1716, 90v, dated 15 May 1716. The partition was effected in March 1717: Hooper, *Reigate*, 43n. See also *V.C.H. Worcestershire*, III, 534; IV, 192.

117 *V.C.H. Hertfordshire*, II, 260.

118 See above, p. 196.

Epilogue

The name of Somers lives on chiefly in connection with the formulation of the Bill of Rights. At a time when he was scarcely launched upon his political career, he was to give substantial direction to a constitutional settlement which was little altered for a century and a half, and which still continues as a fundamental basis for England's government. Few men so new to the business of Parliament have played so significant a part in its deliberations. In the years that followed he remained staunchly attached to the principles adopted by the Convention, and in tune with the moderation that underlay the arrangements he did so much to implement. In his contributions to the refinement and extension of the 1689 settlement he tended to support the *via media*, and thereby dissociate Whiggery and radicalism. Jonathan Swift recalled that Somers deplored that 'the Prerogative of the Crown, or the Privileges of Parliament, should ever be liable to Dispute, in any single Branch of either', in that 'the Publick often suffered great Inconveniences'.[1] He was concerned for the general welfare of England, but his 'public', for the most part, was that body within the kingdom already endowed with direct political influence. He supported certain 'liberal' issues, such as the freedom of the press and the interests of Nonconformists; he recognised the plight of those ensnared in charges of treason; and, while he did little to raise judges and courtroom functionaries above the age-old system of patronage and vested interest, at least he left judicial procedure more reasonable and expeditious than he found it. But there is no evidence that he sought to alter the balance of the national polity by revamping the franchise, and he is said to have had second thoughts as to the wisdom of the Triennial Act.

In his eulogy of Somers, Addison makes particular reference to his 'great Share in the Plan of the Protestant Succession' and to his being the 'chief Conductor' of the union with Scotland and the Regency Bill.[2] These undertakings bore directly and weightily upon the stability of the revolutionary settlement; they were keystones in the bridge over which the British people might cross the turbulent waters of the later Stuart era. They reflect Somers's abiding concern for the permanence of the regime he had helped to found. So does his hostility to France, England's prime rival and the avowed enemy of the new regime. While his francophobia under William may be in part attributable to political survival under a warrior king, its continuance in Anne's later years must have been rooted in a deep-seated conviction. That this conviction was to some extent shaped by partisan considerations, and that it tended to degenerate into prejudice, we may admit. Somers would probably appear a more enlightened figure had he not clung so stubbornly to 'No peace without Spain'. Perhaps, had he been younger and more vigorous, he would have shown more adaptability. But his war-mindedness, however misguided and out of date, however identified with party tactics, was inextricably bound up with the principles of 1689.

Though a man of scholarly interests, one who read and wrote and enjoyed the company of men of letters, he was essentially the practical politician rather than the theorist. Broad doctrinaire concepts were not the mainsprings of his action. He was a distinguished, but hardly a creative, jurist. The political writings that can with some certainty be ascribed to him deal with such practical matters as the serviceability of grand juries, the pattern of the succession, or the right to petition; he nowhere attempts to construct a philosophical system of government or to describe an ideal polity. He is at home with generation after generation of English politicians who have been satisfied with a pragmatic approach to the problems of the day. The political parties of his time had scarcely emerged from an embryonic stage, but he saw in party an effective device to channel opinion, exercise influence and implement policy. His identification with the Whigs was as complete and persistent a partisan association as can be found in his generation. Sunderland, who ought to have known, called him 'the life, the soul and the spirit of his party'. This suggests a monolithic quality which existed among neither Whigs nor Tories. But it is undeniable that at his best Somers gave direction to the Whigs, through the 'great connexion' of the Junto; and he was always a voice to be listened to, until physical and mental decay removed him from the arena.

In his great store of learning and practical experience, he came to be unrivalled among the Whigs. For all Sunderland's expertness and influence, he was untutored compared to Somers, suspect as unreliable, and, in any case, dead by 1702. Wharton never gained ministerial status; a brash and witty aristocrat, he could be devastating in the Lords, but was chiefly useful for delivering votes. Orford was inactive in Parliament in Anne's reign, though valuable for his following in the Commons. Halifax was a man of parts, certainly in matters of finance, and showed marked aptitude as a parliamentary manager; but he appealed to neither William nor Anne, and lacked Somers's staying power. Shrewsbury, by temperament, was effective only by fits and starts. Cowper came relatively late to the scene; his talents were considerable, but more specialised than those of Somers. Walpole was a rising star. Except for Wharton, Somers was the oldest of these men. As a life-long bachelor, without the distractions of family or extensive possessions, he was able to concentrate, as few English politicians have done, for many years on public business. 'No Science in my opinion is worth a Gentlemans while, but Morality, polities, and polite Learning':[3] this he set down among his maxims. Application to business was probably second nature to Somers; Swift accused him of having the 'regularity' of an alderman. But his political success had other sources than efficiency and indefatigability. According to Macky 'very few Ministers in any Reign ever had so many Friends in the House of Commons'.[4] Though no hale-fellow-well-met he had a personal touch, an innate skill, which was effective in political management.

His elevation to the Whig pantheon followed hard upon his death. Addison had no doubt that 'this wonderful Man' would be regarded as 'one of the most distinguish'd Figures in the History of the present Age'. Others, less bound by ties of gratitude, were no less laudatory. Oldmixon called him 'the greatest lawyer, orator, politician and patriot of our Times', while Kennett labelled his services to king and nation as 'truly great and good'.[5] As, with the passing of the years, the Revolutionary Settlement came to be more and more identified with all that the governing classes held dear, and the Whigs enjoyed decade after decade of virtually un-challenged influence, he came to be regarded as a founding father. To Edmund Burke he was the archetype of the 'old Whigs', to whom he addressed his *Appeal*. Goldsmith called him 'the great Somers'.[6] A hundred years after his appointment as Lord Keeper, a collateral descendant went so far as to describe him, among the moderns, as most closely approximat-ing the character of Socrates, outstripping Clarendon and even Bacon.[7] The rearrangement of the constitution in the early nineteenth century had little effect on a reputation which, at the hands of Coxe, Macaulay and Campbell, looms almost heroic.

Now and then the warts have been painted. James Ralph, though admit-ting that he was 'the most Extraordinary Man of his Times', and 'un-doubtedly irreproachable' as Lord Chancellor, regarded him as too com-pliant where William's favour was concerned: 'That firmness which had withstood the Storm, melted in the Sun-Shine; and, having once suggested what was right, he did not think himself oblig'd to withstand what was wrong.'[8] Thomas Somerville gives him full credit for insuring a Protestant regime, but considers his mildness and modesty as personal liabilities, in that he gave way to the judgement of persons 'neither so disinterested, nor well-informed' as himself.[9] Macpherson, too, suggests that his moderation blocked the way to greatness: 'he seemed more calculated to smoothe the current of business, by amending and softening measures already adopted, than to propose and execute those spirited and manly expedients which times of faction seem to demand of a great minister'.[10] His compliance with the Partition Treaties continued to be held against him, and his supposed dalliance with St Germain did not pass unnoticed. Before the nineteenth century was over, a more critical evaluation of his role in the events of 1688–89 was voiced, and his contributions to religious liberty questioned.

However close to the mark such criticism may come, it does not materially alter the outlines of Somers's character and accomplishments. It may be that as a 'new man', without the background and family con-nections then and for generations to come associated with possession of high office, he was less aggressive, more self-effacing, than was warranted or desirable. But if the essential test of Somers's labours was the peaceful accession of George of Hanover in a unified British realm, one may question the need of more aggressive methods. It is hardly likely that more authoritarian tactics could have avoided the anti-military reaction following Ryswick, or the more consequential Tory ascendancy of 1710, with its adverse effects on the Nonconformists and its peace without Spain. And if his co-operation in the Partition Treaties was ill-advised, a few short years were to make that question almost purely academic. Perhaps, could Somers speak more fully for himself, a more egocentric personality would emerge. He was not without an appetite for power, as his association with Sunderland and his manoeuvres in Anne's reign amply demonstrate. He appears at no time as an amateur in politics, but rather as a professional, committed and hard-driving. But his course of action usually rested on a broader base than that of self-advancement. His coat of arms bore the motto 'Prodesse quam conspici'. Such maxims are usually honoured at least as much in the breach as in the observance, but there is relevance in Somers's case. To be conspicuous was secondary; to be serviceable, and thereby possess the substance of power, was the prime consideration.

NOTES

[1] *Drapier's Letters*, ed. Davies, 135.
[2] *The Freeholder*, No. 39.
[3] Add. MSS. 32,095, f. 410.
[4] *Secret Services*, 48.
[5] Oldmixon, 637; Kennett, III, 734.
[6] *The Present State of Polite Learning in Europe* (London, 1759), in *Miscellaneous Works of Oliver Goldsmith*, ed. David Masson (London, 1928), 435.
[7] *Annual Register* (1793), 266.
[8] *History*, II, 784.
[9] *History of Great Britain during the Reign of Queen Anne*, 257–58.
[10] *History*, II, 182.

Index